AT EMPIRE'S EDGE

To my parents,
Arthur and Nancy Jackson

Published with assistance from the Mary Cady Tew Memorial Fund.
Photo credits: © British Museum (6.7); Patrick Godeau (1.6, 1.8, 1.16, 2.3, 2.5, 4.1, 4.2, 5.4, 8.5, 8.6, 8.9, 8.10, 8.22, 8.32, 8.33, 10.1, 10.7, 10.8, 10.9); J.-Fr. Gout, © IFAO (8.2, 8.3, 8.4); James A. Harrell (7.1); Norbert Schiller (8.17, 9.2); Chip Vincent/ARCE (8.30, 8.31). Remaining photos are by the author.

Designed by Mary Valencia.
Set in Quadraat type by à la page, Brooklyn, New York.
Printed in the United States of America by Phoenix Color, Hagerstown, Maryland.

Library of Congress Cataloging-in-Publication Data
Jackson, Robert B., 1961–
At empire's edge : exploring Rome's Egyptian frontier / Robert B. Jackson.
p. cm.
Includes bibliographical references and index.
ISBN 0-300-08856-6 (alk. paper : hbk.)
1. Egypt—Antiquities, Roman. 2. Romans—Egypt. 3. Egypt—Boundaries.
4. Egypt—History—30 B.C.–640 A.D. I. Title.
DT60 .J28 2002
932′.022—dc21   2001004942

A catalogue record for this book is available from the British Library.

1 3 5 7 9 10 8 6 4 2

AT EMPIRE'S EDGE

EXPLORING ROME'S EGYPTIAN FRONTIER

ROBERT B. JACKSON

YALE UNIVERSITY PRESS

NEW HAVEN & LONDON

CONTENTS

ILLUSTRATIONS

FIGURES

MAPS

PREFACE

This book was unwittingly conceived in 1980, when I first traveled to Egypt as a university student. That sojourn lasted less than a fortnight and included visits to the magnificent temples and tombs at Giza and Saqqara and in Upper Egypt. Yet for reasons I cannot fully explain, it was not these monuments that captured my attention, but rather the desert that loomed beyond their tumbled remains, beyond the green fields of the Nile Valley, beyond the dusty skyline of Cairo—the desert that lurks on the edge of every Egyptian horizon. Those vast, mysterious lands guarded ancient secrets like a treasure, and they ignited within me a desire to explore their depths and to learn what lessons of man and nature they might contain.

Between 1981 and 1996, I spent seven years in Egypt, first as a student at the American University in Cairo, then as a teacher at Cairo American College. During that time, I hiked more than 1,500 kilometers through the Eastern and Western

Deserts—either with a camel or carrying water and supplies on my back—and traveled several thousand more kilometers by jeep. In the course of my journeys I encountered remains and artifacts from many epochs of human existence: from flint tools of Palaeolithic man to fuel cans of Allied soldiers. But of all these, it was the remains of the Greco-Roman period that sparked my interest most intensely. I was awed by the sight of Roman fortresses thrusting upward from the desert— dying slowly, defiantly, amidst seas of ancient pottery. In size and historical significance, of course, these structures cannot compare to the Pharaonic ruins of the Nile Valley. But Karnak and Luxor have been excavated, reconstructed, and sanitized, and their hordes of tourists, guides, and hawkers inhibit one's ability to appreciate the temples' spiritual majesty. By contrast, far into the desert, resting in the shadows of the fortresses and water stations that mark Rome's most distant frontier and intoxicated by the stillness, one can sense the presence of the soldiers, merchants, and laborers who once brought life to this desolate world.

As my interest in the Roman period of Egyptian history grew, I sought to learn more about the remains I encountered in my desert travels. To my disappointment, I discovered that no author, academic or popular, had ever attempted to present what is currently known about Rome's Egyptian frontier in a single, concise volume. Indeed, I found that to the extent such information existed, it was scattered among academic journals to which the nonspecialist was unlikely to have access. Although these journals contained highly detailed information pertaining to excavations of frontier sites, the beauty and mystery of the sites themselves were usually lost in scholarly prose. Frustrated at not finding the book that I thought should exist and determined to save other interested individuals from the same disappointment, I decided that the only way to discover what I wanted to know about Rome's Egyptian frontier was to write the book myself.

Foremost among my objectives for this book is simply to provide both the student and general reader of ancient history with a description of the most important sites that constitute Rome's Egyptian frontier and a summary of what is currently known or theorized about the Roman occupation of these sites. But beyond describing the quarries, fortresses, and temples that punctuate the desert frontier, I have tried, when archaeological evidence permitted, to convey at least some sense of what life might have been like for the individuals who inhabited these distant corners of the Roman Empire. Toward this end, I have included translations of inscriptions, graffiti, ostraca, and papyri so that the reader might hear the ancient voices of these people speaking of their business affairs, their passions, and their religious beliefs—and in so doing, better appreciate our common humanity.

A few words of explanation are necessary regarding two technical aspects of this book. First, it focuses on the period spanning 29 B.C. and the end of the fifth century A.D. Thus, it includes the two centuries of the late Roman period, ending at approximately the start of the Byzantine period. The actual distinctions between these eras, however, are imprecise, and the inclusion of certain sites (particularly in Kharga and Dakhleh Oases) that appear to date from the late Roman period does not exclude the possibility that, in the future, they might be more appropriately labeled as Byzantine. Indeed, given that many of the fortresses and settlements of the Western Desert have never been excavated, it is impossible to ascribe dates to them with certainty. Second, concerning my use of the term "frontier," it is not my intention to enter into the academic debate over the location of Rome's *limes* in Egypt. Although I mention the existence of *limes* when their locations are specifically identified by inscriptions or other written sources, I use the term "frontier" to denote the general area of separation between Roman-administered territory and those regions beyond Roman control.

I hope this book provides sufficient geographical detail to enable the reader who is unfamiliar with Egypt to imagine the varied terrain of its Eastern and Western Deserts, but it is not intended as a navigational guide. Many of the places I discuss, particularly those in the Western Desert, are accessible by automobile, and several publications give adequate information on how to visit them.[1] With regard to the more remote sites, however, I have intentionally avoided stating their exact location out of concern for their archaeological integrity. As I state in this book, many of these sites are endangered by vandalism, modern quarrying, and unregulated tourism, and I do not wish to contribute to this destruction. Instead, I hope that for those who are determined to venture into the desert, this book instills a deeper appreciation of the beauty and fragility of these ancient sites and a respect for their enormous archaeological and historical importance. In addition, I hope it attracts the attention of Egyptian government officials, archaeological funding organizations, and adventure tour companies, so that they might take further steps to protect not only Greco-Roman sites, but all of the ancient sites in Egypt's deserts.

Finally, although I have made every attempt to incorporate as much of the most recent information on the frontier as I thought appropriate, this is not the definitive work on Rome's Egyptian frontier. Volumes could be written about many of the subjects and places to which I have devoted only a few pages. Indeed, so much archaeological and historical analysis remains to be done on the desert sites that it would be foolhardy to attempt to write a complete analysis of the frontier at this time. No doubt such a work will eventually be published, but it will be written decades hence. Thus, until that work is written, I offer this book to the reader in the hope that it informs with accuracy and increases public interest in this important period of Egyptian history. To the degree it succeeds at these tasks and to the extent it encourages the continued study and heightened protection of these sites, then I shall have accomplished the goal for which I undertook this adventure.

ACKNOWLEDGMENTS

For their encouragement and assistance throughout the long gestation of this volume, I wish to thank James Harrell, Robert "Chip" Vincent, Michael Jones, Arita Baaijens, Willemina Wendrich, Agnès Honigmann, Jason Thompson, and Evan and Susan Bloom. I extend special thanks to my companions with whom I shared so many desert adventures: Carlo Bergmann, Hatim El-Gammal, Patrick Godeau, Barry Iverson, Norbert Schiller, and Michael Sissons. Finally, I acknowledge a gratitude beyond words to my wife, Sarah, whose unflagging encouragement, patience, and guidance saw me through periods of great uncertainty and truly made the completion of this book possible.

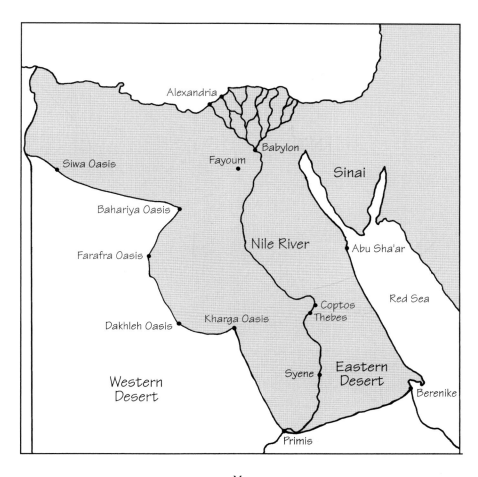

Map 1

INTRODUCTION

For more than five thousand years Egypt has enchanted humankind. In antiquity Mediterranean peoples were fascinated by Egyptian manners and customs, and the mysterious, fabled land inspired countless myths. The Greek historian Herodotus visited Egypt in the fifth century B.C., and his famous description of the land and its people influenced Europeans' opinions about the country for centuries:

> Not only is the climate different from that of the rest of the world, and the rivers unlike any other rivers, but the people also, in most of their manners and customs, exactly reverse the common practice of mankind. The women attend the markets and trade, while the men sit at home at the loom; and here, while the rest of the world works the woof up the warp, the Egyptians work it down; the women likewise carry burthens upon their shoulders, while the men carry them upon their heads. They eat their food out of doors

in the streets, but retire for private purposes to their houses, giving as a reason that what is unseemly, but necessary, ought to be done in secret, but what has nothing unseemly about it should be done openly. A woman cannot serve the priestly office, either for god or goddess, but men are priests to both; sons need not support their parents unless they choose, but daughters must, whether they choose or no.[1]

Among the most remarkable features of Egypt was the river Nile, which the Egyptians revered as a deity for millennia. Indeed, in a desert land nearly devoid of rain, the Nile played the central role in the magnificent flowering of Egyptian civilization that began in 3100 B.C. with the unification of Upper and Lower Egypt under King Narmer. Flowing north from then unknown sources deep in eastern and central Africa, the mighty river bequeathed to Egypt two life-giving essences, water and sediment. The river's flow was constant, but every year during the late summer months the water level rose as the result of heavy monsoon rains falling nearly 6,000 kilometers to the south. By September the river reached its highest level, inundating agricultural lands in the Nile Valley and Delta. As the waters receded, they left in their wake the precious gift of rich, black silt that enabled the Egyptians to plant two crops per year. The annual inundations, however, were never predictable in their intensity, and in years in which the central African rains were light, the resultant lower-than-average rise in the water level endangered the livelihood of Egyptians. On the other hand, in years of heavy rains, the river thundered through the cataracts of the Sudan and Upper Egypt, overflowing its banks and irrigation ditches along the Nile Valley, destroying dams and villages, and drowning crops and livestock. The Egyptians, however, were masters of agricultural planning, organization, and engineering, and generally the disasters brought on by low or high inundations were infrequent enough to permit them to reap an abundance of grain and produce and to build and maintain a civilization that was among the grandest, most prosperous, and longest-lived in antiquity.

Framing this verdant river valley are the unforgiving deserts that today constitute over 95 percent of Egypt's land area and that in ancient times were often referred to as the Land of Fire. Between the Nile and the Red Sea is the Eastern Desert—rugged, mountainous, and forbidding but nevertheless penetrated since ancient times by narrow trails carved out for conducting commerce and accessing the numerous quarries and mines that for more than three thousand years enriched Egypt's pharaohs and foreign sovereigns. To the west of the Nile lies the vast immensity of sand that constitutes the Western Desert. Here, permanent human habitation is possible only in the remote oases of Kharga, Dakhleh, Farafra, Bahariya, and Siwa. Yet it was the very inhospitability of these two great deserts that helped protect successive dynasties from external invasions and pre-serve the peace and security of Egyptian civilization.

Despite the protection afforded by its deserts, Egypt's prosperity made it an at-tractive target for determined invaders. The first successful incursion was made by the Hyksos, a collection of Semitic peoples from Syria and Palestine who swept into Egypt in 1700 B.C. and ruled until their expulsion by the Egyptians in 1575 B.C. From this time onward, Egyptian history was heavily influenced by new groups of people attempting to assert their control over eastern Mediterranean regions: the Hittites, Akkadians, Sumerians, Amorites, Mitannians, and Assyrians. Eventually, even the vast Assyrian empire, which included Egypt, was defeated by Persians in the sixth century B.C. Under successive kings—Cyrus the Great, Cambyses, Dar-ius, and Xerxes—the Persians created an empire that stretched from India to Egypt to Asia Minor before the combined armies of Greek states halted their ex-pansion at the battles of Salamis, Plataea, and Samos. Despite the grand blos-soming of Greek classical culture that followed these victories, however, the Greek states were weakened by generations of political disputes and were collec-tively defeated by Philip II of Macedonia in 338 B.C. Although it was Philip who de-cided to expand further, attacking the Persians and liberating all the regions under their control, his assassination in 336 B.C. left the challenge of that grand campaign to his extraordinary twenty-year-old son, Alexander III.

In a series of spectacular victories, young Alexander defeated the Persians in battle after battle, securing all the major port cities along the coast of Asia Minor and those of Byblos, Sidon, and Tyre in 333 B.C. From there he continued into Egypt, where, after founding the city of Alexandria, he visited the famous oracle of Siwa Oasis deep in the Libyan desert. He went on to become one of the greatest generals in history, founding approximately seventy cities and a multinational em-pire that encouraged commerce and introduced Hellenic civilization into some of the most remote regions of central Asia. His incandescent career, however, ended abruptly when he died at age thirty-three of a fever—compounded perhaps by a heavy bout of drinking—in Babylon in 323 B.C. There being no royal heir to the Macedonian throne, conspiracies and civil wars characterized the years immedi-ately following Alexander's death as his ambitious officers fought for control of the empire. Ultimately, the Hellenistic world was divided into three regions ruled by Alexander's generals: Ptolemy I, Seleucus I, and Antigonus I.

Ptolemy I laid claim to Egypt and founded the thirty-first Egyptian dynasty, the Ptolemies. Under the autocratic rule of the Ptolemies, Greek culture entrenched itself even more deeply in Egyptian society. Alexandria became the largest and most influential city of the Hellenistic world as its great library promoted learning and scholarship in many fields and as its harbors and markets became the economic locus of the Mediterranean. The dynasty reached its economic and political height during the reigns of Ptolemy II (285–246 B.C.) and Ptolemy III (246–221 B.C.), inspiring one ancient writer to extol Egypt's virtues: "In Egypt, there is everything that exists anywhere in the world: wealth, gymnasia, power, peace, fame, sights, philosophers, gold, young men, the shrine of the Sibling Gods, a good king, the Museum, wine—all the good things one could want. And women—more of them, I swear by the daughters of Hades than heaven boasts stars—and their looks; like the goddesses who once induced Paris to judge their beauty!"[2]

The administrative structure established by the Ptolemaic kings dominated Egypt for the next three centuries and created the economic foundation the Romans would later exploit and expand. The Ptolemies divided the country into approximately forty administrative units called *nomes*, within which they officially encouraged Greeks to settle. As payment, soldiers (and select civilians) were given parcels of land known as *kleroi* in the Delta and Nile Valley. This policy served to further entrench Greek culture and language in Egypt. Many Greeks eventually intermarried with Egyptians, thus softening the ethnic distinction between Greek and Egyptian. Indeed, even during the period of Roman domination of Egypt, Greek remained the lingua franca of Egyptian civil administration, Latin being reserved primarily for use in the Roman military.

Along with remolding the Egyptian political structure, the Ptolemies undertook major economic development projects. Most notably, they constructed ambitious irrigation systems that expanded the amount of arable land in the Fayoum (Arsinoite) (see map 4) and the Nile Delta. They also introduced new crops to better suit their needs and tastes, replacing, for example, the traditional emmer wheat with durum wheat and expanding the cultivation of wine in lieu of the traditional Egyptian barley beer. Their most influential economic change, however, was the introduction of currency for use in nearly all commercial exchange. Previously, Egyptians had used a barter system rather than coins for domestic commerce. Although the Ptolemies continued to collect certain taxes, such as those on grain, in kind, levies on other agricultural products required currency. Given the complexities of currency-based economies, the Ptolemies' introduction of gold, silver, and bronze coins had a dramatic effect on the whole of Egyptian society. Political strife, economic problems, and occasional civil wars began to weaken the Ptolemaic dynasty by the second century B.C. Egypt fell increasingly under the influence of Rome, which was fast becoming the major political power in the Mediterranean. Ptolemaic rulers began seeking Roman support to reduce the possibility of an outright Roman invasion and to protect their authority from hostile factions within Alexandria.

It was during this last, turbulent phase of Ptolemaic power that the most famous ruler of that dynasty, perhaps the most celebrated queen of antiquity, acceded to the throne: Cleopatra VII. The reign of this remarkable woman was characterized by her attempts to earn Egypt's independence by engaging in intimate personal and political relationships with powerful Romans: first with Julius Caesar, then Marc Antony. She gave Antony military support for his campaign against the Parthians when Octavian reneged on his promise to send troops to Antony's aid. Her attempts to retain a modicum of Egyptian independence and her success in gaining from Antony nominal control over important regions beyond Egypt contributed to her popularity among her subjects. Ultimately, however, Cleopatra became a client queen of Rome and, as such, could not halt the forces that opposed the man upon whom she depended for her authority. The resultant civil war between Octavian and Marc Antony concluded with Antony and Cleopatra fleeing to Alexandria after their defeat at the sea battle of Actium, guaranteeing that neither Cleopatra nor her Roman overlord and lover could retain the throne of Egypt. Famously entrenched in the royal palace in Alexandria, they awaited their inevitable destruction. Octavian captured Alexandria on August 3, 30 B.C. Antony died that same day, and Cleopatra was asked to help organize his elaborate funeral. After making at least one unsuccessful attempt to starve herself to death, she pleaded with Octavian to permit her children to ascend the throne of Egypt. But such an arrangement was unacceptable to Octavian, who ordered the execution of young Caesarion, Cleopatra's son by Julius Caesar. Although the historical record is imprecise about Octavian's plans for Cleopatra, it is clear that her personal charms and political wiles had little effect on Rome's first emperor. Perhaps Shakespeare's dark version of her future is indeed plausible—a forced return to Rome and inevitable public humiliation:

> Now, Iras, what think'st thou?
> Thou, an Egyptian puppet, shall be shown
> In Rome as well as I. Mechanic slaves
> With greasy aprons, rules, and hammers shall
> Uplift us to the view. In their thick breaths,
> Rank of gross diet, shall we be enclouded,
> And forc'd to drink their vapor.
> . . . and I shall see
> Some squeaking Cleopatra boy my greatness
> I' th' posture of a whore.[3]

Rather than endure such a fate, Cleopatra VII committed suicide on August 12, 30 B.C. and left the throne of Egypt to Octavian.[4]

With the deaths of Antony and Cleopatra, Octavian, now Caesar Augustus, absorbed Egypt directly into the Roman Empire. In light of its importance, Augustus assigned a Roman governor to administer the territory and sent a large contingent of the newly formed Roman Imperial soldiers to defend it from internal and external enemies. The army of Rome consisted of two main components: the Italian legionary troops who formed the infantry and the auxiliary troops composed primarily of non-Roman citizens taken from other Roman provinces. Augustus also assigned three Roman legions, each consisting of 5,600 men, to occupy the country. By A.D. 23, this presence was reduced to two legions, and by the second century A.D. it was further reduced to one.[5] Although their primary task was defensive, the soldiers also engaged in numerous public works, such as building bridges, roads, and canals, guarding trade routes, and serving as administrators in the mines and quarries of the Eastern Desert.

With Egypt now firmly under its control, Rome commenced expanding and exploiting the province's valuable assets. Of highest importance was the grain produced in the Delta, in the Nile Valley, and in the large western oases; the annual output constituted roughly one-third of Rome's total grain consumption. Additionally, Egypt boasted a myriad of other resources originating not in the Nile Valley, but in the Eastern and Western Deserts, including fine ornamental stone from the eastern quarries and gold, silver, and turquoise from its mines. But even such abundance as Egypt offered was insufficient for Imperial Rome, and Augustus expanded his financial ambitions to include the establishment of seaborne trade with Asia and sub-Saharan Africa. This commercial enterprise proved astoundingly lucrative as Egypt became the conduit through which the riches of India and East Africa entered the Roman world. Camel caravans set out from ports on the Red Sea laden with spices, incense, tortoise shell, and pepper. Together with additional commodities such as ivory and rare animals that the Romans obtained from Egypt's southern border with the Sudan and the olive oil and grain produced in the five major oases of the Western Desert, the Egyptian frontier zones constituted an enormously valuable source of wealth for Rome. Because of the area's economic importance, Augustus risked the possible usurpation of the province by an ambitious Roman senator. Consequently, he appointed governors of Egypt from the equestrian ranks of Roman society and issued strict orders that no senator or equestrian could visit Egypt without the emperor's approval.

Unlike the Ptolemies, the Romans did not encourage emigration to Egypt, although they did permit landownership by Romans. Most of the Roman-sounding names that survive in the historical record, however, are Egyptian residents who attained Roman citizenship by proclamation rather than by Roman birth. Throughout the Roman period, Alexandria was the major urban center of Egypt, and, at least initially, until a policy change around the beginning of the third century, only Alexandrine citizens were eligible for Roman citizenship. Egyptian society thus consisted of several distinct groups: Roman citizens, Alexandrine citizens, citizens of major Greek *poleis*, and the rest of the Egyptian population, referred to as *Aiguptioi*. Among the largest towns were Oxyrhynchus and Hermopolis, which had populations of roughly twenty-five thousand and forty thousand, respectively, while the smallest settlements supported fewer than a hundred residents.[6]

Although Egypt continued to develop and prosper well into the middle of the third century, when the rest of the Roman Empire experienced a series of political and economic crises, the province ultimately could not remain immune to the gradual decline in Roman stability. New taxation policies, changes to the administrative structure, and price inflation began to plague Egyptian society. Of profound importance, too, was the gradual Christianization of Egypt. The spread of this new faith affected virtually every aspect of Egyptian life from religious practices and institutions to individual attitudes regarding wealth and politics. Oases and desert populations grew as an unknown number of Christians retreated into Egypt's remote areas, either to escape the early persecutions under emperors Decius, Valerian, and Diocletian or to achieve spiritual cleansing. From these nascent communities emerged the earliest monastic movement in Christianity. Indeed, many of these early Christians left substantial records of their presence in the oases and remote caves of the Western and Eastern Deserts.

Numerous scholarly publications and several general books dealing with the Roman period in Egypt are available to interested readers. This book, however, focuses on issues relating to the remote desert regions of Roman Egypt. Today, archaeologists from nearly a dozen nations are at work in many of these desert areas, and every year they uncover additional evidence that sheds new light on old theories concerning the role of Rome's Egyptian frontier and the nature of its administration. While much has been done by this dedicated group of scholars, much more work remains in every corner of the frontier. Indeed, for those sites that are most remote, the need for excavation is acute—for it is only by intensive gathering and study of the material culture of these sites that their secrets can be saved from the ravages of weather, development, and theft.

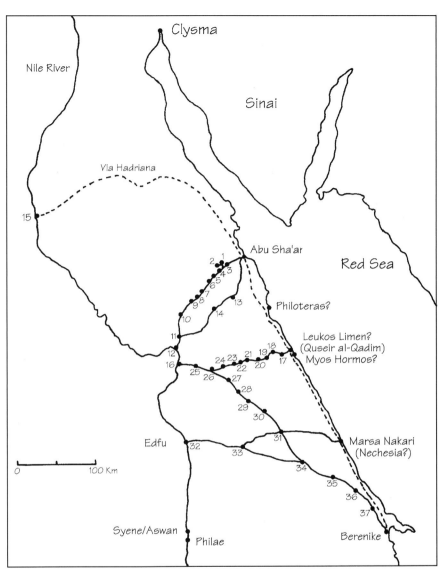

Clysma

Nile River

Sinai

Via Hadriana

15

Abu Sha'ar

Red Sea

2 1
5 4 3
6
9 8 7
13
10
14

Philoteras?

11

Leukos Limen?
(Quseir al-Qadim)
Myos Hormos?

12
16

24 23
25 26
27

21 19 18
22 20
17

28

29
30

Edfu

32
33

31

Marsa Nakari
(Nechesia?)

34
35
36
37

Syene/Aswan
Philae

Berenike

0   100 Km

1. Wadi Umm Sidri	14. Abu Zawal	27. Didyme
2. Mons Porphyrites	15. Antinoopolis/Sheikh Ibada	28. Afrodito
3. Wadi Belih	16. Coptos/Qift	29. Compasi
4. Badla	17. El-Iteima	30. Jovis
5. Umm Balad	18. Seyala	31. Aristonis
6. Wadi al-Qattar	19. El-Hamrah	32. Apollonopolis Magna/Edfu
7. Deir al-Atrash	20. El-Zerkah	33. El-Kanais
8. Bab el-Mukhenig	21. El-Fawakir	34. Falacro
9. El-Saqqia	22. El-Hammamat	35. Apollomos
10. El-Heita	23. El-Muweih	36. Cabalsi
11. El-'Aras	24. Qasr el-Banat	37. Vetus Hydreuma
12. Qena	25. El-Matula	
13. Mons Claudianus	26. Phenicon/El-Laqeita	

Map 2

PART ONE

THE EASTERN DESERT

I

THE HILLS OF SMOKE, GEBEL DOKHAN

But here in the "Hills of Smoke" one thinks of these antiquities with a feeling bordering on veneration. If the workmanship tells of an art that is dead, how much louder does the material cry out the praises of an energy that is also dead?[1]

From the summit of Gebel Dokhan (Mountain of Smoke) in the Eastern Desert, one can see the Red Sea to the east, the Sinai beyond, and all around the vast ruggedness of the Red Sea mountains. Here the air is pure and the silence complete. But these hills were not always peaceful. As the rising sun casts a golden veil over the peaks, one hears the wind whisper a story of long ago when, for nearly four hundred years, the Romans assaulted these mountains with iron and muscle.

The Romans came for porphyry—*porfido rosso antico*—a rare purple stone favored for statuary and used also as a veneer to decorate the walls and floors of palaces. There are three principal kinds of porphyry: one contains white feldspar crystals, a second contains rose-colored feldspar crystals, and a third is black. The so-called Imperial variety contains the white crystals. It is found nowhere else in the world but in the vicinity of Gebel Dokhan, and the Romans spared neither expense, effort, nor human life to extract it from these mountains.

Exactly when the purple treasure of Gebel Dokhan was discovered remains a mystery. A few small porphyry bowls dating from the Old Kingdom (2613–2181 B.C.) have been found, and the remains of an early dynastic hut are not far from the quarries, indicating that the ancient Egyptians sent workers into the area to extract small amounts of the stone. Clearly, however, they did not exploit porphyry to any significant degree. During the Ptolemaic period (323–30 B.C.), the only known evidence that porphyry was quarried and exported is found in the Old Testament. The Book of Esther has the following description of the gardens at the royal palace of Ahasuerus, king of Susa: "There were . . . couches of gold and silver on a mosaic pavement of porphyry, marble, mother-of-pearl and precious stones."[2] Although scholars believe the Book of Esther was written during the Ptolemaic period (sometime between 350 and 125 B.C., the latter date being more likely), there is little evidence that porphyry was used during the reign of the Ptolemies. Instead, it was the Romans who first exploited the stone on a massive scale, and recent excavations by British archaeologists have identified exactly when the Romans came to Gebel Dokhan.

In March 1995, researchers discovered a black porphyry stele in a hut located in the small village of the Bradford quarry.[3] The stele measures 56 centimeters by 40 centimeters and depicts Pan-Min, the ithyphallic god of the Eastern Desert, standing beneath the winged sun disk and two cobras. The inscription to the right of the picture states, "Caius Cominius Leugas,[4] who discovered the quarries of the porphyry stone and knekites and black porphyry and also [found] multicolored stones, dedicated a sanctuary to Pan and Serapis very great gods for the well-being of his children. The 4th year of Tiberius Caesar Augustus Epeiph the 29th."[5]

The date on this inscription corresponds with July 23, A.D. 18, and marks the likely beginning of the Roman exploitation of the vast complex of quarries known today as Mons Porphyrites (Mountain of Porphyry). So impressive is the site that some modern archaeologists consider it "one of the most remarkable manifestations of Roman activity anywhere in the Empire."[6] This is hardly an exaggeration. The remote and hostile location of the quarries, the logistical difficulty of sustaining a large population of workers at the site, and the magnitude of the labor required to extract the stone and transport it to the Nile stagger the imagination.

THE FORTRESS AND TEMPLES

Mons Porphyrites lies at the heart of the Red Sea mountains, 45 kilometers west of the Red Sea and 140 kilometers east of the Nile River (see map 2). It is dominated by Gebel Dokhan[7] and consists of four main quarrying areas located on the

1.1 The remains of the fortress at Mons Porphyrites as viewed from the south. The
five standing granite columns that supported a roof for the cistern
are visible amid the rubble.

upper slopes of both sides of a valley called Wadi Abu Ma'amel (Father of Work-
ings), which runs from south to north. These principal quarries are the Northwest, the Lycabettos, the Southwest (Romulus), and the Lepsius. Such evidence as
an inscription dated July 4, A.D. 29. (Tiberius) suggests that the Northwest quarry
and its village date from the first to the third centuries A.D., while Lycabettos and
its small villages date from the third to the fourth centuries A.D.[8]

The main fortified village, or *castellum*, at Mons Porphyrites stands 6 meters
above the wadi floor on the eastern side. Due to the erosion of its rock foundation
by water flowing down the wadi, it is slowly crumbling into the wadi itself. The
fort is just over 600 meters above sea level, measures approximately 45 by 85 meters, and contains many rooms, a large cistern, and a bakery. While the fort is essentially in ruins (fig. 1.1), detailed architectural studies of the building have
enabled researchers to speculate with some confidence about how it might have
appeared when the Romans occupied it.

Aside from the castellum, the village attached to the Northwest quarry, and numerous small villages adjacent to the other quarries, few buildings have survived at Mons Porphyrites. Indeed, the number of known buildings in the area seem insufficient to house the apparently large number of men who worked the quarries at any given time. Some scholars think that prisoners, conscripted laborers, and slaves might not have been housed in structures that were of sufficient quality to survive for fifteen centuries. It would have been far more practical and economical to house them in lightly constructed sheds or tents. In other quarry sites in the Eastern Desert, such as those at Bir Umm Fawakir in Wadi Hammamat, small crude huts can be found outside the main settlements. It is possible that such huts existed in the main wadi at Mons Porphyrites, but no trace of them survives.

Of course, one of the difficulties posed by the use of such lightly built structures is that if they housed prisoners, their flimsiness increased the possibility of escape. This raises the question of whether the prisoners were put in chains upon their return from the quarries. But another possibility is suggested by the ancient writer Aelius Aristeides, who traveled in Egypt during the second century A.D. Referring to Mons Porphyrites, he stated that in "this renowned convict quarry of porphyry, the prisoners are not guarded by any military force, so destitute is the place of water."[9]

In addition to the buildings that accommodated the residents of Mons Porphyrites, two major temples answered to their spiritual needs. The smaller temple, a few meters south of the fort, is dedicated to Isis. While little remains of the temple itself, the door lintel—now fallen and broken in two—contains an inscription that pinpoints the date and purpose of the structure: "In the time when Marcus Rutilius Lupus was the governor of Egypt, Marcus Papirius Celer, a decurion of the *Ala Vocontiorum*, erected the temple to the great goddess Isis, in the sixteenth year of Trajan's reign."[10]

Further south of the castellum are the remains of the second temple, this one to Serapis, the Sun God. The small but exquisitely crafted structure rests atop a rocky promontory that juts out into the wadi and is reached by a wide staircase (fig. 1.2). The temple had four columns in front, supporting an architrave and an entablature, but these have fallen forward onto the court (figs. 1.3, 1.4). Despite their age, the stones look as if they were recently cut, and a clear inscription dedicates "the temple and the area around the temple to Zeus Helios Great Serapis and gods who share the temple, by Epaphroditus, slave of Caesar, Sigerianus, when Rammius Martialis was Prefect of Egypt, when Marcus Ulpius Chresimus was *procurator metallorum*, and when Proculianus was Centurion."[11] No date is

1.2 The stairway leading to the main temple at Mons Porphyrites.

1.3 Fallen columns and portions of the architrave lying in forecourt of the temple.

1.4 A portion of the dedicative inscription on temple lintel.

visible on the inscription, but Rammius Martialis was the governor of Egypt from A.D. 117 to 119, which gives us an approximate date for the building's construction. The omission of a date, an important element in Roman inscriptions, has led some scholars to speculate that the temple was never completed.[12] But given that the Romans exploited Mons Porphyrites until at least the mid–fourth century, it seems improbable they would have left the temple unfinished for two hundred years.

THE QUARRY RAMPS

Most of the larger quarries in Mons Porphyrites are located near the summits of the mountains on either side of Wadi Abu Ma'amel. The heights of the quarries range from 1,200 meters to 1,600 meters, and the slopes leading to them are perilously steep and covered with loose stones. Access to the porphyry was made possible by narrow, well-constructed paths that zigzag up the slopes to the quarries and their attendant villages. More impressive than these paths, however, are the massive ramps or slipways the Romans built to enable them to lower the quarried stone into the wadi.

These ramps are remarkable feats of engineering and labor. Upon first beholding them, one is inclined to believe, as one early visitor wrote, that "the feats of skill and endurance performed by the workmen under Roman direction take on the character of a miracle tinged with mystery."[13] Of all the slipways at Mons Porphyrites, that serving the Lycabettos quarry is the longest (two kilometers) and the most impressive (figs 1.5, 1.6). From its beginning at the 1,600-meter-high quarry, the ramp descends steeply down the mountain, passes the high quarry village, and then slopes gently down to the west side of Wadi Abu Ma'amel. At its base, approximately two kilometers from the main castellum, is a loading ramp from which the rock was transferred to carts for the continued journey down the wadi to the larger loading ramp at Wadi Umm Sidri. Nearby lie the remains of a small village where masons inspected and further worked the stone blocks that came down to them from the quarries above before sending them on their way.

Exactly how the stones were lowered to the valley remains one of the intriguing mysteries of the Roman presence at Mons Porphyrites. Although there is evidence, particularly at the Romulus quarry, that some porphyry blocks were simply tumbled over the edge to be retrieved by men working below, this could not have been the method employed for the bulk of the stone. Instead, it is certain that the ramps played a vital role in the difficult and dangerous process of bringing the stone to the valley floor.

One puzzling characteristic of the ramps is that they are punctuated on both sides by large cylindrical cairns of expertly packed stones. The cairns are all heavily damaged, but their remains average approximately 1.5 meters high and 3 meters across and are more frequent at those places where the angle of the ramp is steepest. These cairns are found only at Mons Porphyrites and Mons Claudianus; they are not at any other quarry in Egypt (fig. 1.7). They are of a larger diameter and more numerous at Mons Porphyrites because the quarry ramps here are much higher and longer than those at Mons Claudianus. It seems the cairns played a role in the lowering of the quarried stone, but scholars disagree on the exact nature of that role. Several archaeologists who have examined the cairns conjecture that they are piles of stones used in the maintenance and reparation of the ramps.[14] But this explanation seems implausible. The cairns are built with a slightly inward camber—hardly the kind of structure one would build simply to provide a convenient source of replacement stones.

One expert on Roman quarries in the Eastern Desert theorizes that a log might have been laid across the ramp on the uphill sides of a pair of cairns to act as a control barrier for sleds carrying the blocks of stone. This way the blocks could be

1.5 A portion of the two-kilometer ramp leading to the Lycabettos quarry as viewed from the mountains on the east side of Wadi Ma'amel.

1.6 The upper section of the ramp leading to the Lycabettos quarry located near the summit of the mountain. The human figure (barely visible approximately three-quarters of the way up the ramp) gives a sense of the enormous size of the structure.

1.7 Large cairns alongside the ramp leading to Lycabettos quarry.

lowered down the ramps, one pair of cairns at a time, the logs preventing the sleds from sliding uncontrollably.[15] While this explanation offers a logical use for the cairns as safety devices, it does not adequately explain how the heavy blocks themselves were controlled as they were being lowered from one set of cairns to the next. In some places the incline of the ramps is fairly gentle, but in other places it is so steep that it would have been impossible for men holding the sled to control it as it descended the ramp.

Perhaps the cairns served both as emergency brakes for the sleds and as anchor points for ropes used to ease the sleds down the ramp. To be used as anchor points, the cairns, whose stones were not mortared together, might have been sheathed on the outside with wide iron bands that would have spread the weight over the surface of the cairn more evenly. Chains could then have been wrapped around the encased cairn to fasten heavy sets of pulleys, through which ropes could be used to belay the heavy cargo in a controlled descent of the mountain. More plausibly, the workers might have placed logs against the uphill sides of the cairns and fastened pulleys and belaying ropes directly to them. This way, they could ease the sleds down to a log resting against the next set of cairns below, then repeat the procedure. In either case, during the lowering of particularly heavy blocks or columns, two or three sets of cairns could have been used simultaneously to distribute the weight more evenly and reduce the strain on the ropes and men. If sleds were used to convey the stone—as opposed to the larger stones simply being slid down the mountain—the cairns and logs also might have aided in dragging the heavy sleds back up the mountain once the porphyry had been delivered to the valley below.

Unfortunately, archaeologists have yet to discover any remains of iron bands, logs, pulleys, ropes, or sleds that might confirm the use of the system just described. Indeed, some scholars doubt that the cairns could have borne the enormous weight necessary to serve as winches.[16] But the lack of such evidence is not surprising. Almost sixteen centuries of floods, erosion, and scavenging by local bedouin have virtually eliminated all artifacts from Mons Porphyrites that were not made of stone or clay or that were not buried. Only a single, small piece of an iron tool has been found at Mons Porphyrites thus far, and even this item—the tip of a pickax—cannot be dated to the Roman period with certainty.[17]

The ravages of time and severe weather have taken their toll on the mighty ramps, but not all of the erosion has been natural. In November 1932, a European visitor witnessed damage being done to the Lycabettos ramp by workers from the Egyptian Mines Department as they attempted to extract a limited quantity of imperial porphyry for King Fouad. While repairing the ramp up to the western mountain, the workers nearly demolished many of the ancient cairns. The observer added that "the first heavy rain-storm . . . will inevitably undo most of this repair, and the half-ruined butts, which had remained in almost perfect condition for more than fifteen hundred years, will now rapidly follow it into dissolution."[18]

THE QUARRIES

In all of the quarries and on much of the stone debris found in the wadis nearby one can see the inscriptions, wedge holes, toolmarks, and quarry numbers left by the Romans in the process of extracting the stone. Above a precarious ledge in the Lycabettos quarry, for example, the following portion of an inscription is neatly carved in large, squared letters: "I, Pancratius, Centurio *frumentarius*, gave it as a vow . . ." Unfortunately, we shall never know what Pancratius gave as his vow, as that section of rock face is missing (fig. 1.8). But the inscription is helpful nevertheless. The frumentarii were men originally detailed from the Roman legions to collect supplies, but in the third century they came to be used for a variety of special services.[19] Diocletian abolished the frumentarii during his reign (A.D. 284–305), so it is probable that Pancratius inscribed the words to his vow sometime in the mid–third century.[20] This and other inscriptions may aid scholars in dating the working of the quarries—and serve as poignant reminders of the men who struggled there—but the toolmarks and wedge holes found in the stone debris offer more definitive insights into Roman quarrying techniques.

By the Roman period, tools for working stone were made of iron, not, as is popularly believed, wood. To extract the stone, the quarrymen cut a series of wedge holes along a line marking the intended separation of a block from its parent rock. The wedge holes were cut so as to ensure a tight fit with the sides of the wedge itself, but each hole was deep enough to prevent the wedge from hitting the bottom of the hole. Thus the wedge, when struck by heavy blows, pressed more forcefully and evenly on the walls of the wedge holes. Ideally, after sufficient skillful hammering, the rock would split cleanly and the block would break free.

Worked stones remaining in the quarries show that masons sometimes repaired cracks and large chips that occurred during cutting if the fracture was not of sufficient size to render the entire column, block, or sarcophagus unsound. In some cases, masons used iron staples to hold damaged stone together, but if the crack worsened, a column would simply be abandoned or cut up into smaller pieces. Unlike Mons Claudianus to the south, however, which is littered with abandoned granite columns, basins, and pedestals, it seems the Romans left behind only two complete porphyry artifacts at Mons Porphyrites: a pillar, cracked in

1.8 The rock face in the Lycabettos quarry that contains the
partial inscription of Pancratius.

1.9 The broken porphyry bathtub located in the lower village
of the Northwest quarry.

three places and lying high in the Northwest quarry; and a splendid bathtub in the
blacksmith's hut of the Northwest quarry's lower village (fig. 1.9).

Given the enormous volume of stone quarried in Mons Porphyrites, the blacksmiths certainly were kept busy repairing, replacing, and sharpening the iron
tools of the quarrymen. They fueled their forges with large quantities of charcoal
made from the wood of acacia trees. In the villages of Mons Porphyrites and at
many Roman sites in the Eastern Desert, deposits of charcoal indicate where the
blacksmiths worked their furnaces. Surprisingly, after fifteen hundred years,
much of this charcoal is still usable.[21]

THE RESIDENTS OF MONS PORPHYRITES

Aside from the information provided by the inscriptions mentioned above, scholars know relatively little about the people who ran the daily operations of Mons
Porphyrites. Of the hundreds of ostraca found in the rubbish heaps next to the
main settlement, only a few furnish information about the men (and possibly
women) who lived and worked there. One such ostracon, for example, gives a clue

about the military's role at the settlement. At the top, it contains a heading in Greek—"those who go the rounds and visit the posts of sentinels, patrols"—and consists of a partial list of soldiers assigned to each of the four night watches the Romans maintained at the quarry complex.[22] But the question of who performed the wrenching labor of quarrying the porphyry remains a mystery. Until recently most scholars agreed that many, if not most, were convicts. It was common for criminals in Egypt to be condemned to the mines and quarries, especially during the Jewish and Christian persecutions.[23] There is, however, conflicting evidence on this issue. For example, none of the recovered ostraca mention convicts. In addition, we shall see later that the most recent findings from the granite quarries of Mons Claudianus—50 kilometers south of Mons Porphyrites—indicate that the workers there were paid, free laborers. Given that at least during the Antonine dynasty (A.D. 96–192), the two great quarries were similarly organized, there is a strong possibility that the men of Mons Porphyrites were also free. Supporting this theory is the discovery of an ostracon that contains a list of the following civilian occupations at the site: bellowsmen, storekeepers, hammermen, bakers, firewood gatherers, carpenters, and a herald.[24] Of course, the presence of these specialized workers does not eliminate the possibility that they were convicts or that convicts were used to perform some of the nonspecialized heavy manual labor required in the quarrying process, but, again, the documents from Mons Claudianus do not support this theory.

Whether they were criminals or not, the quarrymen faced a difficult and dangerous task as they separated the blocks of stone from the mountainside. The work was made more perilous by the height of the quarries themselves and the extreme steepness of the slopes that had to be negotiated in the process of lowering the blocks of stone to the valley. The first segment of the Lycabettos ramp, for example, slopes down to the quarry village at a 40-degree angle (see fig. 1.6). Because the Lycabettos quarry village rests on a short, narrow col and straddles the main slipway, one assumes the lowering of the heavy stone was well controlled; a runaway sled full of porphyry would have caused a catastrophe.

As in all quarries, however, accidents undoubtedly occurred at Mons Porphyrites. No records of such events have yet been found, but a small graveyard along the ridge to the east of the Lycabettos village may be where men who died in the high quarry were laid to rest. The only gravestone ever found in this cemetery is now in the Egyptian National Museum in Cairo. The stone is a small slab (60 by 18 by 5 centimeters) of roughly shaped porphyry, now broken into two pieces. Interestingly, it belonged to a Christian and states, "John from the hamlet of Nilos of the Hermopolite (nome)."[25] The fact that John received a headstone upon his death makes it improbable that he was a convict. Although he might have been a conscripted laborer, more likely he was a Christian hermit who lived in the area after the Romans abandoned the quarries in the fourth century. If so, then the graveyard dates from the period following Roman abandonment of the quarry. Some literature reports that hermits lived at Mons Porphyrites—as they did in the nearby mountains—but archaeological evidence has not yet confirmed this.[26]

SUSTENANCE FOR THE QUARRY WORKERS

As at all of the Roman stations in the Eastern Desert, the most important requirement at Mons Porphyrites was maintaining an adequate water supply. But other than a few small seasonal pools, there were no permanent natural water sources in the nearby mountains. Water was obtained solely from two large wells dug into the floor of the wadi; these reached pockets of ancient water beneath the valley floor.[27] The wells are still visible and appear to have served the needs of the entire population of soldiers and workers. The first is located near the middle of the wadi, approximately 150 meters west-northwest of the fortress, and the second lies on the east side of the wadi between the fortress and the Bradford quarry.

Of the two wells, the one closer to the fortress is the most interesting. It is a round pit, and along its rim are five pillars made of mortared stone and covered with plaster, which must have once supported a roof made of either woven mats or palm branches[28] (fig. 1.10). From here, men or animals must have carried heavy water bags into the fortress, then emptied them into the large cistern. After fifteen centuries, the well is now a dry depression filled with soil and rocks, but several of the pillars remain in surprisingly good condition. Scratched into their surfaces are graffiti including an Aramaic/Hebrew inscription and a nineteenth-century graffito by an Armenian land surveyor named Hekekyan Bey. The most mysterious graffiti, however, are a series of crudely drawn sailing ships on three of the five pillars.[29] One expert on Roman remains in the Eastern Desert concludes that the drawings are of merchant vessels, but adds that dating the ships is difficult. Two of the drawings are probably of seventeenth-century vessels, while the smallest drawings (11.8 by 19 centimeters and 28 by 43 centimeters) appear to depict the famous sickle boat that has been used on the Nile River throughout Egyptian history (fig. 1.11).[30]

Not surprisingly, in the large, well-preserved village of the Northwest quarry, which sits high up on the mountainside, there is no evidence of a well. Water for this village was no doubt carried up by donkeys and poured into a cistern still vis-

1.10 The main well located in the wadi floor approximately 150 meters from the fortress.

ible in the southeast section of the village. This typical stone tank, approximately 3 meters wide, was sunk into the ground and coated with a thick layer of lime plaster. A ledge on the inside may have supported a wooden cover intended to reduce evaporation.

Of course, the men in the quarries also needed water as they labored throughout the day, and it was carried up to them with difficulty. Footpaths zigzag up the mountain slopes. About halfway along each of these paths are small stone structures whose purpose is uncertain. They could have served as watchtowers, guard houses, or, as some recent evidence hints, small temples (fig. 1.12). The trails leading past these buildings up to the summits are well engineered and well constructed. Even so, in places it would have been hazardous to drive a heavily laden donkey. Thus teams of men were probably employed in the arduous task of hauling goatskins filled with water up to the quarries on their backs. Indeed, the ostracon mentioned earlier, which lists the various occupations of civilians at the site, includes an entry for "water bag carriers for the quarries."

In light of the limited number and size of the wells at Mons Porphyrites, water must have been carefully rationed, compounding the harshness of an already difficult life. Recent discoveries of dated ostraca reveal that quarrying was a year-

1.11 Close-up of one of the columns at the Mons Porphyrites well. The engraved picture of a sailing ship is visible in the plaster in the middle of the column.

1.12 One of the small huts located on a path leading to the high quarries. The hut may have served as a guard post, rest station, or temple.

round operation. During the summer, working in the quarries must have been miserable beyond description. One would like to believe the Romans shifted to a night schedule during the hottest months of the year. This would have reduced the number of deaths, illnesses, and accidents caused by the effects of dehydration and, on a practical level, reduced the amount of water that had to be brought up the mountains. Such a schedule might have been possible during periods of a full or nearly full moon but would have required extensive use of artificial lighting at other times. Archaeologists, however, have not uncovered any evidence of night-time operations.

While the Romans could meet their needs for water by carefully managing local sources, they obviously imported most of their food from the Nile Valley. These imports would have included meat, vegetables, and grains like wheat, barley, and corn. Fish from the Red Sea and such game as ibex, gazelle, desert hares, and ostrich probably supplemented the agricultural foodstuffs brought from the Nile Valley. According to the stories told by local bedouin, these animals were numerous in ancient times. Looking at the landscape today, one finds it difficult to believe that such game was ever abundant. But thousands of years before the Romans came, much of the Eastern Desert was a savanna woodland that must have supported a great variety of wildlife. While it seems there was slightly more perennial vegetation in the Eastern Desert during the Roman period than there is today, the amount of rainfall was about the same, and descriptions of that time indicate that the desert was still regarded as barren. Pliny (circa A.D. 50) stated that as soon as one leaves Qift (on the Nile) for the east, "passing through the desert, we find nothing growing except the thorn called 'dry thorn.'"[31]

The Romans are partially responsible for today's dearth of plant and animal life. Their large, concentrated presence for four hundred years in a fragile desert ecosystem must have had a devastating effect. In addition to hunting animals, the Romans cut down large numbers of acacia trees to make charcoal to forge tools and to separate gold from ore in their gold mines. Once these trees were gone, the food chain was irrevocably altered.[32]

THE FIRST STAGE IN TRANSPORTING PORPHYRY
TO THE NILE VALLEY

Scholars continue to debate the exact method used to lower the stone from the quarries, yet the fact remains that the descent into the valley was only the beginning of a much longer journey. Once at the bottom of the ramps, the stone was still 140 kilometers from the Nile River, 700 kilometers from Alexandria, and 2,500 kilometers from Rome. This longer journey began as the quarried porphyry was pulled on rollers or carts past the fortress, temples, and wells of Wadi Ma'amel and proceeded north until the wadi intersected with eastward-flowing Wadi Umm Sidri (see map 2). This was the only viable route out of the Gebel Dokhan area. Today, Wadi Abu Ma'amel is strewn with fifteen hundred years' worth of stone debris cast down from the mountains by countless floods. But two thousand years ago, the Romans constructed a smooth, paved surface through these wadis, short sections of which are still visible, especially that portion leading from the Southwest village. Along this road, camels, mules, or donkeys pulled carts loaded with porphyry down to a water station approximately eight kilometers from Mons Porphyrites.[33] A single acacia tree in the middle of the wadi now marks the site of the remains of this station. Here, the draft animals were watered and rested before continuing the trip another eight kilometers to the great loading ramp in Wadi Umm Sidri, where the stone was put onto large wagons for the long westward journey to the Nile (fig. 1.13).

1.13 The large loading ramp in Wadi Umm Sidri, approximately 16 kilometers from Mons Porphyrites. The height of the ramp at its far edge is just under 2 meters. Here the Romans transferred loads of porphyry that had been carried down Wadi Ma'amel onto larger wagons for the westward journey across the desert to the Nile River.

From the Wadi Umm Sidri ramp, the Roman route is clearly marked by small cairns as it bends around the eastern foothills of the Gebel Dokhan range. Wheel tracks of the ancient carts—measuring approximately 3 meters across—are still visible in some places along this route. As it approaches Wadi Belih, the road bends to the southwest and passes within a kilometer of the small Roman fort of Wadi Belih. Then it turns west, heading past the Badia station, and continues over the watershed pass to Wadi Qattar and beyond, eventually reaching the Nile at Qena.

THE FORT AT WADI BELIH

Prior to arriving at the Badia fort from the east, one encounters the much-ruined station at Wadi Belih (see map 2). The fort, which dates from the first to second centuries A.D., measures only 28 meters by 25 meters and is the third smallest Roman fort in Egypt. At most, it could have held fifteen to eighteen cavalrymen or twenty-eight to thirty-six infantrymen.[34] Its purpose, however, is uncertain

1.14 Looking toward the southeast, the diminutive fort in Wadi Belih being photographed from a nearby hill.

because it is slightly distant from the road that leads from the Wadi Umm Sidri loading ramp to the Nile and because it does not appear to contain a well, cistern, or animal lines (that is, long troughs for feeding and tethering animals). Its placement in the middle of the wadi, however, implies that such structures may have been erased over the centuries by the powerful floods occurring in these mountains every few years. Despite its size and distance from the main road, some scholars believe that the fort served to monitor traffic from the quarries to the Nile.[35] Another possibility is that it was a forward observation and patrol post, whose primary function was to protect the eastern entrance to the porphyry road and control access to the area around the Badia fort (fig. 1.14).

THE BADIA FORT

Of the eight known stations along the ancient route to the Nile River, none is as enigmatic as that of Badia. Its size leads one to think it must have played a central, although as yet unclear, role in the overall administration of the quarries at Mons Porphyrites. Possibly it was used to manage such supplies as food, tools, and pottery. It also appears to have been a major resting place and water station during the operation of the quarries at Mons Porphyrites, on the other side of Gebel Dokhan. Surface pottery indicates that it was also used in the fourth and fifth centuries after the quarries had been abandoned.

Part of Badia's allure is its setting. Immediately beyond the settlement to the north, Gebel Dokhan rises majestically, while to the southwest the mountains of Wadi Qattar thrust heavenward, forming a dark, forbidding backdrop reminiscent of a Da Vinci painting. The fort itself measures 37 meters by 45 meters and is built of well-stacked local stone. Nine towers punctuate the walls; two of these flank the only entrance gate, which faces south. The collapsed state of the fort does not hide the fact that parapets lined the inner wall: the remains of one are still visible on the northwest wall.

The two halves of a large, broken grinding wheel lie in a room in the southeast corner of the fort. Here the Romans ground wheat and barley imported from the Nile Valley before transporting it over the mountain and into the quarries on the other side. Scholars who have studied the surface pottery and coins have been able to date the fortress to the first to third and fourth to sixth centuries. This seems to indicate that the fort played an important logistical role during the period when the quarries were being worked. It then declined until the fort of Abu Sha'ar on the Red Sea was built, at which point it became a major station along the Abu Sha'ar–Nile route. According to one scholar, it functioned, "no doubt, as part of the *limes* system in place in the region after the early fourth century, if not earlier."[36]

Extensive animal lines are plainly visible to the south of the fortress, but the well is located in a depression 200 meters to the north. Animals were apparently brought to the well from their shelter outside the southern entrance of the fort, then returned after they had been watered in order to prevent them from contaminating the water source. The well itself is still used by local bedouins to water their animals, wash clothes, and fill their containers for domestic use.

The most mysterious feature of the Badia fortress is a circular walled enclosure measuring approximately 40 meters in diameter and located some 50 meters to the west of the fort. The wall, almost 4 meters high in places, is made of stacked stones and surrounds an enormous rock outcropping twice the height of the wall (fig. 1.15). The enclosure, which has a single entrance on the eastern side, contains neither rooms nor inscriptions of any kind, although remains of a catwalk can be seen in some sections of the wall. Scholars speculate about the purpose of this structure, yet to date no one has advanced a generally accepted explanation of why the Romans went to so much trouble to build a stone wall around a rock. There are no marks on the rock except for a large, shallow hole hacked out of the top. In 1949, Leo Tregenza's guide pointed out a place where the granite had been blasted by dynamite and told Tregenza the following story:

1.15 The mysterious walled enclosure near the Badia fortress.

In the Valley there are old books about treasures and gold in the desert. In Qena a Copt once told me that one of the stories is about this place. It says that somewhere inside this rock are hidden the treasures of seven kings; that there is a well-concealed iron door here, and if a man succeeded in finding it and went in, he would come to a slave with a sword guarding it inside. If he showed fear, the slave would kill him; but if he entered fearlessly, the slave would let him pass and the treasures would be his. Some years ago, a man came up from Qena with a *fellah* and some dynamite, and blew away part of the granite here; but finding nothing but the rock inside, he made no second attempt and went away.[37]

This is a charming story, but a more plausible explanation for this structure is that it had some spiritual function. Regrettably, there is no precedent for such a design anywhere else in the Eastern Desert nor, to my knowledge, anywhere in the Roman world.

From the Badia fort, the Romans hauled their loads of porphyry westward along a well-defined route that led deeper into the desert wilderness. The surviving section of the road from the Badia fort back to Wadi Balih offers a good example of just how much effort the Romans put into their desert roads. It varies in width from 20 to 50 meters, and all the larger stones have been meticulously cleared to the side, leaving a smooth, gravel path. The road continues south for four kilometers until it connects with Wadi Balih, then turns southwest toward the Qattar pass. Much of the route to the Nile was undoubtedly as well constructed as this section, but unfortunately, it alone survives. Being on slightly higher ground, it may have been able to withstand the many centuries of floods.

THE FOOTPATH FROM BADIA TO MONS PORPHYRITES

The Romans maintained close communication between the settlements at Badia and Mons Porphyrites by means of a narrow road that served as a shortcut over the mountains. It begins just behind the walled rock at Badia and is marked by small cairns until it dips into the outwash of several small tributary wadis, after which it virtually disappears amidst the chaos of stones. The road heads west-southwest until it rounds a short spur of Gebel Dokhan. There it turns up a wide, steep ravine that leads over a narrow pass and down into Mons Porphyrites on the other side of the mountain (fig. 1.16). Halfway up the ravine, the road passes a small, unexcavated Roman station. During my hikes through the area, I called this the phantom station because it was difficult to see from a distance, even with binoculars.

1.16 The beginning of the footpath that connected Badia with Mons Porphyrites on the other side of the mountains. Note the ancient cairns marking the route.

Like most stations in the region, it was constructed of local stones and is therefore well camouflaged in color and texture. Only the angularity of its shape would enable anyone to recognize it as a human construction. Because the building has been heavily damaged, however, the angularity is limited, especially from a distance. Add to these characteristics the shimmering of early afternoon heat waves, and one can understand why the station is often invisible from the valley below. In reality, however, the phantom station has thick walls with parapets. It is heavily damaged from floods thundering down the ravine, but the walls on its eastern side are well preserved and reach a height of more than 3 meters. Inside are six rooms, four on the northern side and two on the southwestern corner. The southern wall is most heavily damaged and almost entirely collapsed.

From the station, the road changes into a narrow footpath that zigzags its way to the top of the ravine. Because of the loose scree, the footing is treacherous and at times the path is almost completely obscured. At the top of the pass are the remains of a small Roman-era building that must have served as a guard post or administrative station. From this site, one has a magnificent view of Wadi Abu Ma'amel and the fortress of Mons Porphyrites on one side and Wadi Belih on the other (fig. 1.17). It is another two-hour walk down the ravine into Wadi Abu Ma'amel. The Roman footpath is clearly visible and leads directly to the Mons Porphyrites fortress on the east side of the wadi. Coming down this route late one afternoon, my companion and I made our camp near the bottom of the path but high enough that we could look down on the wadi below. As evening fell, a brilliant moon rose over the rim of the canyon walls. Sitting in that cold, silver light, one could not help but be awed by the splendid desolation of these mountains. This is a place where time ceases to exist on any dimension comprehensible to man. To these mountains, the Romans were here only yesterday.

WHERE IS THE PORPHYRY?

What happened to all the porphyry the ancient Romans hewed from these mountains? Scholars are not certain about the quantity of stone extracted from the slopes of Gebel Dokhan, but undoubtedly it was vast. Most of it was carved into columns, ornamental veneer, and various forms of statuary, and much of this can still be seen, primarily in the countries bordering the Mediterranean. In the 1930s,

1.17 A splendid view of Wadi Belih from the pass that connects Badia with Mons Porphyrites. The phantom station (barely visible in this photograph) stands at the base of the dark conical hill near the center of the photograph.

one researcher documented 134 pillars and countless altars, fonts, basins, and sarcophagi still in use in Italian churches. In addition, he stated that 8 giant porphyry columns once stood in the Temple of the Sun in Baalbek, Lebanon, but were later moved to the church of Hagia Sophia in Istanbul.[38] Porphyry columns were also sent to the Holy Land. An inscription discovered at Mons Porphyrites in 1820 by Sir Gardner Wilkinson and dating from about the middle of the fourth century records that a man named Didymus and the chief quarrymen, Paranius and Panachates, carried out repairs (on the ramp and cairns?) in order to lower pillars for the Catholic church of Melitius in Jerusalem.[39]

Although numerous columns were hewn in Mons Porphyrites, only the one mentioned earlier remains there today, near the top of the Northwest quarry. This 7-meter column was apparently abandoned when it broke into three pieces shortly after being separated from its mother rock. The pillars from Mons Porphyrites were not the size of the granite giants the Romans produced in Mons Claudianus to the south. In fact, this abandoned column was probably among the largest pieces produced in Gebel Dokhan. According to a report made in 1845, "The largest red porphyry columns in Rome were a pair in the triumphal arch of San Crisogono and a second pair in San Giovanni in Fonte."[40] Scholars estimate that those columns were no more than 6 to 8 meters long—as opposed to the 15- and even 20-meter columns produced at Mons Claudianus. The stone beds at Mons Porphyrites were not sufficiently massive to permit the extraction of larger pieces.[41]

In addition to columns, porphyry was used for statues and sarcophagi and as paneling for walls and floors. Its unique color seems to have given it an almost sacred significance. Byzantine rulers, who regarded purple as a symbol of hope and promise, lined the birth chamber of the Imperial Palace in Constantinople with porphyry and called it the Porphyra. Children born in this room received the epithet *Porphyrogenitus*, "born in the purple."[42] Rulers who were not fortunate enough to be born in the purple could choose to spend eternity in it instead. Emperor Septimius Severus (A.D. 193–211), for example, carried a porphyry funerary urn with him during his British campaigns and was returned to Rome in it after dying in York on February 4, 211.[43]

Although porphyry is a uniquely Egyptian stone, relatively few original examples of it remain in Egypt. No doubt many ancient pieces were broken up in the Islamic period and used to decorate the niches of some of Cairo's mosques. Among the objects in the Egyptian National Museum is a porphyry bust of the emperor Galerius (A.D. 305–11), the ruthless persecutor of Christians who later rescinded his anti-Christian decrees by issuing the Edict of Toleration from his deathbed.[44] Farther north, in the Greco-Roman Museum in Alexandria, one can examine the porphyry base of a statue of Serapis dated A.D. 20–21, a complete sarcophagus lid, and an enormous headless statue believed to depict Diocletian (A.D. 284–305). This last piece is approximately 2 meters high and constitutes the largest known statue hewn from a single piece of porphyry (fig. 1.18). It dates to the fourth century A.D., but because it is headless, the attribution to Diocletian is uncertain—some believe it could also be the emperor Constantine (A.D. 307–37).

Other examples of statuary exist in Italy, thanks in part to Diocletian, the great military and imperial reformer. He replaced traditional marble with porphyry as the medium of imperial portraiture, perhaps because it is more rare and therefore more impressive. In reality, this transition was unfortunate because porphyry's speckled surface renders it unattractive for human figures. The famous porphyry statue of Diocletian, Maximian (his coemperor), and their lieutenant caesars, which the crusaders looted from Byzantium in 1204 and which now stands at the corner of St. Mark's Cathedral in Venice, is an example of the stern, impersonal style to which porphyry lent itself.

A pair of magnificent sarcophagi in the Vatican Museum, however, are outstanding specimens of just how beautiful well-crafted porphyry can be. The first of these was found in Tor Pignattara and was thought to have been intended for Constantine the Great, the emperor who legalized Christianity throughout the Roman Empire in the early fourth century. Ironically, however, it was used instead by his mother, Helena, who is remembered as a saintly woman, yet was laid to rest in this splendid porphyry sarcophagus decorated with battle scenes of a victorious Roman cavalry defeating barbarians.[45] The second, matching sarcophagus is decorated with vine scrolls and was presumably intended for Constantine's wife, the empress Fausta. But this one was used by their daughter Constantia, who was buried in what is now the Church of Santa Costanza in Rome.[46] Interestingly, the porphyry lid in the Alexandria Museum appears to be almost identical to that found on Constantia's sarcophagus. The discovery of these massive artifacts in Rome implies that Emperor Constantine envisioned being buried there. But as a result of his victory over Licinius at Chrysopolis in September A.D. 324, a victory that made him the sole ruler of the Roman world, Constantine was buried in the city that bore his name, Constantinople—without his porphyry sarcophagus.[47]

Sometime in the mid- to late fourth century A.D., for reasons not yet fully understood, the Romans abandoned their efforts at Mons Porphyrites. The shouts of

1.18 Fourth-century porphyry statue of Diocletian(?) in the
Greco-Roman Museum in Alexandria.

men, the ring of chisels on stone, and the grating of rock slides all ceased. Slowly the wells, fortress, and ramps began their slow dance of decay. Today, the ruins of these bold structures and an occasional ostracon are all that remain of this monument to Roman audacity and determination. In time, these, too, will disappear, the archaeologists will come no more, and the Hills of Smoke will finally know peace.

MONS CLAUDIANUS

Of the twenty-one known Roman imperial quarries in the Eastern Desert, the most famous of them all, Mons Claudianus, lies 50 kilometers south of Gebel Dokhan. From this site, the Romans hewed the enormous columns of speckled, white granite that were to grace some of the most splendid buildings of Roman antiquity, among them Trajan's Forum and the Pantheon itself.

THE SETTLEMENT

Mons Claudianus lies on the north side of Wadi Umm Hussein, 75 kilometers from the Red Sea and 120 kilometers from the Nile River. Although its name suggests that it dates from the time of the emperor Claudius (A.D. 41–54), the earliest known evidence indicates that the settlement was not established until the reign of Domitian (A.D. 81–96), and that it reached its height of activity during the reigns of Trajan (A.D. 98–117) and Hadrian (A.D. 117–38).[1] Like all Roman sites in the Eastern Desert, the settlement was partly a military station, but the imperial government established it primarily to maintain and protect the valuable granite quarries. During the approximately 150 years the settlement was occupied, the Romans modified and expanded its configuration numerous times according to the needs of a particular period. The prominent animal lines and storage area on the west side of the settlement, for example, were added during the latest periods of occupation. When the site was abandoned, the fortress measured approximately 75 meters by 70 meters, the dimensions it has today. Unlike the castellum at Mons Porphyrites, that at Mons Claudianus is magnificently well preserved. As the German traveler Georg Schweinfurth once wrote, "Perhaps nowhere in the world has a Roman settlement come down to us in so perfect a state."[2] The stone walls on the north and west sides are in especially good condition, reaching a height of 4 meters and punctuated by towers in each corner and halfway along each side. These towers served not only as watchtowers for the sentries, but also as buttresses for the long expanse of otherwise unsupported wall (fig. 2.1).

The only entrance to the castellum is a *porta praetoria* (main gate) in the middle of the west wall; its enormous granite posts and lintel are still in place. Inside this gate, the fortress is a labyrinth of rooms, alleys, and stairways cluttered with stone debris. Although many of the rooms originally had roofs made of woven mats, others were covered with granite slabs, several of which are still intact. Amidst the jumble of collapsed stone, the many preserved doorways, niches, and narrow alleys give one the impression that the place was only recently shaken by an earthquake. At each turn, one half expects to encounter a dejected Roman sitting amidst the rubble.

From outside the gate, two streets lead away from the fortress, one to the west and the other to the north. The first passes a large enclosed stable and storage area and the dry remains of a deep, funnel-shaped well before arriving at the open wadi. This street was the main entranceway to the castellum, and its south side is lined with a long stone shelf that served as a public bench. The second street passes an assortment of ruined buildings before it arrives at a broad staircase leading to the temple of Serapis.

The temple, which was built by Epaphroditus Sigerianus, the same man who built the temple at Mons Porphyrites, stands on a small hill approximately 60 meters from the fortress. Numerous inscriptions attest to its purpose and the approximate dates of the settlement's most active occupation. Included among the inscriptions, for example, are the following:

1. A fallen lintel containing a long Greek inscription dated April 23, A.D.118, dedicates "the temple and the area around the temple to Zeus

2.1 The fortress of Mons Claudianus in Wadi Umm Hussein. The main quarries are located on the other side of the hills behind the fortress.

Helios Great Serapis and gods who share the temple, by Epaphroditus Sigerianus, slave, lessee of the quarries, when Rammius Martialis was Prefect of Egypt, when Chresimus, imperial freedman, was *procurator metallorum* and when Avitus, centurion of *cohors I Flavia Cilicum Equitata*, was in charge of the works at [Mons] Claudianus";[3]

    2. A smashed altar that once stood on the terrace of the temple states, "In the twelfth year of the emperor Nerva Trajan Caesar Augustus Germanicus Dacicus: by Sulpicius Simius, prefect of Egypt, this altar was made";[4]

    3. On an altar that now lies on its side in the sand in the center of the temple floor is the Latin inscription, "Annius Rufus, Legate of the XVth Legion 'Appolinaris,' superintending the marble works of Mons Claudianus by favor of the emperor Trajan."[5] This is the first instance of the name Mons Claudianus found to date (fig. 2.2);

    4. Another altar, now in the Cairo Museum, contains the following inscription: "To the Zeus Helios, Great Serapis, for the fortune of our lord Caesar Trajan, when Encolpius was procurator and Quintus Accius Optatus, centurion, Apollonios, son of Ammonios, Alexandrine, architect, dedicated this altar for the preservation of all his work."[6]

2.2 The altar that bears the words "Mons Claudianus," lying on its side in the remains of the principal temple of the settlement.

Among the ruined buildings located between the castellum and the temple is a bathhouse. The Romans placed great importance on maintaining an adequate water supply at Mons Claudianus because it was necessary not only to sustain life, but also—at least for the most privileged individuals at the settlement—to allow for a comfortable life. The scarcity of water did not prevent the Romans from going to considerable trouble to provide themselves with proper bathing facilities. The baths lie just outside the castellum gate, on the west side of the street leading to the temple. The first large room, known as the *apodyterium*, measures approximately 8 meters by 13 meters and was probably open to the sky. Here men would have changed clothes and perhaps exercised before passing through the door in its northern wall to enter the vault-roofed *frigidarium*. This room, which measures 7 meters by 5 meters, contains a plaster-lined bath sunk into the floor in the northern corner. The bath measures 2.5 meters by 1 meter by 0.7 meters and features three steps. Along the plaster-covered walls are small niches that might have held statues, decorative vases, or clay jars filled with aromatic oils. Two rooms to the west of the frigidarium is the vault-roofed *tepidarium*, which measures roughly 2 meters by 3 meters and boasts the visible remains of heating ducts behind its walls and underneath the floor. Finally, just west of the tepidarium is the *caldarium*, now much ruined, in which there is a second sunken bath, but of slightly smaller dimensions than that in the frigidarium. Because water was strictly rationed at Mons Claudianus, there is some question about who had access to these luxurious baths. Although almost certainly not for the exclusive use of the settlement's commandant—as has long been believed—the inner baths are too small to have allowed the numerous quarry workers to soak away the aches of their daily toil in such a splendid setting.

Approximately one kilometer southwest of the main castellum, on the western edge of the narrow valley that connects Wadi Umm Hussein with Wadi Umm Diqal, stand the ruins of another walled settlement connected with Mons Claudianus. Referred to by early writers as the *hydreuma* (fortified water station), it is much smaller than the principal fortress and, according to the latest excavations, appears to represent the original, first-century settlement at Mons Claudianus.[7] As the quarrying operation grew over time, the Romans built the larger castellum in Wadi Umm Hussein, but they continued to occupy the hydreuma and exploit its nearby quarries. The well-preserved fortress retains some walls at their near-original height of 4 meters, and the main enclosure contains several plaster-lined cisterns, the largest of which measures approximately 3.5 by 4.5 meters and is 2.5 meters deep. Despite its name, however, the hydreuma did not contain a well, so water carriers must have brought water in skins or amphora from the wells in Wadi Umm Hussein and emptied them into the cisterns.

The exact system by which the Romans supplied themselves with water at Mons Claudianus—whether at the hydreuma or at the castellum—is not clearly understood. There were at least four and perhaps as many as six wells serving the population of more than nine hundred people. As stated above, one of these is right next to the castellum, but two others are located in Wadi Umm Hussein within a kilometer to the north and south of the settlement. In addition, a large well is located in Wadi Umm Diqal (Mother of Columns), three kilometers west of the castellum.[8] This beautifully constructed well, 3 meters wide and 25 meters deep, contains water to this day and is still used by local bedouin. The well lies at the center of a much-ruined enclosure whose walls have collapsed and are now buried beneath the sand. At the eastern corner of the enclosure, however, stands an enigmatic stone tower that measures approximately 7 meters high and 5 meters in diameter near its base. The exterior of the structure is in relatively good condition, but the upper portion has collapsed (fig. 2.3). Until recently, scholars believed this was a water tower from which the Romans supplied water to the main castellum via one or more aqueducts. Indeed, the partial remains of two low walls (thought to be aqueducts) are still visible heading away from the vicinity of the tower into Wadi Umm Diqal and toward the hydreuma in the valley leading to Wadi Umm Hussein. Recent studies prove, however, that this structure is not a water tower and that the two low walls were designed to protect the quarry road

2.3 The stone tower at the well in Wadi Umm Diqal, three kilometers from the
main settlement at Mons Claudianus.

from being damaged by floods (fig. 2.4). The tower's lower portions are solid to a
height of 4 meters; above this level an opening was built in the outer wall, so the
tower could not have contained water. Furthermore, the well appears to have been
built with stones taken from the fortress at Mons Claudianus itself and therefore
implies a construction date after the Romans abandoned their quarrying operations
at Mons Claudianus in the third century. A more plausible theory thus emerges that
the tower, the well, and the enclosure of which they are a part constituted the center
of a monastic community that developed in the area sometime in the late fifth or
early sixth century. Indeed, the remains of approximately three hundred huts that
could have housed monks dot the edges of Wadi Umm Diqal. Examination of these
huts and of nearby surface pottery corroborate this later date. If this theory is correct, the tower might have served as a cramped place of refuge for a select number
of monks in case of bedouin attack.[9] The enclosure possibly featured one or more
similar towers that did not survive the ravages of floods and scavenging.

THE QUARRIES

There are approximately 130 quarries in the hills surrounding Mons Claudianus.
Many of these contain examples of the variety of objects the Romans fashioned

2.4 A portion of one of the nearly buried walls that extend from
Wadi Umm Diqal to Wadi Umm Hussein. These walls were
designed to reduce damage during flash floods.

from the fine stone but discarded because of cracks or other defects. In the quarry above the hydreuma, for example, lies a beautifully crafted bathtub. In another quarry, less than a kilometer from the main castellum, is a 3-meter granite basin for a fountain (fig. 2.5). As the workers moved this basin from the quarry, however, it cracked across its diameter, and although an attempt was made to secure the two halves by means of iron staples, the overseer of the quarry must have decided that its durability was compromised beyond the point where it could be used. It was abandoned where it sits today, and another was probably hewn and sent on to Rome.

The process by which the workers extracted these massive blocks of granite at Mons Claudianus was similar to that used in Mons Porphyrites. After a particular granite bed was identified, the quarrymen used chisels, picks, and hammers to cut a trench along the intended line of separation, perhaps 30 centimeters wide and 30 centimeters deep. Next, they cut wedge holes at intervals in the bottom of the trench. An average, 13-centimeter wedge hole at Mons Claudianus required about two and a half hours and as many as six thousand hammer blows to create. But the depth of the wedge holes depended on the size of the piece to be separated. A series of 13-centimeter wedge holes, for example, can split a block of granite 2 meters thick, while shallower wedge holes suffice for thinner blocks. The original trench, which was easier to cut than the wedge holes, effectively placed the holes deeper into the stone, thus enabling the quarrymen at Mons Claudianus to split blocks of granite up to 6 meters thick.[10]

As at Mons Porphyrites, there are numerous inscriptions chiseled into the stones and quarry walls. One large block, for example, intended to be used for a capital, bears the inscription, "The property of Caesar Nerva Trajan."[11] Numbers and names are also abundant. "Harpocrates" and "Sophieronym" are identified as overseers in one quarry. Seeing these names etched into the stone walls invites one to imagine the humanity of this strange place: Harpocrates, lean, sunburned, and bearded, shielding his eyes against a platinum sun as he scrutinized the quarrymen hammering incessantly at the granite.

On the slopes of the hills north and east of the castellum are more quarries and a slipway that meets the wadi floor just beyond the northeast corner of the fortress. This ramp is lined with cairns similar to those found along the ramps at Mons Porphyrites. At the top of the ramp is the broken base of an enormous column. This piece retains the protrusions on either side that might have served to secure the ropes needed to move the column. Beyond the top of the ramp, over a low ridge, is Wadi Fatiri, and within a small quarry at the head of this wadi lies the most spectacular and most famous object at Mons Claudianus: a column so enormous that it staggers the imagination. Hewn from a single piece of granite, it is

2.5 Broken basin in a quarry near Mons Claudianus. Note the chiseled holes where staples were placed in an attempt to hold the two halves together.

nearly 20 meters long and weighs approximately 210 tons—possibly one of the largest monolithic columns ever hewn by the Romans[12] (fig. 2.6). Next to it lies the lower portion of another column that appears to have had the same dimensions, but that now measures only 4 meters in length. The remainder was likely broken up into smaller, usable blocks. Even the Romans rarely attempted to incorporate such giant pillars into their imperial architecture. The cutting of such a stone was a difficult undertaking in itself, and very few quarries had beds large enough to extract such a massive stone in one piece. Given, however, that Mons Claudianus was located in the farthest, most inhospitable reaches of the empire, it was the transportation of the columns that constituted a truly Herculean task. Indeed, it appears that this giant column cracked after having been moved only a few meters from the spot from which it was carved. The cracks occurred in the middle of the column along its circumference and at its base. But the amount of labor already spent on the piece led the stonemasons to attempt to save it by inserting iron staples to keep the separating parts together. The repairs, however, were not sufficient to keep the crack from expanding as the workers attempted to inch the column closer to the ramp. Despite their efforts, the column split cleanly in two—beyond any hope of repair—and was abandoned forever.

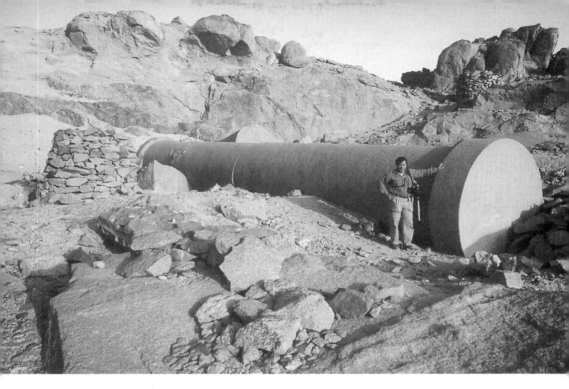

2.6 The great abandoned column in Wadi Fatiri. The precise meaning of the large letters visible on the bottom of the column base is unknown. They were applied with red paint and probably served some administrative function.

Nevertheless, the Romans did successfully extract columns of similar dimensions from Mons Claudianus and other sites, although the exact number is unknown. Today, only four known structures incorporate columns of a height of 15 meters or more:[13]

1. The Temple of Trajan in Rome, built either circa A.D. 105–13 or circa A.D. 118–28),[14] employed perhaps as many as twenty-six 15-meter pillars on its porch. Only fragments of two of the columns remain today, and they originated at Mons Claudianus, according to the latest petrographic analysis.[15] The other columns were presumably also monoliths, but whether they were white granite from Claudianus or red granite from Syene (modern Aswan) is uncertain;

2. The Column of Antoninus Pius in Rome, erected A.D. 161, came from Syene, and the inscription from the lower portion indicates that there were two such columns cut in A.D. 105–06;[16]

3. Diocletian's Column in Alexandria, erected A.D. 297 and incorrectly labeled Pompey's Pillar, consists of a single piece of red granite from Aswan and measures 20 meters (fig. 2.7);

2.7 Diocletian's Column (mistakenly known today as Pompey's Pillar) stands in Alexandria and is among the largest extant monolithic columns produced during the Roman period.

4. The Basilica of Maxentius or Constantine in Rome, built circa A.D. 306–12, employed eight 17-meter columns of Proconnesian marble. One of them now stands in the Piazza Santa Maria Maggiore in Rome.

In addition to these buildings, there are two others that might have incorporated columns of 15 meters or more:

1. The Baths of Trajan in Rome, built A.D. 104–09, has dimensions that suggest it contained either eight or twelve 15-meter shafts; scholars do not know what kind of stone was quarried to make them;

2. The Pantheon in Rome, built circa A.D. 118–28, was originally to have had, some scholars believe, sixteen 15-meter columns on its porch. Supply problems, however, forced the architects to redesign the building and use 12-meter columns instead. These came from both Mons Claudianus and Syene.

Other magnificent Roman buildings like Hadrian's villa at Tivoli and Diocletian's mausoleum at Split also incorporated columns from Mons Claudianus, but they were not as enormous as those mentioned above.[17] As petrographic research continues on the columns used in ancient Mediterranean architecture, it is becoming increasingly apparent that the stone of Mons Claudianus was used only in the most important and magnificent public buildings.[18]

To one standing on a ledge above the quarries of Wadi Fatiri, from which these giant columns were hewn, it seems as if the quarries were abandoned only yesterday. Everywhere, thin black lines mark the places where stones were to be cut, wedge holes and chisel marks are clean and sharp, and thousands of freshly cut blocks lie scattered about as if waiting to be collected and dragged down the narrow, cairn-lined wadi to the loading ramp a short distance away. Adding to this sense of immediacy, the loading ramp is strewn with five complete columns. One of them rests at the lower edge of the ramp itself, as if waiting for the men to return and roll it up the incline onto a cart (fig. 2.8). Nearby, a fragment of a column contains the following Greek inscription cleanly chiseled on its base: "In the time of Valvennius Priscus, centurion of the 22nd Legion; by the architect Heracleides."[19]

THE RESIDENTS OF MONS CLAUDIANUS

Recent discoveries indicate that at some point during its occupation as many as 920 people lived at Mons Claudianus. Of these, at least 60 were soldiers.[20] The question of who constituted the nonmilitary residents at the settlement has puzzled scholars since the rediscovery of the site by Europeans in the nineteenth century. The classic description of quarry life comes from early travelers like Arthur Weigall:

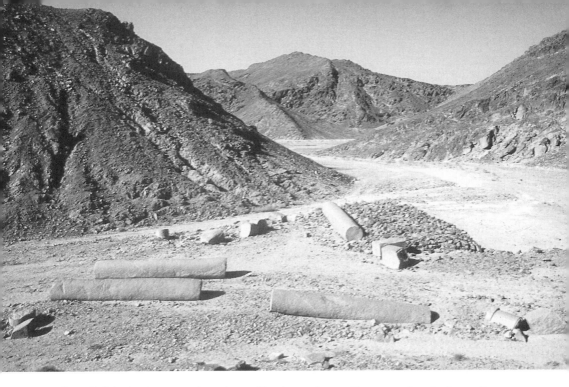

2.8 Unfinished columns and portions of broken columns lie scattered at the base of the loading ramp in Wadi Fatiri.

The persons who worked the mines were mainly criminals and prisoners of war; but with these there were many unjustly accused men of good breeding, and those who had by some political action earned the Pharaoh's or the Emperor's wrath. Frequently, this class of prisoner was banished to the mines, together with all the members of his family, and these also were obliged to labor for the king's profit . . . and all were weighed down with fetters by night and by day. There was little or no chance of escape, for sentries were posted on every hill-top, and the soldiers were ready to give chase through the waterless desert should a man elude the watchman.

The work was carried on day after day without cessation and always the laborers were under the eye of a merciless overseer, who showered blows upon them at the slightest provocation. In order to keep down expenses, no clothes were provided for the prisoners . . . In good or in bad health they were forced to work. . . . Thus the end of a man who had been banished to the mines was always the same: fettered and unwashed, covered with bruises and disfigured by pestilence, he dropped dead in his chains under the lash of the relentless whip.[21]

Scholars who followed Weigall have echoed his description. George Murray, who traveled through the Eastern Desert in the 1930s, described Mons Claudianus as a "concentration camp for political prisoners, who were sent there to be hustled—some quickly, some slowly—-from the burning hell of existence into the outer darkness of eternity."[22]

Today, these horrific descriptions of quarry life are recognized as being inaccurate. Since the late 1980s, international teams of archaeologists under the direction of the Institut Français d'Archéologie Orientale in Cairo have undertaken major excavations at Mons Claudianus. Their efforts have uncovered literally tons of pottery (some of which came from the farthest reaches of the Roman world), more than twenty-five thousand pieces of textile, ten thousand ostraca (the largest discovery of ostraca ever found), bones, coins, jewelry, school texts, and a wide assortment of shoes and other leather items.

Of these artifacts, the most valuable are the ostraca discovered in the rubbish dumps outside the settlement. Although it will take many years for scholars to translate and publish the texts of all these documents, those that have been translated are already helping historians answer crucial questions about the administration of Mons Claudianus and the everyday lives of its residents. The ostraca reveal, for example, that the site was administered by the Roman army, that most of the people at the settlement were Egyptians, and that the workers involved in the extraction of the granite received wages for their labor. These paid workers included adze men, water carriers, side wedgemen, sawers (presumably for rollers and scaffolding because there is no evidence that saws were used in the cutting of stone), stonemasons, hammer men, guards, roller operators, iron hardeners, bellows blowers, and blacksmiths. Interestingly, thus far not a single ostracon attests to the use of criminals in the quarries. Imperial slaves and freedmen, however, did serve as accountants and architects at Mons Claudianus and Mons Porphyrites, according to some of the most recently translated, but unpublished, ostraca.[23] Yet their presence does not point to the kind of slave labor that Weigall and others imagined.

With regard to workers' wages, the ostraca reveal a complex payment system. The workers were divided into two categories: *pagani* and *familia*. The pagani were local, free, skilled workers who came from a variety of towns in the Nile Valley and from Alexandria. Both the pagani and the familia received payment in money and in food, although the amounts of food differed between the two groups. For example, the pagani received one *artaba* (approximately forty kilograms) of wheat plus an unspecified quantity of wine per month. The familia, on the other hand, received one artaba of wheat, lentils and oil, and, once a year, a set of clothes. The pagani had to order their own lentils, oil, and other goods from the Nile Valley on their own, and the cost of these items was deducted from their wages.[24]

Of the thousands of ostraca that scholars have translated, those constituting wage receipts furnish the most precise information ever discovered about Roman wages for quarry workers. One ostracon, for example, reveals that a paganus named Pachoumis earned 47 drachmae per month.[25] This amount—also the wage of 106 other workers—is the most common payment for labor documented to date. It also represents the highest category on a pay scale that ranged between 28 and 47 drachmae.[26] The lower figure was paid to apprentices, of which there were few, while the higher wage went to quarrymen, smiths, and steel temperers.[27] The average pay for a civilian in second-century Egypt was just over 25 drachmae and the highest rate was about 40, so the men of Mons Claudianus were paid better than their counterparts in the Nile Valley. Based on a second-century market price of about 9 drachmae for one artaba of wheat, the highest paid workers at Mons Claudianus received enough money to feed five people.[28] No doubt the remote, desert conditions under which the people lived and the dangerous nature of quarry work made life at Mons Claudianus harsh, but the wages and benefits were obviously high enough to attract a sufficient number of skilled workers to the quarries.

While ostraca that pertain to wages have proven particularly valuable, other types of ostraca have granted scholars intimate glimpses into the lives of the inhabitants of Mons Claudianus and provided them with vital information concerning the administration of the settlement, quarries, and traffic along the desert access roads.[29]

LETTERS

1. Isidorus to his sons Isidorus and Paniscus.[30] I have written to you in a previous ostracon that you should send me the small elbow-rest, because I suffer pain when sleeping and you did not send it. So send it and the ink and two sticks of eye-salve. . . . About the money I have written elsewhere that I shall send it as soon as I have sold the barley. Send me all letters that may have been brought to me from Egypt.[31] I have decided you do not have to shave because you are in the desert. Do not neglect to provide what I have written to you about. Farewell. (early second century)

2. Pthiaus to Peteniphis his father, greetings. Receive from Chennamis the camel driver a basket of meat and one liver.[32] Greet your wife and your children. It was not nice of you to write that I owe you four *staters* that I

do not owe. Write back to me if you receive meat of any sort. Farewell.
(circa A.D. 100–20)

3. Firmus to Exochus, his brother, many greetings. I have heard that you are
moving to Porphyrites. Give my grain to Mescenius and give him back
the money from the woman Tasalis. . . . Greet Amaranthus many times
from me and Mescenius and Barathus . . . and everyone who loves us.
(circa A.D. 100–20)

4. Maximus to Sarapias, his sister and lady, many greetings. I know myself
that I did you no harm, nor did I hate you as you suddenly hated me. I do
not blame Valerius Longus, my brother, for anything, although he neglected me and scorns me, his own brother. But you, you should have said
to him: "Write an ostracon to your brother!" . . . I thank you from the
heart. Palmas went to Kampe. He has four days. About the pig, be free of
care, my lady. I send it to you. Send me the axe. Greet my brother.
Farewell. (circa A.D. 110)

RECORDS FROM THE ARCHIVE OF SUCCESSUS[33]

1. Athenor(?) to Successus, greetings. Please order four highly necessary
yoke straps to be sent so that the column can be . . . Farewell. (circa
A.D. 107)

2. Leontas to Successus, greetings. I wish you to know that my waterskins[34] have all become useless, and the water is sparse. Please send me
new water skins if you will and write to me. If you will not, please choose
from among the old ones until Epaphroditus comes up. And send me a
rope of palm fiber and a double cloak and the ladder, if you will, or a . . .
send me also four wedges and feathers.[35] Farewell. (circa A.D. 107)

3. Leontas to Successus, greetings. Please exchange the two waterskins and
send me two baskets so that the waterskins do not suffer. Farewell. (circa
A.D. 107)

TRAVEL PERMITS[36]

1. Antoninus, centurion, of the statonarii of the Claudianus road, greetings. Let pass four men and twenty donkeys.

2. Antoninus, centurion, of the statonarii of the Claudianus road, greetings. Let pass one woman and two children.

Other ostraca have given scholars some knowledge of the physical ailments
that affected the people. Predictably, these included various lung disorders result-

ing from the inhalation of dust from the quarries, bilharzia, and intestinal para-
sites. One rather mysterious ostracon hints that food was not always adequate, at
least at some of the smaller quarries in the vicinity of Mons Claudianus: "Markos
to Arteimas, greetings. I beg you, brother, to send me three matia of bread by the
intermediary Apollos the camel driver, so that we don't die of starvation."[37] The
letter does not make clear where Markos lived and whether he was actually
suffering from a shortage of food or was simply exaggerating. Most of the letters
uncovered by archaeologists were written by family and friends in the Nile Valley
to men working at Mons Claudianus, but it is probably safe to assume that Markos
lived at Mons Claudianus. None of the other correspondence, however, alludes to
men living in the state of destitution suggested by Markos's letter. Indeed, the
most recent evidence tends to support the idea that, although faced with enormous logistical difficulties, the Roman administrators of Mons Claudianus supplied the majority of their workers with a remarkable variety of food, supplies, and
services.

SUSTENANCE FOR THE PEOPLE OF MONS CLAUDIANUS

Given the great distance between Egypt's breadbasket, the Nile Valley, and Mons
Claudianus and the harshness of the desert environment, that the Romans were
able to sustain a community of nine hundred people is an accomplishment on a
par with their ability to hew and deliver huge, magnificent columns from the quarries. An abundance of archaeological data has enabled researchers to identify a
surprisingly wide variety of foods consumed by the residents of Mons Claudianus.
For example, researchers have unearthed large quantities of animal bones: from
donkeys (and some from horses), camels, pigs, and goats. Many of the bones
show signs of the animals' having been butchered, suggesting that camels and
donkeys were used not only as draft animals, but also as sources of meat. No cattle bones have been found, doubtless because they need too much food and water
to make them practical as draft animals in the harsh desert environment. Archaeologists have also uncovered bones of dogs, fennec foxes—some with skinning
marks—and fish from the Red Sea,[38] as well as amphora containing salted fish.
These items were supplemented by grains and vegetables imported from the Nile
Valley, including barley, wheat, corn, beans, lentils, dates, olives, grapes, and
nuts. Recent excavations have also identified seeds, such as those of globe artichokes, which may mean that some residents grew vegetables in small gardens at
or near the settlement.[39]

Bread, of course, was a staple food at Mons Claudianus. While barley bread appears to have been baked by women at the settlement, other kinds of bread were

imported from the Nile Valley. Some evidence indicates that men who did not live with women at the settlement had their wives and women relations in Qena bake their bread and send it to Mons Claudianus by regular supply caravans. Indeed, because there is no evidence that the town of Qena existed in the Ptolemaic period, it seems it was founded primarily to serve as a base from which to send and receive supplies for the quarries deep in the desert.

As was the case at Mons Porphyrites, water was always a critical issue at Mons Claudianus. Aside from the special allowances the Romans obviously made for the baths of the privileged few, water was strictly rationed. Each man received two to three liters of water per day in winter; no records of the summer ration have been found.[40] Summer temperatures rise well above 40° centigrade, hence the water ration must have been almost doubled if men were expected to work during the daytime.[41] Of course, water was not the only drink available to the residents. Wine was brought to the settlement in amphorae carried by camel caravans from the Nile Valley. Each amphora could carry 24 liters of wine (or oil), and, when full, it would have weighed approximately 35 kilos. Thousands of sherds of such amphorae have been discovered at Mons Claudianus, but thus far archaeologists have not uncovered any documents specifying how much wine was rationed to the residents.

THE END OF MONS CLAUDIANUS

Scholars do not know exactly when or why quarrying ceased at Mons Claudianus. They think it was abandoned sometime in the early to mid–third century A.D. It is certain the Romans did not leave because they had exhausted the supply of granite, for even today the stone continues to be quarried in the surrounding area. Quite possibly the Romans departed as a result of the political and economic upheaval taking place in the empire at that time or, more simply, because the supply of water became insufficient. No doubt scholars will learn more about the life and death of Mons Claudianus as they continue to examine the ostraca and other artifacts recovered in their excavations.

Unfortunately, archaeological research at Mons Claudianus itself is becoming increasingly difficult because the site is threatened both by modern quarrying, which every year destroys valuable inscriptions in the surrounding area, and by the ravages of irresponsible tourism. The site has been accessible to tourists from Cairo and resorts along the Red Sea for only a few years, but already it is littered with water bottles, cans, plastic bags, and cigarette butts. More sadly, however, tourism has directly affected the progress of archaeological research because scholars must now work hastily in order to save artifacts from destruction and theft. As one archaeologist stated, "It became an emergency excavation when we noted how [the ostraca] were being looted by Europeans coming from Cairo."[42] Even the castellum is not immune from the danger. Several granite roofs that were still in place when I first visited the site in 1992 had caved in four years later, and the large tower that dominates the northern wall has been severely damaged by tourists climbing its fragile stones. One can only hope that the Egyptian government will soon take the necessary steps to protect the site from such desecration and, in so doing, ensure that Mons Claudianus forever remains a symbol of Roman power in the Egyptian desert.

QUARRY ROADS TO THE NILE RIVER

W hile Mons Porphyrites and Mons Claudianus have been the focus of much archaeological research, the routes the Romans used to transport the stone from these quarries to the Nile River have received relatively little attention. This is unfortunate because scholars could learn a great deal more about how the Romans overcame the logistical and technical difficulties of moving heavy loads of stone across the desert by studying the ostraca, papyri, and other artifacts that remain buried in and near the *hydreumata* that line these routes. But aside from a few travelers' accounts, thus far only one detailed survey of the roads has been published.[1]

Unlike the other four important transdesert routes (Berenike–Edfu/Coptos, Marsa Nechasia–Edfu, Myos Hormos–Coptos, and the Via Hadriana), the routes from Mons Porphyrites and Mons Claudianus to Qena were not primarily commercial routes during the Roman period (see map 2). Their role was to enable the transportation of stone from the quarries and the movement of troops, supplies, and communications related to those quarrying operations. Later, after the porphyry quarries were abandoned and the fort at Abu Sha'ar was built in the late third or early fourth century, the old Porphyry Road was used to convey supplies and people from the Nile to the coast and back.[2]

THE PORPHYRY ROAD

Beyond the fort at Umm Balad (see below), the Romans built a chain of six hydreumata along the route from Mons Porphyrites to Qena to control communications and travel and to protect vital water sources. After the road turns west near the Badia fort, it gradually slopes upward until it reaches its steepest section just before the watershed pass at Wadi al-Qattar. From that point, the road slopes gently downward, following a series of wadis through the spectacular mountains and across wide gravel plains until it arrives at Qena on the Nile River.[3] In antiquity, large portions of the road probably consisted of the kind of wide gravel path that can be seen near the Badia fort. Today, most of the route is covered with sand, but short sections of the original surface can be seen in numerous places, and small towers, cairns, and occasional wheel tracks from the ancient wagons still clearly mark this Roman highway. Many of the cairns and towers remain in excellent condition, and approximately 125 such structures mark the route from the fort at Wadi Belih to the final station at El-'Aras. These rectangular towers, built of unmortared, stacked stones, measure approximately 2 meters wide and 1.5 meters high, although many are smaller. Whereas the cairns could serve only as route markers, the intervisibility of the towers hints that they served not only as markers, but as platforms from which soldiers could signal each other by using flags, mirrors, or, at night, fire—although no evidence has yet been found on any of the towers of scorching or ashes. Pottery found in the vicinity of these structures suggests that teams from the hydreumata regularly left amphorae of water next to the towers so that those manning the towers, troops on patrol, and other desert travelers could have drinking water.[4]

Today, if one travels from Badia to Qena through the desolate splendor of the desert, it is difficult to imagine just how busy this quarry road must have been. Along these picturesque wadis, large caravans of camels and donkeys must have carried a steady flow of food and supplies to meet the needs of the quarrymen, soldiers, and their animals. The soldiers, in turn, patrolled the road and the nearby desert for raiders and thieves who might descend on a caravan laden with valuable provisions. All of this activity is over now, yet the modern traveler will still encounter the haunting remains of the towers and water stations that sustained this corner of the Roman frontier.

Umm Balad

After leaving the fort at Badia, the Porphyry Road heads west toward Gebel Qattar. Along the way, it passes the intersections of two short roads that lead north to the fort of Umm Balad. The first road is approximately 15 meters wide, while the second, which leaves the main Porphyry Road farther west than the first, measures approximately 8 meters wide. Both are in excellent condition and constitute two of the most intact sections of Roman road in the Eastern Desert (fig. 3.1).

The Umm Balad fort nestles in the foothills of the Gebel Dokhan range (fig. 3.2). It is a fortress rather than a hydreuma and contains many small rooms and a large rectangular cistern. The fort appears to have served some role in the quarrying operations in the Dokhan region. The site has never been excavated, but analysis of surface pottery indicates that when Mons Porphyrites was abandoned, Umm Balad ceased to be an important station and played little or no role in the Nile–Red Sea traffic that took place in later centuries.[5]

3.1 The narrower of the two roads heading south from the fort at Wadi Umm Balad as viewed from a hill near the fort.

3.2 The fort at Wadi Umm Balad with the mountains of Wadi al-Qattar
in the background.

Qattar

The fort in Wadi al-Qattar measures 34 meters by 44 meters and was originally protected by six towers, one at each corner and two flanking the entrance gate. The walls were surmounted by a catwalk and a parapet. To the west of the main gate are the faint remains of what appear to be animal lines. Pottery samples show that the fort was occupied from the first to the fourth century. Unfortunately, almost two thousand years of floods and earthquakes have reduced the fort to nearly a complete ruin. Compounding these effects of nature, engineers from a nearby mining operation deepened the original Roman well in the 1920s or 1930s and constructed a small basin next to the wellhead (fig. 3.3).[6]

Further up Wadi al-Qattar, to the south of the fort, is Wadi Naqqat. Although the lower surface of this narrow wadi contains few, if any, material remains from the Roman period, its eastern and western walls are decorated with countless petroglyphs and ancient graffiti. The majority of these fascinating scenes depict such animals as ibex, giraffes, gazelle, and camels, but some include sickle boats and humans engaged in hunting and in battle. These drawings represent an enormous span of time. The giraffes, for example, probably date from the Epipalaeolithic and predynastic periods (approximately 9,000–3,200 B.C.), while the camels and scenes featuring horses with riders date from the Roman period or later (fig. 3.4).[7] The eastern wall contains a particularly interesting and unusual group of figures executed in red paint. The scene is extremely faded, but it depicts two warriors, one standing above and slightly to the left of the other, each carrying a sword in his left hand and an oval-shaped shield in his right.[8] It appears they are facing a horse or camel that bears a rider who is carrying a long spear. Below and to the right of the warriors are three animals walking in a line to the right and carrying baggage. Although it is difficult to state with any certainty, perhaps this scene records an attack by members of a desert tribe on a Roman supply caravan.

The plethora of graffiti and petroglyphs in Wadi Naqqat attests to thousands of years of human habitation in the area. Even today, bedouin still manage to live in the rugged, unforgiving environment. One of the secrets to their survival lies several kilometers further up Wadi Naqqat at its headwall. There, in a stunning example of natural contrast, two waterfalls flow down the shear face of the canyon wall into shallow green pools shaded by the overhanging rock and wild fig trees.

3.3 The well inside the fort in Wadi al-Qattar. The scattered stones are the remains of the wall that originally surrounded the fort.

3.4 Petroglyphs of camels from Wadi Naqqat.

The falls originate in an enormous natural basin that lies atop the 35-meter canyon wall. This basin, which nourishes half a dozen palm trees, fig trees, and maidenhair ferns, collects water that runs off the barren slopes of the surrounding mountains. In the late summer, the water in the basin is stagnant and the falls are reduced to a seeping trickle. But after heavy rains, such as those that hit the region in November 1996, the falls become torrents, and the narrow wadi below is transformed into a turbulent river, powerful enough to move boulders the size of automobiles.

In the late Roman and early Byzantine periods, this remote area of Wadi Naqqat was home to a significant number of Christian monks and hermits who sought spiritual strength in the extreme isolation of the wilderness. Some rather remarkable evidence of their presence still exists. Overlooking the high basin from a massive ledge some 10 meters above is a roofless L-shaped church in almost perfect condition. Surely it ranks as one of the most remote houses of Christian worship on earth. Superbly built from unmortared flat stones, it includes three rooms, two with windows, and a portico with two stacked-stone columns (fig. 3.5). A short distance away, the small stone huts of Christian hermits dot both sides of the ravine leading to the church. In 1823, Sir Gardiner Wilkinson visited the site and discovered a Greek inscription on a block of granite next to the

3.5 The c. fourth-century church atop the headwall of Wadi Naqqat.

church. The inscription, which dates from approximately A.D. 339, states, "Flavius Julius, the most eminent leader of the Thebaid, built here a public church, at the time when Hatres was the bishop of Maximianopolis [Qena]."⁹ On a more personal level, another ancient source relates the following account of a Christian hermit who lived in the vicinity of Qattar, and quite possibly at this very site, in the late fourth century: "Living in the Porphyry district for a year I met no man during the whole year, nor heard a voice, nor tasted bread. I kept myself alive on small dates and the plants I found growing wild. Once, when these failed me, I went out of the cave to return to the inhabited world. After walking a whole day, on looking about me I saw a horseman having the appearance of a soldier, with a helmet on his head. Thinking he was a soldier, I hurried back to the cave."¹⁰

Deir al-Atrash

After the fort in Wadi al-Qattar, the next Roman station on the Porphyry Road is Deir al-Atrash. This fort measures approximately 55 meters square and is the first hydreuma along the route from Badia that contains extensive mud-brick construction in addition to walls of stone. The entrance is on the south and is flanked by two mud-brick towers (fig. 3.6). Extensive animal lines are still visible outside the fort to the east, while inside there are remains of a large well, a cistern, and mud-brick arches and vaults. Because the fort was used up to the seventh century, however, it is difficult to determine whether these mud-brick structures were part of the original Roman construction. Pottery analysis has revealed that the fort was used extensively in the first and second centuries, then again from the fourth to the seventh centuries. Scholars have found more pottery from the later period than from the first and second centuries, although numerous bits of porphyry lying about and a long trough and exterior cistern dating to the earlier period attest to the fort's use as a water station on the quarry road during the operation of the Mons Porphyrites quarries.¹¹

Bab al-Mukhenig

The much-ruined station of Bab al-Mukhenig lies at the base of a hillock in the sandy plain where Wadi al-Atrash and Wadi al-Ghazza intersect. The small structure consists of at least six rooms and what appears to be a cistern with a plaster-lined trough leading to it from an external well. Unlike the other structures along the Porphyry Road, this one does not appear to have been surrounded by a defensive wall. The distinct remains of animal lines lie at the base of another small hill slightly west of the main buildings. Large water vessels and amphorae constitute

3.6 The southern entrance to the Roman fort known as Deir al-Atrash

the majority of the surface pottery sherds, implying that the site did serve as a watering station during the early and late Roman period and thus reinforcing the theory that the station supported the quarry operations at Mons Porphyrites.[12]

The route from Bab al-Mukhenig to El-Saqqia and El-Heita contains several sections in which the tracks of ancient quarry wagons are still detectable on the gravel surface of the wadi. The gauge of these tracks differs depending on the size of the load being carried, but they average about 2.5 meters wide. Near the third- or fourth-century well at Bir Salah on the road to El-Saqqia, at least two sets of tracks are now visible, one with a gauge of 2.2 meters and the other of 2.3 meters.[13] On the way to El-Saqqia, these tracks often pass between the pairs of cairns marking both sides of the old road. A third set of tracks, measuring 3.35 meters and discovered in the 1950s by an explorer crossing the Naq al-Teir plain, is no longer observable.[14]

El-Saqqia

The diminutive fort of El-Saqqia (19 meters by 24 meters) stands in the midst of a vast, empty landscape of sand and low, gravel-covered hills. Its small size,

3.7 Looking south across the enormous well depression adjacent to the ruined fort at El-Saqqia. The animal watering trough and cistern are visible on the far side of the depression.

however, belies its role as one of the most crucial water stations on the route to Qena. This significance stems from its location at the intersection of the Porphyry Road and the road from the Abu Zawal station on the route from Mons Claudianus. Situated at this important junction and serving travelers on both roads, the station had to satisfy a great demand for water. To meet this demand, the Romans constructed two massive wells. The largest of the well depressions lies to the south of the fort and measures 55 meters in diameter. On the southern rim of this depression is an elevated animal watering trough that appears to have been filled from a rectangular stone cistern measuring 5 meters by 6 meters. A well-preserved staircase in its northwest corner afforded access to the cistern. The entire well depression is surrounded by a square earthen embankment whose sides are almost 100 meters long. Their enormous size implies that they served as water catchment systems to supplement the water that could be obtained from the wells within (fig. 3.7).

In addition to boasting the largest wells in the area, the fort of El-Saqqia is the only station on the Porphyry Road containing painted plaster in one of its rooms. The room, which is in the center of the north wall of the fort, is now almost completely buried in sand. But beneath the sand, one can still see the red plaster that once decorated its walls. Several scholars have speculated that, in light of the station's importance, a fairly high-ranking officer may have been assigned there to oversee its operations. The red paint could have been an attempt to make his humble accommodations in this desolate place a bit more acceptable.[15]

El-Heita

Before arriving at the El-Heita station, the quarry road enters Wadi Qena and passes through several areas of soft sand on its way to the station. To enable the heavily laden wagons to get through, the Romans paved over these sandy sections with irregularly shaped stones.

There are actually two forts at El-Heita, one on the gravel bank of the wadi and one approximately 100 meters away, strategically positioned atop a 50-meter hill (fig. 3.8). The fort on the hill is constructed almost entirely of mud brick, and some of its walls are 7 meters high. Local bedouin used to refer to it as Qasr al-Ginn, or the Castle of Ghosts. Three corner towers accessible by means of internal staircases survive, but virtually none of the fort's interior structure remains. Although at least one early traveler conjectured that the hilltop fort served as the "officers' quarters" for the station,[16] the lack of pottery in the vicinity and the apparently unfinished northern wall impart the sense that the fort was never completed.

The lower fort is built of stone and mud brick, and although most of its west side has been destroyed by floods, it still contains numerous rooms, a well, and two towers: one, which contains a room, is next to the entrance gate, and the second, which is solid and served an unknown purpose, stands closer to the center of the fort. The fort also features examples of barrel vaulting in the base of its corner towers and in the rooms that appear to be storage magazines, located in the middle of the fort. In the summer of 1949, Tregenza discovered numerous ostraca in one of these rooms, mainly consisting of receipts and letters. The most interesting of these was written in Greek and appeared to be a letter from a woman to her lover: "Isidora to her lord and master . . . , greetings. First of all, I hope you are well as I am. As I begged you before, please do not forget me. Receive from Primus [the wagoner?] this salted fish. I would like you to send me the earthenware bottle and ink so that I may be able to write to you."[17]

Coincidentally, years earlier Sir Flinders Petrie had found two ostraca at Qift (ancient Coptos) dating from the first century A.D. The ostraca related that a woman named Isidora was an active member of the Nicanor family transport company, which operated from 6 B.C. to approximately A.D. 68, and indicated that

3.8 The upper and lower forts at El-Heita.

she may have lived at the port of Myos Hormos on the Red Sea coast.[18] Another ostracon, dated May 15, A.D. 41, and also ascribed to her, acknowledged receipt of some articles, including eight rush mats from merchants in the Nile Valley. Each ostracon, however, ends with, "[so and so] wrote this for her because she does not know how to write."[19]

For years scholars thought that the Isidora ostracon found by Tregenza at El-Heita was written by the same woman who composed the ostraca discovered in Coptos. This theory was based on the mistaken belief that Myos Hormos was located at the end of the Porphyry Road, at the Red Sea port now known as Abu Sha'ar. As I discuss in more detail below, recent excavations at Abu Sha'ar reveal that the site was constructed in the early fourth century and therefore did not exist when Isidora lived. Furthermore, most scholars now accept that Myos Hormos was actually located near the more southern port of Quseir al-Qadim. While the Isidora of the Coptos ostraca might indeed have lived at Myos Hormos, and while it is possible that she could have sent fish to someone at El-Heita via Coptos, it nevertheless seems unlikely that, as a businesswoman, she would have requested an ink bottle from someone stationed at El-Heita. Isidora was a common name at that time, so presumably Tregenza's Isidora was not the author of the two ostraca discovered in Coptos.

Like the other stations on the Porphyry Road, El-Heita has never been exca-vated. It undoubtedly contains ostraca and other artifacts that would enable schol-ars to learn more about life at the fort and the regulation of traffic along the quarry road. Unfortunately the site stands at the end of an old paved road that comes up from the south through Wadi Qena. This road makes El-Heita rather easily acces-sible and consequently leaves it vulnerable to vandalism. Sometime in 1995, bull-dozers inflicted terrible damage on the lower fort by gouging several deep trenches inside and outside the fort and all but destroying the northeast and southeast corners of the fortress walls.

El-'Aras

The final Roman station on the long road to Qena, El-'Aras is located approxi-mately 30 kilometers further down Wadi Qena from El-Heita. It is the most ruined of all the stations. Today virtually the only structure above ground is a modern wellhead. Despite its current decrepit state, one can imagine that in the Roman period this fortress was a welcome sight to the weary men and animals who strug-gled to transport the stone from the distant quarries. From El-'Aras, only 23 kilo-meters separated them from the chance to luxuriate in the flowing waters of the Nile.

While the original purpose of the stations along the Porphyry Road was to serv-ice the quarrying operations, the forts continued to be used even after the quarries were abandoned. From the late third to the seventh centuries, literary texts report that there were repeated threats to the Eastern Desert from nomadic tribes, espe-cially the Nobatai and Blemmyes. These raiders posed a threat to the security of the Nile Valley itself. To control these tribes, protect the routes, and maintain some sort of early warning system, the stations were refurbished and maintained at various periods depending on the security needs of the time. At some point, for example, the gate at El-Saqqia was narrowed, as was the one to the south at the El-Zerkah station on the Quseir road. We will not know much about the frequency, purpose, or intensity of these raids until archaeologists are able to undertake thorough excavations of the desert stations.

ROUTES FROM MONS CLAUDIANUS TO THE NILE

Less is known of the exact route used by the Romans to haul stone from Mons Claudianus to the Nile than is known about the Porphyry Road. In part this is so because, unlike the Qena–Abu Sha'ar road, the Claudianus road was not heavily used after the Romans abandoned Mons Claudianus and, therefore, its attendant stations and wells were not maintained. Yet based on what is known of the area, one can follow the probable route that enabled the provisioning of the quarrymen and the removal of the giant columns from Mons Claudianus to the Nile.

From Wadi Fatiri (where the giant pillar now rests) and its neighboring quarries, blocks and columns were pulled through a series of wadis that run southwest from the quarries, past the Roman mining settlement at Fatireh al-Beida and on to the major water station of Abu Zawal. Between Fatireh al-Beida and Abu Zawal, on a rocky outcrop not far from the road, a Latin inscription from circa A.D. 113 honors Emperor Trajan: "For the Emperor Nerva Trajan Caesar Augustus, Conqueror of Germany, Conqueror of Dacia, Chief Pontiff, with Tribuician Power, Consul, Father of his Country; in the procuratorship of Flavius Diadumenus, freedman of the Emperor, by the agency of Flavius Fortunatus, his dependent."[20] Surrounded by a carpet of pottery sherds, Abu Zawal resembles other water stations in the Eastern Desert: rectangular, with thick walls and a well sunk in the middle of the structure. Outside are the animal lines and drinking troughs for the draft animals that hauled the stone. This site appears to have been used in Ptolemaic times as a center for gold mining. The Ptolemies washed the ground quartz they extracted to separate it from the gold, and after many years of such activity the quartz residue formed a large mound around the well. The mound made an ideal foundation for the Romans when they built their fort because it enabled them to secure the water source and it elevated the building above the wadi floor, thus ensuring some safety in case of a flood. The Romans deepened and enlarged the well to about 20 meters.[21] Today, the well is still in excellent condition, and the water, although salty, is used frequently by local bedouin. The remains of the shadoof lifting mechanism and water conduits can still be seen.

From Abu Zawal, the Romans used two routes to haul their stones to the Nile Valley, taking advantage of wells that have in all likelihood been obliterated by heavy floods over many centuries. The main route leaves the Abu Zawal station and heads almost due west to the El-Saqqia station (see above), located along the Porphyry Road almost 35 kilometers away. The second route leads southwest from Abu Zawal toward the well of Qreiya, some 40 kilometers south, which now lies next to the main tarmac road connecting Qena with Port Safaga. From here the ancient road continued to El-'Aras and finally to Qena.

TRANSPORTATION OF EGYPTIAN STONE BY LAND AND SEA

Although researchers know approximately which routes the Romans used to move stone from Mons Porphyrites and Mons Claudianus to the Nile, the specific techniques they employed to do so remain a mystery. The wide-gauged tracks described above belonged to enormous wagons called *hamaxai*. Besides these tracks, however, and an ostracon from Mons Claudianus that refers to a "twelve-wheeled wagon,"[22] archaeologists have uncovered little evidence pertaining to the design of vehicles capable of transporting massive loads over long distances.[23] The vehicles would presumably have been made of wood and had fixed, nonturning axles, but no wooden fragments that could have belonged to a wagon have ever been recovered. If exposed to the elements, the wood would have decayed over the course of two thousand years. But a more likely reason for its disappearance is the probability that the remains of the giant carts were scavenged by local tribes and used for other purposes, possibly even for firewood. Trees, after all, are a precious commodity in the Eastern Desert, and the desert tribes would certainly have used any wood they happened upon. Over the course of sixteen hundred years, generations of bedouin had ample opportunity to use or consume whatever Roman artifacts they might have discovered. The salvaging instinct exists even today among the desert bedouin, although their lives have been changed by modern technology. A British archaeologist working at Mons Claudianus told me his team returned from the off-season to discover that bedouin had almost succeeded in extracting a steel survey rod the team had erected the year before. Only the fact that the rod had been set deeply in concrete prevented the bedouin from walking away with a useful piece of steel.

The presence of loading ramps at all of the quarries provides some clues about the design of the ancient stone-carrying wagons. First, it confirms that some kind of vehicle was used to transport at least the majority of columns from the quarries to the Nile and that the columns were carried on top of rather than underneath the cart.[24] (As mentioned above, the largest of these ramps is in Wadi Umm Sidri, near Mons Porphyrites. At 2 meters high, it is slightly larger than the ramps at Mons Claudianus, despite the fact that the columns from Claudianus were much bigger than anything quarried in Mons Porphyrites.) Second, given that the height of the ramp would have at least equaled the height of the wagon bed, we can get some idea of the maximum height of the platforms and the maximum size of the wheels: neither the height of the platform nor the diameter of the wheels could exceed the height of the ramp, but they could be less. Additionally, the tracks still discernible along the quarry roads demonstrate that the axles of the ancient wagons varied from 2 to 4 meters wide.[25] Thus, notwithstanding a paucity of archaeological evidence, it is possible to theorize about the structure of the wagons. Most such theories are based on the idea that the columns were rolled sideways up the ramps and onto the wagon platforms. Support for this notion comes from several ramps at Mons Claudianus that still bear columns in the sideways position at their bases (see fig. 2.8).

While this technique seems logical for the 6-meter columns that were the most common product of Mons Claudianus, it might not apply to the transportation of the 18-meter giants. These were rarely produced, so perhaps the Romans constructed special carts for them. Such vehicles might have featured six or more axles and much larger, wider wheels to support the great weight, and the columns could have been loaded onto the wagon bed via rollers from the rear. Indeed, the columns could have remained on their rollers—once firmly wedged into place—for the duration of the journey to simplify the unloading process at the Nile. As is shown by the following calculation, the size and number of wheels on these carts would have been critical to their ability to carry their cargoes across the desert: "A large wheel with a 50 cm wide tyre might have a ground contact area of 2,500 cm², which with 12 wheels would give a total contact of 30,000 cm². A column weighing 207,000 kg would thus exert a pressure of 6.9 kg per cm², which is not particularly excessive, nor would it be beyond the powers of a competent carpenter to make a spoked wheel which would bear such a load."[26]

Although such estimates suggest that the Romans could have transported their largest columns by wagon, when one stands next to the actual pillars in Mons Claudianus, it is difficult to imagine that any wooden wagon with primitive axles could have carried such massive objects across 120 kilometers of desert. Perhaps instead of special wagons, the Romans moved their biggest pieces by laboriously rolling them along the wadi floors on logs or stone rollers. This would have required considerably more time for the journey, but the relative simplicity and safety of the technique might have outweighed the cost in time. One problem with this theory, however, is that columns like the giant in Wadi Fatira feature raised collars at either end—thus making the efficient replacement and recovery of rollers more difficult as the column moved along the ground. In any case, moving the columns to the Nile was undoubtedly a backbreaking, lengthy ordeal requiring anywhere from one to four weeks depending on the size of the load and to some extent on the time of year.[27] To ensure that the columns survived the journey, the Romans made the roads as flat and smooth as possible, but because of the damage done to the wadis by floods over many centuries, ascertaining the degree to which they succeeded is problematic. Nevertheless, smooth, wide sections of quarry roads still exist, and in my hikes throughout the region, I never saw a single abandoned column along these routes.

Whatever device was used for transport, the column itself—or the vehicle on which it rested—would have been moved by either animal or human power. Here, too, scholars disagree. Many early writers assumed that oxen were the most likely draft animal, but oxen are ill-suited to the desert; it would have required an enormous effort to meet their needs for food and water, even if the removal of the columns was restricted to the winter months.[28] Moreover, cattle bones have not been found at Mons Claudianus or Mons Porphyrites.

Today considerably more evidence points to camels as the designated beasts of burden.[29] Numerous camel bones have been excavated at Mons Claudianus, and documentation from there and other sites supports the use of camels. A stone-cutter's contract on papyrus, for example, refers to the use of camels for carrying stone, although it is not clear if it is saying that camels were always used for stone transport or simply stating the maximum load a camel can carry.[30] Another papyrus, dated December 29, A.D. 118, refers to the removal of a column, probably from Mons Claudianus, but does not specify which kind of animal was used for the task:

> To Apollonios, the most honored. Greetings. Chaeremon, the man present-
> ing this letter to you, is not unknown to you, brother, for last year I left him
> with you for the consignment of cloaks. Now I have sent him for the con-
> signment of barley. I enjoin you to aid him in all things and to hand over to
> him all of the barley currently in your nome, and to render assistance, so
> that once he has quickly loaded all of the barley he can swiftly convey it to
> Kaine, for we have a great number of animals for the purpose of bringing
> down a fifty-foot column, and already we are nearly out of barley. You would
> render me a very great favor in this, brother, if the barley. . . were to arrive
> swiftly. In the third year of the reign of Hadrian Caesar, the third day of the
> month of . . .[31]

A document dating from A.D. 162–63 relates that four camels belonging to a man named Satabous, who lived at Socnopaios Nesos,[32] were requisitioned by the military to transport porphyry columns down to Qena.[33] This limited evidence suggests that the Romans might have used camels as the primary draft animals on the quarry roads. By the second century A.D., camels cost twice as much as oxen in Egypt, but they had many advantages over oxen in the harsh climate and were used extensively in Egypt in the Roman period for tasks less onerous than hauling quarried stone.[34] Numerous ostraca and papyri attest to camels being used by sol-diers to patrol the desert, by merchants to carry supplies, food, and water, and by mail carriers. Reliefs and clay tablets from Tunisia and Libya substantiate that the Romans used camels to pull chariots and to plow fields perhaps as early as the first century B.C.[35]

Donkeys, too, may have served as draft animals on the quarry roads. They are well known for their ability to survive in harsh environments and for their strength, and they, along with mules, were used as draft animals throughout the Roman empire. Indeed, donkey bones are the most abundant animal bones uncovered in the excavations at Mons Claudianus. Given that loads in excess of 200 tons occasionally needed to be hauled from Mons Claudianus—as was the case with the largest columns—one writer estimates that as many as 450 donkeys would be required for the task.[36] Obviously, harnessing and controlling so many animals would have been a remarkable feat in itself.

The difficulty of yoking and controlling hundreds of animals, camels or donkeys, has given rise to the theory that humans pulled the heaviest columns across the desert. Certainly human traction was common in ancient Egypt and had the advantage that large numbers of men could quickly obey commands to turn or pull in unison. Based on analysis of evidence from Pharaonic Egypt and assuming that wagons were used on smoothed tracks, it has been estimated recently that a maximum of 360 men would have been needed to haul the largest columns from the quarries to the Nile.[37]

Whatever the engine of their movement, when the columns and the wagons of stone arrived at Qena, their journey was still far from over. The columns were first placed on large river barges, then sailed to Alexandria, where they were transferred to even larger seagoing ships for the long, dangerous journey to Italy. Although no descriptions or illustrations of the process of moving the columns down river in the Roman period have been discovered, a Pharaonic relief on the walls of the temple of Deir al-Bahari at Thebes depicts two obelisks being transported from Elephantine, in Aswan, to Thebes. They were placed end to end on a barge measuring 78 meters and towed by three rows of boats, nine boats in each row, with a tenth in the lead. The whole operation of quarrying and transporting the obelisks took seven months. They were erected at the entrance to the Luxor Temple in honor of Hatshepsut.

The ships that carried Egypt's granite columns to Italy must have been enormous, but scholars have yet to uncover any documentary evidence specifically describing these trans-Mediterranean stone carriers. Instead, we have written accounts of the famous grain ships that hauled the agricultural wealth of Egypt across the sea to the hungry citizens of Rome.[38] Regrettably, no grain ship has ever been discovered; our limited knowledge comes from ancient descriptions and pictorial representations, rather than extensive archaeological evidence.[39] The ships probably featured two or even three masts, a relatively flat bottom, a frame of hardwood such as oak, and soft wood planking 10 to 15 centimeters thick. Like most large seagoing ships of the Greco-Roman period (up until at least the second century A.D.), the ships were most likely covered with a sheath of lead to preserve the wood and protect the cargo from moisture.[40] One surviving description, by a Greek who saw a grain ship in Piraeus, states that the enormous vessel was capable of carrying 1,200 to 1,300 tons. A single anchor stock discovered off the coast of Malta—probably from just such a ship—weighed two tons.[41] Perhaps these grain ships were modified to carry heavy loads of stone to Rome, but the Romans may conceivably have built a fleet of ships specifically for that purpose. In the first century A.D., for example, Emperor Caligula ordered the construction of a vessel to carry an obelisk from Egypt to Rome. The obelisk and its pedestal, which now stand in the center of St. Peter's Square, weighed 496 tons, and its ballast weighed another 800–900 tons—the entire load therefore equaling approximately 1,300 tons.[42]

IV

PORTS ON THE RED SEA COAST

The Romans were not the first rulers of Egypt to recognize and exploit lucrative trade opportunities with regions south and east. Ptolemy II Philadelphus (285–246 B.C.) and his descendants constructed ports along the Red Sea in Egypt, Sudan, and Ethiopia and possibly as far south as Somaliland. Through these ports came exotic merchandise, including the elephants and gold that Ptolemy II used to wage war and to pay his mercenary troops. But by the time Octavian defeated Cleopatra VII, the last of the Ptolemaic rulers, and added Egypt to the Roman Empire in 30 B.C., the Romans were a world power, and they quickly became the dominant force in the east–west trade. No longer desiring to employ elephants in war and possessing enough gold within their empire to meet their needs, the Romans used their knowledge of the monsoon winds and turned their attentions to the luxuries of the east, including incense, spices, and ivory.

At the height of the Roman period, from the late first century B.C. to the second century A.D., seven main ports were operating on the Egyptian Red Sea coast. Although most of these were established by the Ptolemies, the Romans greatly expanded their economic importance. From north to south, these ports were Clysma, Abu Sha'ar, Philoteras, Leukos Limen, Myos Hormos, Nechesia, and Berenike (see map 2).[1]

CLYSMA

At the northernmost point on the Red Sea, the Ptolemaic port of Clysma (modern Suez) was the terminus for a canal that during the Roman period began near the old city of Babylon on the southern fringes of modern Cairo.[2] Numerous ancient sources refer to this canal, but whether it was first built in the Middle Kingdom by Pharaoh Necho II or by such later rulers as Darius I (521–486 B.C.) or Ptolemy II is unknown. What is certain is that Emperor Trajan (A.D. 98–117) excavated the canal and reestablished access to the Red Sea from the Nile.[3] This made the transporting of goods from Alexandria eastward more economical by eliminating the need to carry them across the desert by camel caravan. Because the canal did not commence in Alexandria, however, such a voyage would have required that commodities from Egypt's north coast be carried southward by boat before gaining access to the entrance to the canal, whose primary purpose seems to have been to facilitate the exportation of bulky cargoes like grain, wine, and textiles originating in the southern delta region and the Fayoum Oasis (ancient Arsinoite Nome). The Fayoum produced these items in large quantities during both the Ptolemaic and Roman periods, and they constituted some of the more important Egyptian exports to South Arabia and India.[4] Over the centuries, the canal was repaired many times, but it appears to have remained only intermittently navigable until the Arab conquest of Egypt in A.D. 642–43. At that time, the Umayyad caliph ordered that the canal be thoroughly dredged to enable grain shipments and pilgrims from Egypt to sail for Mecca and Medina.[5] Today, however, few traces of the canal exist, and scholars are uncertain of its exact route and dimensions.

Given the relatively easy passage between the port of Clysma and the Nile River and thus to Alexandria, one would expect (mistakenly) that Clysma was Roman Egypt's most vital port on the Red Sea. Indeed, a twelfth-century monk from Monte Cassino named Peter the Deacon is partly responsible for perpetuating this misunderstanding of Clysma's importance during the Roman period. Writing a book about holy places in 1137, Peter borrowed material from a travelogue written by a remarkable nun named Egeria who had visited the holy sites of the Middle

East and Egypt in the late fourth century. In his book, entitled *Liber de locis sanctis*, Peter described Clysma as follows:

> It is on the shore, right by the sea. It has an enclosed harbor which makes the sea come right inside the fort, and it is the port from India, which is to say that it receives ships from India, for ships from India can come to no other port but this in Roman territory. And the ships there are numerous and great, since it is a port renowned for the Indian merchants who come to it. Also the official [*agens in rebus*] known as the *logothete* has his residence there, the one who goes on embassy each year to India by order of the Roman emperor, and his ships lie there. The children of Israel came to this place on their way out of Egypt when they were escaping the Pharaoh, and the fort was built later on, to be a defense and deterrent against Saracen raids.[6]

Although the validity of this picture of Clysma was accepted for centuries, scholars now think that Peter the Deacon took his information about the site from a secondhand document that dated from the sixth or seventh century. His description was obviously inaccurate for the late fourth century, when Egeria passed through Clysma on her way to the Holy Land. In Egeria's day, Clysma was a desolate outpost whose nearest source of potable water was at Ain Musa (Moses' Spring), roughly ten kilometers to the southeast. Indeed, Egeria neither stated that Clysma was a port nor gave the impression that its fort served as one of four staging posts on the road to Arabia. Of her arrival she merely wrote, "The place was now known [from the fort there] as Clysma."[7] Certainly Clysma was not the bustling port of Peter the Deacon's fancy, and it was never a major Red Sea harbor during the Roman period.

In spite of its proximity to Trajan's canal, Clysma was not well situated as a port for international trade. As anyone who has visited the Egyptian or Saudi Arabian coasts can attest, strong northerly winds blow year-round, and these gusts made sailing up the Red Sea extremely difficult in antiquity. Thus it appears that over its long history, Clysma functioned primarily as a port of embarkation and export, rather than as a major site for the importation of foreign commodities.[8] Documentary evidence indicates that the more southerly ports of Myos Hormos and Berenike were Roman Egypt's main centers of importation because their locations made them far easier to reach by sea. One writer in the first century B.C. stated that Berenike, the southernmost port, was the only harbor through which goods from India, Arabia, and "such Ethiopian merchandise as is imported by the Arabian Gulf" passed.[9] Although this might have been true at the time it was written, recent archaeological finds show that by the first century A.D., Myos Hormos also received goods from the east.

ABU SHA'AR

For more than a century since its rediscovery in the early 1800s, Abu Sha'ar was thought to be the famous ancient port of Myos Hormos (Mussel Harbor) mentioned by Strabo.[10] Excavations carried out in the 1990s, however, have confirmed that Myos Hormos was located elsewhere.

Today, the fort at Abu Sha'ar is almost completely buried by sand from years of storms and wind, and it will soon be surrounded by an explosion of five-star hotels.[11] The fact that the area is swiftly becoming a center for beach resorts is ironic in light of what Sir Gardner Wilkinson said about the location when he visited it in 1823: "No place can be more unhealthy. During the summer months the atmosphere is charged with damp vapour, exceedingly oppressive, and resembling that of a Turkish bath. In the time of prosperity of Myos Hormos, many were, doubtless, the victims of its unwholesome air."[12]

Recent excavations at Abu Sha'ar attest to the fact that, unhealthy air notwithstanding, it was an important stronghold in the late Roman period. One of the largest Roman-Byzantine forts east of the Nile, it measures 77 meters by 64 meters and has walls that were 4 meters high and 1.5 meters thick and included catwalks and parapets. There were two gates, one in the center of the north wall and one in the center of the west wall. These gates were closed by doors made of pine and acacia wood. The fort contained barracks, headquarters offices, storage magazines, and a colonnaded street that connected the main east–west street with the north–south street. All of these inner structures were made of igneous cobbles in their lower portions and mud brick in their upper sections; the outer walls were built of igneous cobbles and white gypsum and were punctuated by twelve towers, two flanking each entrance. In one of these towers, researchers discovered six stone catapult balls that weighed an average of nine kilos each. Very few other weapons were discovered at the site and no battle damage was discernible: apparently Abu Sha'ar was peacefully abandoned.[13]

Because Abu Sha'ar is so close to the sea, the absence of fresh water must have been a major obstacle to the settlement of the site. To overcome this problem, the Romans constructed a well approximately one kilometer west of the fort consisting of an ingenious closed-pipe system that worked under pressure. The water came from a nonflowing artesian well that produced up to 74 liters per minute.[14] Three sets of terra-cotta pipes emanated from this well. The longest pipeline was composed of nearly two thousand sections of pipe and led directly to the western gate of the fort. The other two lines were shorter and connected the well to an elaborate semicircular *tepidarium* that boasted a stone floor and glass windows.[15] A second, more traditional well, Bir Abu Sha'ar, was located approximately six kilometers west of the fort against the base of the coastal mountains. Roman-period structures in the vicinity indicate that although this may well have provided additional water for the fort, it also may have been used to irrigate the surrounding land, enabling the Romans to grow grain and vegetables for the garrison. These provisions would have supplemented the food they obtained from the sea, including fish, shellfish, and sea turtles, and items such as beer and wine that they imported from the Nile Valley.[16]

The most exciting discovery during the Abu Sha'ar excavations was a monumental Latin inscription in twenty-five fragments that originally hung above the west gate. The inscription states that the fort was built (or rebuilt) around A.D. 309–11 by Aurelius Maximinus, the same Roman governor who built the fort at Luxor, who dedicated this fortress in the name of the following emperors: Galerius (A.D. 305–11), Maximinus II (A.D. 310–13), Licinius I (A.D. 308–24), and Constantine I (A.D. 307–37).[17] The text of the inscription makes it clear that Abu Sha'ar was part of a *limes*[18] that was garrisoned by members of a mounted camel unit, the Ala Nova Maximiana, based at the major legionary fort in Luxor. The barracks discovered inside Abu Sha'ar indicate that approximately two hundred men were once stationed there, and their primary job appears to have been to protect merchants.[19] From guard posts situated in the nearby mountains, they monitored the movements of potentially troublesome desert tribes such as the Blemmyes and patrolled the various desert routes leading to and from Abu Sha'ar, including the Via Hadriana and the Porphyry Road. An ostracon written in Greek on the bottom of a broken plate describes the rotational system used by the soldiers in the guard stations: "After serving in a guard post the man gets a day off, and the next day he has to serve in another post."[20] Supporting the theory that Abu Sha'ar was intended to protect commerce, the term *mercator* (merchant) appears among the inscriptions above the west gate. Unfortunately, the excavations failed to uncover evidence of the specific goods whose protection required the establishment and maintenance of this military installation.

The initial military occupation of Abu Sha'ar lasted for most of the fourth century. The second, longer period of occupation occurred from the early fifth century to the early seventh century. Sometime after the Roman military abandoned the fort, Abu Sha'ar was occupied by Christian monks or hermits who converted the headquarters room into a church and may have used the fort to assist pilgrims traveling from Upper Egypt to the monasteries of Saint Anthony and Saint Paul in the Eastern Desert, to Saint Catherine's monastery in the Sinai, or to Jerusalem.[21]

Inside the church, researchers discovered human remains wrapped in cloth—possibly those of a saint or martyr who had been the focus of a religious cult.[22] Christian pilgrims covered the walls of the north gate with graffiti, and the arch over the gate bore the following inscriptions:

> 1. I implore you, Lord, oh God of our Fathers Abraham and Isaac and Jacob and of all the saints and of the Holy Mary, the Mother of God, of (?) holy Trinity, have mercy upon our sins and upon your poor servants, being there (?) at your coming, Lord Jesus Christ.
>
> 2. There is one God only, Christ.[23]

Inside the fort, researchers discovered the short prayer "Lord Jesus Christ, save and have mercy on your servant Salamanis"[24] and uncovered a complete fifth-century papyrus constituting a letter from Apollonios to Abba John and his daughter Sarah. After the usual greetings, Apollonios writes, "The Lord testifies for me that I was deeply grieved about the capture of your city, and again we heard that the Lord God had saved you and all your dependents."[25] Scholars do not know which captured city is being referred to here, or why the recipients of the letter were in Abu Sha'ar.

These discoveries, coupled with the realization that Abu Sha'ar was a relatively late Roman fort, have led most scholars to conclude that the site can no longer be regarded as the possible location of Myos Hormos.[26] Some historians believe that Myos Hormos remains undiscovered somewhere along the coast north of Abu Sha'ar, but most scholars think the famous port lies 165 kilometers south of Abu Sha'ar, at or near Quseir al-Qadim. As we shall see below, however, the evidence supporting this latter theory is inconclusive.

PHILOTERAS

The Ptolemaic town of Philoteras has never been discovered. Strabo (16.4.5) mentions that it was located before the "hot, salt springs," which could place it in the vicinity of Ain Sukhna (Hot Spring) some 50 kilometers south of modern Suez. Several modern scholars, however, speculate that it is south of the modern port of Safaga.

LEUKOS LIMEN

Leukos Limen (White Port), has traditionally been associated with Quseir al-Qadim (see map 2). Indeed, several documents uncovered by archaeologists working in Quseir al-Qadim possibly contain the name Leukos Limen. As we shall see below, however, some contrary data indicate that Quseir al-Qadim might be the site of Myos Hormos, in which case the true location of Leukos Limen is uncertain.

MYOS HORMOS (QUSEIR AL-QADIM?)

The exact location of Myos Hormos remains the subject of heated debate among scholars. One theory holds that it is located at the site of Quseir al-Qadim (Old Quseir), while an older belief is that Quseir al-Qadim is the location of Leukos Limen. Whichever ancient name is correct, it is certain that Quseir al-Qadim was an important Roman-era port (fig. 4.1).

Quseir al-Qadim was not the best natural site for a harbor on the Egyptian coast, but it was the closest point on the Red Sea to the Nile River. The eastward bulge of the Nile between Nag al-Hammadi and Armmant meant that the town of Quseir al-Qadim was only 175 kilometers from Coptos (modern Qift), which was the major trading center on the Nile River during the Roman period (see map 2). Its proximity to the Nile significantly reduced the time and cost involved

4.1 Excavated room at Quseir al-Qadim. Although many scholars believe this could be the site of the ancient harbor of Myos Hormos, others argue that Quseir al-Qadim is actually the site of Leukos Limen.

in transporting goods from the coast to Coptos. Despite its less-than-ideal harbor, therefore, Quseir al-Qadim became the logical site for a port.

With the exception of its splendid setting on the shores of the Red Sea and a Swiss beach resort nearby, there is little at Quseir al-Qadim to interest a modern visitor. The harbor itself is no longer visible to the casual observer, having silted up over many centuries, while construction of the modern coastal road cut an 80-meter-wide swath through the ancient site. Today, a high mound of sand and gravel built up by ancient dredgings marks its location, divulging that, even in their day, the Romans struggled to keep the harbor clear. The town that served the port was located to the north and west of the harbor, but only a few structures exist above ground. Excavations carried out between 1978 and 1982 by the University of Chicago, however, revealed that the layer of hard salt pan that covers the site and makes archaeological work extremely difficult preserved a wealth of material underground in excellent condition.[27]

After an arduous process of excavation, archaeologists were able to see that the harbor of Quseir al-Qadim and its surrounding town were carefully laid out along the classical grid pattern of blocks and streets called hippodamian. Unlike the fort at Abu Sha'ar, here there is no evidence that the Romans built an enclosure wall to protect the settlement. In addition to some mud brick, they used local white limestone to construct the buildings, thus giving some credence to the long-standing theory that the town was actually Leukos Limen. The broadest side of the town faced the sea, and most of its streets ran parallel to the coast to take advantage of the cooling northern breeze.

From the remains of buildings along these streets, archaeologists identified a central administrative building that served as a storage and customshouse and recovered an abundance of Roman artifacts dating to the first and second centuries A.D. These included cloth, basketry, wooden bowls and pulleys, seeds, papyrus, faience bowls, glassware, and terra sigillata, a fine, polished red-ware from Italy.[28] Of these, glass and cloth represented the two main Egyptian exports to the east during the Roman period. Researchers also uncovered a large number of fishnets, hooks, and piles of fish bones.[29] Judging from the artifacts, it is apparent that during the Roman period, Quseir al-Qadim was used primarily for trading staple products rather than luxury items.

As is often the case at Roman sites in the Eastern Desert, and particularly at those such as Quseir al-Qadim where water was scarce, a large variety of amphorae was present. Some, dating from the first and second centuries A.D., were inscribed with Tamil graffiti in the Brahmi script and likely came from Arikamedu in southern India (not far from the modern town of Pondicherry).[30] These constitute the first Indian Tamil inscriptions ever found in Egypt, and their discovery, next to a small iron forge, raises the possibility that a small community of Indian merchants or metalworkers lived at Quseir al-Qadim.[31] As further testimony to Quseir al-Qadim's role in Rome's trade with India, researchers found items typical of the east, for example, teak and cloth made from jute.[32] In addition to the amphorae, archaeologists discovered an abundance of plaster plugs used to seal the amphorae and other containers. Some of these plugs were inscribed and revealed that slaves and freedmen often acted as agents for their masters and patrons at Red Sea ports like Myos Hormos and Berenike. Two such plugs at Quseir al-Qadim record the business activities of imperial freedmen: the first was in the wine business, and the second mentions a Titus Flavius, who appears to have been a freedman of one of the Flavian emperors (A.D. 69–96).[33]

The textual discoveries at Quseir al-Qadim are of great significance. Most of the ostraca were written in Greek, but some were in Latin or Demotic Egyptian, and one was in Himyarite, the Sabaean language of Yemen.[34] Scraps of papyrus included writing in both Greek and Latin. Five of the Latin texts refer to a military presence in Quseir al-Qadim. On the basis of these pieces, researchers have determined that the total military strength at the town was anywhere from fifty to one hundred men and that on any given day as many as twenty-five of them might have been on patrol in the neighboring desert. In addition, one ostracon requested that three jars of wine be sent out to a commander with the unusually high rank of *tribune*, who was temporarily away from the town.[35] Another text included a roster of soldiers who were on duty away from the town, in all likelihood patrolling the nearby desert. Interestingly, of the names on the list, 25 percent are Roman, 50 percent Greek, and 20 percent Egyptian. Because similar ratios for military detachments have been discovered elsewhere in Egypt, those with Roman names like Saturninus conceivably represent legionary soldiers, while those of Greco-Egyptian origin belong to members of an auxiliary unit.[36]

These textual discoveries do not, however, answer many basic questions concerning the nature of the trade conducted through Quseir al-Qadim. Scholars remain uncertain about the volume of trade and the extent to which it was undertaken by private businessmen as opposed to the Roman government of Egypt.

For the ethnically diverse collection of people who sought their livelihood at Quseir al-Qadim, life was certainly difficult and tenuous. The port was almost completely dependent for its survival on the importation of food and provisions from the Nile Valley, although residents did manage to supplement their diet with seafood. Even water was not locally available. The nearest well was Bir Kareim, at least 20 kilometers away. Because of these difficulties, it is possible that Quseir al-Qadim was fully inhabited only during those times of the year when the monsoons enabled the Romans to conduct their trade by sea. However many months per year people resided there, the lack of life-sustaining amenities helps explain why the town did not survive after the Romans peacefully abandoned it sometime in the third century.[37] As at other Roman sites in the Egyptian desert, the sustaining of viable communities in remote and hostile areas required tremendous organizational skill, logistical effort, and a determined commitment to a broader purpose—in this case, promoting the lucrative trade with the east. Once the Romans departed, those who followed no longer had the same interest in trade, so they were either unwilling or incapable of meeting the challenges necessary to make long-term human habitation of the ancient site possible. Indeed, as recently as 1930, the modern town of Quseir, which is eight kilometers south of Quseir al-Qadim, was the only village in the 1,000-kilometer stretch between Suez and Sudan.[38]

The most recent evidence pertaining to the issue of whether Quseir al-Qadim is Myos Hormos or Leukos Limen is helpful. At the El-Zerkah station (known during the Roman period as Maximianon), located on the ancient road connecting Quseir al-Qadim with the Nile Valley (see map 2), archaeologists have uncovered several vase inscriptions and eight ostraca dating from the second century A.D. Each of the inscriptions on these items reveals that Myos Hormos was located at the end of the road from Coptos, that is, at or near the site of Quseir al-Qadim. One such letter, for example, was written in response to a request for fish by a man named Gaios Apolinarios. Given that the stations along the desert road would have needed to import their food and other provisions from either the Nile Valley or the Red Sea, and that, for El-Zerkah, the Red Sea was the closer of the two sources (65 kilometers), the residents of El-Zerkah may well have obtained their fish from Myos Hormos. Supporting this theory are the following ostraca (the first three were written in Greek, the fourth in Latin) found at El-Zerkah:[39]

1. Ioulios Maximos to his brother Gaios Apolinarios, many greetings. I want you to know that the boats did not come back to Myos Hormos while I was there. I was going to send you the fish. So don't reproach me, brother, for you know what duty is. If it is possible for me to go, I shall see to it. Write me what you want. Greet those who are friends with you. For as far as I can see, we stay here a few days. Take care.[40]

2. Sarapias to her father and lord Ammonios, many greetings. I do obeisance on your behalf to the lady Philotera. I received from Nestareus 6 loaves of bread. If I come to Myos Hormos, as I announced to you, I shall send you a jar of fish-sauce with the first donkeys.[41] For I care as much

about you as if you were my own father. And if I find the linen for you I shall buy it. If you have a drinking-cup, send it to me. My brother salutes you. Don't forget to send me the scalpel. Receive 1 jar [and] write to me about yourself. Greet Proklos.[42]

3. Sarapias to Ammonios her Father and lord, many greetings. I constantly pray that you are well and I do obeisance on your behalf to Philotera. I left Myos Hormos quickly after giving birth. I have taken nothing [with me] from Myos Hormos. Recently I sent from Myos Hormos drachmas in order that you bring me slices [of?]. Send me 1 small drinking cup . . . and send your daughter a small pillow. I have received small loaves of bread. I hope you are well.[43]

4. To Domitius Nemonianus, greetings. I send you two bunches of green with Saluianus, the cavalryman. Tell Amat[ius?] Antoninus to collect a letter and a bunch [of vegetables?] which Caienus sent him from the donkey-drivers (?) who carry the food supply to Myos Hormos. Take care.[44]

Although these ostraca suggest that the ancient port of Myos Hormos was indeed located at the end of the Coptos road and that its ruins are to be seen at Quseir al-Qadim, several leading scholars are not convinced by the evidence. They argue that Myos Hormos remains undiscovered at another location along the Red Sea coast, perhaps under the modern town of Quseir, just south of Quseir al-Qadim. The proximity of the two sites would explain why the above texts hint that Myos Hormos was located at the end of the Coptos road. At the time the ostraca were written, the port might have been situated at the current location of Quseir. Over time, however, the harbor might have silted up, requiring that the port and harbor facilities be relocated farther north at the site of Quseir al-Qadim. This could mean that Quseir al-Qadim might be Leukos Limen—as was thought traditionally—rather than Myos Hormos. More research and additional excavations must be conducted before this debate will be settled.[45]

NECHESIA

This ancient port has never been positively identified, but a recent theory holds that it could be at Marsa Nakari, approximately 19 kilometers south of Marsa Alam (see map 2). While the results of preliminary (summer 1999) excavations have not been published as of this writing, researchers working on a survey of the Berenike region identified an ancient road that linked Marsa Nakari with Edfu in the Nile Valley.[46]

BERENIKE

By the mid–first century A.D., then later from the fourth through the fifth centuries, Berenike was one of the two busiest and most vital harbors on the Egyptian Red Sea coast.[47] Founded by Ptolemy II Philadelphus in 275 B.C. and named after his mother, the port was originally intended to facilitate the importation of gold, ivory, and forest elephants from Ethiopia (that is, lands south of Egypt). The elephants were transported on special ships called *elephantagoi* from Adulis on the Zula Gulf in modern Eritrea to Berenike and were used in warfare, carrying towers filled with archers into battle.[48]

At first glance, it seems odd that the Ptolemies, and later the Romans, established this major port so far south on the Red Sea and at such a great distance from Edfu and Coptos, the two major commercial centers of the Nile Valley during the Ptolemaic and Romans periods, respectively. But the constant northern winds and the treacherous reefs and currents that characterize the Red Sea made sailing further north than Berenike extremely hazardous. Just north of Berenike, for example, captains planning to sail further north along the coast opted to portage their ships for ten kilometers rather than risk sailing around the great peninsula of Ras Banas, which juts 30 kilometers out into the Red Sea just north of Berenike.[49] In addition to these navigational problems, piracy was a constant concern in the Red Sea, especially in the Roman period, when the ships were known to carry extremely valuable cargoes. Thus, even though remote, Berenike became the preferred port for ships engaged in the lucrative trade with the east.

Berenike was a large town, occupying an area of about seven hectares. The harbor was located southeast of the main settlement. Numerous small buildings housed a population of least five hundred inhabitants, although the number would have fluctuated widely over time. The houses were generally constructed of coral blocks, white gypsum, and igneous cobbles.[50] As at Quseir al-Qadim, the town was laid out roughly in a grid pattern of blocks and streets. Well situated on a rise about 7 meters above the high tidemark and bounded on the north and south by the wadi depressions, the site nevertheless suffered from countless storms and floods over the centuries.[51] Today, aside from portions of the temple of Serapis, no standing buildings remain above ground.[52] The temple sits atop a small hill on the west side of the settlement and contains cartouches that mention Marcus Aurelius and Lucius Verus, Roman coemperors from A.D. 161–69. Several larger buildings on the eastern side of the site appear to have served as administrative buildings, warehouses, customs buildings, small-scale manufacturing centers, and facilities to repair ships. Unlike many other Roman structures in the Eastern Desert, Berenike appears not to have been surrounded by a defensive wall.

In 1994, however, archaeologists did notice that four flat-topped mounds appear to have been strategically built on the outskirts of the town, perhaps serving as watchtowers.[53]

Since excavations began at Berenike in 1994, archaeologists have uncovered numerous outstanding artifacts spanning nearly eight centuries (fig. 4.2). These include papyrus fragments and ostraca, Persian Gulf and Indian pottery, enameled glass, Axumite (Ethiopian), Indian and Sri Lankan beads, coins, Indian resist-dye textiles, coconut, rice, teak wood, pieces of shell jewelry, an ivory bracelet, emeralds, and several fake emeralds made of chloride that may have come from St. John's Island, which lies 85 kilometers southeast of Berenike.[54] In addition to these items, archaeological and literary sources reveal that goods from the following territories constituted the bulk of the merchandise that the Romans imported via Berenike:

> Ethiopia—ivory, tortoise shell, rhinoceros horn, aromatics, myrrh
> Northern Somalia—myrrh, frankincense, slaves, ivory, tortoise shell
> Arabia—myrrh, white marble, aloe, frankincense
> India (northwest)—costus, bdellium, nard, myrrh, indigo, turquoise, lapis lazuli, onyx, agate, ivory, cotton cloth, fine cotton garments, silk cloth and yarn, Chinese pelts, pepper
> India (south and southwest)—nard, malabathron, pepper, pearls, ivory, tortoise shell, transparent gems, diamonds, sapphires, silk cloth, fine cotton garments
> India (northeast)—nard, malabathron, pearls, ivory, fine cotton garments.[55]

Although not all modern scholars would agree, there is strong evidence that shippers operating out of Berenike (and Myos Hormos) concentrated on importing luxuries, especially pepper, that were destined for wealthy homes and palaces throughout the Roman Mediterranean. Loaded with such luxuries, the cargo of a single ship could earn merchants staggering profits, despite the 25 percent tax levied on all goods imported into Berenike. One papyrus relating specifically to the India trade gives a good idea of how lucrative such an investment could be. The papyrus concerns a shipment from Muziris, India, to Alexandria that included 700 to 1,700 pounds of nard, more than 4,700 pounds of ivory, and 790 pounds of textiles. The total value of this merchandise was 131 talents, enough to purchase 2,400 acres of the finest farmland in Egypt. But this shipment was only a small portion of the entire cargo. Even if the ship that carried these goods was modest (500 tons), it could carry as many as 150 such consignments.[56]

4.2 An excavation area at Berenike that reveals portions of the foundation dating from the earliest period of Roman settlement.

Because of the Romans' demand for expensive goods and the fact that Roman Egypt exported mainly low-priced commodities like wine, olive oil, cloth, coral, and metals, historians have argued that a severe trade imbalance emerged between Rome and Asia. Supporting this theory are the musings of the ancient Romans, including Emperor Tiberius: "How shall we reform the taste for dress? How are we to deal with the particular articles of feminine vanity, and in particular with that rage for jewels and precious trinkets, which drains the empire of its wealth, and sends, in exchange for baubles, the money of the Commonwealth to foreign nations, and even the enemies of Rome."[57] Pliny the Elder also added a warning: "The subject is one well worthy of our notice, seeing that in no year does India drain us of less than 550,000,000 sesterces giving back her own wares, which are sold among us at fully 100 percent their first cost."[58]

Romans were not the only ones to comment on the nature of their trade with India. A Tamil poem from the second or third century A.D. includes the following passage: "The beautiful vessels, the masterpieces of the Yavanas [Westerners], stir white foam on the Periyar, river of Kerala, arriving with gold and departing with pepper."[59] Despite the discovery in southern India of some six thousand silver *denarii* and gold *aurei*, which seems to corroborate these statements, scholars disagree about whether such an economic imbalance actually occurred. Certainly the Romans spent vast sums of money on Asian luxuries, but they might also have used a barter system. Roman amphora, pottery, glass, lamps, and other items have been excavated in India, Sri Lanka, and Arabia, and Roman beads (gold or silver, set in glass) have been uncovered in the Rufiji Delta of Tanzania.[60] Indeed, from this latter site the Romans obtained ivory, high quality tortoise shell, and rhinoceros horn in exchange for spears, axes, knives, awls, and, as noted above, "numerous types of glass stones."[61] In addition, the Greek/Egyptian author of the *Periplus Maris Erythraei* (Circumnavigation of the Red Sea) identifies specific places where bartering was or was not possible. Ports along the northern coast of India were amenable to exchanging goods while those of the southern coast were not. Regarding the southern Malabar coast, for example, the *Periplus* recommends that Roman merchants bring "mainly a great amount of money."[62]

The value and volume of commerce passing through Berenike during the harbor's centuries of peak activity must have been impressive, and no doubt transformed the settlement from a desolate backwater into a bustling, international port town. We know relatively little of the people who actually inhabited Berenike, but archaeologists continue to uncover clues that offer glimpses into the makeup of this colorful society. For example, on the basis of material discovered in recent excavations—mainly bracelets, earrings, and other jewelry—we know that women were present at Berenike. Although the bones of a fetus or prematurely born child were discovered at Berenike during the 1995–96 excavations, the general paucity of evidence of the presence of children there suggests that the women were not wives and mothers.[63] Archaeological evidence also implies that a broad mixture of people, including Africans, Indians, Greeks, and Arabs, must have passed through the town and, further, that a variety of ethnic groups lived permanently or semipermanently in the community. Among these groups were Nubians, Egyptians from the Nile Valley, Romans, and, possibly in the later periods, nomadic tribesmen.

One of the most intriguing questions concerning the inhabitants of Berenike pertains to the relations between the Romans and the indigenous desert tribes who lived between Berenike and the Nile River, specifically, whether members of these tribes might have occasionally resided at the port. The question stems from the abundance of handmade (as opposed to wheel-turned) pottery discovered at the site. This burnished and decoratively inscribed pottery, hitherto found only in the Nile Valley, mainly between Primis (Qasr Ibrim) and Talmis (Kalabsha), is now attributed to the Blemmye people who lived in the region during the Roman period.[64] As I shall discuss in detail later, the Blemmyes and another desert people known as the Nobatai have traditionally been regarded as marauding nomads who constituted the primary threat to Roman settlements and trade routes in the Eastern Desert. Indeed, there are convincing data to support this theory. We know, for example, that Blemmye criminals or prisoners of war were brought to Rome to fight in the arena: "Three hundred pairs of gladiators were also produced, with several Blemmyans who had been paraded in the triumphal procession fighting, as well as some Germans."[65] In addition, from the reign of Diocletian (A.D. 284–305) to that of Justinian I (A.D. 527–65), the Roman government annually paid the Blemmyes and the Nobatai a fixed sum of gold in an attempt to prevent them from raiding Roman territory.[66]

The presence of Blemmye pottery at Berenike raises the possibility that, however deep the enmity between the two peoples, the Romans actively engaged in trade with the Blemmyes and even that a certain number of them actually lived at Berenike. That most of the Blemmye sherds in Berenike date from the late Roman period could mean that the two groups, although in conflict during the first and second centuries, achieved a certain modus vivendi by the third to sixth centuries. Indeed, analysis of food remains at the site indicates that at least two distinct groups, a desert people and a coastal (or Nile Valley) people, inhabited the settlement simultaneously during the later period. In addition, recent examinations of an ancient text disclose that relations may have occasionally involved a military alliance.[67] According to one researcher, the text hints that in A.D. 524, Emperor Justin I ordered Timothy, the patriarch of Alexandria, to write to Elesboas, the king of Axum (the capital of ancient Ethiopia), and encourage him to wage war on the Jewish king of the Himyarites in southwestern Arabia. To support Elesboas, Timothy apparently promised to send ships from Berenike with contingents of Blemmyan and Nubian troops.[68]

Although the degree of Roman military occupation at Berenike is not yet clear, Roman troops certainly were present at the settlement. Archaeological evidence has affirmed that Roman soldiers enforced customs regulations at the harbor, collected taxes on all imported goods, guarded the harbor and town from attacks from land and sea, and generally monitored the movement of people into and out of the coastal region. Their presence even influenced people's eating habits. Archaeologists have determined that the inhabitants of Berenike maintained a highly Romanized diet including pork, chicken, and *garum*, the fish sauce of which the Romans were so fond—"all products which usually follow in the wake of the Roman military."[69] Further grounds for a military role at Berenike, at least at the beginning of the third century, are furnished by a Greek inscription from September 8, A.D. 215, honoring Emperor Caracalla. The two limestone blocks on which the dedication is written formed the base of a large bronze statue of a god-dess discovered in 1995. Numerous cult artifacts such as offering tables and incense burners uncovered near the statue suggest that the local residents worshiped the goddess into the early fifth century. The inscription, by a Palmyrene auxiliary sol-dier, reads as follows: "For the eternal power and permanence of our lord, Lord of the World, Marcus Aurelius Severus Antoninus Pius Augustus [and] for Julia, *mater castrorum*, the Lady Augusta and [for] their whole house, [has dedicated] Marcus Aurelius Mocimus, son of Abdaeus, Palmyrene, Antonine archer,---. Year 24, Thoth 10."[70] "Julia" refers to Julia Domna (A.D. 170–217), Caracalla's mother and the wife of Emperor Septimius Severus. Palmyrenes were present in Egypt as traders, but they also served as military archers who guarded desert roads and set-tlements. In addition to the inscription above, researchers in Coptos discovered an inscription by a Palmyrene archer dedicated to the Palmyrene god Hierobolos, and an additional Palmyrene-Greek inscription was uncovered in Berenike during the excavations of 1997.[71]

To sustain themselves in this remote location, the military and civilian resi-dents of Berenike imported sheep, cattle, fowl, and pigs from the Nile Valley and, at some point, began raising these animals on their own. They also supplemented their diet with dates and palm fruits, vegetables, sorghum, and rice. Not surpris-ingly, a wide variety of fish was also a critical food source—but it appears that the people of Berenike, unlike those at Myos Hormos, ate few sea turtles. There was a fish-processing center located in the town, and one room of this site contained ex-tensive fish remains and a large, intact jar containing *garum*. Seashells were also an important commodity, and researchers identified the remains of more than seventy species of shellfish, some of which were of edible varieties, while others were used primarily for jewelry making.

As elsewhere in Roman Egypt, water was a major problem at Berenike. So far, three wells have been identified, but these are brackish, as they no doubt were in the Roman period, and could have supplied water suitable only for animals. It is likely, therefore, that the residents of Berenike relied upon sources in the outlying areas of the desert, especially the two hydreumata in Wadi Kalakat, approximately eight kilometers southwest of Berenike, and the small hydreuma at Siket, approx-imately seven kilometers northwest of Berenike. This water may have been trans-ported to the port via pipeline or caravan. No matter what the logistical difficulties involved in such a system, recent discoveries of the remains of at least fifty species of vegetables suggest, remarkably, that at least in the cooler months the water supply was adequate for limited kitchen gardening. Among the types of produce grown in these gardens were onion, garlic, coriander, watermelon, cucumber, and beets.[72]

Besides the main town adjacent to the harbor, the Romans built and occupied several settlements west of Berenike. The Vetus Hydreuma, approximately 30 kilometers northwest of Berenike, for example, was the first water station on the route from Berenike to the Nile Valley (see map 2). The purposes of the other settlements in the area are presently unknown, but they appear to have been directly connected to the commercial activity of Berenike itself. These include two forts in Wadi Kalakat, approximately eight kilometers southwest of Berenike, Hitan Rayan, approximately 20 kilometers southwest of Berenike, and Shenshef, approximately 25 kilometers south-southwest of Berenike and 12 kilometers from the coast. Of these, the largest fort is in Wadi Kalakat. It features nine round watchtowers, catwalks, parapets, and an enormous cistern measuring approximately 30 meters in diameter. The settlement at Shenshef, however, is the most intact of Berenike's outlying settlements. It stands in a rugged, mountainous area, and its ruins contain several exceptionally well-preserved buildings. The site actually comprises two areas, a settlement and its adjacent cemeteries in the wadi and a hilltop fort. The lower settlement, consisting of some one hundred houses with small courtyards and about fifty other small buildings and shrines, rests on shallow terraces on both sides of the wadi. One early traveler referred to it as "a slave dealer's stronghold where slaves were herded till they could be shipped from Berenice."[73] Another investigator thought that it was the winter habitation for the people of Berenike because it was close to a potable water source and the weather did not permit shipping at that time.[74] Although the town was built in several phases, the pottery from the site indicates that it was inhabited only during the fifth and sixth centuries (that is, during the latest phase of Berenike's occupation). But the fort that appears to guard the settlement from atop a hill just east of the town, from which one can view the Red Sea, dates from the beginning of the first century or earlier. This time span makes it unlikely that the fort and the lower village are contemporary, thus raising puzzling questions about the fort's purpose. A great deal of research remains to be done to determine what roles Shenshef—and indeed each of the outlying settlements—played in the defense, operation, and administration of Berenike itself.[75]

Archaeological discoveries analyzed to date strongly support the idea that Berenike's periods of greatest activity were in the first century and the fourth to fifth centuries A.D., although the settlement continued to be occupied until the sixth century.[76] These times of prosperity correspond roughly to those of great economic activity throughout the eastern Roman Empire. Conversely, the spans of lower activity at Berenike might reflect the direct and indirect impacts of such events as the severe plague that hit Egypt in A.D. 166 and the political instability and invasions that occurred in the second half of the third century.[77] The extensive excavations planned for the coming years will undoubtedly shed more light not only on the nature and duration of Berenike's occupation, but also on its role in Roman and Byzantine international trade.

V

DESERT TRADE ROUTES

In addition to the quarry roads discussed earlier, at least four major Roman roads crossed the Eastern Desert to link the Red Sea with the Nile Valley.[1] Unlike the quarry roads, however, which served no commercial purpose other than the quarries, these transdesert routes carried the wealth of India and Africa from Red Sea ports to the great emporium at Coptos. From north to south, these roads were as follows: Via Hadriana; Myos Hormos to Coptos; Marsa Nakkia (Nechesia?) to Edfu; and Berenike to Edfu/Coptos (see map 2).

VIA HADRIANA

The Emperor Trajanus Hadrianus Augustus . . . opened the new Hadrian Way from Berenike to Antinoopolis through safe and level country, with stations of plentiful water, rest stops, and guard-posts along the route.[2]

The rationale for constructing the Via Hadriana is uncertain. It was significantly longer than either of the two more southerly roads to Coptos, and thus it would have been more expensive for merchants to transport their goods from the coast to the Nile. One recent theory, however, proposes that the road was intended primarily for administrative and military use rather than for commercial purposes.[3] Certainly there were compelling reasons for investing in such an expensive project, but they will remain unclear until researchers survey the route in much greater detail.

The traditional story of the origins of the Via Hadriana is as follows: Hadrian (A.D. 117–38), the emperor famous for solidifying Roman frontiers and for building the celebrated wall across northern England, spent eight to ten months touring Egypt with his wife, Sabina, in 130–31. By most accounts, he enjoyed his imperial visit immensely and engaged in a variety of activities such as hunting lions in the Western Desert and listening to the mysterious song of the Colossi of Memnon (fig. 5.1). Accompanying the emperor was Antinous, Hadrian's handsome young lover, whose influence on the emperor eventually brought him the ultimate honor of deification: "Egypt . . . received a new god when the emperor of the Romans deified his lover Antinous with the most solemn honours, just as Zeus took Ganymede up to heaven; for one cannot easily cut short a passion which took no account of shame."[4]

But Hadrian's sojourn in Egypt ended tragically when, during their sailing voyage up the Nile, Antinous was found floating in the river, dead. The reasons for his death are not known, but two traditional accounts relate that Antinous either dreamed he would inadvertently bring harm to Hadrian and, rather than permit this to happen, chose suicide or offered up his life in a mysterious sacrificial rite. Whatever the case, Hadrian was inconsolable. At the scene of the greatest loss of his life, he founded the Greek city called Antinoopolis (modern Sheik 'Ibada). To ensure that the new city prospered, he built a road from Antinoopolis all the way to Berenike, approximately 800 kilometers, thereby tapping into the lucrative Red Sea trade. The road headed almost due east from Antinoopolis, apparently through Wadi Tarfah, Wadi Ragalah, Wadi Hawashiya, and, after passing the foot of Gebel Abu Had, arrived at the coast approximately near Ras Gharab today (see map 2).

In 1925, George Murray attempted to follow the southern portion of the Via Hadriana:

> From Bir Abu Nakhlah, I traced it southwards as a well-cleared track, 12–20 meters wide, marked with little cairns on either side at about 20 meter intervals. Further south, it is known to the Ababda not as Sikkat el-'agal (road of wheels), but as Sikkat el-'agam (road of the foreigners). South of Myos

5.1 The Colossi of Memnon on the west bank of the Nile River was among the ancient sites Emperor Hadrian visited during his grand tour of Egypt in A.D. 130–31.

Hormos, it turns inland to Bir Umm Dalfa, where I saw two Nabataean inscriptions but no other remains. The road leaves the foothills again near Gebel Abu Bedûn; and there is a station in the Wadi Abu Kariah. It reaches the coast near the mouth of Wadi Barud, and thence southwards it is generally obscured by the present day camel-track. There is a *hydreuma* and a bitter well at the mouth of Wadi Safaga. Then come the ruins of Philoteras at the mouth of Wadi Guwesis. There is another *hydreuma* at Kuwe, which I was led to discover in 1922 by following up a divergence from the main road. . . . Beyond Kuser, the old road is very noticeable south of Bir el-Essel, where it is 26 m. wide . . . One gets the impression that the Via Hadriana, circuitous and, in the northern half, waterless, was little used except for local traffic between ports. It was probably planned however as a great trade-road to divert the traffic from all the ports to Antinoe in order to give that artificial foundation a solid commercial basis.[5]

The exact course of the Via Hadriana was unmapped until June 1996, when two American researchers succeeded in tracing its route from the Nile Valley to the Red Sea coast. Since then, they have explored approximately 450 kilometers of the road from Sheikh 'Ibada (Antinoopolis) to Safaga on the Red Sea coast.[6] The remaining 350 kilometers between Safaga and Berenike will be surveyed in the near future. Like other roads in the Eastern Desert, the Via Hadriana consists mainly of a wide gravel track from which larger stones were pushed aside to form a distinct border. In addition, cairns of varying sizes marked the course of the road, also in keeping with other Roman-era desert routes. Markedly absent from the east–west section, however, are indications that any fortified structures existed to protect the road, suggesting that threats to its security were either nonexistent or undetected. If in fact the transdesert portion of the road was not heavily used, as Murray states, then perhaps it did not warrant the attention of marauders.

The recent surveys reveal that much of the surface on the transdesert portion of the road has survived in excellent condition. The survey team identified at least five wells between the Nile and the coastal fort of Abu Sha'ar, all surrounded by large earthen mounds. The team also discovered an abundance of amphorae, most dating to the fifth century A.D. The presence of this untouched pottery at the wells suggests that these sites have remained virtually unvisited for more than fifteen hundred years.

MYOS HORMOS ROAD[7]

Long before the arrival of the Romans and for centuries after their departure, the scenic Myos Hormos Road between the Red Sea and the Nile served as a vital artery through the Eastern Desert. Halfway along its path, in Wadi Hammamat, an astounding collection of graffiti and inscriptions attest to its commercial and political importance from the Predynastic period (prior to 3200 B.C.) to the Islamic era (late seventh century A.D. onward).[8] These inscriptions, for example, reveal that Queen Hatshepsut's famous expedition to the land of Punt began along this route to the sea.[9] During the Roman period, the road was heavily used to transport the products from mines and quarries in the surrounding mountains to the Nile Valley and also as a major trade route for valuable commercial goods destined for Coptos and beyond.

Hydreumata

The Romans' determination to expand maritime commerce with the East via the Red Sea harbors led them to recognize the importance of securing and maintaining this ancient desert highway. To this end, they constructed or rebuilt at least ten hydreumata and more than sixty-five watchtowers along its 180-kilometer route. The primary purpose of the hydreumata was to enable the Roman military to protect and sustain commercial and military travelers and to defend the vital wells from attacks by marauding desert peoples like the Blemmyes and Nobatai.[10] Traveling from east to west, caravans would have encountered the following stations:

Ancient Name	Modern Name
Simiou (?)	El-Iteima
unknown	Seyala
unknown	El-Hamrah
Maximianon	El-Zerkah
unknown	El-Fawakir
Porsou	El-Hammamat
Krokodilo	El-Muweih
unknown	Qasr al-Banat
Phoenicon	El-Laqeita
unknown	El-Matula[11]

The Romans obtained water along the Myos Hormos road by digging wells or deepening existing ones and by constructing stone walls and cisterns that collected water during the flash floods that followed the infrequent but severe rains. Some of the stations contained large wells within their walls; others had cisterns to which water was brought from outside the station. In addition, there can be little doubt that numerous smaller wells dotted the route in antiquity, but these have been destroyed by flooding over the centuries. Although several of the wells within the stations still contain water, it is difficult to determine how much of the vital liquid they were able to provide in the Roman period. Human and animal traffic along the road was probably greatest during the summer, when the monsoons enabled ships to sail up the Red Sea, so the demand for water must have been considerable. Because it had the most abundant, most easily accessible water, El-Laqeita was a suitable point for the intersection of the Myos Hormos–Coptos and Berenike–Coptos roads.[12] Although no parts of this site remain above ground today, two inscriptions were found: one, a dedication to the god Pan, dates from the Claudian period (30 B.C. to A.D. 68), and the second mentions a centurion named C. Papirius Aequus, who belonged to the III Cyrenaica, one of two Roman legions stationed in Egypt during the first century.[13]

Unlike the quarry roads further north, over which enormous, heavily laden wagons were hauled through occasionally sandy terrain, the Myos Hormos road was not paved. Traders loaded their goods not into wagons but onto camels, which were able to walk easily over the firm gravel beds of the wadis that determined the course of the road. The distance between stations along this route averages just 16 kilometers, but this is almost certainly not the distance a camel caravan covered in one day. According to the following account, a typical caravan would travel between 25 and 35 kilometers per day: "Formerly, the camel-merchants travelled in the night, directing their course by observing the stars, and, like mariners, carried with them a supply of water. But now watering-places are provided: water is also obtained by digging to a great depth, and rain-water is found, although rain rarely falls, which is also collected in reservoirs. It is a journey of six or seven days."[14]

Today, with the exception of the El-Zerkah station, most of the hydreumata on the Myos Hormos road are in advanced states of ruin (fig. 5.2).[15] Nevertheless, their basic structures are discernible and reveal that the stations are architecturally quite similar. The stone outer walls were typically about 1.5 meters thick and 2 to 3 meters high, featuring semicircular, solid towers at their corners. Occasionally, as at El-Iteima, towers were also placed halfway along each wall. Multiple stairways permitted soldiers and sentries to gain access to the towers and to the walkways along the tops of the walls. Several stations appear to have had parapets, which added more height to the walls and afforded greater protection to the stations' defenders. Inside, the stations consisted mainly of an open courtyard around the well or cistern, with numerous small rooms abutting the walls of the fort. Roofs made of wood, palm matting, and fabric probably covered these rooms, but these materials have long since decayed or been removed. Such roofs must also have covered the cisterns, which otherwise would have lost significant quantities of water through evaporation. Given the absence of animals lines outside any of these stations, it appears that pack animals and their baggage were brought inside the walls for the night.[16]

The hydreumata were occupied, damaged, and repaired over the course of many centuries, so it is difficult to determine the date of their construction with certainty. But there is little doubt that the Roman military was primarily responsible for developing this route as a commercial road, and analysis of the abundant surface pottery at the stations indicates that they generally date from the first and second centuries A.D. In addition, inscriptions along the route, such as one on the large rock outcrop near El-Muweih, refer to a Thracian named Dida, who, as a member of a Roman cavalry unit, was assigned to the El-Muweih station for five months[17] (fig. 5.3). Another inscription, found in Coptos and dating from A.D. 43–50, lists several dozen troops (from units of either the III Cyrenaica or the XXII Deiotarianan legions) who worked on stations in the Eastern Desert: "By those whose names are written above wells were built and dedicated at Apollonos Hydreuma on December 25, at Compasi on 1 August, Berenike on December 14, at Myos Hormos on 15 January they built and repaired a camp."[18]

Although the Myos Hormos road was the best defended of all the trade routes in the Eastern Desert, not all the water stations appear to have been fortified. The

5.2 The Roman station of El-Zerkah on the Myos Hormos road. Just beyond the station is the modern road connecting the town of Qift in the Nile Valley with Quseir on the coast.

large gold mining settlement at Wadi Fawakir, for example, shows no signs of fortification, although ostraca discovered at the site indicate that soldiers were stationed there.[19]

Towers

Approximately sixty-five square towers mark the route of the Myos Hormos road. Almost identical in structure and built of local fieldstone, they were solid, approximately 2.5 meters high by 3 meters wide, and located on the hilltops or lower slopes of the mountains that line the road (fig. 5.4). Although many have collapsed over the centuries, recent studies have shown that each tower along the route was probably visible from the towers to its east and west. This implies that they served primarily as signal posts, by which news of the arrival of a ship or ships at Myos Hormos could be quickly communicated to both the hydreumata below and to Coptos itself.[20] In addition, some evidence suggests they were used as sentry towers, from which guards could spot bands of marauders that threatened caravans and the stations themselves. From their high vantage points, the

5.3 An inscription from the Roman station at El-Muweih on
the Myos Hormos road.

5.4 Looking west from a watchtower on the Myos Hormos road. A second tower is visible on the next hill.

guards who manned these towers could have easily warned their fellow guards in the hydreuma of any approaching danger.[21]

Taxation and Tolls

The maintenance of the roads and water stations in the Eastern Desert was costly for the Roman military. To pay these expenses, they established a tariff system for civilians who used the desert routes. In the late nineteenth century, excavations at the tollhouse in Coptos uncovered an inscription, dated A.D. 90, giving the various rates of fees charged for people and animals crossing the desert:[22]

For a captain in the Red Sea trade	8 drachmae[23]
For a lookout man	10 drachmae
For a shipwright	5 drachmae
For a sailor	5 drachmae
For an artisan	8 drachmae
For courtesans	108 drachmae
For women of marines (?)	20 drachmae
For women of soldiers	20 drachmae

For a camel's permit	1 obol
For a seal on the permit	2 obol
On the return journey, for each man coming up	1 drachma
On the return journey, for each woman coming up	4 drachmae
For a donkey	2 obol
For a covered wagon	4 drachmae
For a mast	20 drachmae
For a yardarm	4 drachmae
For a funeral (to the cemetery and return)	1.5 drachmae

In addition to identifying the exact costs of travel, this tariff schedule seems to reveal an attempt to limit the presence of women on the desert routes and in the Red Sea ports by charging them high rates. Given the large number of soldiers and marines employed to protect the caravans, stations, and ships, the government might have considered the presence of women disruptive to military discipline. This theory is supported by the Roman policy that prohibited auxiliaries and legionnaires, who were Roman citizens, from marrying for the duration of their service. The law prohibiting marriage was likely enacted by Augustus (27 B.C.–A.D. 14) during his efforts to improve military discipline in the aftermath of Rome's civil wars. Although the law was highly problematic, it remained Roman policy until the reign of Septimius Severus (A.D. 193–211). Septimius owed his position and authority to the Roman army and, in return, enacted reforms such as the following that improved the life of the soldier:[24] "To the soldiers he gave a very large sum of money and many other privileges that they had not had before; for he was the first to increase their pay and he also gave them permission to wear gold rings and to live in wedlock with their wives. All these things are normally considered alien to military discipline and an efficient readiness for war."[25]

Although the pre-Severan prohibition against marriage seems to have stemmed from the desire to maintain discipline among soldiers, we cannot assume that the higher tariffs for women were established for the same reason. It is well documented, for example, that many soldiers openly formed and maintained relationships with local women, which probably explains the reference to "women of soldiers" in the Coptos tariff schedule. In addition, the numerous existing documents concerning the taxation of prostitutes in Egypt, which do not include elements of moral condemnation, suggest that the Roman government regarded prostitutes as merchants like any other: a potential source of income for the state.[26] Instead of taxing prostitution out of existence, the high tariff was probably the rate for a group of women rather than a single woman; moreover, the existence of a group rate might suggest that prostitutes were common at the desert stations and Red Sea ports and that their presence was a method of maintaining rather than undermining discipline in men who would otherwise be deprived of female company.[27]

The traffic on the road would have been most intense during the summer, especially in July, when the northerly winds enabled ships bound for Africa and India to depart from Myos Hormos and Berenike, and in the late spring, when the southeasterly winds permitted the heavily laden ships to return to their Red Sea ports. In light of the number of people who lived and worked in the ports, stations, and quarries of the Eastern Desert, it is a fair guess that there was a considerable volume of traffic year-round. On the basis of recent estimates, it is reasonable to think that roughly two hundred to five hundred camel loads per month were required to bring goods and supplies to Berenike.[28] But given the current debate about the exact location of Myos Hormos and thus the uncertainty of its size, scholars have little evidence upon which to base their opinions regarding the volume of trade Myos Hormos handled. If Quseir al-Qadim is in fact Myos Hormos, its small size relative to Berenike implies that it witnessed considerably less commercial activity. On the other hand, Strabo says that during his lifetime (circa 63 B.C.–A.D. 24), Myos Hormos was more important than Berenike.[29] In any case, for those fortunate enough to be involved in the Eastern trade, the profits could be enormous—both for the merchants and for the Roman officials who taxed them heavily and levied tolls for the use of the desert roads. Papyri record that the Roman government and the Ptolemaic administration before it made 25 to 50 percent profit on the value of the imported commodities.

The system of tariffs and taxation raises questions about the prevalence of smuggling in the Eastern Desert. It seems likely that for individuals who were clever and daring enough to transport goods from the coast to the Nile Valley via numerous obscure desert tracks the potential for profit was extremely high. Military patrols were no doubt charged with detecting and apprehending smugglers and imposing severe penalties on them. We cannot be certain, of course, that merchants were inclined to engage in such activity. If, in fact, the desert tribes posed a serious threat to caravans—and most evidence suggests they did—then it is probable that merchants willingly paid the taxes and tariffs to ensure the safe delivery of their goods to Coptos and then simply increased the final sale price accordingly.

MARSA NAKARI (NECHESIA?)–EDFU

Researchers began examining the Marsa Nakkari–Edfu route only recently, and little definitive information is available. The road may have been an extension of the Ptolemaic road from Edfu to the gold mines at Barramiya, which lie approximately midway between the Nile and the Red Sea. If so, it would have approximately bisected the Roman road from Berenike to Coptos.[30]

BERENIKE–COPTOS

Berenike's status as the main port on the Red Sea coast significantly lengthened the distance over which trade goods needed to be transported by caravans across the desert. But in those years in which the springtime southerly winds were not strong enough or died out early, ship captains rarely struggled further north along the Red Sea coast to reach a port whose westward road would have been more direct. Thus Roman merchants or their agents carried their precious goods along the 370-kilometer route from Berenike to Coptos, a journey that typically took twelve days. As one would expect of a vital and vulnerable commercial road through the desert, this route is lined with hydreumata that feature thick walls, solid towers, and large cisterns. At least ten major water stations punctuate the main route heading northwest from Berenike to Coptos (see map 2):

Ancient Name	Modern Name
Vetus Hydreuma	Wadi Abu Qreiya
Cabalsi	Wadi Ghusan
Apollonos	Wadi Gemal
Falacro	Wadi Dweig
Aristonis	Wadi Gerf
Jovis	Wadi Abu Greiya(?)
Compasi	Bir Daghbag
Afrodito	Wadi Menih el-Heir
Didyme	Khashm el-Menih
Phoenicon	El-Laqeita[31]

During the Ptolemaic period, the main road from Berenike went to Apollonopolis Magna (Edfu), but in the Roman period the principal route went to Coptos (Qift) (see map 2). In both periods, the road was approximately the same until it split at the Falacro station in Wadi Dweig, one branch leading to Edfu and the other to Coptos. Banditry was apparently a danger along both routes, and numerous inscriptions and votives can be found in rock shelters along the way. One such inscription is located in a sanctuary of Pan at El-Kanais, the penultimate station on the Berenike–Edfu road: "Akestimos, Cretan of Kourtolia, to Pan of the good road, for having returned safe and sound from the land of the Troglodytes."[32]

No doubt such concerns were common among those engaged in the eastern trade. Once a ship laden with Asian and African treasures anchored at Berenike, merchants contracted with companies or individuals to transport their precious cargoes quickly and safely across the desert to Coptos by camel caravan. From there, the merchandise would continue its long voyage to the Mediterranean. A papyrus from the mid–second century A.D. is an example of such a contract:

> I will give your camel driver 170 talents, 50 drachmae, for use of the road to Koptos, and I will convey your goods inland through the desert under guard and under security to the public warehouses for receiving revenues at Koptos, and I will place them under your ownership and seal, or of your representatives or of whoever of them is present, until loading aboard at the river, and I will load them aboard at the required time on a seaworthy boat on the river, and I will convey them downstream to the warehouse that receives the duty of one-fourth at Alexandria, and I will similarly place them under the ownership of you or your representatives.[33]

Although the existence of the Berenike–Coptos road has been known to modern scholars for many years, it has only recently been thoroughly explored and surveyed. No doubt when the results of these surveys are published, they will yield a great deal of fascinating information concerning the nature and volume of the commercial traffic that in the Roman period trudged along the road's now silent tracks.[34]

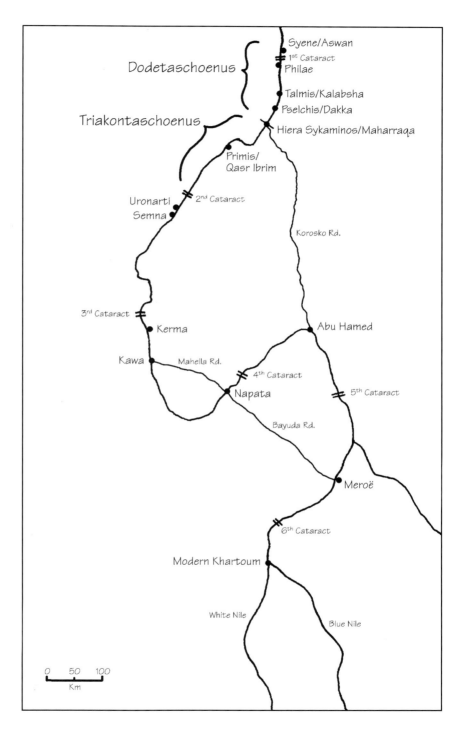

Map 3

PART TWO

THE UPPER NILE VALLEY

VI

THE GATEWAY TO AFRICA: ASWAN, ELEPHANTINE, AND PHILAE

Just north of the modern city of Khartoum, Sudan, where the Blue and the White Nile merge into a single mighty river, one encounters the first of six cataracts that punctuate the Nile at intervals extending into southern Egypt (see map 3). From Khartoum the river flows northward along its serpentine path, surging over the turbulent rapids, cutting through vast expanses of desert, and bringing life to the Nubians and Egyptians who inhabit its banks. The final series of cataracts is located in the Egyptian town of Aswan, 1,000 kilometers south of Alexandria. Here, throughout history, the first cataract—so named because it is the first obstacle one encounters on a southward journey—has prevented boats from sailing farther upriver without a long portage to the southern end of the rapids. Tamed since 1970 by the completion of the Aswan High Dam,[1] the Nile River today flows gently around the nine kilometers of small islands and black granite boulders that constitute the first cataract at Aswan. In antiquity,

the presence of the cataracts made Aswan (ancient Syene) a necessary halting place for any journey up the Nile, and many of the cataract's boulders and
cliff faces still contain the inscriptions of generals, soldiers, and explorers who
visited this remote, enchanting place over the course of its long, fascinating
history.

Located on the eastern bank of the river, at the northern end of the rapids,
Aswan was well suited as an entrepôt, administrative center, and launching point
for military and commercial expeditions into Nubia and beyond. For this reason,
the Romans turned Aswan into their headquarters for protecting and administer-
ing the southern frontier region. But in addition to Aswan's strategic importance,
the surrounding area contained valuable resources. Just east of Aswan, for example, are ancient amethyst mines, while the hills to the southeast of the town were
an excellent source of fine granite in beautiful hues of red, yellow, and brown that
the Romans and ancient rulers before them prized for obelisks, statuary, and royal
architecture.[2]

THE SITES

During the Roman period, there were actually three important settlements in the
vicinity of Aswan: Syene itself, Elephantine Island, and Philae. Scholars know relatively little about Syene because most of the ancient city now lies beneath the
modern, ever-growing town of Aswan. Today, only the southeastern portion of the
old town is visible, but this section includes the remains of a well-preserved temple of Isis built by Ptolemy III (246–222 B.C.) and portions of the defensive wall
that once surrounded Syene. As was typical of such structures at that time, the wall
featured staircases and towers at its corners and probably at intermediate points
along its lengths. Within the settlement, archaeologists have uncovered narrow
streets running north to south, intersected by smaller lanes and lined with houses
and other buildings dating from the Ptolemaic through the Late Roman period.[3]
Although much of the ancient city is buried under modern roads and buildings
constructed in the past forty years, little of Greco-Roman Syene remained even in
the nineteenth century, when wealthy Europeans began traveling to Aswan to bask
in its warm climate and explore its ruins. In 1839, the Scottish artist David Roberts
visited the site and wrote the following description: "We walked over the ruins of
the ancient city which crown the height of a rock jutting out into the stream, a corresponding one being on the island of Elephantine opposite. The remains of a
high Roman wall flank the rocks on that side and on the rock from which this
rises, as well as on the land side, are hieroglyphics. Nothing remains of the ancient town but the brick walls"[4] (fig. 6.1).

6.1 David Roberts' lithograph of the ruins of Syene and Elephantine at Aswan in 1839.

Despite this less-than-inspiring description, Aswan has always been a place of mystery and enchanting beauty. It was in Aswan, for example, that a scribe informed the great historian Herodotus (484–425 B.C.) that the bottomless source of the mighty Nile could be found: "Between Syene, a city of the Thebais, and Elephantine, there are two hills with sharp conical tops; the name of one is *Crophi*, of the other, *Mophi*. Midway between them are the fountains of the Nile, fountains which it is impossible to fathom."[5] Skeptical of this account, Herodotus ascended the Nile himself as far as Elephantine and inquired further about the great river. Although no one could inform him of its ultimate source, he learned that beyond the first cataract one could proceed upriver by boat only for four days before jagged rocks and rapids forced one to land on shore. After trekking overland for forty days, one arrived at a calmer part of the river, where "you go on board another boat and proceed by water for twelve days more, at the end of which time you reach a great city called Meroë, which is said to be the capital of the Ethiopians."[6]

The city of Elephantine, from which Herodotus made his inquiries, was an even older town than Syene. Located on the southern end of an island measuring only two kilometers long and half a kilometer wide, just offshore from Syene, Elephantine contains evidence of human settlement dating from the early dynastic period (approximately 3,000 B.C.). Various theories have been proposed as to the origins of the name Elephantine. One explanation suggests that the enormous black boulders of the island and nearby cataracts resemble elephants. Another possibility is that the island, whose ancient Egyptian name is Abu, meaning "elephant," derived its name from its role as a central trading post for ivory—although other commodities such as ebony, leopard skins, gold, and slaves were also imported through Elephantine from the deeper regions of Africa.[7] It was Rome's newly acquired taste for such items that inspired Juvenal, the brilliant early-second-century satirist, to express his disdain for contemporary opulence. Whereas once even a wealthy Roman was content with simple food and furnishings, now he could not be satisfied unless "the broad slabs of his dinner-table rested upon a ramping, gaping leopard of solid ivory, made of the tusks sent to us . . . from the portal of Syene."[8]

But Syene and its neighboring settlements at Elephantine and Philae were also important for noncommercial reasons. For much of its pre-Roman history, Elephantine Island was regarded as the home of Hapi, the god of the Nile, while the major temple in the city center was dedicated to Khnum, the ram-headed god of the first cataract, and his two consorts, the fertility goddesses Satet and Anuket (fig. 6.2). The majority of the buildings comprising the temple of Khnum were constructed during the New Kingdom (1552–1027 B.C.) and later added to by the pharaoh Nectanebo in the early Thirtieth dynasty (380–343 B.C.). Four centuries later, Roman emperors rebuilt and improved the great temple. Antoninus Pius (A.D. 138–61), for example, famous for restoring the Roman Colosseum and for building the temple of the deified Hadrian, added numerous decorations to the temple of Khnum. The Romans also constructed and occupied mud-brick barracks around the temple to house the troops stationed on the island. Today, graffiti the Roman soldiers left behind can still be seen in the large paving stones of the temple. Among these drawings are pairs of sandled feet, occasionally signed and left by worshipers who wished to leave a record of their having paid homage at the temple (fig. 6.3).[9] The temple of Khnum, of course, was not immune to the enormous religious changes that occurred throughout the Roman world. After Emperor Theodosius I made Christianity the official religion of the Roman Empire and forbade pagan worship in A.D. 391, portions of the Khnum temple were converted into a church.

Elephantine was also the site of the famous experiment by Eratosthenes (?276–?194 B.C.), the Father of Geography, who served as director of the great library of Alexandria.[10] He was the first scientist to calculate the circumference of the earth. On June 21, the summer solstice, he recorded that the sun cast no shadow on the walls of a well on Elephantine island, while in Alexandria it cast a

6.2 The pedestal and feet of a royal statue in the main courtyard of the Temple of Khnum on Elephantine.

shadow of 7.5 degrees. Based on the difference between the two, he calculated the circumference of the earth.

Because the annual flooding of the Nile was of vital import to the survival of all Egyptians, it is little wonder that the Romans were keen to maintain access to another essential feature of Elephantine Island, its two famous Nilometers. The first, newer device is on the eastern edge of the island, just opposite the banks of modern Aswan and includes a scale measuring the high-water marks in Demotic and Greek (fig. 6.4). While it appears that the Romans might have repaired and used this scale, the older Nilometer, south of the temple of Khnum, consists of a large square cistern that includes two scales: one measures the height of the flood above a low-water mark, and a second measures the level of flood waters above agricultural land. Quite probably it was this second Nilometer that Strabo, the famous geographer, described on his visit to Elephantine in 25 B.C.:

> The Nilometer is a well upon the banks of the Nile, constructed of close-fitting stones, on which are marked the greatest, least, and mean risings of the Nile. . . . Those who examine these marks communicate the result to the public for their information. For it is known long before, by these marks, and by the time elapsed from the commencement, what the future

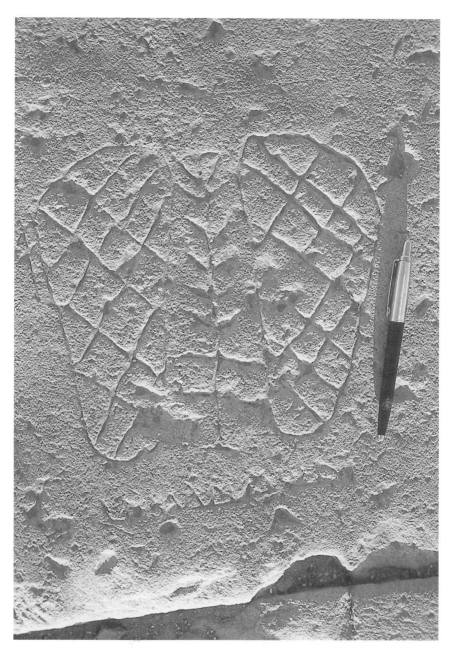

6.3 Sandled feet etched into the paving stones of the temple of Khnum by a worshipper during the Roman occupation of Elephantine.

6.4 The outer wall of the ancient Nilometer as it appears today. The building above
the Nilometer houses a small museum.

rise of the river will be, and notice is given of it. This information is of service to the husbandmen with reference to the distribution of water; for the purpose also of attending to the embankments, canals, and other things of this kind. It is of use also to the governors, who fix the revenue; for the greater the rise of the river, the greater it is expected will be the revenue.[11]

A writer from the first century A.D. gave a more detailed description of what the measurements from the Nilometer meant to the Egyptians:

An average rise is one of seven meters. A smaller volume does not irrigate all localities and a larger one, by retiring too slowly, retards agriculture; and the latter uses up the time for sowing because of the moisture of the soil while the former gives no time for sowing because the soil is parched. The province takes careful note of both extremes: in a rise of five-and-a-half meters it senses famine and even at one of six meters it begins to feel hungry, but six-and-a-half meters brings cheerfulness, six-and-three-quarters complete confidence and seven meters delight. The largest rise up to date was one of eight meters in the Principate of Claudius and the smallest a little over two meters in the year of Pharsalus as if the river were attempting to avert the murder of Pompey by a sort of portent.[12]

The third notable site in the Aswan region was Philae, which was south of Aswan on the upstream side of the cataracts; today it lies between Aswan and the High Dam. So that traffic might pass efficiently and safely around the cataracts in antiquity, a seven-kilometer road on the east bank connected two small river harbors located at the northern and southern ends of the rapids—thus linking Syene with the sacred temples and settlement at Philae. Along the eastern side of this road, a high wall protected travelers and their belongings from marauding bandits. The mud-brick wall was filled with granite rubble and averaged 10 meters high, with a 3-meter-wide catwalk and protective parapets at the top to permit sentries to defend the wall. Thus far, however, no staircases or intermediate towers have been identified.[13]

For many years scholars believed that the Syene-Philae wall might have been built by the Romans, but this theory has been disproved. Archaeologists discovered Middle Kingdom pottery sherds in the material for the bricks, and the bricks themselves bear the same unique finger markings of those used to build the wall at Elephantine. In addition, a similar wall was discovered at the second cataract protecting the road between the Middle Kingdom settlements of Semna and Uronarti (see map 3). Thus, it seems most likely that the wall leading to Philae was constructed sometime during the Twelfth dynasty (1991–1786 B.C.).[14] Although pottery sherds discovered at the base of the wall reveal that the structure was used during the Roman period, Strabo, who traveled this route in 25 B.C., did not mention the wall in his writings even though it must have been a prominent feature of the road.

At the southern end of the cataracts, the protected road leads to the river harbor of Konosso. Nearby, the Legio I Maximiana was stationed in two camps just opposite the triumphal arch of the Tetrarchs at Philae. Inside the walls of the larger camp, excavators found two executioner's trenches containing a total of 102 bodies, evidence of the unhappy end of some insurrection against Roman authority or perhaps an unsuccessful raid from the Eastern Desert against Philae or its environs.[15] Given that the wall originated at the fortified town of Syene and connected it with these fortified camps at Philae, one can regard the entire region thus enclosed as a portion of the large defensive system that protected the eastern and southern borders of Roman Egypt. To further enhance the security of the area, watchtowers like those that line the Myos Hormos Road were built on the hilltops along the eastern banks of the Nile. Several such towers can be seen east of the Syene wall, but they are more numerous between Syene and Edfu.[16] The towers provided the fastest possible means of communication between such distant frontier zones as Qasr Ibrim and the rest of Roman Egypt, although we do not know exactly how they were employed for this purpose. Thin-walled sherds made of pink clay and pieces of faience discovered in the vicinity of the towers date from the first century B.C. and the early third century A.D., indicating that the construction of the towers took place prior to that time.[17]

At the southern end of the protected road was the plain of Shellel, and just offshore the sacred island of Philae, long known as the City of Isis. For ancient and modern travelers alike, Philae is often highlighted as one of the most splendid sites in Egypt. Although it measures only 500 meters long by 150 meters wide and lacks the grandeur of Karnak, its picturesque setting amidst the islands of the Nile made it the ultimate destination for many Victorian tourists. Numerous paintings and written descriptions from the nineteenth century attest to its power to enchant: "Excepting the Pyramids, nothing in Egypt struck me so much as when, on a bright moonlight night, I first entered the court of the great temple of Philae. The colours of the paintings on the walls are as vivid in many places as they were the day they were finished."[18]

Forty years later, Amelia Edwards visited Philae and wrote that the temples impressed her not because of their size but because of their

> perfect grace and exquisite beauty. . . . The approach by water is quite the most beautiful. Seen from the level of a small boat, the island, with its palms, its colonnades, its pylons, seems to rise out of the river like a mirage. Piled rocks frame it on either side, and the purple mountains close up the

distance. As the boat glides nearer between glistening boulders, those sculptured towers rise higher and even higher against the sky. They show no signs of ruin or age. All looks solid, stately, perfect. One forgets for a moment that anything is changed. If a sound of antique chanting were to be borne along the quiet air—if a procession of white-robed priests bearing aloft the veiled ark of God, were to come sweeping round between the palms and pylons—we should not think it strange.[19]

Of all the magnificent structures at Philae, the largest and most important is the temple of Isis, portions of which were added during the Greco-Roman period. At the south end of the east colonnade, for example, is the small temple of Arsenuphis, a Nubian god, and halfway along the colonnade is a Roman-period chapel of Mandulis, another Nubian god. The Romans also rebuilt the kiosk of Nectanebo I, the grand east and west colonnades, and the gate of Hadrian. The most beautiful building on Philae, however, is the so-called temple of Trajan (fig. 6.5). Although the names of Trajan are inscribed in reliefs on the inner sides of the temple's walls, it is unlikely that such an enormous structure could have been planned and nearly completed during his imperial reign (A.D. 98–117). The size of the building gives the impression of power typical of the beginning of the Roman period, but its architectural form is consistent with a construction during the late Ptolemaic period.[20]

Today, the walls of the Philae temples are covered not only with their original hieroglyphic texts, but also with inscriptions and graffiti from virtually every period of occupation. This abundance of writing provides information about religious rituals, records offerings from rulers, and divulges that the keepers of the Isis temple were instructed to permit only certain people into the sanctuary and that they were to be intimidated "neither by important personages, nor by ordinary people."[21] In addition to scripts written in Egyptian hieroglyphics, Demotic, Greek, Latin, Coptic, and even crude pictographs inscribed by desert tribes, the temples of Philae contain examples of Meroitic, the language of the Kushite kingdom that had its capital in the fabled city of Meroë.

Although a few scholars can read the Meroitic script, the language is far from fully comprehended. Luckily, the Meroites occasionally wrote in or had their messages translated into Demotic, hieroglyphics, and Greek. Of the few examples of Meroitic graffiti at Philae, several passages date from the time of Roman occupation. In the first century A.D., for example, delegates and priests from distant Meroë held permanent offices at Philae. One of these individuals inscribed the following statement over a gate, reflecting what must have been a common fear of travelers crossing the desert from the south: "I have come to Egypt, having sung a song of triumph over this desert, thanks to the care and protection of Isis, the

6.5 The temple of Trajan.

great goddess, because she heard our prayer and brought us safely to Egypt. . . .
Oh, my lady, you who distribute lands to the gods, see to me that I be brought back
to Meroë, the beautiful city of your beloved son [King Teqridamane] and keep me
in good health in this fierce desert with the goods for which I have come, to bring
them to your beloved son King Teqridamane . . . and the tributes which the King,
my father, gave me saying: 'Bring them to Isis!' I brought them."[22] Even such
pious individuals as this traveler, however, were not without their weaknesses. A
papyrus from Philae that dates from 180 B.C. records how a priest named Petra,
son of Pa-sheri-Pa-wer, was censured for reveling in the temple: "You know exactly what you have done. You have drunk wine in the house of the garden trees,
which refresh King Osiris Wennofre. You have committed an outrageous act
against Isis, because you have drunk the wine of the night, when the divine Ladies
[the goddesses Isis and Nephtyhs] were mourning. You have called on your wife:
'Tefnet—there is no divinity like you!' The mourning wives were standing with
their bosoms uncovered, but you brought singers and spent a happy time revel-
ling. You woke the soul of Osiris from his sleep and you opened the bottle of wine
sacred to the New Year [rites], drinking together with the Blemmyes."[23]

Isis, the divinity whom the priest offended, was the great Egyptian fertility goddess: wife of Osiris, the god of the afterlife, and mother of Horus, the falcon god

of the sky. From the middle of the seventh century B.C. to the end of the fourth century B.C., the cult of Isis at Philae seems to have had relatively few devotees. Herodotus, for example, did not mention the sanctuary, and there is little evidence that it had much influence beyond the vicinity of Philae.[24] But the Ptolemies saw in Isis a divinity similar to their Olympian goddesses, and eventually made her the most popular deity in Ptolemaic Egypt.[25] The cult ultimately spread throughout the Mediterranean world, mainly as a result of Greek traders who brought it from Egypt to their homeland and its territories. Celebrating her divinity, Ptolemy II Philadelphus (285–246 B.C.) and Ptolemy III (246–222 B.C.) constructed a new temple to Isis at Philae.[26] One of several hymns to the goddess discovered in the sanctuary of this temple dates from Ptolemy II and reveals the fondness and piety with which she was venerated by Egyptians:

> O Isis, the great, God's Mother, Lady of Philae,
> God's Wife, God's Adorer, and God's hand,
> God's Mother and Great Royal Spouse,
> Adornment and lady of the Ornaments of the Palace.
>
> Lady and desire of the green fields,
> Nursling who fills the palace with her beauty,
> Fragrance of the palace, mistress of joy,
> Who runs her course in the divine place.
>
> Rain-cloud which makes green [the fields] when it descends,
> Maiden, sweet of Love, Lady of Upper and Lower Egypt,
> Who issues orders among the divine Ennead,
> According to whose command one rules.
>
> Princess, great of praise, lady of charm,
> Whose face loves the joy of fresh myrrh.[27]

By the time Egypt was joined to the Roman Empire in 30 B.C., the Isis cult was widespread, even in Rome. In the beginning, Augustus was uncertain about the degree to which he should adopt and protect the cult. After all, Cleopatra VII, his onetime enemy, had worshiped Isis. By 9 B.C., however, the emperor gave in and built a temple, most of which is now gone, at the northern end of Philae. Other emperors added reliefs and inscriptions to the buildings, and several engaged in new constructions. Claudius (A.D. 41–54) built the small temple of Harendotes, which was heavily damaged in the Christian period; Trajan (A.D. 98–117) continued work on the great kiosk that bears his name but remained unfinished; Hadrian (A.D. 117–38) built the gateway and vestibule near the temple of Harendotes; and Diocletian (A.D. 284–305) probably built the triumphal arch that was later turned into a ceremonial gateway at the northern end of the island.[28] Among the reliefs and inscriptions within the gate of Hadrian is a particularly interesting one depicting the source of the Nile. It features a large pile of stones, on top of which stand a vulture (representing Upper Egypt) and a hawk (representing Lower Egypt). Seated inside a small chamber under the stone mountain is Hapi, the god of the Nile, who holds a vessel in each hand as he prepares to pour the life-giving waters of the Nile into the lands of Upper and Lower Egypt (fig. 6.6).

Just as the cult of Isis had spread north through Egypt and the Mediterranean, it moved south into the Kushite kingdom of Meroë. As early as the third century B.C., the Meroitic king Ergamenes (c. 285–205 B.C.) demonstrated his devotion to Isis by enlarging the temple of Arsenuphis at Philae.[29] Indeed, it was in the territory extending between Aswan and the Nubian settlement at Maharraqa, a region known in antiquity as the Dodekaschoenus, that the cult of Isis took its strongest hold—so much so that the entire region was regarded as the personal estate of Isis, and its revenues were the principal means of support for the temple and priests at Philae (see map 3).[30] As one scholar writes, Philae thus became the spiritual capital of the region's inhabitants: "Within the microcosm of the Nile lands, the worship of Isis became the first truly international and supra-national religion, no longer claimed as the proprietary cult of any one temporal ruler but sanctioned by, and conferring its blessings upon, several. Philae became a holy city and a place of pilgrimage alike for all classes and all nationalities: Greeks, Romans, Egyptians, Meroites, and desert nomads."[31] When the emperor Theodosius I issued a decree in A.D. 391 forbidding pagan worship anywhere in the Roman Empire, only Philae was exempted from the imperial decision. The Romans had wisely accepted the Ptolemaic incorporation of the Nubian god Mandulis into the cult of Isis and regarded his temple on Philae as a means of strengthening their ties with the Nubians. The Romans recognized the potential danger to their southern frontier zone if they closed the temple at Philae. No doubt the Kushites and nomadic tribes like the Blemmyes and Nobatai would have revolted against the decision. Sixty years later, in A.D. 451–52, after the Blemmyes had continued to raid Roman-occupied Upper Egypt, the emperor Marcian ordered his general Maximianus to launch an attack on the Blemmyes, which he did successfully. In the subsequent peace treaty, the Blemmyes promised not to attack Roman territory for one hundred years, and the Romans permitted them not only to worship and offer sacrifices at Philae, but to occasionally borrow the sacred statue of Isis. Eventually the cult was destroyed by Christianity when the new faith moved south into Nubia—but important elements of its spirituality, for example, virgin birth and resurrection after death, survived in their new, Christian form.

6.6 A relief located in Hadrian's arch depicting Hapi, the god of the Nile River.

THE ROMAN OCCUPATION OF THE ASWAN REGION

By the time the Romans occupied Egypt, Syene had been a frontier town for hundreds of years. From here pharaohs launched the earliest knows expeditions into Africa. Later, the Ptolemies extended their control further south in order to secure access to the gold mines of Wadi Allaqi (180 kilometers southeast of Aswan). They also built temples in the newly occupied Kushite territories at Pselchis (Dakka) and, of course, at Philae. The Kushite kings, who were the descendants of Twenty-fifth dynasty pharaohs, were retained by the various occupiers of their lands: Persians, Ptolemies, and the Romans. At any time, however, they could have attempted to reassert their authority over the occupied lands, thus posing a threat to occupying authorities. But it appears that for the majority of the inhabitants, life went on as it always had, following the rhythms of the river, regardless of the nationality of the occupying power. From time to time, the Ptolemies made extended incursions further south as far as the second cataract, probably in response to Kushite attempts to interfere in the internal affairs of Egypt.[32]

Predictably, the region remained a place of occasional tension even after the Romans asserted their control over Egypt. Three Roman cohorts remained stationed in and around Syene for at least 130 years and possibly into the third century. Because of their proximity to each other and their common duty to defend the Nubian frontier, the three cohorts that constituted the Syene forces were commanded by the prefect of one of the cohorts. One of these prefects, Iunius Sabinus, left the following inscription on the south pylon of the Isis temple at Philae: "Iunius Sabinus commander of the Ituraean cohort [?] came here leading the multitude of the Syene forces, solemnly celebrating with new chants Isis who knows how to save the world. Having conquered the Nubian tribes that raged against the sons of Romulus, he came here with his troops. [——] in the fray, you will say, then, Caesar's man [——] put on the crown."[33] Of the approximately twenty-two thousand soldiers Emperor Augustus stationed in Egypt in 29 B.C., only three cohorts (fifteen hundred men) were deployed in Syene, Elephantine, and Philae.[34] Although Strabo recorded that nomadic tribes from the desert surrounding Syene and Elephantine directed numerous attacks against the Roman occupiers, he also stated that the tribesmen and the local townspeople were militarily weak and therefore did not constitute a major threat to the Roman forces. Accordingly, it seems that the three cohorts were adequate for the task of protecting this vital southern region. Unlike Thebes (modern Luxor), which is located on the Nile approximately 180 kilometers further north, Aswan was not a center of social and political unrest in Upper Egypt.[35] Nevertheless, the Roman presence in Aswan was vital for the protection of Roman interests further south in Nubia. Of the people of this region, Strabo wrote, "The remaining parts towards the south are

6.7 The bronze head of Augustus that invading Kushites stole
from Aswan in 25 B.C.

occupied by Troglodytae, Blemmyes, Nubae, and Megabari, Ethiopians above
Syene. These are nomads, and not numerous or warlike, but account so by the an-
cients, because frequently, like robbers, they attacked defenseless persons. Neither are the Ethiopians, who extend towards the south and Meroë, numerous nor
collected in a body; for they inhabit a long, narrow, and winding tract of land on
the riverside . . . nor are they prepared either for war or the pursuit of any other
mode of life."[36]

Immediately upon the incorporation of Egypt into the Roman Empire, the Romans turned their attention to this region. Negotiating with the representatives of
the Kushites, the dominant kingdom that ruled from Meroë and that controlled
the territory south of Syene, the Romans initially established their southern frontier at Syene. Because the Romans were primarily interested in the wealth of Egypt
itself and most of their valuable trade with East Africa and Asia was conducted via
the Red Sea ports, they did not see the need to directly control the Kushites.
Rather, they appear to have adopted their usual frontier policy of granting the
Kushites the status of a client kingdom. By naming a viceroy in charge of the entire Triakontaschoenus (see map 3) and possibly over the Dodekaschoenus as
well, the Romans effectively reduced the Kushites to the position of tributaries.[37]

The imposition of Roman authority was hardly to the liking of the Kushites or, for that matter, to the various tribes who lived in the eastern and western deserts that flanked the Kushite territories. These peoples did not have to wait long before the Romans gave them the opportunity they needed to revolt against their new over-lords. In 25 B.C., after the Roman forces in Syene had been temporarily removed to fight a disastrous campaign in Arabia, and despite Strabo's declaration that they were "not warlike," the Kushites sent an army of thirty thousand men north-ward, sacking Syene and Elephantine, enslaving their inhabitants, and demolish-ing statues of Augustus[38] (fig. 6.7). Today, scholars debate whether the revolt was the result of anger over Roman taxation policy or whether it stemmed from a Kushite desire to reassert and possibly extend their own territorial claims. What-ever the case, the attack on Syene began a period of tension and, at times, military conflict between the Romans and the peoples south of Syene, tension that was to characterize the Roman occupation of Lower Nubia for the next five hundred years.

VII

ROMAN NUBIA

The land of Nubia, or Kush, as it was called in antiquity, lies south of Aswan and extends from the first cataract to approximately the fourth cataract (see map 3).[1] But unlike the Nile Valley north of Aswan, which permitted extensive cultivation of a wide flood plain along its banks, the river valley south of the first cataract narrows to the point where, at times, the river is bounded on both sides by the high cliffs of the Eastern and Western desert plateaus. This difference in the quantity of arable land helps explain why throughout much of its history, Nubia was too poor to resist the political and cultural imperialism of Egypt. For despite its poverty and the fact that the ancient Egyptians usually referred to the land as miserable or abominable, they nevertheless invaded Nubia many times in an effort to secure access to gold, ivory, and slaves. By the New Kingdom (1552–1070 B.C.), Egyptian control of Nubia extended all the way to the fourth cataract.

THE PEOPLES OF NUBIA

After the New Kingdom, however, Egypt began its long, slow decline from the glories of the Pharaonic ages, and Egyptian control of Nubia waned. But its influence remained strong, particularly in the southern city of Napata. A highly Egyptianized Kushite ruling class eventually emerged in Napata and seized power.[2] These rulers turned on their former northern overlords and successfully attacked and subjugated all of Egypt, forming the Kushite dynasty (the Twenty-fifth dynasty), which reigned from 751 to 656 B.C.[3] After being dethroned by the Assyrian invasion of Egypt, the Kushites then suffered an attack by the Egyptian pharaoh Psammetichus II, who destroyed Napata in 591 B.C. Sometime in the following century, the Kushites formed a new capital to the southeast at Meroë, the city that gave the Kushites their new name, Meroites.[4] There, on the Middle Nile, amidst the splendor of more than two hundred pyramids and temples, the rich, sophisticated Meroitic culture endured for nearly a thousand years before finally fading from the historical record sometime during the fourth century A.D. (fig. 7.1).

Upon the death of Alexander the Great in 323 B.C., the throne of Egypt passed to his able general Ptolemy I Soter, who began the Macedonian dynasty that ruled Egypt until the death of Cleopatra in 30 B.C.[5] The Ptolemies divided Nubia into two major regions: the northern portion, referred to as Lower Nubia and extending from approximately Aswan to Wadi Allaqi, was called Dodekaschoenus[6] and was controlled by the Ptolemies; the southern portion, incorporating the territory between Wadi Allaqi and the second cataract, was the Triakontaschoenus,[7] which the Ptolemies granted the Meroites the right to control.[8] After their defeat of Antony and Cleopatra and the official absorption of Egypt into the empire, the Romans continued to use these territorial designations. The Meroites nominally continued to control the Triakontaschoenus after their peace treaty with Augustus in 21 B.C.

Although the primary role of the Roman military in Egypt was to protect state interests against rebellion by the Egyptians themselves, rather than to ward off invasion, the general stability of the Nubian frontier was broken by clashes between the Romans and the various peoples who inhabited Nubia and its surrounding deserts. As mentioned above, the first and most important group in this category was the Meroites, whom the Romans simply referred to as Ethiopians, meaning "burnt-faced people."[9] In addition to the Meroites, ancient sources identified several desert tribes in the region: the Blemmyes and the Megabari, who lived on the eastern banks of the Nile and were subjects of the Meroites; the Troglodytes, who lived in the mountains along the Red Sea coast; and the Nobatai, who inhabited the deserts to the west of the Nile and who were independent of the Meroites.[10] Although Strabo stated that none of these tribes posed a serious threat to the

7.1 Meroitic pyramids and reconstructed chapels at Meroë (north cemetery), Sudan.

Roman occupiers of Egypt, his assessment of the pacifism of the desert dwellers was premature. Of the tribes he mentioned, two appear to have been of particular significance during the Roman period: the Blemmyes and the Nobatai.

The Blemmyes

Like most nomadic peoples, the Blemmyes left few records of their passage through history. Aside from several documents they commissioned, which are written in the still-undeciphered Meroitic script, most of our knowledge about the Blemmyes comes from the scattered and biased accounts of Greek and Roman writers who regarded them as enemies. Predictably, these accounts describe the Blemmyes as savage warriors who preyed upon the settlements, garrisons, and monasteries of the Nile Valley. Although relatively little is known about the Blemmyes, they were a unique cultural and political entity and as such played a significant role in the affairs of more powerful and better known civilizations.

The Blemmyes inhabited a vast region of the Eastern Desert that was demarcated on the east by the Red Sea and on the west by the Nile River and fell approximately between the latitudes of Coptos to the north and Axum in Ethiopia to the south. Ancient sources record their existence over a span of more than two thousand years, but the period of their greatest political influence lasted roughly from A.D. 250 to 550. One early reference to the Blemmyes comes from a stele in honor of Anlamani, a Kushite king who ruled during 623–593 B.C. and engaged a desert tribe in battle somewhere near Kawa, on the eastern bank of the Nile (see map 3). The stele does not describe the actual battle, but its early passages report that the king launched his offensive into the land of the Blemmyes; the later passages describe the consequences of his victory: "A great slaughter was made among them. The number [of enemy dead] thereof was not known. Their [captives] were four men. They were brought back as prisoners. They took captive all their women, all their children, all their flocks, all their possessions. He made them to be male and female servants for each of the gods. This land was rejoicing in his time. There was no saying, 'Would that I had this or that!' Every man slept until dawn. There were no desert dwellers in rebellion in his time so greatly did his Father Amun love him."[11]

Over the centuries, archaeologists have discovered other fragmentary references to the Blemmyes, both in Egyptian and Demotic texts. While these do not furnish an abundance of cultural or political information, the Upper Egyptian sites in which they were found reveal that, although the majority of the tribe dwelled as nomads in the Eastern Desert, some members lived in Syene, Apollonopolis Magna (Edfu), and maybe Thebes (Luxor) and were to some degree integrated into Egyptian society.[12] Yet, despite their presence in the region for more than a thousand years and the possibility that they interacted culturally and politically with both the Egyptians and the Meroites, several Roman sources perpetuated fantastical descriptions of the Blemmyes, which served to reinforce notions about their uncivilized nature: "In the middle of the desert some place live the Atlas tribe and next to them the half-animal Goat-Pans and the Blemmyes and Gamphasantes and Satyrs and Strapfoots. . . . The Blemmyes are reported to have no heads, their mouth and eyes being attached to their chests."[13] Even during the fourth century A.D., descriptions of the Blemmyes were not without their mysterious elements. One Roman writer, for example, stated that the Blemmyes were of large stature, dark skin, and slender waists (literally, dried intestines) and that their arms and legs were marked by protruding muscles. In addition, he remarked that they always ran barefooted over the soft sand but did not leave so much as a footprint.[14]

The Nobatai

The Nobatai (also referred to as the Noubae, Noubades, and Nubians) brought the Nubian language to the Nile Valley, but their origins are unclear. Classical writers such as Procopius stated that the Nobatai first inhabited the Western Oasis (that is, Kharga Oasis), but the unreliability of his sources on this issue discredits this assertion. Although it is now known that the Nobatai did not come from Kharga Oasis, modern scholars are still uncertain about the tribe's provenance. Some believe they moved east to the Nile from the region of Kordufan in west-central Sudan. Others argue that they originated on the Upper Nile and migrated northward, mainly along the west bank of the river, and eventually settled in Lower Nubia. Sometime during this migration, for reasons that remain a mystery, one branch of Nubian-speaking people left the river valley and headed southwest across the desert to the region of Kordufan, where the Nubian dialect is still spoken by the inhabitants of the hill country. Whichever of these interpretations is correct, the Nobatai, Procopius notwithstanding, do not appear to have been a significant presence in Nubia until the second quarter of the fifth century A.D.

ROMAN FORTRESSES AND TEMPLES IN LOWER NUBIA

The Romans were but one in a long line of conquerors of Egypt who occupied large parts of Nubia. During the Middle Kingdom's Twelfth dynasty (1991–1786 B.C.), for example, the Egyptians built a series of large fortresses along the banks of the Nile from Syene to Semna, some 80 kilometers south of the second cataract (see map 3). Two remarkable stele erected at Semna by Sesostris III unmistakably identify the location of Egypt's southern frontier and reveal that the Egyptians constructed these fortresses to defend the border and to control commercial traffic along the river.[15] The first inscription reads as follows:

> I have made my boundary further south than my fathers, I have added to what was bequeathed me. I am a king who speaks and acts, what my heart plans is done by my arm. One who attacks to conquer, who is swift to succeed, in whose heart a plan does not slumber. Considerate to clients, steady in mercy, merciless to the foe who attacks him. One who attacks him who would attack. Who stops when one stops, who replies to a matter as befits it. To stop when attacked is to make bold the foe's heart, attack is valor, retreat is cowardice, a coward is he who is driven from his border.
>
> Since the Nubian listens to the word of mouth, to answer him is to make him retreat. Attack him, he will turn his back, retreat, he will start attacking. They are not people one respects, they are wretches, craven-hearted. My majesty has seen it, it is not an untruth. I have captured their women, I have carried off their dependents, gone to their wells, killed their cattle, cut down their grain, set fire to it.
>
> As my father lives for me, I speak the truth! It is no boast that comes from my mouth. As for any son of mine who shall maintain this border which my

majesty had made, he is my son, born to my majesty. The true son is he who champions his father, who guards the border of his begetter. But he who abandons it, who fails to fight for it, he is not my son, he was not born to me.

Now my majesty has had an image made of my majesty, at this border which my majesty has made, in order that you maintain it, in order that you fight for it.[16]

The second inscription reads as follows:

Southern boundary, made in the year 8, under the majesty of the King of Upper and Lower Egypt, Khakaura Sesostris III who is given life forever and ever; in order to prevent any Nubian from crossing it, by water or by land, with a ship, or any herds of the Nubians; except a Nubian who shall come to do trading in Iken,[17] or with a commission. Every good thing shall be done with them, but without allowing a ship of the Nubians to pass by Heh, going downstream forever.[18]

During the Roman period, troops occupied dozens of sites in Lower Nubia by building settlements or reoccupying Pharaonic and Ptolemaic fortresses and temples along the Nile. There were at least ten major settlements between Syene and Hiera Sykaminos (Maharraqa). Because the main threat to security came from the Blemmyes in the Eastern Desert, most of the fortresses were located on the west bank, the river serving as an additional barrier. Some of the forts, however, had small satellite-posts on the eastern bank just opposite the main settlement. To maintain access to these posts, the Romans built bridges across the river that could be withdrawn during an attack from the Eastern Desert. In addition, archaeologists have identified numerous smaller Roman military camps throughout Nubia: two opposite Philae, one at Qertassi, one at Dakka, and two north of Qasr Ibrim (see map 3). Further upstream, on the west bank of the second cataract, is another camp, this one overlying the Middle Kingdom fortress of Mirgissa. Other Roman forts may have existed at Batn al-Hajar and between the second and third cataracts.[19]

The relatively few surviving details about the history of the Roman occupation of Nubia have led modern scholars to disagree on the role these settlements might have played or exactly how long the Romans occupied them. Some argue that they were Roman forward-positions (that is, beyond the actual Roman frontier), in territory nominally controlled by the Meroites. Thus, with their true frontier located at Syene, the Romans could maintain a military presence in the region and yet be seen as permitting the Meroites a modicum of independence.[20] Other scholars believe that while the Romans might have maintained forward positions, the true border between Roman Egypt and the Meroitic Kingdom shifted over the centuries: initially it was Syene, then Primis (Qasr Ibrim), Hiera Sykaminos (Mahar-raqa), and, finally, back to Syene.

Whether the Nubian fortresses were forward positions or not, the Romans needed an efficient means of communication between the settlements. Syene, of course, was below the first cataract, so the Romans simply used the Nile as a means of transport and communication all the way to Alexandria. But to enable communication above the cataracts in Nubia, the Romans constructed watch-towers on hilltops near the Nile, just as they did along the caravan routes in the Eastern Desert—although the towers in Nubia do not appear to have been nearly as numerous. One lonely soldier manning a tower on the west bank south of Talmis (Kalabsha) simply states, "The soldier Visina of the Cohortis I, Lusitano-rum 7, centuria Flavi."[21] This regiment was part of the Nubian forces from A.D. 105 to 131, so Visina must have been stationed at the tower sometime during this period. On a stone below the watchtower is an interesting, well-executed relief of a man riding a horse, suggesting that horsemen as well as infantrymen may have been assigned to the towers.[22]

With regard to transportation in Nubia, it seems most likely that the Romans traveled by land much more than by river. Numerous trails connected the ancient settlements with each other, and major caravan routes periodically branched off into the desert to distant oases and cities. The exact location of these routes, how-ever, is uncertain. It is known that, beginning in the Old Kingdom (2686–2181 B.C.), much of the trade in the region was conducted overland because the cataracts of the Nile made river travel difficult except for the portion between the first and second cataracts. One account dating from the Sixth dynasty (the last of the Old Kingdom), for example, described how a man named Harkuf made four journeys deep into Nubia, to a place he called Yam, which scholars believe to be Kerma, south of the third cataract (see map 3). Although his description of the route he and his father took is vague, it is clear they traveled overland rather than by water, leaving Elephantine via the "Oasis Road" on the west side of the Nile. Harkuf's tomb inscription states that they returned north with three hundred donkeys laden with incense, ivory, ebony, and other valuables.[23] The Oasis Road to which he refers was probably the route that headed west from Syene, then branched into at least two major desert roads: the first, leading south, eventually arrived at the west bank of the Nile, approximately 15 kilometers north of Qasr Ibrim; the second veered west-northwest toward the distant Greco-Roman for-tress of Kysis (Dush), the southernmost major settlement in the Kharga Oasis.[24] Further south in Nubia, three major desert routes shortened the distance between settlements on the Nile: the Bayuda Road, which connected Napata with Meroë; the Maheila Road, which connected Napata with Kawa; and, most important during the Roman period, the Korosko Road, which connected Abu Hamed with Korosko, halfway between the first and second cataracts (see map 3).

During the Roman period the population of the Dodekaschoenus reached its height. Gold mines and granite quarries—at places like Qertassi, where the names of Antoninus Pius, Marcus Aurelius, Caracalla, and Gordian were discovered[25]—were magnets for Roman exploitation as the empire and its appetite for riches expanded. Large garrisons were necessary to guard the access to the mines, and industries were needed to support the garrisons. Trade between the Romans and the Meroites must have played a large part in the prosperity of this region because, as we have seen, the potential for agricultural production in the area was low. Although some food came from the Meroitic side, the garrisons were no doubt supplied with food and other goods from Syene.

Unfortunately for modern scholars, most of the settlements, smaller fortresses, and cemeteries the Romans visited, constructed, and occupied were destroyed by the creation of Lake Nasser. Five of the most impressive sites, however, were saved by a massive relocation program that coincided with the construction of the High Dam from 1962 to 1971.[26] From north to south, the structures are as described below.

Tafis (modern Taifa)

Nothing of this ancient town remains. During the construction of the Aswan Dam, however, the Tafis temple was dismantled and sent abroad as a gift from the Egyptian government to the people of the Netherlands. The temple, which was dedicated to Isis and graced the banks of the Nile River for two thousand years, now stands inside the National Museum of Antiquities in Leiden, Netherlands.

Talmis (Kalabsha)

With the exception of the magnificent temple at Abu Simbel built by Ramses II, the sandstone temple of Kalabsha is the most splendid of the Nubian monuments to have been saved from the flooding of Lake Nasser. Originally Kalabsha temple was located at Talmis, but since 1970 it has stood with two other relocated temples—Qertassi and Beit al-Wali—on an island just south of the Aswan Dam, approximately 50 kilometers north of Talmis.

Dedicated to the Kushite sun god, Mandulis, Kalabsha is the largest temple in Nubia, measuring approximately 75 meters by 25 meters. Although it was probably started by Tutmose III, major portions of it were constructed under the reign of Augustus (27 B.C.–A.D. 14) (fig. 7.2). Later in the first and early second centuries, Caligula and Trajan added reliefs and inscriptions. The temple consists of

7.2 The relocated temple of Kalabsha.

enormous pylons, a forecourt containing fourteen columns, a hypostyle hall with eight columns, a sanctuary, and two outer vestibules. Facing the water, the great imposing pylons in front of the temple are decorated only around the entrance. Just inside is a depiction of Emperor Augustus before the god Horus, and throughout the temple's interior are numerous inscriptions attesting to its many periods of occupation. On the northwestern wall at the back of the forecourt, for example, are the following inscriptions from the Roman and Late Roman periods:

1. A Greek inscription by Silko, king of the Nobatai (late fifth or early sixth century A.D.);
2. A picture of a man in Roman dress, astride a horse, receiving a wreath from the winged Victory (fig. 7.3);
3. A decree by Aurelius Besarion, governor of Ombos and Elephantine (circa A.D. 248), ordering the expulsion of pigs from the precincts of the temple.

The most noteworthy of these inscriptions is that of King Silko: "I, Silko [king] of the Nubians and all the Ethiopians, I came as far as Talmis . . . I fought against the Blemmyes, and God granted me the victory. I vanquished them a second time, three to one; and the first time I fortified myself there with my troops. I vanquished them and they supplicated me. I made peace with them, and they swore to me by their idols. I trusted them, because they were a people of good faith. Then

7.3 An engraving from the inner wall of the temple of Kalabsha depicting a soldier in Roman dress receiving a wreath from the winged Victory.

7.4 Blemmye pictographs of camels and horses located near the ceiling
in the temple of Kalabsha.

I returned to my dominions in the Upper Country."[27] But, as we shall see below, a
papyrus discovered at Qasr Ibrim implies that it was the Blemmyes who defeated
Silko in the first war, then occupied Kalabsha and made it their capital. Many of
their tombs can be found in the surrounding hills, and numerous Blemmye pictographs remain visible on the temple walls just below the ceiling (fig. 7.4).

Beyond Kalabsha's forecourt, inside the hypostyle hall, the emperor Trajan
(A.D. 98–117) is seen making an offering to Mandulis, Isis, and Osiris. Inscribed
on a nearby wall is the following prayer by Decurion Maximos:

> Be benevolent, O Mandulis, Son of Zeus, and nod to me in acquiescence!
> Save me and my beloved wife and my good children! I call upon Thee con-
> stantly that my companions and the female slaves, free from disease and
> toil, may return to our country.
>
> How happy is the people which lives in the holy [town of] Talmis, loved
> by Mandulis, the Sun God, and which is under the scepter of Isis, of beauti-
> ful hair and many names![28]

Just south of Kalabsha, the beautiful temple of Qertassi stands atop a small
rise, overlooking the Nile. It was not originally part of the Kalabsha complex and
came from a Ptolemaic quarry site located about 40 kilometers south of Aswan.

7.5 The temple of Qertassi, built to honor two Nubian gods,
Srupkithis and Pursepmunis.

Built to honor two Nubian gods, Srupkithis and Pursepmunis, the splendid little
kiosk contains a single chamber surrounded by exquisitely cut floral capitals and
two columns topped by heads of the goddess Hathor (fig. 7.5). From within its
walls, priests presided over the quarrying and transportation of the stone. Originally, the temple stood next to a fortress with stone walls 6 meters high that surrounded a temple to Isis. Neither the fortress nor the temple to Isis contained
within it were saved, however, during the construction of the Aswan Dam; they are
now covered by the waters of Lake Nasser.

During the dismantling of Kalabsha in preparation for its move north, a Ptolemaic shrine and its monumental gateway were discovered to have been reused by
the Roman builders of the temple. The gateway was given to Germany in appreciation for its work in saving Kalabsha and now stands in the Egyptian Museum in
Berlin. The Ptolemaic shrine and a small statue of an elephant were relocated to
the southern tip of Elephantine Island (fig. 7.6).

Pselchis (Dakka)

The small temple of Dakka was begun by the Meroitic king Ergamenes (third century B.C.) and added to by Ptolemy IV (221–205 B.C.) and Roman emperors. Now

7.6 A statue of an elephant from the temple of Kalabsha. Now located on the southern tip of Elephantine Island near Aswan.

located at Wadi al-Sabua near the Maharraqa temple, it was once the dominant structure in the lost ancient town of Pselchis, which stood on the west bank, just across the river from the entrance to Wadi Allaqi—the location of numerous gold mines.

Hiera Sykaminos (Maharraqa)

The settlement of Hiera Sykaminos once stood on a slight rise on the west bank, along a desolate section of the Nile. Even in the early twentieth century, little remained of the riverside town that was eventually submerged by Lake Nasser. In 1961, however, the temple from the site was dismantled and moved almost 50 kilometers south to the higher ground of Wadi el-Sebua, where it joined two other relocated temples: the temple of Wadi el-Sebua, built by Ramses II, and the small temple of Dakka. The Maharraqa temple consists of a small hall formed by pillars that are joined together by walls. The north and south sides contain six pillars each, while the east and west sides contain three. The entrance is on the eastern side, near an unusual spiral staircase located in the northeast corner. The most interesting feature of the temple complex, however, was actually discovered on an adjacent building:

> Between the main temple and the water there is another construction, the plan of which is not easy to determine. It stands somewhat to the axis of the (main) hall, and its north wall seems to have formed the side of an entrance passage leading to the main temple. On the north face of this wall there is a most remarkable relief, executed partly in the Roman and partly in the Egyptian style. It represents a full-faced figure of Isis, seated under the sacred sycamore tree, and clad in Roman costume. Above her a hawk hovers, while another rests in the branches of the tree. She stretches out her arm to an approaching figure of a boy clad in a toga and representing Horus, who brings a vessel of wine to her. Above him are three small figures representing Min, Isis, and Serapis, these again being portrayed in the Roman style. To the left of this scene, Thoth is shown in the Egyptian conventional style, and to the right is Isis, also portrayed in the Egyptian manner.[29]

Nearby, on one of the fallen stones of the ruined temple, was the following inscription: "The vow of Verecundus the soldier, and his most pious parents, and Gaius his little brother, and the rest of his brethren."[30]

Although scholars know few details about the original site from which the Maharraqa temple was removed, the historical evidence strongly suggests that, for more than three hundred years after the Romans and the Kushites signed the treaty of Samos in 21 B.C., it served as the true southernmost political and cultural border of Roman Egypt. The location of the settlement not only provided further protection for Syene, Elephantine, and Philae, but also gave the Romans access to the gold mines in Wadi Allaqi and control over several strategically vital caravan routes.

Primis (Qasr Ibrim)

Of all the surviving monuments in Nubia, only Qasr Ibrim (ancient Primis) remains in its original location.[31] Situated approximately 100 kilometers south of Maharraqa, atop a 75-meter bluff on the east bank of the river and enclosed by massive walls, Qasr Ibrim was built in an ideal defensive position: it commands a superb view of the surrounding deserts and the Nile Valley below (fig. 7.7). The site was originally constructed during the later part of the New Kingdom (1552–1072 B.C.), shortly after which Egyptian control of Nubia waned, and the region was gradually depopulated as the inhabitants migrated south to the fourth cataract. But the discovery at Qasr Ibrim of a mud-brick temple built by the Nubian pharaoh Taharqa (689–664 B.C.) and the presence of other structures from

7.7 The hilltop fortress of Qasr Ibrim as it appeared to David Roberts during his visit in 1839. After the construction of the Aswan High Dam and the subsequent formation of Lake Nasser, the fortress of Qasr Ibrim became an island, with water lapping against its lower walls and endangering the unexcavated archaeological remains at the site.

this period imply that the Nubians may not have abandoned the region to the degree once believed by scholars.[32] Indeed, thirty plus years of archaeological excavations at Qasr Ibrim clearly indicate that it played a major religious, economic, and strategic role in the history of Lower Nubia for nearly three thousand years and was almost continuously occupied from the time of its construction to its final abandonment in 1811, by a garrison of Bosnian mercenaries whose predecessors were first stationed at Qasr Ibrim in 1517 by the Ottoman sultan Selim I.[33]

As a result of its long occupation and the generally good condition of its artifacts, Qasr Ibrim has offered scholars an exceptional opportunity to piece together at least part of the fascinating history of Lower Nubia. To date, researchers have uncovered an enormous and invaluable collection of artifacts and documents from essentially every period of its occupation. The majority of the documents were uncovered from refuse deposits that measured as much as 4 meters deep. In the hyperarid climate of Lower Nubia, these trash dumps preserved both organic and inorganic archaeological material in excellent condition.[34] The finds have included a stele of Amenophis I (reigned from 1545 B.C.), two monumental stele in cursive Meroitic, tens of thousands of pottery sherds, intact vessels, fragments of textiles, boots and sandals, coins, and hundreds of whole and fragmentary documents written on papyrus in Demotic, Greek, Latin, Coptic, and Arabic.[35]

Of the items that pertain to the Roman period, some of the most interesting appear to date from the initial Roman occupation of the region by Petronius in 25–23 B.C. Just a kilometer north of the fortress archaeologists have discovered, for example, the remains of two Roman camps dating from the first campaign of Petronius to annex Kushite territory. In addition, in 1978, archaeologists uncovered a deposit of Roman-era artifacts including clothes, coins, lamps, and thousands of stone ballistae. Near a bronze 8-drachmae coin of Cleopatra VII (51–30 B.C.) lay a scroll of papyrus written in Greek dating from 22–21 B.C. and a fragment of papyrus containing Latin writing. Upon close inspection, the Latin text proved to be a page from a book of elegiac verse written by Cornelius Gallus.[36] Gallus, the victor over Marc Antony and Cleopatra and the first Roman governor of Egypt, was also a highly renowned poet and military commander. He counted Virgil and Ovid among his literary friends and is credited with giving a new direction to Latin literature. Although Ovid had once prophesied that Gallus's "literary fame would reach as far as his military commands, and last longer," prior to the discovery of the Qasr Ibrim verses only a single line of his poetry was known to exist, and his talent was acknowledged only because other writers had praised him.[37] No doubt the verses found their way to Qasr Ibrim in the rucksack of a Roman officer assigned to a lonely tour of duty on the farthest outpost of the empire. The first pertains to Julius Caesar's plans for a grand military campaign that was to begin with an attack on the Parthians and end with the conquest of the territory from the Caspian Sea to Gaul (the wars never took place, partly because Julius Caesar was assassinated three days before he was scheduled to leave): "My fate will then be sweet to me, Caesar, when you are the most important part of Roman history, and when I read of many gods' temples the richer after your return for being hung with your trophies." The second epigram is addressed to the critics Viscus and Valerius Cato: "At last the . . . Muses have made poems that I could utter as worthy of my mistress. . . . the same to you, I do not, Viscus, I do not, Cato, fear . . . even if you are the arbiter."[38] Neither Gallus's once-distinguished military record nor his poetic talents, however, could prevent him from ending his governorship in disgrace from charges of embezzlement and eventually committing suicide in 25 B.C.

Scholars continue to debate the question of how long the Romans occupied Qasr Ibrim. The few historical accounts that survive lack sufficient detail to enable one to draw firm conclusions, and none state when or whether the Romans abandoned the fortress.[39] Furthermore, the archaeological evidence, abundant though it might be, has not yet given historians a convincingly clear picture of the nature and purpose of the occupation. The traditional interpretation states that Roman troops commanded by Prefect Petronius occupied Qasr Ibrim for a period of only two years after they routed the Kushites, marched 800 kilometers to the south, and sacked their capital at Napata in 23 B.C. When those two years were over, and after the conclusion of the treaty of Samos in 21 B.C., the Romans withdrew to Hiera Sykaminos (Maharraqa), which remained their primary frontier outpost for three hundred years. The degree to which Qasr Ibrim was visited or occupied by Romans after 21 B.C. is uncertain. Apparently, after about A.D. 100, the fortress reverted to Nubian control, as is hinted at by the construction about that time of a large Meroitic temple complex surrounded by houses, shops, and a tavern. And yet, researchers have uncovered more than 150 Roman coins dating between the second and fifth centuries that were apparently deposited as offerings on the floor of the temple, along with numerous inscriptions left by pilgrims visiting the temple. Furthermore, the discovery of a third-century letter written by the commander of a Roman legion affords evidence of a Roman presence at Qasr Ibrim not limited to commercial, religious, and diplomatic purposes.[40]

Another interpretation is that Qasr Ibrim remained a Roman garrison for the duration of the first century A.D.[41] In this case, the fortress was probably not a proper frontier garrison, but an advanced outpost in non-Roman controlled territory, beyond the actual limits of Roman settlement and administration.[42] Eventually, after the region was more thoroughly settled by Meroites, the fortress was handed over to their control. This explanation assumes that the Roman presence in Lower Nubia was not primarily intended as a defense against the Meroites, who, if anything, seemed to be concentrating their base of political and military authority further south. The more serious threat seems to have come from the Blemmyes, who constituted "the most powerful opponents of the Roman rule in Nubia."[43] Although the Roman occupation of Qasr Ibrim could not prevent the Blemmyes from attacking Roman Egypt from the Eastern Desert, it could preclude them from taking the fortress, thereby attaining an easily defended permanent position in Nubia.[44] Furthermore, the Romans might have encouraged the settlement of the area by Meroites because they were not regarded as threats to Roman control of the frontier region or Upper Egypt itself. In return, the Meroites might have accepted the presence of the Roman garrison as a means of preventing Blemmye attacks on their own settlements and commercial interests. This danger appears to have been well founded, because when the Romans did withdraw from the region the Blemmyes attacked and temporarily occupied Qasr Ibrim. According to Olympiodorus, who visited the fortress in A.D. 423, the fort and surrounding region were under the control of the Blemmyes.[45] As we shall see, however, they were eventually ousted and dispersed by Silko, "king of the Nubians and all the Ethiopians" during the late fifth or early sixth century.

One of the most noteworthy discoveries from Qasr Ibrim pertains to the relations between the Blemmyes and the Nobatai. In 1975, researchers unearthed the following fifth-century(?) A.D. letter, written in Greek, from the Blemmye king to his rival:

The most illustrious Phonene, King of the Blemmyes To Abouni, King of the Noubades and Mouses his sons. First of all I send many salutations to your Majesty with all the inhabitants of your country and wishes for the safety of your people. For this is in the forefront of my immediate prayers. I now write to your Valiancy since your Valiancy wrote to me that . . . For you have a child and I too have a child, Breeitek, and my brother Eienei and others . . . but do not imagine that he is of anything but the most noble birth. For no one sees these things which have happened except God and our child Breeitek and brother Eienei. I desire Breeitek and the brothers of Eienei to inquire into the death of Eienei. You summoned Breeitek and the brothers of Eienei, but I prevented them [from obeying the summons]. For nobody can go to war unless I have ordered it. But these same people of yours do not listen to you, but you listen to the words of these people. As [your Valiancy] wrote to me that 'I desire that we being of one mind between each other should hold in common my cattle with your cattle, pasturing [them] with each other, and treat [our] sheep with all kindness.' If you so desire, you and I will remain peaceably within our [respective] homelands. For first I defeated Silko and took Talmis, and now you have conquered [me] and taken Talmis and occupied my territories. You said: 'Give me sheep and cattle and camels in order that your lands may be given [back] to you,' and I gave them all and you treated [me] with contempt but I restrained myself. And I wrote to Eienei with a view to peace and sent ambassadors with sworn undertakings. And you expressed contempt and killed the phylarchs and hypotyranni and seized the prophets in the place Phontauou. It is possible that wars should come, but it is not allowable to treat men with contempt and to kill men [who come] with letters of credence. As to what happened to Silko, for which you treated Eienei with contempt, on this account I was grieved and came down and waged war. For I have passed over the conversations of Silko and Eienei—or perhaps I should rather say the fate of Eienei and Silko. For now I and you can create with each other a time of peace as brothers and sovereigns in collaboration. Evacuate my territory and return [the images of the] gods to the temple in order that I and you may establish a time of peace. And you indicated to me [your demand] concerning silver and sheep and camels. These were procured. And I sent you [a letter] under my own hand [saying] 'if you please, give me [back] our territories and the [images of the] gods [so that] I may establish with you an honorable peace.' Let me inform you that if you withhold from us our territories and the [images of the] gods, we cannot endure to leave everything to go to ruin . . .[46]

Throughout their occupation of Lower Nubia, the Romans had to deal with the same issues of territory and security that drove the Blemmyes and the Nobatai to war. Not surprisingly, therefore, the Romans themselves occasionally engaged in combat with the inhabitants and would-be inhabitants of the region.

ROMAN MILITARY CAMPAIGNS IN NUBIA

After absorbing Egypt into the Roman Empire in 30 B.C., the Romans lost no time in securing their southern border. But the first years of imperial occupation were anything but peaceful, and the location of the frontier itself changed three times over the next decade. The first Roman governor of Egypt, the poet-general Cornelius Gallus, met with Kushite leaders on the island of Philae and established the border at Syene. This agreement did not last, in part because of Gallus's summons to Rome and eventual suicide.[47] Whether Gallus returned to Rome much before his death is not known, but the latest evidence of his presence in Egypt is a stele on Philae dated April 15, 29 B.C. He likely left Egypt, therefore, sometime between the spring of 29 B.C. and 27 B.C., the approximate time his successor, Aelius Gallus, assumed the governorship of the province.[48]

Unlike his predecessor, however, Aelius Gallus was not a talented general, and his disastrous campaigns have inspired at least one modern scholar to refer to him as "a bungler of the first order."[49] In 25 B.C., only a few years after becoming governor, Aelius Gallus was ordered to launch an attack on Arabia. Using troops he removed from their positions in Upper Egypt and Syene, Gallus departed from the Red Sea port of either Myos Hormos or Berenike for what was to be his last battle. Realizing that the southern frontier was weakened by the reduced number of Roman troops, the Kushites launched a surprise attack against Syene, Elephantine, and Philae and "enslaved the inhabitants, and threw down the statues of Caesar."[50]

By now, Aelius Gallus had been removed from office and was replaced by Publius Petronius.[51] It was under Petronius that the Romans reacted to the Kushite attack on their southern border. With a force of ten thousand infantry and eight hundred cavalry, Publius Petronius launched his first campaign against thirty thousand Kushite forces in the closing months of 25 B.C. and succeeded in forcing them to retreat south to Pselchis (modern Dakka). During the ensuing negotiations, the Kushites demanded three days to consider the Romans' demands for the return of the people and objects captured from Syene. When the three days passed with no Kushite attempt to meet the Roman terms, Petronius attacked again, and the poorly armed Kushites fled in disarray "being badly commanded and badly armed; for they carried large shields made of raw hides, and hatchets for offensive weapons; some, however, had pikes, and others swords. Part of the insurgents were driven into the city [Pselchis], others fled into uninhabited country; and such as ventured upon the passage of the river escaped to a neighboring island, where there were not many crocodiles on account of the current."[52]

Among the Romans' many captives were generals serving under Candace, the one-eyed queen of the Kushites (reigned 41–12 B.C.).[53] Petronius sent these men, along with the rest of the prisoners from the battle, to Augustus in Rome via Alexandria.[54] But the capture of Pselchis apparently neither accorded the Romans an adequate buffer zone on their southern frontier, nor taught the Kushites a sufficiently strong lesson in Roman retribution. So Petronius led his forces further south, along a desert route, in pursuit of the Kushites and successfully attacked and occupied Qasr Ibrim. From there, the Roman troops advanced even deeper into Kushite territory to Napata, then the capital of the Kushite Kingdom, located approximately 600 kilometers south of Qasr Ibrim, just below the fourth cataract. There, the Romans hoped to confront Candace herself, but the queen had fled the city and sought refuge in another town. When the Romans arrived at the outskirts of Napata, they were met by ambassadors from Candace, who offered to return the prisoners taken from Syene and the royal statues in exchange for peace. But the deal was unacceptable to Petronius, who was determined to subjugate the Kushites to Roman rule. Rather than accept Candace's terms, he destroyed Napata, enslaved its residents, recaptured what had been looted from Syene, and, not wanting to linger in the increasing heat of early summer, returned with his troops to Egypt. Along the way, however, he strengthened the fortifications at Qasr Ibrim and stationed a garrison of four hundred troops there with enough provisions for two years. The southern border of Roman Egypt was redrawn. Once back in Alexandria, he sold some of the surviving Napatan slaves at public auction and sent the remaining thousand slaves to Augustus.[55]

Remarkably, the destruction of the capital of Napata was not a crippling blow to the Kushites and did not frighten Candace enough to prevent her from again engaging in combat with the Roman military. Indeed, it seems that Petronius's attack might have had a revitalizing influence on the kingdom.[56] Just three years later, in 22 B.C., a large Kushite force moved northward with the intention of attacking Qasr Ibrim. Alerted to the advance, Petronius again marched south and managed to reach Qasr Ibrim and bolster its defenses before the invading Kushites arrived. Although the ancient sources give no description of the ensuing battle, we know that at some point the Kushites sent ambassadors to negotiate a peace settlement with Petronius. By the end of this second campaign, however, Petronius was in no mood to deal further with the Kushites, and he ordered them to direct their complaints to the emperor himself. Moreover, if the Romans had actually extended their southern border south to Qasr Ibrim (and there is strong evidence to support that theory), then Petronius in all likelihood would not have had the authority to negotiate with the Kushites himself. Roman Egypt was regarded as the personal property of the emperor, and if Lower Nubia was now annexed by the Romans, then Augustus was the proper authority with whom the Kushites should negotiate the peace treaty.

The Kushites attempted to stall the negotiations by claiming that they did not know who Augustus was, so Petronius appointed several officers to escort them to the Aegean island of Samos, where Augustus was spending the winter of 21–20 B.C. while preparing for a voyage to Syria. As a result of this meeting, Augustus granted the ambassadors "all that they desired,"[57] including the cancellation of the tribute Petronius had apparently imposed in the emperor's name when he subjugated the territory between Syene and Napata in his first campaign.[58] In addition, the Romans agreed to withdraw their frontier to the old Ptolemaic border of Hiera Sykaminos (Maharraqa), located about 80 kilometers south of Syene (Aswan), where it appears to have remained for the next three hundred years.[59] With a few notable exceptions, this period marked a time of peace and economic vitality in Lower Nubia. Trade between Roman Egypt and the Meroitic Kingdom increased, and the region became more populated than at any other time in its history.[60]

From the time of Augustus until the reign of Nero (A.D. 54–68), the ancient records are strangely silent on the subject of the southern Roman frontier. According to one source, Nero sent an expedition south from Syene in A.D. 61, with the intention of discovering the source of the Nile River. The expedition consisted of a party of Praetorian soldiers under the command of a tribune and two centurions. After traveling up the Nile and then across the Eastern Desert, they reached Meroë, some 1,000 kilometers from Syene. There they saw parakeets and monkeys and the tracks of rhinoceros and elephant. The Meroites supplied the Romans with a military escort and recommendations to the neighboring southern tribes. The explorers continued their journey up the White Nile until, as they told one historian upon their return to Rome, they "came to immense marshes" where "the plants were so entangled with the waters" that they were impermeable except, perhaps, to a one-man canoe.[61]

Evidently the expedition managed the remarkable feat of reaching the Sudd, a vast, almost impenetrable swamp in southern Sudan that in the rainy season covers an area the size of England. In 1850, the English explorer Samuel Baker managed to cross the Sudd during his own quest for the source of the Nile. He wrote,

A short distance above the present town of Malakal, the river turns west, the air grows more humid, the banks more green, and this is the first warning of the great obstacle of the Sudd that lies ahead. There is no more formidable swamp in the world than the Sudd. The Nile loses itself in a vast sea of papyrus ferns and rotting vegetation, and in that fetid heat there is a spawning tropical life that can hardly have altered very much since the beginning of the world . . . crocodiles and hippopotamuses flop about in the muddy water, mosquitoes and other insects choke the air . . . for black and white men alike the Sudd contained nothing but the threat of starvation, disease and death.[62]

If it really was the Sudd that forced the return of Nero's expedition, then their unparalleled journey was the most southerly overland penetration of Africa during the Roman period.

Seneca's writings imply that Nero's men aimed to discover the source of the Nile, yet the true purpose of the journey is not clear. The expedition may have been a reconnaissance for a Roman attack deep into the reaches of the Upper Nile. By the time of Nero's reign, Rome had scrapped its former policy of permitting the existence of client kingdoms just beyond its frontiers, replacing it with a new system of direct control of strategic regions. The implication is that, once again, Rome was falling back into an expansionist mode, and it seems reasonable that, despite the earlier, unsuccessful attempts by Augustus, Nero planned to annex the Meroitic Empire. Some scholars disagree with this theory, arguing that Rome retained client kings in the east until Trajan annexed the Nabataean Kingdom in A.D. 106 after the death of its king.[63] If in fact Nero was preparing for a military expedition deep into southern territory, the plan was never attempted, possibly because the Jewish revolt against Roman rule in A.D. 66 and his death two years later put an end to his ambitions in sub-Saharan Africa. In any case, immediately after Nero, Roman emperors seem to have had little interest in conquering Nubia. After all, they obtained slaves, animals, and ivory from eastern Africa (via Berenike and Myos Hormos) rather than from Nubia, and the enormous expense of defeating the Meroites and subjecting them to Roman rule could hardly be justified in light of the limited economic returns that the lands south of Lower Nubia might offer.

After Nero's ambitious expedition, the only existing indication that the Romans might have militarily engaged the Kushites in the late first century A.D. is a papyrus fragment of an official Roman military report, which records that the Romans fought a major battle with the Meroites (including their auxiliary forces of Troglodytes) sometime between A.D. 89 and 91. The location and cause of the battle are not known, but it involved the use of cavalry, and the Roman forces were commanded by Mettius Rufus, the prefect of Egypt.[64]

But the Kushites were not the only potential adversary of the Romans in Nubia. By the late third century, Roman Egypt was undergoing a period of civil strife and economic hardship, the Meroitic Kingdom appears to have been weakening, and, once again, tensions were increasing on the southern frontier.[65] The Blemmyes, apparently no longer subjects of the Meroites by this time, took advantage of Egypt's weakness and launched an invasion sometime during the reign of Emperor Decius (A.D. 249–51). Decius, who allegedly used African lions in his wars against rebels on the Palestinian frontier, decided to employ equally unusual measures against the Blemmyes: "Decius . . . brought from dry Libya poisonous snakes and dreadful hermaphrodites and released [them] at the Egyptian frontier because of the barbarians, the Noubades and the Blemmyes."[66] After Decius's victory, the Nubian frontier appears to have been quiet—or at least there is no surviving record of a military engagement—until the reign of Emperor Gallienus (A.D. 260–68), when the prefect of Egypt, L. Mussius Aemilianus, found it necessary to reinforce the defenses of the southern border. The exact reasons for this effort, however, and whether it involved warfare with the Blemmyes, are undetermined.[67]

But the long period of general unrest in Egypt meant that the southern border could not remain quiet for long. The Romans again engaged the Blemmyes in combat during the reign of Emperor Aurelian (A.D. 270–75). This conflict also involved the Palmyrenes, who had unsuccessfully attempted to invade Egypt in A.D. 268 and 270. Palmyrenes had been present in Egypt for many years, and a sizable contingent of rich, influential Palmyrene merchants lived in Coptos, where they were heavily involved in the Red Sea trade. In A.D. 272, however, a wealthy Alexandrian businessman named Firmus apparently supported a rebellion by the Palmyrenes, and at least one source indicates that he enlisted the assistance of the Blemmyes in the enterprise as well.[68] Given that scholars generally regard the Blemmyes as having been the primary threat to the caravans involved in the Red Sea trade, this purported alliance between the Palmyrenes and the Blemmyes seems odd, but it might be a reflection of how little historians know about the degree of political power the Blemmyes wielded at that time and, consequently, about the nature of their relations with the Romans and other groups in Egypt. In any case, the uprising was defeated, and Emperor Aurelian placed Blemmyes captured in battle at the head of his triumphal procession in Rome.[69]

Aurelian's victory, like other Roman victories before it, however, did not put an end to the Blemmye problem. During the reign of Probus (A.D. 276–81), the Blemmyes captured the Upper Egyptian cities of Coptos and Ptolemais (near the modern town of Sohag) and had to be ousted by Roman forces, led by Emperor Probus himself. Once again, Blemmye prisoners of war were featured in a Roman victory parade,[70] yet, once again, the parade represented a triumph limited to one battle, rather than a decisive defeat of the Blemmye people, who continued their insurgencies against Roman forces in Egypt.

In an effort to deal directly with political and economic crises that triggered violent uprisings in Alexandria, Coptos, and other cities, and to finally end the intermittent hostilities with the Blemmyes, the emperor Diocletian (A.D. 284–305) traveled to Egypt in 297. By killing an upstart named Aurelius Achilleus, who had declared himself emperor, Diocletian restored order to Alexandria in early 298.[71] He then moved on to secure the southern frontier by first attacking both the Kushites and the Blemmyes. At the end of this military engagement, however, Diocletian decided to withdraw all Roman troops from the Dodekaschoenus and to consolidate the frontier at Syene by strengthening the military outposts at Philae and in the area of the first cataract and by redistributing Roman forces in Egypt.[72] Upon the withdrawal of the Roman forces in Nubia, Procopius, the only ancient historian whose account of the withdrawal survives, claimed that Diocletian invited the Nobatai to occupy the recently abandoned region and thus serve as a buffer between the Blemmyes and the Roman troops in and around Syene:

> From the cities of the Axumites to the boundaries of Roman rule, where the city called Elephantine is located, the way is a thirty day journey for an unencumbered man. But many nations are situated there, among them the Blemmyes and the Nobatai, very numerous people. The Blemmyes dwell in the center of the country, whereas the Nobatai possess the area around the Nile River. In earlier times this was not the case, for the most distant part of

the Roman realm extended seven days' [journey] further on. When Diocletian, the ruler of the Romans, came there, he judged that the tribute from these lands was very small, for the arable land happens to be very narrow there. Very high rocks rise not far from the Nile and fill up the rest of the country. Since ancient times a great number of soldiers had been garrisoned there whose maintenance was an excessive burden on the public.

And at this period the Nobatai who had previously dwelt around the city Oasis [that is, Kharga Oasis in the Western Desert] had begun to plunder the entire region. He persuaded these barbarians to relocate from their usual [land] and to settle around the River Nile, and he agreed to give them both the great cities and a big country much better than the one in which they had dwelt. He thus supposed that they would no longer harass the land around the oasis and, having acquired a land of their own, that they would repel the Blemmyes and the other barbarians, a reasonable assumption.

This pleased the Nobatai, and they immediately migrated, doing just as Diocletian had commanded them. They took over all the cities and land of the Romans on both sides of the river from Elephantine upward [south]. Then this emperor ordained for both them and the Blemmyes a stated amount of gold each year upon the condition that they would not plunder Roman land. The same is true in my time [that is, the sixth century], but, nonetheless, they overrun the country. Hence with all the barbarians the only way to make them keep their word is through fear of soldiers. Indeed, the emperor, having found an island in the Nile near the city of Elephantine and having placed there a strong garrison, established shrines and altars for both the Romans and the barbarians and settled there priests of both nations to firm up the friendship between them by the sharing of similar sacred things. Whereupon, he named the place, Philae.[73]

For years, this account was accepted by the majority of scholars. But Procopius wrote it 250 years after the events took place, and his description understandably contains several crucial errors. For example, although the Dodekaschoenus might have been poor in resources, its location at the head of land and river routes into Africa made the region militarily and commercially strategic; a Roman emperor would not be inclined to give it up easily. Thus, Procopius' explanation for Diocletian's withdrawal seems less plausible than the possibility that the Romans retreated because Blemmye power had reached such a degree that the emperor recognized his control over the region was militarily untenable.

According to modern scholars, however, the main problem with Procopius's account is that he brought the Nobatai onto the scene more than a hundred years before they became a substantial force in Lower Nubia. No other ancient source even mentions their presence in the region until the fifth century, at the end of which King Silko finally defeated the Blemmyes and at least temporarily asserted control of Lower Nubia.[74] Instead of the Nobatai, who were present in Lower Nubia during Procopius's day, it may have been the Meroites who filled the void created by the withdrawal of the Romans from Maharraqa to Syene. The fact that in A.D. 336, the Meroites (and the Blemmyes) sent a party of officials to Constantinople to celebrate the thirtieth anniversary of Constantine's rise to power shows that the Meroites may still have been a considerable political power in the fourth century. In addition, the presence of the name of the Meroite king Yesbokheamani (circa A.D. 283–300) in the lion temple at Meroë, on a stone lion from Qasr Ibrim, and at Philae, connotes that the Meroites had managed to retain control of their traditional territory until the fourth century A.D.[75] The degree of this control is uncertain, however, and there is little doubt it was fading: by the middle of the fourth century, the once-powerful Meroites disappeared from the historical record. In their wake came the Nobatai, who, along with the Blemmyes, were to continue to occupy the attention of the Romans, but for different reasons than before.

EPILOGUE

Constantine's defeat of his rival coemperor, Licinius, in A.D. 324 and his subsequent accession to the position of sole emperor marked a dramatic turning point in the history of the Roman Empire. Not only did the new emperor move the capital from Rome to Constantinople (formerly Byzantium) in Asia Minor, but he officially legalized Christianity in A.D. 313 by issuing the Edict of Mediolanum (Milan) and actively supported the expansion of the Christian church.[76] Upon his death, however, the western portion of the empire began a long century of decline until, in A.D. 476, in the face of political chaos and barbarian invasions, the last of the western emperors, Romulus Augustulus, simply abdicated the ancient throne and retired to his home on the Gulf of Naples. Rome, the eternal city, was sacked. Despite the collapse of the western empire, however, the eastern realm, now known as the Byzantine Empire, continued to flourish until Constantinople fell to invading Muslims in 1453.

Egypt, of course, became part of this new Christian empire. But the Romans who now ruled from Constantinople were no longer interested only in securing their borders. After the adoption of Christianity, the conversion of pagan peoples who lived along its frontiers became a high priority. By the reign of Emperor Justinian (A.D. 527–65) and his wife, Theodora, the inhabitants of Egypt's southern frontier experienced the fervor of this new crusade as the couple competed against each other for the souls of the Nobatai and the Blemmyes. Justinian wanted them to become Chalcedonians, but Theodora was determined that they should adopt the Monophysitic doctrine.[77] To further her cause, Theodora enlisted the services of a clergyman named Julianus who was keen to Christianize the Nobatai, who were "not only not subject to the authority of the Roman Empire, but even receive a subsidy on condition that they do not enter or pillage Egypt."[78] While the empress decided to send Julianus, Justinian ordered another man, a supporter of the Council of Chalcedon, to convert the Nobatai. Determined to have her way, the empress wrote the following letter to the ranking official of the region: "Inasmuch as both his majesty and myself have purposed to send an embassy to the people of the Nobadae, and I am now dispatching a blessed man named Julianus; and further my will is that my ambassador should arrive at the aforesaid people before his majesty's; be warned, that if you permit his ambassador to arrive there before mine, and do not hinder him by various pretexts until mine shall have reached you and shall have passed through your province and arrived at his destination, your life shall answer for it; for I shall immediately send and take off your head."[79] The dutiful imperial officer did as Theodora commanded, and Julianus, laden with expensive gifts, arrived first, warmly welcomed by King Silko of the Nobatai. Upon receipt of the gifts, and after hearing Julianus's instructions, the people joyfully "yielded themselves up and utterly abjured the errors of their forefathers, and confessed the God of the Christians, saying, 'He is the one true God, and there is no other beside Him.' "[80] By the time the erstwhile ambassador of Justinian arrived, the Nobatai were prepared, and they rejected the "wicked faith" to which he attempted to convert them. Thus sanctified, King Silko led the Nobatai against the Blemmyes and attempted to convert them to Christianity. After his initial military victory, the king ordered the following statement inscribed in the Blemmye temple of Talmis (Kalabsha): "I do not allow my foes to rest in the shade but compel them to remain in the full sunlight, with no one to bring them water to their houses. I am a lion for the lands below, and a bear for the lands above."[81] In A.D. 536, in a final attempt to force the Blemmyes to adopt Christianity, Emperor Justinian ordered that Philae's temple of Isis be closed. The temple's statues were brought to Constantinople and the priests removed from office. Thereafter, a Christian community inhabited the island and turned the great hall into the church of Saint Stephen.[82] Christian crosses were carved into the walls, sometimes destroying the earlier sculptured reliefs of the ancient gods. In the doorway leading to an antechamber of the Isis temple, a Greek inscription, written by Abbot Bishop Theodore in the fifth century, simply states, "The Cross conquered and will ever conquer." Thus, the ancient rites and beliefs that had been preserved for five hundred years of Roman rule in Egypt came to an end, and new peoples, with new ideas and new armies, came to occupy and defend Egypt's southern frontier.

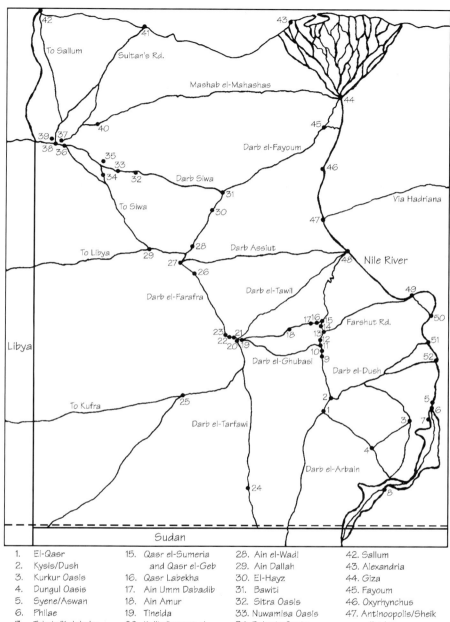

1.	El-Qasr	15.	Qasr el-Sumeria
2.	Kysis/Dush		and Qasr el-Geb
3.	Kurkur Oasis	16.	Qasr Labekha
4.	Dungul Oasis	17.	Ain Umm Dabadib
5.	Syene/Aswan	18.	Ain Amur
6.	Philae	19.	Tineida
7.	Talmis/Kalabsha	20.	Kellis/Ismant el-
8.	Primis/Qasr Ibrim		Kharab
9.	Qasr el-Zaiyan	21.	Amheida
10.	Qasr el-Ghieta	22.	Seir el-Haggar
11.	Hibis	23.	El-Muzzawaka
12.	Bagawat	24.	Bir Tarfawi
13.	El-Deir	25.	Abu Ballas
14.	Ain Mohammed	26.	Bir Dikka
	Toleib	27.	Qasr Farafra

28.	Ain el-Wadi	42.	Sallum
29.	Ain Dallah	43.	Alexandria
30.	El-Hayz	44.	Giza
31.	Bawiti	45.	Fayoum
32.	Sitra Oasis	46.	Oxyrhynchus
33.	Nuwamisa Oasis	47.	Antinoopolis/Sheik
34.	Bahrein Oasis		Ibada
35.	El-Areg	48.	Assiut
36.	Al-Zaytun	49.	Farshut
37.	Abu Sharuf	50.	Thebes/Luxor
38.	Siwa Oasis	51.	Latopolis/Esna
39.	Balad al-Rum	52.	Apollonopolis
40.	Qara		Magna/Edfu
41.	Paraetonium/Marsa		
	Matruh		

Map 4

PART THREE

THE WESTERN DESERT

OVERVIEW OF THE WESTERN DESERT

The Nile River provides a constant and abundant source of water, enabling farmers in the Nile Valley to produce two or even three harvests per year and sustaining a rich variety of plant and animal life. But only a few kilometers from either side of the river, the cultivated lands end abruptly at the desert's edge. Seen from the air, this separation is as distinct as a winding green line painted across a great sand-brown canvas. To the east of this line lies the mountainous Eastern Desert, while to the west lies the Western, or Libyan Desert, whose silent barrenness constitutes the most inhospitable region of the Sahara. Bordered on the north by the Mediterranean Sea and on the east by the Nile River, this vast immensity of sand and rock stretches westward to the outlying oases of Fezzan and Tripoli in Libya and southward to Darfur and Kordufan in the Sudan and to the Tibesti Mountains of Chad—covering an area of approximately 1.4 million square kilometers.

The portion of this desert that lies in western Egypt is characterized by enormous fields of shifting sand dunes. The dunes are mostly crescent-shaped Barchan dunes, which extend southward in parallel lines carved by the prevailing northern winds. In the eastern portions of the Western Desert, where all but one of the Egyptian oases are located, the lines of dunes are narrower and more isolated, averaging six or seven kilometers wide. Although they are smaller than those found further west, these dunes nevertheless cause considerable problems as they descend into the inhabited depressions and gradually bury roads, power lines, and cultivated fields. Predictably, however, the single greatest problem of the oases is water, for aside from infrequent winter rains falling on the narrow strip of land along the Mediterranean coast and an occasional thunderstorm in the interior, the Western Desert is almost entirely rainless.

But even in antiquity, before pipelines and diesel-powered pumps, the absence of measurable precipitation did not render Egypt's Western Desert completely uninhabitable. As it is today, this sea of sand and rock was punctuated by five isolated depressions carved by wind erosion out of the limestone of the Libyan Desert plateau.[1] From southeast to northwest, these oases are Kharga, Dakhleh, Farafra, Bahariya, and Siwa. At the bottom of these depressions, which range in depth from 30 to 120 meters above sea level, the porous sandstone that underlies the limestone is fairly close to the surface, making the water contained within the sandstone accessible either by the digging of wells or, in some cases, simply by the tapping of natural springs. The water itself comes from rain that has fallen far to the south in the Sudan and from seepage that occurs in the upper reaches of the Nile River. In both instances, the water infiltrates the sandstone and gradually flows northward under the depressions of the Western Desert, where, when tapped, it has enabled sizable populations of people to live in the oases and support themselves by farming.[2] Upon seeing these small cultivated areas for the first time after days of exhausting travel, one surprised nineteenth-century explorer described them as "tufted isles that verdant rise amid the Libyan waste."[3]

Although the early history of the oases is unclear, it is certain that they have been inhabited since prehistoric times. Attesting to such ancient origins are the abundance of both Paleolithic and Neolithic stone implements that lie scattered about the desert floor and the numerous pictographs of animals long extinct from the region.[4] Equally uncertain is exactly when the Western Desert oases fell under the control of the Egyptians who ruled the Nile Valley; we do know that the Egyptians were present in the oases in the Archaic period, the Third dynasty, and the Sixth dynasty.[5] From the Pharaonic period onward, inhabitants of the oases left evidence of their presence in the form of cemeteries, fortresses, and temples, but it was during the Roman period that the oases, particularly Kharga and Dakhleh, attained their greatest prosperity.

During the Roman period, the western oases were divided into three groups: Siwa Oasis was one unto itself, but Bahariya and Farafra were jointly named the Small Oasis, and Dakhleh and Kharga were united as the Great Oasis. Each of these oases was connected to its neighboring oasis by one or more desert tracks, while additional caravan routes snaked eastward to the Nile Valley. Although it is unclear exactly when the Romans first traveled these ancient routes and occupied the western oases, archaeological evidence suggests that they established authority over their desert-dwelling subjects soon after they took control of Egypt in 30 B.C. The Romans decided to occupy these remote areas for both strategic and economic reasons. Certainly they could not permit a relatively large population of potentially hostile people to live within striking distance of Roman interests in the Nile Valley. The oases could serve as a security buffer between hostile nomadic tribes and the Nile Valley. More important, however, the Romans saw that the oases could contribute a considerable income to the imperial coffers through taxation and agricultural revenues. In addition, it is probable, although as yet unproved, that a limited amount of trade was conducted—via Kharga and Dakhleh—between Roman Egypt and both the people of Darfur in the Sudan and the inhabitants of Kufra Oasis in what is now eastern Libya. For these and other reasons, the Romans marched across the Western Desert and settled in the oases. Depending on the size of an oasis's population and its potential for agricultural production, the Romans dug wells, constructed elaborate irrigation systems, repaired ancient temples, and built impressive mud brick fortresses from which they proceeded to govern and defend one of the most distant frontiers of the Roman Empire.

The local people apparently were viewed by the Romans as being of a different race from the so-called proper Egyptians who lived in the Nile Valley. A document dating from A.D. 202, for example, describes a certain slave as "of the Oasis race."[6] The appellation Oasites, however, did not apply to the inhabitants of Siwa, who, as we shall see, were referred to as Ammonites because of the important temple to Amon located at the heart of that oasis. Today, it is difficult to speak with certainty about the ethnicity of any of the oases' original inhabitants, but there is little doubt that they were primarily a mixture of Egyptian, Libyan, and Sudanese stock and that their dominant languages were Coptic and Greek.[7] By the third and fourth centuries A.D., however, the ethnicity of the original inhabitants was further diluted by the long presence of Greeks, Romans, and the various peoples from around the Roman Empire who served in the Roman army units that occupied the oases. Indeed, it was during this period that classical Greek names began to appear frequently in the graffiti scribbled on the walls of many of the buildings within the oases. The most common of these was Appollon, but others, including Theophilos, Satyrion, and Alexandros, also appear in abundance. In addition, documents from this period include a variety of Greek, Egyptian, and Latin names as well as a few foreign names such as Saracen Abram.[8]

The people of the oases were not, however, the sole inhabitants of the Western Desert. They shared this vast, inhospitable land with nomadic tribes like the Goniotai, Mastitai, Blemmyes, Nobatai, and Maziques, who from the third through the sixth centuries periodically raided the oases and pillaged, killed, or enslaved their peoples.[9] Occasionally, these tribes joined forces with the Libyans and attacked villages in the Nile Valley. In A.D. 258, for example, the Libyans attacked the village of Kaminon in the Fayoum, and documents indicate that the Nile Valley towns of Hierakleopolis and Oxyrhynchus suffered numerous attacks throughout the third century.[10]

VIII

THE GREAT OASIS

KHARGA

The Kharga depression is the largest inhabited depression in Egypt's Western Desert. Located approximately 200 kilometers west of the Nile Valley, it lies on a north–south axis, measures roughly 185 kilometers in length, and varies from 20 to 80 kilometers in width. Its northern and eastern edges are bounded by sheer escarpments measuring up to 400 meters high. Within this area, small villages cluster around the precious wells that dot the floor of the depression. In the winter months, Kharga's hyper-arid climate is pleasantly warm during the day and cold at night, but in summer the white sun turns the air into a furnace. The residents of Kharga sometimes refer to a particularly hot day as Abu Farrar, or Father of Axes, for the heat has the power to kill. Throughout the summer months, anyone venturing on foot through the deserts surrounding the oasis will suffer terribly in the ovenlike atmosphere. In the words of the poet Wilfred Blunt,

How the earth burns! Each pebble underfoot
Is a living thing with power to wound.
The white sand quivers, and the mute footfall
Of the slow camels strikes, but gives no sound,
As though they walked on flame, not solid ground.
'Tis noon, and the beasts' shadows even have fled
Back to their feet, and there is fire around
And fire beneath, and overhead the sun.
Pitiful Heaven![1]

Throughout its history, Kharga's intense heat and remote location made the oasis an ideal place to banish undesirables.[2] Domitius Ulpianus, a third-century lawyer and writer, stated that Roman laws actually designated the oasis for this purpose, but it appears that banishment to the oasis was generally limited to a period of six months to a year.[3] Among the well-known figures to suffer this punishment was the poet Juvenal, who was also temporarily banished to Aswan for having offended the emperor Domitian (A.D. 81–96).[4] Other famous people who spent time in Kharga included Saint Athanasius, the fourth-century Greek patriarch of Alexandria, and Nestorius, the Syrian-born, fifth-century patriarch of Constantinople.[5] Two of Nestorius's letters have survived. In one he mentions his banishment, and in the other he describes his capture by the Blemmyes: "After the Oasis was, as I mentioned above, taken by the barbarians [Blemmyes], and completely laid waste and devastated by fire, they who, for what cause I know not, carried me off, suddenly took compassion and dismissed me, adding threats, however, if I did not instantly leave the country, for they said the Mazici were to take possession as soon as we left it."[6] Marauding tribes were not the only fearsome aspect of life in the oases; travel to and from the oases across the open desert could also be a harrowing ordeal. Ancient documents contain terrifying descriptions of the desert as a burning, inhospitable wasteland in which heat, sandstorms, and lack of water killed many unfortunate travelers.[7] About A.D. 357, for example, St. Athanase of Alexandria wrote that the oases were where "one goes to die if one has been lucky enough to reach them alive and if one has not died on the desert tracks leading to them."[8]

In A.D. 362, two priests, Eugene and Macaire, were exiled to Kharga by Emperor Julian, the Apostate, who reigned A.D. 361–363.[9] The writer Symeon Metaphraste described the dreadful experience as follows: "Julian sends them to the Oasis . . . because this region carries illness, mainly due to the devastating winds which sweep it; as a result, not a single one of those who were sent there has ever survived more than one year; on the contrary, they all died very quickly over there, succumbing to serious illnesses."[10] Another writer, Philostorgius, later wrote that the priests died after forty days.[11] In A.D. 396, Timasius, a general in the army under Emperor Theodosius I, was exiled to Kharga, but there are slight differences in the two surviving accounts of his fate. The first version depicts Timasius as unable to even attempt an escape: "Timasius was sent to live in the Oasis. He was sent there in the custody of public guards who accompanied him. This place was very arid and those who were sent there could not escape because the surrounding area is sandy, perfectly deserted and uninhabited, thus we do not know anything further about those who leave for the Oasis, since the wind covers tracks with sand and there are no plants or buildings which could serve as landmarks for the travelers."[12] In the second version, Timasius escapes but does not gain freedom: "He [Timasius] died near the border between Egypt and Libya, while escaping the sentence to which he had been condemned; moreover, he died in the sands, as the whole area through which he was fleeing lacked water and was uninhabited."[13]

Despite Kharga's harsh climate and a constant northern wind, the remains of numerous mud-brick fortresses and the visible traces of ancient cultivation suggest that the oasis was a prosperous agricultural area during the Roman occupation. To profitably cultivate sizable tracts of land with barley and millet, however, the Romans needed access to large and constant sources of water. Given that there were few if any natural springs at that time, this water had to be obtained by the laborious digging of wells. A hydrologist who worked in Kharga in the early twentieth century wrote the following:

It is interesting to speculate on the conditions which obtained in Kharga before the first borings were made, as at present day we cannot point, so far as I am aware, to a single natural efflux of water on the ground of the depression. Surface water, of quite a different character from the deep-seated water, is met with at comparatively shallow depths in various localities, and may either represent drainage water from the flowing wells and cultivated tracts, or be water which has escaped from the underground sandstone and found its way to the surface through fissures. . . . Nothing is known as to when flowing wells were first obtained, or by whom the original deep borings were made, and no trace of the implements used [has] been discovered. Many of these ancient wells, frequently over 120 meters in depth, continue to flow at the present day, although in most cases with a greatly diminished output; a few, however, are still running day and night at the rate of several hundred gallons a minute.

In some parts of the oases water-bearing sandstone occurs at or near the surface, and from these beds the Romans obtained additional supplies by the excavation of underground collecting tunnels . . . they are frequently of great length, cut throughout in solid rock, and connected with the surface above by numerous vertical air-shafts. Many of the latter measure 30 to 50 meters in depth, so that the construction of these and the horizontal carrying channels must have involved an immense amount of labour.[14]

The Romans thus went to extraordinary lengths to secure their water and ensure the success of their agricultural enterprises. The exact period of this prosperity, however, is unclear. Numerous inscriptions indicate that the Romans moved into the oasis soon after taking direct control of Egypt, and many of the temples and fortresses in the oasis date from the early or even pre-Roman period, yet most archaeological evidence dates from the late Roman period, during which Kharga seems to have experienced a rapid conversion to Christianity.

A word of caution concerning the term "fortress." Although no fewer than twenty such buildings still exist in the oasis, and although it is probable that soldiers were stationed at all or most of them, some scholars argue that their role as defensive structures is unproved and that their presence does not necessarily indicate that a high level of hostility or violence characterized the Roman occupation of the oasis.[15] Indeed, some historians have pointed out that in light of the limited evidence of the presence of a serious internal or external threat, the degree to which the Romans needed to defend their position in the oasis is uncertain.[16] As mentioned earlier, however, other sources reveal that during the declining years of the Roman Empire, the settlements in Kharga Oasis were raided with increasing frequency by desert tribes from the south and west.[17] If this was the case, and I believe it was, it helps explain the presence of the numerous fortresses that appear to date from the late Roman and early Byzantine periods. In addition, the fact that the largest fortresses were built near the base of the eastern escarpment might imply that the Romans thought the social and political upheavals in Upper Egypt posed a threat to the oasis. There is little doubt, however, that especially during the later part of the Roman era, the fortresses discussed below controlled access to and from the oasis, served as the military and administrative centers of the oasis settlements, and, to the extent that they incorporated religious temples, acted as spiritual centers as well.[18]

THE SOUTHERN SETTLEMENTS

El-Qasr

The southernmost Roman fort in the Kharga Oasis, El-Qasr is located approximately 15 kilometers southwest of Dush. The building measures 30 by 20 meters and features walls 9 meters high. An abundance of Roman-era pottery sherds attests to the age of the site, but until the structure is excavated, scholars will be unable to determine whether the site served primarily as a military station to guard against attacks from the south or whether it was intended to control commercial traffic along the Darb el-Arbain.[19]

Dush

Located 95 kilometers south of the modern town of Kharga, the temple, fortress, and surrounding town of Dush (ancient Kysis) are among the oldest Roman ruins in the oasis[20] (fig. 8.1). The temple was probably erected by Domitian and later added to by Trajan (A.D. 98–117) and Hadrian (A.D. 117–38). It consists of a monumental gateway leading to a courtyard that contains five columns, a second gate and courtyard, a hypostyle hall containing four columns, and the sanctuary itself. The building was originally dedicated to Osiris, whom the Greeks transformed into Serapis, but a column decorated during the reign of Trajan also honors Isis: "For the fortune of the Lord Emperor Caesar Nero . . . Trajan Optimus Augustus Germanicus Dacicus, under Marcus Ruffinus Lupus, Governor of Egypt, to Serapis and the supreme gods, those of [Cyrene?] having written, erected from a principal of piety this building. The nineteenth year of the Emperor Caesar Nero Adrian Optimus Augustus Germanicus Dacicus."[21]

The main temple is located within the massive mud-brick walls of a fortress that stands atop the only hill in a wide desert plain. In antiquity, this surrounding area consisted of agricultural land, and the fortress boasted a commanding view of both the fields and the thriving town of Kysis. (A second, much smaller Roman-era temple with vaulted ceilings lies a short distance from the fortress.) Portions of the fortress probably date from the Ptolemaic or even Persian period, but undoubtedly it reached its current dimensions during the Roman era. Situated at the terminus of five important desert roads, Dush was strategically positioned to protect a large segment of Roman Egypt's southern frontier in the Western Desert.

French archaeologists, excavating at Dush since 1976, have unearthed an impressive collection of pottery, ostraca, coins, and papyrus. In 1989, their efforts were further rewarded with the discovery of a gold-plated leaden statue of Isis wrapped in cloth, a small bronze statue of Horus, and another bronze statue of Osiris. Located near these objects, however, was a discovery of which archaeologists dream—a magnificent cache of religious jewelry, exquisitely crafted in gold and hidden in a large pottery vessel buried in the fortress. This Treasure of Dush, now on display in the Egyptian National Museum in Cairo, received international attention when it was discovered. In addition to their artistic value, these rare votive objects continue to provide scholars with an invaluable opportunity to further

8.1 The southern wall of the Roman fortress at Dush. In the foreground is a portion of the large quantity of broken pottery uncovered by French archaeologists.

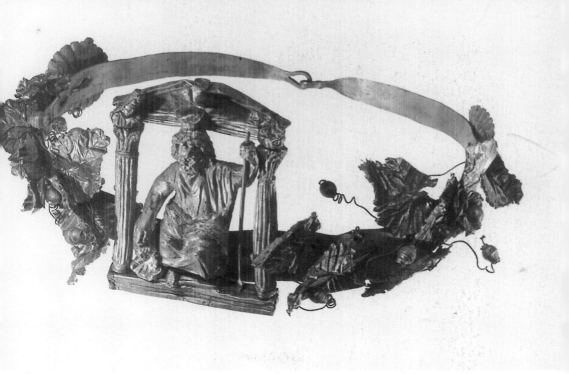

8.2 The exquisite golden crown discovered by French archaeologists
at Dush in 1989.

their knowledge of religious worship in Roman Egypt. The collection includes the
following items:[22]

1. A crown decorated by leaves along both sides, with a figure of Serapis
in the front. The god is seated between two columns that are surmounted by
small busts of Isis and connected by the architrave of a temple. Serapis's left
hand is elevated and holds a staff, while his right hand is lowered with its
fingers resting on the head of Harpocrate. The crown, which was worn by
priests during religious ceremonies, probably dates from the late first or
early second century A.D. (fig. 8.2);

2. Two bracelets, each decorated with leaves and inlaid with a large
piece of semiprecious stone. The setting of one of the bracelets is rectangular, as is the black stone it contains, while the other setting and its piece of
orange agate are circular. Both items probably date from the late first or
early second century A.D. (fig. 8.3);

3. Intact pendants originally designed to be worn on a thin wire or chain
around the neck. Most of the pendants are stylized busts of Serapis and Isis,
and many include depictions of the Apis bull and dovelike birds. The pendants probably date from the late second or early third century A.D.;

8.3 One of the two gold bracelets from Dush. The inlaid stone is orange agate.

4. A large, complete necklace consisting of seventy-seven pendants, mainly depicting the Apis bull and Serapis. Also affixed to the necklace is a coin, the obverse side of which displays a detailed profile of Faustina the Younger, the sole surviving daughter of Emperor Antoninus Pius (A.D. 138–61) and wife of the great philosopher-emperor Marcus Aurelius (A.D. 161–80).[23] The reverse side depicts the goddess Cybele seated at a throne with two lions crouching at her feet. Along the edge of the coin are the Latin words MATRI MAGNAE, meaning Great Mother. As suggested by the presence of the coin, the necklace probably dates from the late second or early third century A.D. (fig. 8.4).

Less spectacular, although collectively no less important, was the discovery of hundreds of ostraca from the two temple courtyards. A few Demotic and Coptic ostraca were recovered, but the great majority were written in Greek and appear to date from the early fourth to the early fifth centuries A.D. For the most part, these ostraca consist of receipts and payment orders relating to the grain supply of the Roman army, but there are also lists of names of soldiers and civilians. In addition to an interesting blend of Egyptian, Greek, and Roman names, these lists include numerous biblical Hebrew names, evidence that Christianity was

8.4 The necklace discovered at Dush features seventy-seven pendants, most of which depict the Apis Bull and Serapis.

firmly in place at Dush, and possibly throughout the oasis, in the fourth century. An occasional, brief private letter also appears in the ostraca from Dush, and more than any other type of document these enable one to peek through a key-hole in the door of history and recognize its most human elements. In the example below, an official writes a private letter to a dishonest tax collector, chastising him for cheating someone by falsely measuring their grain: "To my lord, my brother Chrestos, Peteuris greets you. You acted badly when you deceived our brother Kephalos on his measure of wheat, and therefore, hurry to satisfy him. I wish you good health."[24]

The five desert roads that intersect at Dush originated at Esna, Edfu, Aswan (via Kurkur Oasis), Tumas (approximately 20 kilometers north of Qasr Ibrim but on the west bank of the Nile), and Darfur in the Sudan (see map 4). Given the steepness of the escarpment that lies approximately ten kilometers east of Dush, and the great distance from the edge of the escarpment to the Nile Valley, few western travelers have attempted these crossings during the past century. Today, even the local Egyptians travel to the Nile by bus or automobile along one of two paved roads located further north. Nevertheless, the ancient routes are known to a handful of men in Kharga, and on occasion some of them still make the arduous journey. In 1979, a team of French scholars visiting Dush encountered a small caravan that had traveled from Esna (ancient Latopolis) with the intention of selling several camels in Kharga.[25] In addition, the frequent occurrence of bleached camel skeletons attests not only to the route's waterless desolation, but to its continued, albeit rare, use into modern times.[26]

Of the five desert routes that intersect at Dush, the Darb el-Dush, which connected Dush with Esna and Edfu, was the most important and the most heavily traveled during the Roman period. Archaeologists working at Dush have uncovered graffiti and ostraca indicating that the fortress was manned by troops sent out from the larger garrisons at Esna and Edfu (ancient Latopolis and Apollonopolis Magna) in the Nile Valley.[27] This route actually begins approximately ten kilometers east-northeast of the fortress, at the base of a boulder-covered natural ramp leading up the escarpment.[28] Over many centuries, the strong north wind has deposited enormous quantities of sand over certain portions of this ramp, but in other places the narrow trail is still visible, as are numerous stone cairns. No doubt most of these route markers are not ancient, but at least one large, well-built cairn about halfway up the route appears to date from the Roman period (fig. 8.5). Pottery sherds dating from the third through the fifth centuries A.D.—and occasional pieces from as early as the first century A.D.—are also abundant along the trail. The path to the top of the escarpment rises steeply in an easterly direction, then, once close to the summit, turns northward, traversing a short

8.5 One of the stone cairns that mark the ancient route up the escarpment at the beginning of the Darb el-Dush.

plain of wind-eroded stone before actually reaching the narrow corridor called Bab el-Dush (Door of Dush), which brings one to the plateau itself. Because of the heavy drifting of sand along the route, it is difficult to determine how long the ascent might have taken in antiquity, particularly with heavily laden camels, which are not by nature well suited to ascending or descending steep inclines. Today, unencumbered by a pack or animal and assuming one knows the trail, one can reach the top of the escarpment in two hours.

From the Bab el-Dush, stone cairns and broken pottery mark the numerous trails that pick their way eastward across the plateau toward the Nile. Initially, the terrain is among the most treacherous in the Western Desert. A constant north wind blows sand across the jagged stone surface of the plateau, scouring the limestone into long, knife-edged ridges and sculpting boulders and other protrusions into fantastic, otherworldly designs. But 15 kilometers further east, the difficult terrain gives way to an eight-kilometer-wide, gravel-floored depression, beyond which the ancient camel tracks head east-northeast across alternating sandy and gravelly terrain. Cleared roads of uncertain age cross these gravel plains. Approximately 40 kilometers from Bab el-Dush, a wide track branches off to the southeast toward Aswan, some 180 kilometers away. The main route gradually bends to the northeast, and after 100 kilometers the trail splits, the northern branch heading to Esna and the second branch heading almost due east to Edfu. Although no evidence of wells has ever been discovered along this route, the Romans probably maintained tented camps or water stations at intervals of approximately 30 kilometers, with larger rest stops being located at the intersections of major caravan trails. While a thorough study of such stations along the Darb el-Dush has yet to be completed, they can be identified along other routes in the Western Desert by the sudden appearance of enormous quantities of broken amphorae. The soldiers who used this route to march from Esna and Edfu to Dush would have taken seven or eight days for the journey, but a rider on a fast camel could have covered the distance in less than three days.[29]

The second major route into Dush came from Selima Oasis in the Sudan but originated in Darfur. During the Middle Ages, this became the famous Darb el-Arbain, or Forty Days Road, so named because it took approximately that amount of time to travel its distance between Darfur and Assiut in the Nile Valley (approximately 1,800 km). Along its way north, it passed through Bir Natrun, Lagia, Selima Oasis, and Kharga Oasis. Until the nineteenth century, slave dealers dragged their pitiable human merchandise northward along this stretch, while in the twentieth century the road enabled smugglers to haul natron and salt into Egypt. Although it was used from the early Pharaonic period until modern times, no evidence has yet been uncovered that could shed light on the importance of this route during the Roman period.[30] During the period of the Meroitic Kingdom, the Nile was probably the primary trade route across Roman Egypt's southern border—although illegal traffic may have taken desert routes in the hope of bypassing the customs stations along the river. After Meroë collapsed in the fourth century, however, and traffic along the river was disrupted by the Blemmye occupation of the former Meroitic lands, it is possible that trade along the Darb el-Arbain might have increased accordingly.

During the nineteenth century, two major caravans per year traveled along this route.[31] Consisting of thousands of camels, each caravan was divided into two or three large groups that traveled several days apart so that the wells along the route would not be exhausted. In 1817, the great French explorer F. Cailliaud witnessed the arrival in Assiut of an enormous caravan that had traversed the Darb el-Arbain from Darfur. The caravan consisted of sixteen thousand people, including six thousand slaves: "They had been two months travelling in the deserts, in the most intense heat of the year; meager, exhausted, and the aspect of death on their countenances, the spectacle strongly excited compassion."[32]

8.6 The entrance to the sandstone temple at Qasr el-Zaiyan
in the southern Kharga Oasis.

Qasr el-Zaiyan

Moving north along the main route from Dush, the Roman-era traveler would
have encountered numerous wells and small farming villages at which to rest or
spend the night. Today, the ruins of Qasr el-Zaiyan, one of the largest and most
important of these settlements, can still be seen approximately 75 kilometers due
north of Dush (see map 4). The site contains a small sandstone temple dating
from the Ptolemaic period; it was restored during the reign of Antoninus Pius
(fig. 8.6). A Greek inscription above the south-facing entrance to the temple is
dated August 11, A.D. 140, and states that the temple was dedicated to Amenebis
(Ammon of Hibis), who was the god of Tchonemyris, the unexcavated ancient
town that surrounded the temple: "To Amenebis, the great god of Tchonemyris,
and to the other gods of the temple, for the eternal preservation of Antoninus Caesar our Lord, and his whole house. The cell of the temple and the vestibule were
repaired and renewed under Avidius Heliodorus, governor of Egypt; Septimius
Macro being commander-in-chief, Plinius Capito being general of the forces, in
the third year of the Emperor Caesar Titus Aelius Adrianus Antonius Augustus,
the Pius."[33] The name Tchonemyris corresponds closely to the ancient Egyptian

name Takhoneourit, meaning "the great well," indicating its importance as a major source of water in antiquity.[34] Even today, the site stands amidst well-watered cultivated fields. In light of the availability of water and the sizable population that must have inhabited this prosperous ancient town, it is not surprising that a major desert road led from Qasr el-Zaiyan directly east to Esna.

Qasr el-Ghieita

Northward, the next major Roman settlement was Qasr el-Ghieita, a magnificent fortress that stands atop a prominent hill and dominates the surrounding desert plain. The fort, which possibly served as the headquarters for a Roman garrison, consists mainly of numerous mud-brick buildings and rooms contained within a high surrounding wall. As is common with such structures, the high mud-brick walls of the fortress enclose a small, much older temple. In this case, the temple dates from the reign of Darius I (521–486 B.C.) but also contains the names of several Ptolemaic monarchs, including Ptolemy III (246–222 B.C.), Ptolemy IV (222–205 B.C.), and Ptolemy X (reigned twice: 116–107 B.C. and 88–80 B.C.). The sandstone temple was dedicated to the Theban Triad of Amun, Mut, and Khonsu—the same gods to which the great temple of Karnak in Luxor was dedicated—and consists of a courtyard, a richly decorated hypostyle hall containing four columns with exquisite capitals, and a sanctuary.

Today, the wells that brought life to this ancient settlement still provide enough water to sustain a sizable community of farmers who cultivate the land immediately below the fortress and temple and who live a life not significantly different from that of their ancient ancestors (fig. 8.7). Yet just beyond their hard-wrought, verdant fields, the desert looms menacingly in all directions. Its constant presence makes it even more remarkable that long before the Roman period, this was a large and prosperous agricultural town. During the Middle Kingdom (2050–1786 B.C.), for example, Qasr el-Ghieita was called Per-ousekh and was famous throughout Egypt for the excellent wine that came from its vineyards.[35] Unfortunately, the results of recent excavations by the Egyptian Supreme Council of Antiquities have not yet been published, so little is known about the role Qasr el-Ghieita may have played during the Roman occupation of the oasis.

HIBIS AND ITS ENVIRONS

Hibis Temple

Situated on a plain at the southern end of Gebel el-Teir (Mountain of the Birds) and shaded by palm groves, the majestic Hibis temple is among the most impor-

8.7 The hilltop fortress of Qasr el-Ghieita.

tant ancient structures in the Western Desert (fig. 8.8). Built of sandstone on
the edge of a small sacred lake and dedicated to the god Amon-Ra, the earliest
temple was probably begun by Pharaoh Apries in 588 B.C.; it was completed by the
Persian king Darius I, who ruled Egypt as a province from 521 to 486 B.C. and
whose name appears in the decorations on the temple walls.[36] The main temple
lies on an east-west axis and measures 45 by 20 meters, with walls 6 meters
high. Three separate pylons stand just east of the main entrance. In antiquity, the
temple was the center of the town of Hibis (or Hibiton Polis), "the city of the
plow," the ancient capital of the Great Oasis. Although much of the town is now
buried under agricultural land, excavations in and around the temple have furnished researchers with a wealth of information concerning the history of the
site.[37] The temple itself contains numerous inscriptions from the Roman period.[38] In one well-known example, a certain Cnoeus Virgilius Capito wrote the
following:

> I have both heard long ago some unjust expenses and false charges to be
> made by certain persons avariciously and shamefully abusing their powers:
> and I have just now been informed, that in the territory of the Libyans cer-
> tain things are consumed by those seizing them under pretense, as it
> were, because of their necessities, as being set apart for their expenses and

8.8 Hibis Temple.

entertainment; which charges are neither true nor admissible: and in like manner under the name of the service of couriers. Wherefore I command those traveling through the nomes, soldiers, and horsemen, and sergeants, and centurions, and tribunes, and all others, to take nothing nor to exact the privileges of couriers, except certain have my warrants; and these passing along only indeed to be accommodated with lodging: and that it be laid down, that no man do anything, beyond what were established by Maximus. But if any individual may give, or consider anything as given, and exact as for the public services, I will exact ten times the amount of what he has exacted from the nome, and give a four-fold portion to the informer out of the property of the condemned. The royal scribes, and the village clerks, and the clerks of the districts in each nome, shall keep a register of all that is expended by the nome upon any one: that, if this or any thing else has been irregularly committed, they may be recorded, and may repay sixty-fold. But the inhabitants of the Thebaid may four months come up to the tribunals of accounts: and let them address themselves to Basilides, the freedman of Caesar, an officer of the tribunal of accounts, and to the comptrollers; that, if any thing may be adjudged or done contrary to what is just, I may in like manner put this in order.[39]

Another outstanding discovery was a complete wooden codex, written in Greek, which contained two separate texts.[40] While the second of these is simply an accounting list of names and sums of money, the first text is a draft of an official report written circa A.D. 246/249 by a government official named Aurelius Geminus. It was written for two individuals named Marcellus and Salutaris, the ranking members of a special commission based in Alexandria, who were charged with reinvigorating Egyptian agriculture in the wake of a period of decreased production and tax yields. As part of a broader survey of agricultural resources in Egypt, the commission asked Aurelius to examine the condition of water sources in and around the capital of this remote oasis. Upon completing his survey, Aurelius made this draft of his notes, then wrote the formal report on papyrus before sending it to Alexandria. The text begins with a phrase that translates approximately to, "In response to the letter from . . . , I report . . . " and consists of a list of the names, locations, and conditions of eighty-six basins or pools of artesian water in the vicinity of Hibis. Interestingly, he discovered that while some of these reservoirs were located amid cultivated land, almost 75 percent of them existed in either unused desert or in land that had once been cultivated but for some reason had been abandoned. On the basis of this information, one could assume that the agricultural commission might have taken steps requiring the more efficient use of existing water sources, thus increasing the amount of land under cultivation. Unfortunately, Aurelius's account does not include any such information, and no archaeological evidence has hinted that reforms were attempted.[41]

It is unclear how long Hibis remained the capital of the oasis. Excavations of the Christian-era buildings south of the main temple, which appear to date from approximately A.D. 350, revealed that the structures were destroyed by a great fire. Quite possibly, therefore, the destruction of the town occurred as a result of the Blemmye invasion of A.D. 450, during which the invaders sacked the ancient town and carried off numerous inhabitants as prisoners, including the exiled Nestorius. This attack marked the beginning of the gradual disintegration of the temple and the city, as the burned houses were not rebuilt and water from nearby fields was permitted to settle close to the temple, saturating the foundation and ultimately causing the collapse of the temple's portico and roof.[42] All this destruction, however, does not necessarily mean that Hibis was abandoned, as the following Coptic graffito, discovered in the foothills of nearby Gebel el-Teir, suggests: "In the year of Diocletian 500+, I Severus, the son of the Pagarch of Hibis. . . ."[43] The presence of a *Pagarch*, or chief administrative officer, in Hibis sometime between A.D. 784 and 883[44] may mean that the town continued to survive for hundreds of years after the Blemmye invasion.

Nadoura

Just two kilometers southeast of Hibis stand two temples and the buried remains of the small settlement of Nadoura, meaning "The Lookout." The main temple, standing strategically atop a hill and offering an excellent view of Hibis and the surrounding farmland, was constructed during the reign of Antoninus Pius. The crumbling walls enclose a courtyard containing a three-room sandstone temple. The inside walls of the temple contain numerous figures and hieroglyphics, but the most interesting feature of the temple is an unusual bas-relief located on the lintel above the southwest entrance. Although badly damaged, it depicts two standing figures (one is male, the second either male or female) facing forward. One early traveler remarked that they possessed "something of the roundness and character of Grecian sculpture."[45] The heads and lower legs of each are effaced, but above each figure is an arch resembling a small rainbow or a large halo. Just above the arch of the right-hand figure is a horizontal row of four stars. Scholars have been unable to determine whom the figures represent.

Bagawat

One kilometer north of Hibis, near the southern base of Gebel el-Teir, stands a church surrounded by a vast expanse of domed, mud-brick mausoleums, constituting the oldest major Christian cemetery in the world. The tombs date from between the fourth and seventh centuries A.D., and although they were built in a variety of styles, most consist of a small chapel built over the tomb. Many exteriors of the buildings have ornate facades complete with faux columns and arches, all constructed of mud brick (fig. 8.9). The buildings lie on either side of a series of interconnecting narrow streets, giving one the eerie feeling of walking through a deserted town. Inside the mausoleums, the actual tombs were located beneath the earthen floors and consisted of a deep, central pit, the sides of which contained shelves for the body or bodies and the various items, such as pottery, with which the bodies were interred. Sadly, virtually all of the 263 tombs at Bagawat have been plundered over the centuries by thieves searching for valuable ornaments and coins that might have been buried with their owners. In the process, the thieves dug up the embalmed mummies, broke them apart, and then threw them outside to decay—thus destroying a great deal of valuable archaeological information pertaining to the Christian community in Kharga. Indeed, the fact that Christians adhered to the ancient pagan ritual of embalming is in itself a rather remarkable discovery: "The introduction of Christianity produced great and sudden changes in the minds, habits, and customs of believers; but a length of time was no doubt often necessary to root out many of the prejudices of the people; and it

8.9 Ornate facades in the Christian cemetery of Bagawat in Kharga Oasis.

is very possible, that the practice of embalming may have been continued as a necessary mark of respect to the dead, long after the doctrine had been entirely exploded, in accordance with which the custom had originally been established."[46]

Several of the mausoleums feature vivid paintings of biblical scenes on their plaster walls and domes. The two with the most impressive paintings are the chapel of the Exodus and the chapel of Peace. The interior of the dome of the chapel of the Exodus is decorated with an astonishing array of scenes, mostly from the Old Testament: Adam and Eve, Noah's Ark, Pharaoh Ramses II and his army, Moses, the Israelites in the Sinai, Abraham and Isaac, Daniel in the lion's den, Jonah in the whale, Job, Sarah in prayer, and the martyrdom of Saint Thekla. Similarly, the chapel of Peace, which stands in the southwest corner of the necropolis, contains at least fifteen biblical scenes, including the sacrifice of Isaac, Adam and Eve after the Fall, and the Annunciation of the Virgin Mary (fig. 8.10).

In addition to the paintings, numerous graffiti and inscriptions are still legible on the crumbling walls:[47]

"If God is for us, who can be against us?"[48]
"[Christ] Remember us, Lord, when your kingdom comes."

8.10 Scenes from the Old Testament painted on the interior dome of the chapel of Peace in Bagawat.

"I am Kyros, son of Athanasius, a most humble fisherman; God help me and Esdra and, make our final voyage a good one."

In the foothills of Gebel el-Teir, two kilometers behind the necropolis of Bagawat, hundreds of Demotic, Greek, and Coptic graffiti, spanning more than seven centuries, can still be seen on the boulders and rock faces nestled in a narrow, dead-end valley that served as an ancient limestone quarry. The Demotic texts are divided into two main periods, the first dating from Ptolemy VIII (145 B.C.), and the second from the reigns of Augustus (27 B.C.–A.D. 14) and Tiberius (A.D. 14–37). The majority of the Greek texts were written during the first two centuries A.D. Although many of the texts are merely names, several are of particular historical importance. A Demotic graffito, for example, dates from the reign of Cleopatra VII and contains the oldest known use of the word "Kysis," the ancient name for Dush.[49] Other texts carry the voices of their ancient authors across the centuries. A Greek inscription, for example, attests to the use of this site as a quarry, "Good luck to all the quarrymen," while another records the presence of "Heraklion, the good and the intelligent."[50] Predictably, most of the Christian graffiti are in Coptic, but the following text dating from the late Roman period was written in

Demotic: "Jesus Christ. Esdra the priest. Apa Papnouthiou, assistant of Esdra the priest."[51] Interestingly, Father Esdra's name also appears elsewhere in the quarry and at Bagawat.

Tahunet el-Hawa and Columbarium

Looking north from the highest point at Bagawat, one can see the ruins of the monastery of Mustafa Kachef, a Christian-era fortress, and approximately two kilometers beyond, a high tower, Tahunet el-Hawa, standing on the open plain west of Gebel el-Teir. Built of mud brick, the tower measures 6 meters by 6 meters at the base and contains a single entrance on the south side; the structure rises to a height of 12 meters. Although empty now, it originally contained several floors connected by a staircase. The tower has never been thoroughly studied by archaeologists, so the date of its construction and its actual purpose are not known. Certainly its primary function was that of a watchtower and signal tower. But because it stands at the approximate intersection of two major desert routes—one leading north from Hibis to the large settlement of Ain Umm Dabadib, another heading west along the southernmost route to the Dakhleh Oasis—the tower might also have functioned as a sort of lighthouse, guiding desert travelers into the main oasis at night (fig. 8.11).[52]

Several kilometers northeast of Tahunet el-Hawa stands another unusual structure, a well-preserved columbarium, or pigeon house. The base of its walls measures approximately 5 meters by 5 meters, and the building reaches a maximum height of roughly 7 meters. Numerous small niches inside the structure were nesting spaces for the pigeons, and a central staircase enabled workers to collect the large amounts of guano the birds produced, which was used as fertilizer.

THE NORTHERN SETTLEMENTS

El-Deir (Deir el-Ghanayim)

Twenty kilometers northeast of the capital city of Hibis is the enormous fortress known today as El-Deir, "the monastery."[53] Located near the foot of the eastern escarpment, just north of Gebel Umm el-Ghanayim, El-Deir appears to have guarded the beginning of the main desert road that headed east across the desert to Farshut and the caravan route to Assiut, which exited the northernmost portion of the Kharga depression via the Ramia pass.[54] The site has never been excavated, so the exact date and purpose of its construction are unknown. Most likely, the fortress dates from the reign of Diocletian (A.D. 284–305) (fig. 8.12).[55]

8.11 The Roman-era tower (Tahunet el-Hawa) in Kharga Oasis.

8.12 The large fortress of El-Deir guarded the point where the Farshut road from the Nile Valley entered the Kharga depression.

The mud-brick fortress is rectangular and boasts twelve rounded towers, one at each corner and two at intermediate positions along each of its unusually thick walls.[56] Entrances are located on the northern, eastern, and western sides. A wide parapet surmounted the walls, accessible by staircases from the interior of the fortress. Inside, a spacious courtyard contained a deep well and numerous chambers. Although most of the interior has crumbled, several rooms on the southern side of the courtyard remain intact. The plastered walls of these rooms do not contain ancient inscriptions, but they are covered with graffiti left by British soldiers who were stationed at the fortress during World War I to defend the oasis against attacks by the Sanussi of Libya.[57]

To the north and west of the fortress are the remains of large, cultivated fields. These were irrigated by means of an ingenious system of three underground tunnels that converged at the well in the courtyard of the fortress. As the tunnels approached the surface of the low-lying fields, they took the form of trenches covered with flat stones to prevent them from becoming clogged with blown sand.

Behind El-Deir, to the northeast, a pass makes its way to the top of the escarpment. This was the beginning of the shortest and probably the most important ancient route to the Nile Valley from Kharga. It arrived at the Nile near Farshut, then joined the Farshut–Luxor road, which headed south, cutting across the base of the river's great Qena bend, and finally terminated on the west bank of the Nile slightly north of Luxor (ancient Thebes). There, at the edge of the plateau, just before the trail descends to the river, archaeologists have discovered the remains of a Roman tower that commanded a superb view of the valley below. The presence of the tower, which appears to date from the late third century A.D., may point to the existence of a Roman military or police force to control incoming and outgoing traffic along the desert road and possibly to patrol the road as a precaution against brigands.[58] Whether such a force might also have guarded the Farshut to Kharga portion of the road is at present unknown, but the presence of the fortress at El-Deir implies that the security of the route was an important concern during the Roman period.

Qasr el-Sumeria and Qasr el-Geb

The two small, unexcavated fortresses at Qasr el-Sumeria and Qasr el-Geb are the most northern of the Roman outposts in Kharga. The more southerly of the two, El Sumeria, stands amid a sea of pottery in the middle of the narrow, upper reaches of the depression, approximately 45 kilometers north of Hibis, and directly on the ancient route that enters and exits the depression via the Ramia pass. Built on the desert floor, the mud-brick building is square, its walls measuring 14 meters long and 7 meters high, and contains several rooms, all of which are now collapsed and filled with sand and debris. Aside from the rounded towers at its corners and an entrance in the center of the southern wall, the structure contains few distinguishing architectural or decorative features.

Located two kilometers north of El Sumeria is the fortress of El Geb. In antiquity, it was the last source of water in the depression. Although similar in structure to El Sumeria, El Geb is larger and was built atop a hill, from which the guards within could easily observe all of the terrain between the eastern and western escarpments and thus detect anyone attempting to enter or exit the depression via the Ramia pass. The eastern wall is now totally collapsed, but the remaining walls are in good condition and retain such important features as a beautifully constructed arched doorway in the center of the southern wall and a stairway leading up to the parapet that encircled the top of the fortress. Like El Sumeria, the fortress is square, and its thick walls, which measure 17 meters long and attain a maximum height of 11 meters, feature rounded towers at each corner. Inside, one can still see the inner courtyard, the remains of six vaulted chambers along the eastern and western walls, and the holes that held the wooden beams supporting the upper floors.

Ain Mohammed Toleib

Located some 18 kilometers north of Hibis, at approximately the same latitude as El-Deir (15 kilometers to the east), are the ruins of a late Roman village now called Ain Mohammed Toleib. The two-story rectangular fortress stood at the center of a larger settlement than either of those at El Sumeria and El Geb. Like them, however, it was situated along the main caravan route heading to Assiut.

Qasr Labekha

Midway between Ain Mohammed Toleib and El Sumeria, but approximately 12 kilometers to the west, is the splendid settlement of Qasr Labekha, which lies in a wadi near the base of the northern escarpment (see map 4). Labekha's strategic location suggests that it served as an important checkpoint and as a garrison for troops assigned to guard the intersection of two important caravan routes: one that entered Kharga from the north and continued south to the capital at Hibis, and a second that headed west from Labekha toward Dakhleh Oasis.

At the northern end of the settlement, an impressive three-room temple dating possibly from the third century A.D. rests atop a hill dominating the wadi floor. A second, rock-cut temple, completed during the reign of Antoninus Pius and still featuring some of its original painting, is located on a low hill to the west of the settlement.[59] The fortress stands a kilometer further south, beyond the silted remains of an enormous well that appears to have provided most of the water needed to support the sizable community that once lived here. Just south of the fortress, thorn bushes struggle to survive in the drifting sand, and a cluster of palm trees taps what little groundwater remains, standing guard over these silent, mysterious ruins. Although much smaller than the fortress of El-Deir, Labekha's high walls and massive rounded towers bear a strong similarity to its eastern neighbor (fig. 8.13). The entrance is on the eastern wall, but inside, the fortress is a chaos of collapsed walls and chambers that have never been excavated. Recently, Egyptian archaeologists from the Supreme Council of Antiquities have begun studying the area immediately below the western and southern walls on the outside of the fortress. Their efforts have unearthed several small statues and large quantities of pottery, most of it late Roman. Detailed descriptions of these and other artifacts have not yet been published (fig. 8.14).

Clustered throughout the low, rocky hills that form the western limit of the Labekha settlement are at least fifty-three ancient tombs. Although most were simple chambers hewn into the solid rock, several were constructed with multiple chambers and vaulted ceilings and in some cases decorated with plaster walls and painted with religious symbols (fig. 8.15). Many of the tombs still contain

8.13 The fortress at Qasr Labekha.

8.14 A late-Roman-period vessel near the fortress at Qasr Labekha.

8.15 A tomb in the hills west of Qasr Labekha.

mummies in excellent condition, but it appears that virtually all of the burial chambers have been ransacked by thieves, some very recently. Egypt's Supreme Council of Antiquities is making an effort to excavate as many of the tombs as they can in order to recover whatever artifacts might be of archaeological or artistic value. They have discovered painted burial masks and beautiful statues depicting various divinities, but, again, photographs and detailed descriptions of these artifacts have not been published.[60]

There are several desert tracks leading west from Labekha toward the settlement of Ain Umm Dabadib (see map 4). The main route first heads southwest, then turns northwest in a wide arc that would have enabled camel caravans to circumvent the numerous fingerlike ridges extending several kilometers southward from the escarpment. At least two other tracks from Labekha, however, head almost due west, requiring a traveler to ascend and descend the many ridges between the two settlements. These shorter, more arduous trails were probably used by messengers and small groups of individuals traveling on foot or by donkey. Although the stone cairns still marking these trails are of uncertain date, numerous pictographs and graffiti as well as Roman-era pottery sherds along the paths attest to their use in antiquity. One recent scholar identified Coptic, Latin, and hieroglyphic graffiti along one of these tracks.[61]

Ain Umm Dabadib

Approximately 20 kilometers due west of Labekha, situated at the base of the northern escarpment, is the expansive settlement known today as Ain Umm Dabadib (see map 4). Nestled in the northern reaches of a wide, flat plain that is bordered on the east by a long ridge of the escarpment and on the west by fields of high sand dunes, this magnificent site was once a bustling, well-populated town. Today, its buildings are slowly crumbling into the sandy earth from which they were raised, inhabited only by snakes and scorpions lurking within its deserted chambers and by skinny foxes that scurry along its silent, ruined alleys in the cool of the night.

As at Labekha, the fortress at Dabadib stands at the southern end of the settlement. Even today it is an imposing structure, with walls measuring 20 meters long and 13 meters high. Unlike Labekha, however, the Dabadib fortress and the smaller buildings that stood below its southern and western walls were all contained within an enclosure wall measuring approximately 100 meters per side, whose entrance is to the south. In addition, the four massive towers at the corners of the fortress are rectangular, not rounded, thus rendering Dabadib the only structure of its style in the Western Desert and suggesting that it is of more recent construction than the other fortresses in the oases (fig. 8.16). The southeastern tower is the best preserved of the four and still contains the remnants of a spiral staircase leading to its summit, while a window near the top opens onto a panoramic view of the vast expanse of desert to the south. The upper stories of the fortress have collapsed, but several rooms at or beneath ground level remain intact.

Numerous tombs and buildings, some with vaulted roofs, dot the landscape to the east of the fort, while just next to it are the remains of a small church. Until recently, this structure was partly buried in sand. Sometime in 1998, however, treasure hunters used heavy equipment to break through walls and dig into the floor in search of artifacts. The damage is extensive but the church survives. Inside, the crumbling walls and pillars retain some of their original red-painted plaster. Some of the walls also contain Greek and Coptic graffiti, consisting mainly of names, such as, "I am Isaiah" and "John, son of Serge," but also a few invocations, such as, "Lord Jesus Christ, help the unhappy Papnoute."[62]

Half a kilometer north of the fortress are the ruins of the ancient town, containing hundreds of small buildings that served as homes and shops. Flanking the town on the west is an improbable row of enormous trees, and beyond these, a wide, flat plain extends southward past the fortress. Within this area, one can still see the square outlines of countless cultivated plots and the irrigation trenches that watered them. Standing on the cracked soil of this once-fertile plain, with

Figure 8.16 The fortress at Ain Umm Dabadib. The spiral staircase inside the highest corner tower remains partially intact.

ears ringing in the total silence of the desert, one cannot help but marvel at the extraordinary amount of determination, planning, and labor required of the ancient residents of Dabadib to survive and prosper in this desert. The secret to their success was their ability to obtain large quantities of water by digging an elaborate network of underground aqueducts.

Aqueducts are found elsewhere in Kharga and at other oases in the Western Desert, most notably at Bahariya. But none approach the magnitude and sophistication of the aqueducts at Ain Umm Dabadib. Four separate, parallel tunnels began in or near the cultivated areas and ran north to the escarpment along the sides of three narrow valleys. The first and longest tunnel began approximately 500 meters west of the fortress and covered a distance of approximately 6 kilometers. The second began just north of the village, and the third and fourth began 500 meters east of the settlement and headed north along opposite sides of a single valley. In total, the four tunnels, all of which are now dry, wind and bend for 15 kilometers underground, their locations being easily identified from the surface by the regular occurrence of vertical shafts that served as air vents and as a means of access into the tunnels, both during construction and later to keep them clear of silt.[63]

In 1900, a local Kharga sheikh named Hassan Hanadi hoped to get enough water flowing through one of the aqueducts to cultivate a small tract of land nearby. He employed seventy-five men for the task, and they labored at it for the entire summer of that year.[64] Today, as a result of their efforts, this aqueduct, the second from the west, is the only one of the four that can be entered, albeit at considerable risk. The aqueduct begins just north of the settlement and zigzags through several kilometers of solid, multicolored rock. At its entrance, the tunnel is about 2 meters high by more than 0.5 meter wide, although it tapers in at the bottom—forming a distinct coffin shape (fig. 8.17). Gradually the tunnel narrows to the extent that one must proceed sideways. Every 20 to 30 meters, the ceiling gives way to rectangular air shafts measuring roughly 1.5 by 0.75 meters in diameter and rising to the surface of the desert floor. Although a few of the shafts are open to the sky, most are still covered by large flat stones, placed there to prevent the tunnel from filling with sand. As one proceeds northward along the tunnel, the land above gradually rises, so the air shafts become correspondingly deeper, causing the air within the tunnels to become more oppressive. At the northernmost end of the tunnel, the shafts leading from the surface are more than 50 meters deep. Within the final half kilometer, the tunnel floor becomes damp from water seepage and rises closer to the ceiling as a result of years of silting. At this point, one can proceed only, first, by crawling on hands and knees, then slithering on one's stomach through the narrow channel, until finally the way is entirely blocked by sand that has blown down an open shaft and filled the tunnel.[65]

Although it is no longer possible to reach the end of the aqueduct without extensive digging, a British hydrologist who wished to determine not only how the water entered the tunnel but also whether its final meters contained any valuable inscriptions, penetrated the tunnel to its termination in 1908. After being lowered down the ninth air shaft from the escarpment by means of a windlass, he proceeded north and recorded his journey as follows:

The air was bad enough at the start, but seemed to get worse as we proceeded. I trusted, however, to finding a distinct improvement in the neighbourhood of the shafts, but to my dismay each one in turn proved to be hermetically sealed with masses of rock just above its junction with the tunnel, and there was not the slightest suspicion of any circulation of air, so that the only relief they afforded was the possibility of resting in an upright position. Three hundred metres, as I afterward calculated the total distance to be, may seem little enough in the open, but to grope one's way this distance by the light of a feeble candle along a passage so restricted that one has to proceed not only with bent head and shoulders, but half sideways, in a hot, steamy, stagnant atmosphere, is quite a different matter. My

8.17 Inside one of the four underground aqueducts that supplied water for the
ancient inhabitants at Ain Umm Dabadib.

companion, being of small build and stature, was able to walk upright in comparative comfort, without continually bumping his head and bruising his shoulders, so that the want of air did not tell on him to the same extent; while I became more and more fatigued, owing to the difficulty experienced of getting sufficient oxygen from such an atmosphere in the cramped position I had of necessity to assume. On more than one occasion I sank exhausted into the water, the huge gasps of breath which I took seeming powerless to relieve the horrible sensation of stifling, and with the unpleasant prospect of getting drowned if I escaped suffocation. Yet there seemed to be ten thousand devils tempting me onwards, and although I did not know how long life could be supported under such conditions, a mad desire possessed me to see the thing through; so that whenever I was able to progress a few yards it was towards the head of the tunnel.

When finally we reached our destination, some 15 to 20 metres beyond the last man-hole, it was only to find that the tunnel just stopped. There was no more water emerging from the rock at the end than I had seen entering at a dozen small fissures along the course we had traversed; there was no vertical excavation downwards; there were no traces of inscriptions; nothing, in fact. After all our trouble, we had drawn a blank.[66]

Although it is often assumed that the aqueducts of Dabadib were hewn during the Roman occupation, this theory has yet to be proven. The similarity between these tunnels and those used in ancient Persia have led some scholars to speculate that the Dabadib irrigation system actually dates from the reign of Darius I (521–486 B.C.), the Persian builder of the Hibis Temple. Given, however, that archaeologists began excavating at Ain Umm Dabadib in 1998, perhaps their efforts will soon yield answers to these and many other questions concerning the age and purpose of this fascinating settlement.

Routes Leading to and from Ain Umm Dabadib

Ain Umm Dabadib stood at the intersection of two major desert roads. The first, discussed above, arrived at Dabadib from the fortress of Labekha, continued west toward the temple and settlement of Ain Amur, and eventually arrived at Dakhleh Oasis. The second road led directly to the capital at Hibis, approximately 45 kilometers to the south-southeast, passing the eastern foothills of Gebel Tarif (Mountain of the Border) along the way.[67] Where these roads entered the broad wadi in which Ain Umm Dabadib is located, it appears that guards were posted at stations to observe and possibly control access to the settlement. The remains of these circular stone structures can be seen about one kilometer south of the Dabadib fortress on the road to Hibis and approximately five kilometers southwest of the fortress on the road to Ain Amur. In addition to the two roads just mentioned, at least one track headed northwest from Dabadib, climbed the steep face of the escarpment, and, after approximately 70 kilometers, connected with the Darb el-Tawil, or Long Road, which linked Dakhleh Oasis with Beni Adi in the Nile Valley.[68]

The route from Dabadib to Ain Amur is roughly 50 kilometers long. Initially, it passes through enormous dune fields before reaching the flat, stone-littered plains that characterize most of the route prior to its arrival at the base of the Abu Tartur Plateau. Although this track was probably used extensively in antiquity, a more southerly road, which originated at Hibis, actually served as the main road to Ain Amur. As we shall see below, this latter road was one of two principal routes from Kharga to Dakhleh Oasis.

Ain Amur

Dramatically situated on a broad ledge halfway up the northern slopes of the Abu Tartur Plateau, Ain Amur is the most remote and enchanting ancient site in the Western Desert (see map 4).[69] Although severely damaged by centuries of flash floods and rock slides that, on rare occasions, thunder down from the cliffs behind the site, the remaining structures indicate that this was once a large and important halting place on the road to Dakhleh Oasis. Today, only short sections of the thick walls that surrounded the site remain standing, and these reach a maximum height of 11 meters. The walls formed an irregular, four-sided enclosure, the longest side being the northern, which measured at least 90 meters in length. The main entrance to the enclosure is located on the northern half of the eastern wall, while a smaller postern is found at the intersection of the southern and eastern walls. With the exception of a small temple and well, however, no other structures exist above ground level within the enclosure (fig. 8.18).

The well, complete with an ancient stone watering trough, lies in a small, weed-choked depression toward the rear of the enclosure. Although the water is murky and unpleasant tasting, it is potable, and, after days of walking through the desert on limited rations, its abundance is a welcomed luxury. As a result of the presence of water, a plethora of hearty shrubs and two clusters of palm trees grow in a wide area both inside and outside the settlement. In addition, the water and rich plant life appear to sustain a significant population of gazelle, whose tracks crisscross the surrounding terrain.

The most interesting feature of Ain Amur is the temple, which stands on the northern side of the settlement (fig. 8.19). The walls of the building were constructed from superbly cut and fitted sandstone blocks, while limestone was used

8.18 Looking north across Ain Amur. The remains of the temple are visible in the center of the photograph.

for the large slabs that form the roof and lintels. The temple lies roughly on an east-west axis, its gate facing and in line with the main entrance to the settlement. Hinge holes are clearly visible in the jambs of the gateway, indicating that thick wooden doors were once used to seal the temple. Originally, the temple contained three rooms plus an inner sanctuary, but today all except the eastern and western ends of the building have collapsed. Nevertheless, a few decorations and numerous graffiti survive on the remaining walls. Regrettably, these give no clue to the temple's construction date.[70]

The most important decorations, on the outside of the western wall, include hieroglyphics, an eroded relief of the ram-headed god Amun, and two relief fragments, one of an unidentified winged figure and a second of a skirted, male torso (fig. 8.20). In addition to these decorations, traces of blue and red paint can be seen on the eastern wall near the temple doorway. According to an early-twentieth-century traveler, these were once "elaborate paintings of a king worshipping Amun and Min."[71] The ancient graffiti on the temple include such names as Merkurios and longer texts in uncommon languages. One unusual graffito, for example, resembles the writing of certain pre-Islamic tribes of northern Arabia and has been translated as follows:

[Inscription] of Sayyar.
Now he was faint from thirst,
he went alone through the desert,
he is journeying on foot,
he came to it [water] in the latter part of the night,
it saved him.[72]

Despite its remote location, vandals and thieves in search of salable antiquities have caused widespread damage at Ain Amur in recent years. Many of the tombs in the surrounding hills have been plundered of their mummies and artifacts, and "robber pits" are becoming more numerous, both inside and outside the enclosure. The greatest destruction, however, has been to the temple, from which at least two sandstone blocks containing hieroglyphics and portions of reliefs were removed sometime in 1995.[73]

DESERT ROUTES FROM KHARGA TO DAKHLEH

From antiquity until the present, two major routes have connected Kharga and Dakhleh Oases (see map 4). The longer, more southerly road was the 150-kilometer-long Darb el-Ghubari. The modern tarmac road between Kharga and

8.19 The main entrance to the temple of Ain Amur.

8.20 The damaged relief depicting a skirted male torso located on the
outer western wall of the temple at Ain Amur.

Dakhleh approximately follows this track, which began at Hibis, headed south-west under the southern foothills of the Abu Tartur Plateau, then arched north-west and arrived at Teneida, the most easterly settlement in the Dakhleh Oasis. The terrain through which this road passed was flat, desolate, and waterless, yet, because it contained no steep grades, it was the preferred route for large caravans. Prior to the construction of the modern road, Roman-era pottery sherds could be seen along the entire distance, but they were most heavily concentrated at four sites that served as halting places for the ancient caravans.[74] The most notable qualities of this route are two areas of detached sandstone hills and boulders con-taining large concentrations of pictographs and graffiti dating from the late Palaeolithic period (35,000 to 10,000 B.C.) through the twentieth century. Some of the drawings are of giraffes, ostrich, and other animals long since extinct from the region, while others depict hunters and various *wusm*, or tribal symbols.

The slightly shorter but more difficult route from Kharga to Dakhleh was the Ain Amur road.[75] Approximately ten kilometers west of Hibis, this track branched off from the Darb el-Ghubari and headed northwest across a vast, sandy plain to-ward the northeast corner of the Abu Tartur plateau. At irregular intervals along this route, short hills and rocky outcrops rise from the desert floor, offering a trav-eler patches of much-welcomed shade in which to rest and providing easily visi-ble places to leave pots of water for subsequent thirsty travelers. Today, pottery sherds from ribbed amphora and other types of vessels litter the sand surround-ing many of these outcrops, and ancient graffiti can be seen on several rock faces. Upon reaching the northeastern foothills of the plateau, the road ascends the mountain at a gentle angle until it finally arrives at Ain Amur. From behind the settlement, the trail winds up a narrow canyon to the top of the plateau. Today, this rocky path has been made treacherous by centuries of severe erosion, but even in antiquity its steepness made the ascent difficult for camels, thus explaining why heavily laden caravans have always preferred to use the slightly longer but flatter Darb el-Ghubari when traveling between Kharga and Dakhleh.

After attaining the summit of the plateau, the road heads southwest in the di-rection of Dakhleh. The terrain is hard, stony, and monotonously flat, but the an-cient route is clearly marked with stone cairns and the parallel ruts scuffed into the desert by the feet of countless camels and donkeys (fig. 8.21). Aside from the cairns, no man-made structures exist on the plateau, and there are no more than a handful of natural protrusions that could shelter a traveler from the intense sun and constant northern wind.[76] There are at least three *mahatteh* (resting places) along the route, however, and at these the desert floor turns to auburn from the large concentrations of pottery sherds that centuries of travelers left behind when they rested and camped at these places. Upon reaching the western edge of the

8.21 The High Road across the Abu Tartur plateau leads from Ain Amur to Dakhleh Oasis. Note the ancient cairns and parallel ruts worn into the surface of the plateau by centuries of passing camel caravans.

plateau, the road drops into the spectacular upper reaches of Wadi el-Battikh, then gradually descends to the floor of the Dakhleh depression, and finally arrives at Tineida (fig. 8.22).

DAKHLEH OASIS

Known in antiquity as the Inner Oasis, Dakhleh lies to the west of Gebel Abu Tartur and encompasses an area of more than 2,000 square kilometers. The arable land that has always been the economic foundation of life in the oasis consists of rich clay soil irrigated by hundreds of artesian wells, many of which date from the Roman period. The oasis is bounded on the north by a 400-meter-high limestone escarpment, on the east by the Abu Tartur Plateau, and on the west by one of the greatest expanses of barren desert on earth: the Great Sand Sea.

Like Kharga to the east, Dakhleh was a prosperous, well-populated oasis during the Roman period. Although much smaller than its neighbor, it contained numerous farms and villages and at least four major settlements, the ruins of which have been well preserved over the centuries by the dry desert environment. These farms produced an impressive variety of cereals, vegetables, and fruits and exported olive oil and wine to the Nile Valley. Today, the oasis is divided into two main areas separated by a 15-kilometer-wide stretch of desert. (This uninhabited strip led early European visitors to remark that the two areas appeared to be separate oases.)[77] Although the easternmost portion of the oasis contains the oldest evidence of habitation, the western regions were also heavily settled during the Roman period. In the vicinity of Maghoub alone, for example, at the western end of the oasis, there are at least fifty Roman sites consisting of isolated farmsteads, cemeteries, a major temple, and several villages. There is little evidence that this area was inhabited prior to the Roman era, and scholars are still working to understand why it became so populated during Rome's occupation of Egypt.[78]

Some evidence supports the notion that the settlement of the western regions of the oasis during the Roman period could have resulted from a government-sponsored relocation and development plan. Sometime in the middle of the first century, for example, an agricultural disaster of some kind struck the Fayoum, creating a surplus of farmers. Shortly afterward, it appears that a substantial number of farmers—quite possibly including many from the Fayoum—migrated to Dakhleh. As we shall see, it was also at this time that the Roman government constructed the temple of Deir el-Haggar, whose sanctuary is decorated with the names

8.22 Searching for the ancient trail leading down from the western edge of the Abu Tartur plateau into the Dakhleh depression via Wadi el-Battikh.

of first-century emperors. Furthermore, the fact that many of the farms in the west were spaced at regular intervals implies that they resulted from governmental planning. Given that several of the major agricultural settlements clearly lasted at least through the third and fourth centuries, and that they produced an abundance of food, it appears that the official development scheme was highly successful. This success, however, could not endure the dramatic environmental changes that seem to have occurred at the end of the Roman period, thus causing a decline in agricultural production and leading to a rapid decrease in the population.[79]

One immediately noticeable difference between the Roman-era structures located in Kharga and those of Dakhleh is the apparent absence of fortresses. Indeed, in the entire Dakhleh oasis only two structures might be identified as Roman-era fortresses: Qasr al-Halakeh (Castle of the Ring), located on a wide plain approximately four kilometers east of Ismant el-Kharab, and Qasr al-Qasaba further to the southwest (fig. 8.23).[80] The absence of such structures may signify that Dakhleh was less susceptible to attack, particularly from the south, than was Kharga. But it also reinforces the idea that the fortresses in Kharga, which straddled the main east-west and north-south caravan routes, were primarily intended to serve the dual role of defending that oasis from attacks from the Nile Valley and, at the same time, acting as a buffer against attacks directed at the Nile Valley from the west. Because Kharga could protect Dakhleh's eastern and southern flanks and because Libyan tribes do not appear to have been hostile enough to cross the Western Desert during the four centuries of Roman occupation of Dakhleh, there appears to have been little need to fortify the oasis.[81]

Although there are numerous Roman-era sites within the Dakhleh Oasis, only a few of them constitute major settlements. Today, archaeologists and historians are focusing their attention on the extensive Roman remains at the sites of Tineida, Ismant el-Kharab (ancient Kellis), Amheida, Deir el-Haggar, and El-Muzzawaka.[82]

Tineida

Tineida lies at the eastern edge of the Dakhleh Oasis.[83] Although the site contains few above-ground ruins dating from the Roman period, Roman-era structures likely lie buried under the surrounding cultivated lands. Despite the inaccessibility of these sites to archaeological excavation, the territory between Tineida and Belat unquestionably was inhabited in antiquity. Only eight kilometers northwest of Tineida, for example, at the site of Ain Asil (Spring of the Origin), archaeologists discovered rare clay tablets containing hieroglyphics that date from the Sixth dynasty—thus constituting the oldest known evidence that Dakhleh Oasis was

8.23 Qasr al-Halakeh, one of only two known Roman fortresses
in the Dakhleh Oasis.

actually linked to the Nile Valley. Indeed, it stood near the terminus of the Darb el-
Tawil, the only direct route from the oasis to the Nile Valley. But although Ain Asil
probably served as the capital of the oasis during the Old Kingdom, it appears to
have been abandoned before the Ptolemaic period and thus contains no evidence
of Roman occupation.

The most important Roman site in the Tineida area is the temple at Ain Birbiyeh. The primary deity of this stone temple was a previously unknown god
named Amun-nakht, or Amun the Mighty One. The gateway of the temple was
constructed and dedicated under the reign of Augustus, and its decorations have
provided scholars with valuable information, not only about the building, but also
about the obscure deity in whose honor it was constructed. The following text, for
example, is from the temple gateway: "[Amun-nakht] who runs fast over the
desert, while he makes an end of the enemy. He has overthrown the enemy in this
wadi."[84] Amun-nakht was known by numerous epithets, although Lord of Ain
Birbiyeh and Lord of the Desert appear to have been the most common. All of his
titles, however, bear a strong resemblance to Horus, son of Osiris and Isis. In fact,
an inscription at the temple of Deir el-Haggar relates that Amun-nakht, in the aspect of Horus, first visited Dakhla Oasis during his search for the scattered limbs
of his murdered father, Osiris. The temple at Ain Birbiyeh attests to Amun-nakht

having made the second of two known visits to Dakhleh Oasis from the Nile Valley, in this case, so that he might defeat his enemies.[85] Moreover, the text quoted above calls to mind the mythology of Horus, who, according to such inscriptions as one in the Temple of Edfu, also hurries through the desert in pursuit of his enemies.

Much work remains to be done at Ain Birbiyeh, and, given that it is one of only four temples in Kharga and Dakhleh to have been excavated—the others being Hibis, Deir el-Haggar, and Dush—archaeologists hope that it might shed additional light on the emergence of pagan cults in Dakhleh Oasis and on the nature of pagan spiritualism in general.

Two additional sites near Tineida are probably of the Roman period, but they remain unexcavated. The first is located about two and a half kilometers north and consists of three mud-brick buildings standing on a wide sandy plain. One building measures 25 meters long and contains vaulted ceilings and arched niches in its plastered walls. One early traveler believed that at least one of the three buildings served as a columbarium or tomb for urns. The second Roman site stands about four kilometers northwest of Tineida and consists of two buildings, including a temple-like structure, on a north-south axis. The main entrance to the temple appears to be on the south at the arched gateway of a 6-meter-wide pylon that was originally topped with a limestone lintel. Inside, the first room was vaulted and measures approximately 14 meters long by 4 meters wide. Beyond this were two smaller chambers, probably vaulted, that measure 4 meters square. Both of these northern sites are littered with Roman-era pottery, including faience and red-slip ware.[86]

Ismant el-Kharab (Ismant the Ruined)

Ismant el-Kharab[87] marks the ancient site of the once-thriving, well-populated market town known as Kellis.[88] Located in the eastern half of Dakhleh Oasis (see map 4), the remains of the town have undergone extensive excavation and examination by archaeologists for nearly twenty years. In the course of their work, the researchers have unearthed a vast and invaluable collection of artifacts dating from the Roman occupation of the oasis—artifacts that have made Kellis one of the most important sites for the study of Roman Egypt. The excavated area comprises roughly a square kilometer. Within this space are a number of structures, including houses, churches, four wells, a bathhouse, numerous freestanding tombs, and, most prominently, a large walled enclosure containing a stone temple, four brick shrines, and various storage buildings. The site lies deeply buried by blowing sand, a problem that may have contributed to its abandonment. But the heavy blanket of sand that obscured the settlement for so many centuries also preserved its most important buildings to heights of 2 to 4 meters.

The spacious temple complex dates from the late first century A.D., and its main building includes paintings of religious processions, columns of hiero-glyphic inscriptions, and other decorations based on a mixture of Pharaonic and classical styles.[89] The following Greek inscription, recovered from the vicinity of the temple, shows that, unlike any other surviving temple in Egypt, the temples at Kellis were dedicated to the god Tithoes (ancient Egyptian Tutu), the Master of Demons and son of Neith, the archer goddess and protector of the dead:[90] "To Good Fortune. To the supreme god Tithoes and to the gods adored in the same temple, for the eternal reign of the Emperor Caesar, son of the divine Hadrian, grandson of the divine Trajan, victor over the Parthians. . . ."[91]

West of the main temple is a smaller shrine, built of mud brick but containing stone doorjambs and a stone-lined sanctuary. The site was first excavated in 1981 to examine its architectural plan. At that time, archaeologists discovered that two of the temple's doorjambs bore carved reliefs:

> The "outer" jamb bears the sunken relief carving of a king, facing right, into the doorway. The figure is standing, the right arm raised to shoulder height and the left hand holds a scepter and a staff. He wears a white crown, a col-lar and a kilt. In front of the figure are three columns: each bear the remains of cartouches and terminate at head level, the outer, at the block edge, de-scends to the bottom of the scene. The "inner" jamb is worked in high re-lief and bears a depiction of two female figures. A goddess (Neith?) faces right, towards the doorway, holding an *ankh* in one hand and a staff in an-other, and wearing an elaborate headdress of double plumes and cobras on a vulture. She is being adored by a second female figure, whose back is to the doorway, with arms upraised. Between the figures there are five panels, intended for columns of hieroglyphics, which are left blank."[92]

After the reliefs were recorded, archaeologists re-covered the temple with sand in order to hide its location and to protect the reliefs from sun and wind damage. When the sand was removed from the temple during the 1990–91 excavation sea-son, however, the archaeologists discovered that sometime between February 1988 and January 1991 thieves had sawed off the face of each block containing the reliefs. The blocks have never been recovered.

Although the temples of Kellis have yielded valuable data about the pagan spir-itual life of the town's inhabitants, the most important religious discoveries per-tain to the rapid emergence of Christianity in the community sometime during the fourth century. These discoveries came not from churches, but from several modest houses, the excavations of which produced an astounding collection of both secular and spiritual texts. Of the four houses excavated so far, for example, one contained two intact wooden books, or codices, forty-four inscribed boards, some two hundred coins, and more than three thousand fragments of inscribed papyrus. The texts were written in Greek, Coptic, and Syriac and include administrative and financial documents, private letters, and early Christian writings, including rare Manichaean texts.

The two wooden codices, each with its original binding cords attached, constitute the best-preserved examples of wooden codices ever discovered from this period. Not only are they important for the information they contain, but they are an invaluable contribution to scholars' understanding of the gradual transition from the use of scrolls to the development of books.[93] The first codex contains three Cyprian Orations of Isocrates, while the second is a detailed record of a farmer's harvest accounts spanning a four-year period. Neither of these documents was considered a permanent record: the farm accounts were probably transferred to a papyrus ledger, and the Cyprian book was most likely copied from another source for the purpose of reading and study.

The accounts book consists of eight leaves, whose surfaces were smoothed by plane and pumice stone and then coated with gum arabic to prevent the ink from feathering. The wood appears to be that of the willow tree. A pair of shallow notches were cut into each leaf to show the order of the pages in the event the book came apart and had to be repaired. The accounts book belonged to Fonstianos, son of Aquiana, and was written by an estate agent while the family lived in Hibis.[94] Probably written in the A.D. 360s, the book records the transactions of the supervisor of a group of warehouses (not all of which were in Ismant el-Kharab) managed by various individuals. Written in columns, the accounts record the kind of commodity received, its amount, and its origin. The commodities included barley, wheat, fodder and straw, sesame, cotton, olive oil and wine, chickens, and pigs. There are also references to bed makers, bird keepers, and sandal makers. Interestingly, most of the transactions are in kind rather than in cash. Cash seems to have been used only for such official payments as taxes and for transactions with soldiers who might have been stationed at a nearby garrison. The records also allude to monthly donations to a church, apparently headed by a deacon name Peter.[95]

The Cyprian Orations is a nine-leaf book of speeches composed sometime between 372 and 365 B.C. in Athens. Addressed to Nicocles, son of Evagoras, king of Salamis, who was murdered by his guards, they discuss the responsibilities of kings and their relationships with their subjects. During the Roman period, the Orations of Isocrates were regarded as excellent models for the study of oratory. The presence of numerous marginalia glossing words and phrases confirms that the texts were studied intently by either a student or a teacher of Greek literature or rhetoric.[96]

Of the thousands of papyrus texts from Kellis, the most important pertain to the emergence of Christianity in the oasis. These texts reveal that the people of Kellis experienced an active and enthusiastic period of spiritual growth as Christianity rapidly took hold in the fourth century. Of particular interest are those texts relating to the presence of a Manichaean community.[97] Scholars estimate that Manichaean missionaries arrived in Egypt sometime before A.D. 260 and appear to have concentrated their efforts in Middle and Upper Egypt, most probably in the major cities of Antinoopolis (modern Sheik 'Ibada) and Lycopolis (modern Assiut). By A.D. 300, they reached Dakhleh Oasis, where their unique version of Christianity added yet another ingredient to the spiritual soup of Egyptian and Greco-Roman paganism—and possibly Catholic Christianity—that already existed there. The distinctions among these theologies in the early fourth century, however, and the relations the communities maintained with each other are as yet unclear. Although there is no doubt, for example, that by the time Kellis was abandoned sometime in the late fourth or very early fifth century, it had become a Christian town,[98] it is uncertain whether the Catholic Christians or the Manichaeans were the dominant sect in the oasis. At least one theory holds that, although Christianity was moving rapidly across Egypt and the empire in the early fourth century, Catholic Christian missionaries might have reached the outlying oases relatively late, thus enabling the Manichaeans to present themselves as "true Christians" to the pagan population.[99] On the other hand, the enormous political and religious changes that took place in the empire during the fourth century make it doubtful that the Manichaeans were ultimately successful in converting the majority of Dakhleh's inhabitants to their faith. After all, it was just shortly after A.D. 324—less than a hundred years after the Manichaeans arrived in Egypt—that Emperor Constantine gave valuable support to the Catholic Christian church by discouraging pagan sacrifices, building magnificent new churches in Bethlehem and Jerusalem, and, most important, helping to define Christian orthodoxy more precisely by summoning the western and eastern bishops to the Council of Nicaea. As the impact of this adherence to Catholic Christianity trickled down to Egypt's oases, the Manichaeans would have confronted diminishing receptiveness to their message.

In addition to their religious significance, the papyrus texts afford detailed insights into numerous aspects of the daily lives of the people of Kellis. It is clear, for example, that a great many residents were bilingual, Coptic dominating for domestic, informal use and Greek for administrative and formal communication.[100] Following are examples from the ever-expanding collection of Kellis documents:

Manichaean Letter Dating from the early fourth century, this elegantly phrased letter reveals the presence of a community of Manichaeans living alongside the growing population of Christians. This and other texts imply that Manichaean missionaries lived in Kellis and translated Manichaean texts from their original Syriac to Coptic. Apparently two Manichaeans, Pausanius and Pisistratos, had requested a letter of recommendation from the author of the letter and had also sent him a basket and other items. The author, whose name is now lost, responded to their request and acknowledged the articles:

> To my lords sons who are most longed-for and most beloved by us, Pausanius and Pisistratos, N.N. sends greetings in God. Since your good reputation is great and without limit in our mind and in our speech, I wish to reveal this as much as possible and to extend it through this letter. For this has been recorded and testified to by the most sincere mind in you. And yet, knowing that this letter will gladden [you] in due measure, consequently we hasten to make use of this and to send off to the—word of the divinely generated conceptions which we cherish inside towards your pious character. For we are most pleased and rejoice when [or: that?] we shall receive both the indications of your sympathy and the welcome letter of yours, I mean . . .; and now we benefit from a few fruits of the spirit and [later] again we benefit also from the soul of the pious . . . , of course; and filled with both we shall set going every praise towards your most luminous soul inasmuch as this is possible for us. For only our lord the Paraclete is competent to praise you as you deserve and to compensate you at the appropriate moment. We have received the basket and we give in to your most pious preference and we have given the objects destined for the lord -ryllos. Likewise, we also received the . . . May you remain so helpful for us all we pray; . . . [101]

Christian Amulet This fourth-century amulet was written on a board that served as a page in a notebook:

> Masters . . . eternal God . . . of the Lord . . . your mighty hand, your lofty arm, full of healing and well-being, full of power and life. Keep away from him every disease and every infirmity and every spirit of illness, so that having received your mercy men can worship and thank you [all] the days of their lives. For you are our Savior and refuge and helper of our assistance, for your all-holy name has been given and is exalted for ever and ever. [102]

Business Letter This simple letter dates from the second half of the fourth century:

> To my lord brother Eumathius, Siris sends greetings. Immediately after receiving my letter, collect from the farmers for barley and dates two thousand

talents of silver [. . .], and give them to brother Elias. But don't be neglect-ful; give them to him. I pray for your health, brother, for many years.[103]

Legal Document This papyrus, written in A.D. 362, contains details of the latest known sale (including a price) of a slave in Roman Egypt:

> The Aurelii Psais son of Pekysis, grandson of Palitous, and Tatoup his wife, both from the village of Kellis in the Mothite nome, resident in the hamlet of E——, to Aurelius Tithoes son of Petesis, carpenter, from the same village in the same nome, greetings. We agree that we have sold and conveyed to you from now and for all time the slave girl belonging to us, raised from the ground and reared by me the aforementioned wife with my own milk, at a price agreed between us of two nomismatia of imperial, unalloyed, and newly minted gold, total 2 nomismatia, which we have received from you from your hand in full on all the terms written herein to which we give as-sent, in order that you the purchaser from henceforth possess, own and have proprietary rights over the slave girl sold to you and have the right to control and manage her in whatever way you choose, the guarantee resting on us the vendors throughout against every litigant or claimant. Let the sale, having been written twice under the signature of him who is subscribing for us, be authoritative, guaranteed and legal everywhere it may be produced and having been formally questioned we have assented. In the consulate of Mamertinus and Nevitta, viri clarissisimi, Thoth, according to the Greek calendar.
>
> I, Aurelius Demosthenes son of Polykrates, from the village of Kellis, am a witness.
>
> I, Aurelius Horion son of Timotheos, from the village of Kellis, am a witness.[104]

Legal Document This document concerns a slave who was granted her freedom in A.D. 355. One of very few emancipation documents from Roman Egypt, it reveals an interesting combination of Christianity and paganism:

> Copy of the deed of manumission. Aurelius Valerius son of Sarapion, ex-magistrate of the city of the Mothites, to my own Hilaria, greetings. I ac-knowledge that I have set you free because of my exceptional Christianity, under Zeus, Earth and Sun, together also with your peculium, and [because of] your loyalty towards me, in order that from here onwards you shall have your freedom unassailed by anyone who shall try to lay claim upon you with regard to this deed of manumission made through the most reverend father Psekes ——. Let this deed of manumission be authoritative and guaranteed

and lawful wherever it is produced and in response to the formal question I
have answered positively. After the consulate of Constantius *Augustus* consul
for the seventh time and of Constantius *nobilissimus Caesar* consul for the
third time. I the aforementioned Aurelius Valerius, ex-magistrate, have
drawn up the deed of manumission as written above and in response to the
formal question I have answered positively. I, the aforementioned Aurelius
Psekes, priest, am present and witness.

Legal Appeal Among the numerous accusations of thefts of donkeys and other
property was the following complaint about the beating of a woman, a crime that
appears to have been relatively common:

> To Aurelius Faustianus, former magistrate of the city of the Mothites in the
> Great Oasis, *defensor* of the country. From Aurelius Pamouris son of Psais,
> from the village of Kellis of the city of the Mothites.[105] If for everybody
> deeds of willfulness will have success and if the severity of the laws would
> not usually follow, these times would be insupportable for us—. Now, Sois
> son of Akoutis, comarch of the same village of Kellis, who is constantly
> plotting against me, [is harassing] me every day in violation of everything,
> stirring up the locally present soldiers and *officiales* and *expunctores* against
> my wife and being a constant pain in the neck for me. For yesterday, during
> my absence, he burst the—door open with an axe, went in with his son Pse-
> namounis the carpenter from Pmoun Pamo, though being neither a liturgist
> nor happening to be a fellow villager of mine, he assaulted my wife with a
> club and beat her up with blows so that these are visible on her body, as if
> they are not subject to the laws. As such is the mentality of the said comarch
> and his son Psenamounis, and because I cannot live in peace, I present this
> petition to your clemency and I ask that these things be relayed to the brave-
> ness of my lord the *praeses* Valerius Victorinianus *vir perfectissimus*, in order
> that their reckless act get a fitting vindication. Farewell. After the consulate
> of our lords Constantinus Augustus consul for the sixth time and Constan-
> tinus *nobilissimus Caesar* consul for the first time, Tybi 11. I, the aforemen-
> tioned Aurelius Pamouris son of Psais, have submitted [the petition]. I,
> Aurelius Phibion, ex-magistrate of Hermopolis, have written on his behalf
> because he is not able to write.[106]

Loan of Money This unusual loan of money, occurring during the second half of
the fourth century, was documented as a letter rather than as a legal contract:

> To my lord Pisistratos, Palammon sends greetings. You have on loan from
> me on account of the balance of the price of the wagon one myriad of silver

talents, total 1 myr. Tal., on condition that I shall give them [back] to you on the 30th of the month of Tybi according to the Egyptian calendar without dispute and without looking for pretexts and I have handed over this letter to you for your surety. If, however, on the fixed time I turn out to be careless as regards the repayment I shall pay the said money in talents with —- interest according to the local custom until the repayment of the said one myriad of talents. I pray for your health, my lord, enjoying prosperity for many years. I, Flavius Makarios son of Ptou, have signed for him at his request because he does not know how to write.[107]

Letter Pertaining to a Loan As in every age, the possibility of someone defaulting on a loan was a constant risk. In this case dating from the second half of the fourth century, the creditor threatens to get soldiers involved in the affair if he is not paid promptly:

> To my lord brother Psempnoutes, Timotheos the carpenter sends greetings. Before all I send you many greetings along with all your family. I am surprised that after such a long time you have not been willing to pay the money. Therefore, when Pachoumis comes to you, give the three thousand talents to him, for I have already received them from him. For be informed that if you are unwilling to give them to him, I will get them dunned from you by soldiers. See to it that you are not neglectful. I pray that you are well for many years.[108]

Request for a Notebook Wooden notebooks were a rare commodity in Egypt, broken pottery sherds and papyrus being far more common materials upon which to write. Nevertheless, the following letter from the early to mid fourth century contains a request for just such a volume:

> To my beloved son Theognostos, from . . . , greetings in God. If your brother Psais is with you, take heed [concerning] your sobriety and —-. greet all by name. Your brothers greet you. I pray that you are well in God, beloved [friends]. Send a well-proportioned and nicely executed ten-page notebook for your brother Ision. For he has become a user of Greek and a comprehensive reader.[109]

Personal Letter This affectionate letter was written in the mid fourth century:

> To his most honored and truly most longed-for lord brother Psais, Pamouris send greetings in God. First of all I and my wife and sons each individually send many greetings to your reverence, being well up until now through the providence of God. Greet for us our lord brother Theognostos

and his son Andreas. About your coming to us, most honored one, every day we —- from long ago since you wrote. And, I swear by God, it was on your account that I remained here, not departing for Antinoopolis to transact pressing business with my brother Pekysis. But look, he summoned me there many times and since I was expecting you, I did not leave. Indeed I wrote this very thing to him too that "I am expecting my brother and his children here." So don't neglect to come. Please bring with you a small hatchet and a bronze oven dish. Please greet each by name for me. I am amazed that, while so many have come to us, you have not deemed us worthy of even a letter for such a long time; but I myself, too, had decided not to write, and yet I was unable to endure, particularly since Philammon is here. Or don't you know that we are thirsting for your letters? Greet Kapiton for me and Psais, son of Tryphanes, with their wives and children. Give many greetings for me to mother Maria and the little Tsempouthes. Please send the girl to me. I am giving you her travel money and each year I will give you a present of wool for a cloak as her hire. Farewell my lord.[110]

In addition to the documents described above, the abundance of nontextual material excavated from Kellis provides a more concrete picture of what life might have been like in this remote corner of the empire. From an analysis of pottery sherds, for example, one can surmise that the people of the oasis were in contact with the Nile Valley, and, based on the presence of North African ware, quite possibly maintained at least limited economic relations with Cyrenaica. Furthermore, the analysis of seeds and animal droppings from the excavated soil reveals that the residents of Kellis appear to have eaten a surprisingly varied and healthy diet. They grew not only such staples as lentils, fava beans, and wheat, but also exotic vegetables, fruits, and nuts like artichokes, figs, apples, pomegranates, sugar dates, grapes, and pine nuts.[111] Despite this diet, the physical hardships of agricultural life and the limited knowledge of medicine conspired to keep the average life span short. Recent studies of mummies exhumed at Kellis, for example, indicate that life expectancy at birth was only seventeen years, and 90 percent of the people died before they reached fifty. Indeed, based on recent studies, the mean age of death for men was thirty-six years and for women, forty-three.[112]

Judging from the fact that coins from the site do not bear dates beyond the late fourth century and that the latest recovered document dates from A.D. 389, it appears that people abandoned Kellis at about this time, possibly owing to a lack of water or the encroachment of the desert. Fortunately, however, the same dry sands that buried the ancient town also preserved a great abundance of artifacts. Further excavations at Kellis will advance understanding of the administration, economy, religious life, and culture not just of Kellis itself, but of Dakhleh Oasis and Roman Egypt in general.

Amheida

Only a few kilometers south of the modern town of Qasr Dakhleh, spread along an area of low hills in the middle of a wide plain, lie the ruins of Amheida. The town, whose remains are scattered over a hundred hectares, appears to have been occupied from the first through the late fourth centuries and must certainly have been one of the largest Roman settlements in Dakhleh (fig. 8.24). The tops of the walls of numerous ruined buildings—once covered by vaulted ceilings—dot the landscape, but the vast majority of the settlement remains buried under centuries of sand and debris. The site is dominated by a large building standing atop a slight rise at the northernmost part of the town. Limestone chips, a pair of molded doorjambs, and a sandstone block bearing a relief of Amon and two other figures indicate that this structure served as the temple for the settlement.[113]

8.24 Bedouin women leading a small flock of sheep through the unexcavated Roman settlement of Amheida in Dakhleh Oasis.

The most spectacular discovery thus far is a series of surprisingly well executed Roman paintings adorning the walls of a chamber inside a multiroomed building located near the center of the settlement. The paintings, which date from the late third to early fourth centuries, are proof that a high degree of artistry was present even in this remote corner of the Roman empire. The chamber once featured paintings on all of its walls, but only those on the northern and eastern sides have survived. On the northern wall, to the left of the door, is a painting of Perseus, about to rescue the beautiful Andromeda only a moment before she is to be devoured by a sea monster.[114] In this remarkably skilled painting, Perseus, who is nude except for a maroon cloak draped over his right arm, holds the sword of Hermes in his right hand, while his left hand clutches the pale, snake-haired head of the slain Medusa. From the sea between Perseus and Andromeda rises the purple-gray sea monster with a fishtail, long, erect ears, and a vicious, gaping mouth from which a bright red tongue protrudes. The fair-skinned Andromeda stands awaiting her death, in the posture of a classical standing nude, fastened by thick gold anklets to the rock.[115]

To the right of the door, on the northern wall, is another beautifully executed painting of the famous scene in which Odysseus is recognized by his aged nurse, Eurycleia. The painting captures the very moment when, upon recognizing an old scar on the leg of the man whose feet she is washing, Eurycleia realizes that Odysseus has returned after a twenty-year absence from Ithaca. But determined not to let his presence be known, Odysseus swiftly commands her to be silent:[116]

> Bending closer
> she started to bathe her master . . . then,
> in a flash, she knew the scar . . .
> That scar—
> as the old nurse cradled his leg and her hands passed down
> she felt it, knew it, suddenly let his foot fall—
> down it dropped in the basin—the bronze clanged,
> tipping over, spilling water across the floor.
> Joy and torment gripped her heart at once,
> tears rushed to her eyes—voice choked in her throat
> she reached for Odysseus' chin and whispered quickly,
> "Yes, yes! you are Odysseus—oh dear boy—
> I couldn't know you before . . .
> not till I touched the body of my king!"
> . . . "Nurse," the cool tactician Odysseus said . . .
> "Just be quiet. Keep your tales to yourself.
> Leave the rest to the gods."[117]

In the painting, Odysseus wears a long reddish robe with a narrow gold stripe and sits on an elaborately detailed stool with a sheepskin cushion. He is leaning forward with his right hand extended toward the lips of Eurycleia, who gazes at his face as she kneels before him bathing his feet. The gray-haired Eurycleia wears a long yellow dress with a pinkish mantle, and next to her stands a black pitcher from which she has poured water into the red foot-basin in which she bathes Odysseus's feet. On the far right of the scene, Odysseus's wife, Penelope, despairing of the siege of abusive suitors and unaware that her husband the king has returned, sits passively on a low stool, wearing a white, tasseled mantle. Her ornately dressed hair is parted in the middle, she wears two gold bracelets on each wrist, and a rectangular pendant on a gold chain hangs around her neck.[118]

The eastern wall of the same chamber is divided into two horizontal registers containing painted figures that are smaller than those found on the north wall. Between the two registers, a gray band contains the Greek names of the figures depicted in the lower scenes. Only the bottom portions of the upper register survive, and although these clearly show that the register contained scenes of humans and animals, not one is complete enough to be identified. On the left is a templelike building with four columns and what appear to be the remains of an architrave. Below the temple are the city walls, and to the right sits a female figure labeled Polis, or city. The woman gestures toward the building with her right hand, while holding a golden scepter in her left. Although it is unclear which polis is being depicted in this painting, at least one scholar posits that it is Amheida itself: "Under the earlier Roman empire, a 'polis' had a very specific municipal status, but by the time of our paintings the term was being more generally applied. It is therefore not unlikely that, while Amheida never enjoyed any official or meaningful status as a 'polis,' the female allegorical figure painted here was nevertheless a personification of that city."[119]

The lower register also depicts Aphrodite, the goddess of love, and Ares, the god of war, captured in adultery by a clever ruse of Aphrodite's crippled husband, Hephaistos, who trapped the lovers in bed by means of an invisible net of chains:

> Halting there at the gates, seized with savage rage
> he howled a terrible cry, imploring all the gods,
> "Father Zeus, look here—
> the rest of you happy gods who live forever—
> here is a sight to make you laugh, revolt you too!
> Just because I am crippled, Zeus's daughter Aphrodite
> will always spurn me and love that devastating Ares,
> just because of his stunning looks and racer's legs
> while I am a weakling, lame from birth, and who's to blame?"[120]

In this painting, the gods, including Helios, Herakles, Apollo, Dionysus, Poseidon, and Hephaistos himself, hurry toward the offending couple. Aphrodite raises her gold-braceleted hands in surprise, while the startled Ares prepares to defend himself by lunging for his shield, helmet, and weapons, which lie in a pile nearby.[121]

An enormous cemetery holding between two thousand and three thousand tombs occupies the area to the south of Amheida. Most of these are simple pit-graves, but others are more elaborate, vaulted structures, and several tombs contain paintings of spiritual scenes. One such tomb is an aboveground, two-roomed brick building. On the white plastered wall of the outer chamber, the goddesses Isis and Nephthys are painted on either side of the doorway leading to the inner chamber. The inner room, which measures approximately 5.5 meters by 3.5 meters, features paintings of funerary scenes on all four walls. These scenes include the weighing of the heart, the mummification of the body by the god Anubis, the presentation of the dead to Osiris, and Osiris being carried in a basket by falcon-headed attendants. Unlike other tomb paintings in the oasis, such as those at the nearby site of Muzzawaka, these were executed in a typically Egyptian style, with little classical influence. Thus, in all likelihood they date from the first century B.C. and mark the earliest period of settlement at Amheida.[122]

Deir el-Haggar

The magnificent temple of Deir el-Haggar, whose ancient Egyptian name is Set-ouha and whose Arabic name means Monastery of Stone, is located in the area of Magoub, in the western portion of Dakhleh Oasis[123] (fig. 8.25). Dedicated to Amun, Khonsu, and Thoth, it was constructed during the reign of Nero (A.D. 54–68), whose cartouche appears in the sanctuary. The temple walls also bear the names of Vespasian (A.D. 69–79) and Titus (A.D. 79–81). But other emperors played a role in the construction of the temple as well. The gateway, for example, was decorated during the reign of Domitian (A.D. 81–96), and the astronomical ceiling dates from Hadrian's rule (A.D. 117–38). Thus far, the latest inscription discovered in the temple dates from the third century.

South of the main entrance to the temple complex is a secondary gate in the temenos wall of the sanctuary. It features a dense collection of Greek graffiti and dipinti of gods and sacred animals on the wall of the doorway. The majority of the inscriptions are brief devotional statements written by individuals who wished to leave a lasting spiritual record of their visit to the sacred temple. The more prominent paintings include a bust, executed in red, of the god Serapis wearing the crown of Osiris and bearing the staff of Hermes. Just beneath Serapis is a depic-

8.25 The entrance to the partially reconstructed temple of
Deir el-Haggar in Dakhleh Oasis.

tion in red and black of a divine baboon and a divine ram facing each other across
an offering table laden with gifts. The baboon appears to sit on a pedestal whose
decorations resemble the hieroglyph for "irrigated land" (fig. 8.26). A third important painting, located on the wall opposite the two just mentioned, is that of a
soldier on horseback, bearing a lance in his left hand and featuring a star on top
of his head. Although difficult to identify with certainty because the face and torso
of the figure were vandalized in antiquity, the painting probably represents the
military god Castor, twin son of Zeus, who was a popular deity with Romans[124]
(fig. 8.27).

Within the sanctuary itself is the spectacular astronomical ceiling. This sandstone ceiling, measuring approximately 3.3 meters by 2.4 meters, is highlighted
by an elaborate spiritual scene carved in shallow relief. Although it was originally
plastered and painted, only traces of the paint remain—particularly the light blue
background.[125] The arching figure of the goddess Nut surrounds all the other
scenes of the relief; her hands rest in the northwest corner of the ceiling and her
feet in the northeast corner. The north side of the relief is dominated by the
curved figure of the androgynous god Geb, who symbolizes the earth. Enclosed
within the space of Geb's curled-up body is the constellation Orion, which represents the god Osiris. The ceiling features an exceptional representation of the

8.26 A wall at Deir el-Haggar featuring Greek graffiti and paintings of gods and sacred animals. Pictured here is the god Serapis.

8.27 Another painting from the courtyard wall at Deir el-Haggar, this one possibly depicting the Roman military god Castor.

divinities engaged in their eternal task of maintaining order in the cosmos, thus ensuring the continuation of the natural cycles of days and seasons that renew both humanity and earth.[126]

As mentioned in the discussion of Ain Birbiyeh, an important first-century A.D. inscription from the sanctuary of Deir el-Haggar provides the earliest known record of a visit to Dakhleh Oasis by the god Amun-Nakht, who, in the appearance of Horus (the god of the temple Amun-Re at Karnak), came to find the "limbs" of his father, Osiris.[127] The inscription has helped scholars understand the process by which this particular element of ancient mythology came from the Nile Valley and established itself in the oasis.

A famous story concerning the experiences of the German explorer Gerhardt Rohlfs was told to a later British explorer, Harding King, when he visited Deir el-Haggar in the early part of the twentieth century. Rohlfs arrived at the site in 1873 determined to discover the treasures buried within its ruins, whose presence he was assured of by a "treasure book" in his possession. But the treasure was protected by a spirit who thwarted Rohlfs's efforts. Finally, the explorer ordered all of his assistants, with the exception of one "black man," to leave the temple. Whereupon Rohlfs supposedly immolated the black man as a sacrifice to the spirit of the temple. Thus propitiated, the spirit revealed the location of the entrance to the treasure vault to Rohlfs, who discovered that it did indeed contain an abundance of gold, silver, and diamonds. The men who related this tale to King believed that Rohlfs absconded with the treasure when he left the oasis.[128]

El-Muzzawaka (The Decorated Hill)

Located within the larger area of Maghoub, this Roman cemetery consists of hundreds of tombs cut into three separate hills (figs. 8.28, 8.29). The area has been known to local residents for many years, and almost all of the tombs have been plundered in search of salable artifacts. To date, the most interesting discoveries are of two tombs with colorful frescoes executed in a combination of Pharaonic and classical styles. The first is the single-chambered tomb of Petubastis, and the second is the double-chambered tomb of Padiosir Petosiris. The walls of each tomb feature recessed shelves intended to hold the mummified body of the deceased—although it remains unclear whether anyone was actually buried in either tomb. The tomb of Petubastis, which dates from the first century A.D., contains a crude portrait of the man himself in a burial niche on its eastern wall and a ceiling decorated with a funerary zodiac. The tomb of Petosiris, dating from the first quarter of the second century, contains the judgment of Osiris in its inner room and a more complex zodiac that, in addition to Aries, Libra, Pisces, and others,

8.28 Roman-era tombs cut into the hills of El-Muzzawaka in western Dakhleh Oasis.

8.29 The interior of an unexcavated tomb containing Roman period mummies. The simplicity of the burial wrappings and the absence of any interior decorations suggest that the individuals laid to rest in this tomb were probably of moderate means.

8.30 The south wall of the inner chamber of the tomb of Petosiris. These scenes
depict the weighing of the deceased heart before Osiris, Isis giving a
libation to the deceased's spirit, a fertility figure, and a goddess
with offerings, fruit trees, and corn.

includes figures of birds, crocodiles, a scarab-sun, and the god Horus (fig.
8.30).[129] On the north wall of the outer chamber is a full-length depiction of
Petosiris (fig. 8.31). Wearing a long pink toga of Roman style and holding a papyrus scroll in his left hand, his figure is flanked by the following hieroglyphic inscription: "May you take wing as an ibis, may you alight as the alighting hawk,
without your *ba* [soul] encountering any obstacle in the Underworld, for ever!"[130]
Dressed in Roman clothes, yet surrounded by representations of ancient Egyptian
rituals, the frescoes from the tomb of Petosiris demonstrate the remarkable blend
of religious traditions that characterized early Roman Egypt.

Although many tombs at El-Muzzawaka have yet to be excavated, it is doubtful
that any will possess decorations as important as those of Petubastis and
Petosiris. Thus far, for example, archaeologists have discovered only simple inscriptions such as the following in the neighboring tombs: "Hatres, son of Pae-
sios, grandson of Koryphos."[131] But even these bits of information provide
archaeologists with important clues concerning the ethnicity, demography, and
spiritual beliefs of the people who inhabited this distant oasis during the Roman
period.

8.31 The north wall of the outer chamber of the tomb of Petosiris at El-Muzzawaka. The large figure on the left is Petosiris himself.

Deserts Routes from Dakhleh

In addition to the two roads mentioned earlier that arrived in Dakhleh from Kharga, another vital route, the Darb el-Tawil, linked the oasis with the Nile Valley to the east.

Darb el-Tawil (The Long Road)

From its beginning at Balat in eastern Dakhleh to its termination near Beni Adi in the Nile Valley, the aptly named Darb el-Tawil covered a distance of more than 250 kilometers (fig. 8.32). Access from the oasis floor was gained via several steeply sloped passes in the northern escarpment, the most important being the Balat pass, located 15 kilometers northeast of the village of Balat, and the Asmant pass, which lies due north of Ismant el-Kharab. The former route, which consists of a single, narrow defile leading to the top of the plateau, appears to have been the principal exit and entrance to the eastern portion of the Dakhleh Oasis for travelers headed to and from the Nile Valley. Indeed, it leads directly to the ancient site of Ain Asil, where archaeologists have uncovered clay tablets of hieroglyphics dating back to the Sixth dynasty, the earliest known evidence of an official link between the Nile Valley and Dakhleh Oasis.

No wells currently exist along the great length of the Darb el-Tawil, but there are signs that this might not have been the case during the Roman period. In the early part of the twentieth century, Harding King discovered an ancient road leading to a well located approximately 60 kilometers northeast of Balat pass. According to King, "a long, low, flat-topped hill with a small peak at its eastern extremity" marked the point where the road to the well veered west, away from the Darb el-Tawil.[132] The route soon passed through a rocky tract of desert that featured a man-made road from which all the stones had been cleared. King was certain that this road was not the work of bedouin, and his description of it indicates that it was similar in appearance to Roman roads in the Eastern Desert, although no comparable road has ever been positively identified in the Western Desert. Further along, at a point called the Naqb Shushina (Shushina pass), where the road descended an escarpment, "the road down onto the lower level had been notched out of the side of the scarp in a way that would not have done discredit to a modern engineer."[133] Somewhere within the sandy plain that lay at the bottom of this pass, King's guides led him to a place at which he observed the foundations of walls, broken pottery, and the remains of a well measuring 2.5 meters across and 2 meters deep. Buried in the sand of this well, his guides discovered pieces of purple glass and copper coins dating from the Ptolemaic period. One side of the well contained a ramp leading to the bottom, and the walls were reinforced with palm-

8.32 The desolate landscape along the Darb el-Tawil between Dakhleh Oasis and Beni Adi in the Nile Valley.

tree trunks. King speculated that the site was constructed during the Ptolemaic period and served as a fortified water station for travelers using the Darb el-Tawil.[134] Thus the well possibly continued to function into the Roman period.

Although the Darb el-Tawil was used well into the twentieth century by caravans carrying Dakhleh's date harvest to market in the Nile Valley, archaeologists have never surveyed the route. One nineteenth-century traveler, Sir Archibald Edmonstone, journeyed from the Nile Valley to Dakhleh via this ancient road and wrote of its desolation: "Nothing was to be seen but a vast immeasurable plain of sand, extending itself in all directions, over which the eye searched in vain for an object to rest upon. . . . Not a vestige of cultivation, nor even a blade of grass, were to be seen, and, except for the carcasses of camels which lined our path at no great intervals for the whole extent of our course, there was nothing to remind us that this route was ever frequented."[135] Edmonstone wrote that after several days the sandy plains gave way to gravel and rolling hills, but he did not mention noticing any Roman-era artifacts along the route. Instead, it appears that his most interesting observation was of a large pile of ropes and assorted cordage. His guides told him it was the grave of a man who, while traveling this route in summer, suffered the deaths of all five of his camels. When his last camel collapsed, the man decided to become a hermit and live the rest of his days at the site. Sustained by food and water given to him by passing caravans, he survived for some time, at least long enough to be considered a holy man. When he died, he was regarded as a preserver of camels, and passing caravans would add cordage and fodder of their own dead camels to the saint's hermitage in the hope of being blessed with a safe passage for themselves.[136]

In addition to the Darb el-Tawil, three less-traveled roads connected the residents of Dakhleh with the outside world. These trails were the Darb el-Tarfawi, the Darb el-Kufra, and the Darb el-Farafra (see map 4).

Darb el-Tarfawi

The Darb el-Tarfawi begins in the village of Mut in Dakhleh and proceeds south. After approximately 75 kilometers, it divides, one route heading southwest for more than 500 kilometers toward Gebel Uweinat via the well-known hill named Abu Balas (Father of Pots), and the other track leading 250 kilometers further south directly to Bir Tarfawi, and then on to Selima Oasis in the Sudan. The route has yet to be examined for evidence that might indicate the degree to which it was used during the Roman period.

Darb el-Kufra

Kufra is a major oasis located in eastern Libya, approximately 600 kilometers west-southwest of Dakhleh. Although the Great Sand Sea now covers much of this territory, it is probable that long before the dunes moved so far south, one or more major caravan routes connected the two oases. Local residents of Dakhleh speak of the existence of such roads, and traces of these ancient routes have been noted by European travelers.[137]

Darb el-Farafra

The 185-kilometer Darb el-Farafra leaves Dakhleh via the steep, sandy Bab el-Gasmund pass, which rises to the high plateau just north of Qasr Dakhleh (fig. 8.33). From the summit of the pass, the road first crosses a broad stretch of sharp, wind-eroded limestone, then proceeds northwest for 140 kilometers between parallel rows of enormous, 50-meter-high sand dunes. Within this distance, however, there are wide gravel plains containing sections of a cleared road that closely resemble the one Harding King described on the Darb el-Tawil. But without a closer examination, it is impossible to determine whether this road dates from the

8.33 The steep Bab el-Gasmund pass just north of Qasr Dakhleh.

Roman period. Approximately 140 kilometers from Bab el-Gasmund, a small stand of decrepit palm trees mark the site of the silted-up well known as Bir Dikka. From there, the route arcs several degrees more to the west before finally arriving at Qasr Farafra, some 35 kilometers away.[138]

By camel, the Darb el-Farafra can easily be traversed in four days; travelers in antiquity would thus have likely established at least three rest stops along its length. Unlike the large concentrations of pottery found at intervals along the roads from Dush to Edfu and from Kharga to Dakhleh, however, the Darb el-Farafra reveals only an occasional minor scattering of badly worn sherds, even at Bir Dikka. This paucity of pottery may mean that this route was not heavily traveled in antiquity. Indeed, given that the population of Farafra was far smaller than that of Dakhleh and that—as we shall see later—Farafra's main contact with the outside world took place via Bahariya Oasis, there does not appear to have been a great incentive for people to make the journey. Of course, another explanation for the lack of pottery along the route is that—to the extent that travelers did leave evidence of their passing—the constantly shifting dunes through which the route passes might have obscured any significant concentrations of sherds that would mark ancient halting places.[139]

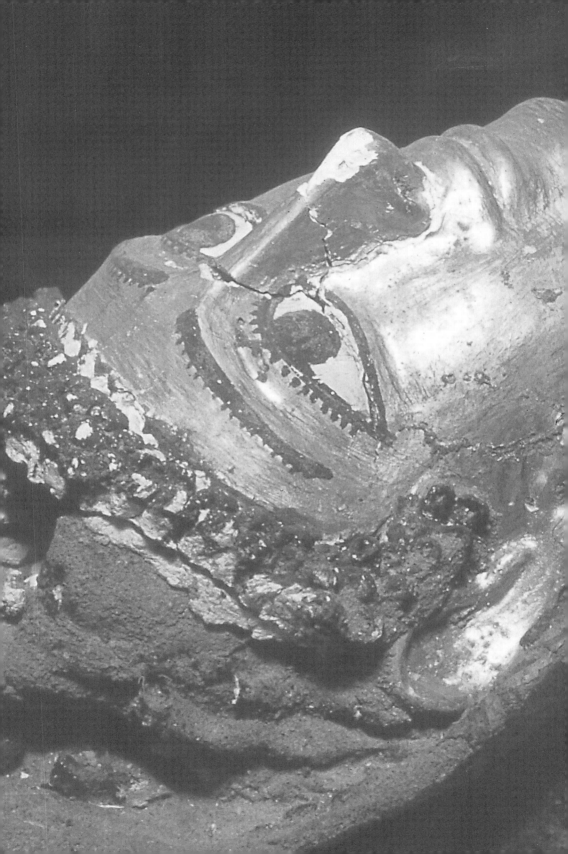

IX

THE SMALL OASIS

The two modern oases of Farafra and Bahariya constitute the single region known in antiquity as the Small Oasis. Relatively little is known about the political, economic, and social life of Farafra and Bahariya during the Roman period. Of the two, Bahariya was the more populated and prosperous. Because it not only sustained large-scale agriculture, but also was situated closer to the Nile Valley than Farafra, the Romans understandably would have exploited its economic and strategic value. Their fortification of the oasis served to protect the farming settlements in Bahariya as well as Roman interests in the Nile Valley, both of which were at risk of attack by Libyans and the various desert tribes that frequently raided Roman Egypt from the third through the sixth centuries.

FARAFRA

In antiquity, Farafra was known as Ta-iht (Land of the Cow) because of its close association with the goddess Hathor. Located in a triangular-shaped depression, it is 210 kilometers northwest of Dakhleh and 175 kilometers southwest of Bahariya (see map 4). Although its modern population is the lowest of the inhabited oases in the Western Desert, the depression itself is vast, measuring approximately 200 kilometers long by 90 kilometers wide. The most remarkable feature of the depression is the northeastern portion, which is characterized by a surface of brilliant white chalk forming a magnificent, otherworldly landscape of wind-eroded boulders and towering ridges.

Farafra's ancient history is still somewhat of a mystery. Although archaeologists have yet to discover any artifacts dating from the Pharaonic period in the oasis, several ancient texts record that Farafra's inhabitants maintained at least limited commercial relations with neighboring oases and the Nile Valley as far back as the Fifth dynasty (circa 2494–2345 B.C.).[1] By the Nineteenth dynasty (circa 1320-1200 B.C.), Farafra's ancient name appeared on a list found in Luxor Temple of places that produced minerals and dates during the reign of Ramses II (circa 1304–1237 B.C.). Quite probably, these exported minerals consisted of the iron pyrites and marcasite, which lie in abundance on the surface of the desert surrounding Farafra.[2]

The few known ancient sites in Farafra all date from the Roman period or later, but even these are relatively insignificant. Thus, although it is probable that the Romans stationed a contingent of soldiers and administrative officials in the oasis to guard access to the caravan routes and wells and to collect taxes, it is likely that the oasis was only sparsely inhabited during the Roman period. The single fortress that probably stood at the center of the oasis is now either completely destroyed or buried beneath the modern town of Qasr el-Farafra.[3] According to Ahmed Fakhry, who made numerous, albeit brief, visits to Farafra over a period of thirty years in the middle of the twentieth century, only three important Roman sites (aside from several clusters of rock-cut tombs) are in Farafra.[4]

Ain Bishai

Although this is possibly the major Roman site in Farafra, it has little to impress a visitor today. Located approximately 12 kilometers southwest of the main town of Qasr el-Farafra, it contains a cemetery, two brick buildings, and what appears to be a small, uninscribed chapel of limestone blocks.

9.1 The cluster of palm trees marking the location of the spring of Ain Hadra just west of Ain el-Wadi in Farafra.

Ain el-Wadi

Located in Wadi Hannis, a picturesque depression one day's journey (approximately 40 kilometers) north of Qasr el-Farafra, Ain el-Wadi was an important water station for caravans traveling between Farafra and Bahariya. The principal spring, Ain Hadra, lies nestled in a small cluster of palm trees and is still a source of excellent water (fig. 9.1). Although the area surrounding the spring has never been surveyed or excavated, the abundance of pottery sherds and the remains of several buildings attest to the fact that the wadi was inhabited and lightly cultivated during the Roman period.[5] Amidst these ruins, Fakhry discovered one small bronze amulet of the goddess Sakhmet and another of Harpocrates as well as a Roman coin too worn to be dated.

Ain Dallah

This site does not actually lie within the Farafra depression; it is located 75 kilometers to the north, on the other side of the Abu Said plateau. From antiquity through modern times, however, it served as an important water station on the desert tracks from Farafra to Siwa and Libya. Fakhry noted in 1939 that the remains of at least two ancient brick buildings with plastered walls stood near the spring, but these structures are now either destroyed or buried beneath the sand.[6]

DESERT ROUTES FROM FARAFRA

In addition to the Darb el-Farafra, which joins Farafra with Dakhleh Oasis to the south (see above), other routes connect Farafra with Bahariya, Siwa, Assiut, and Libya. Given that, with the exception of Siwa, Farafra is the most westerly of the oases and that it lies 300 kilometers due west of the Nile Valley, travel to and from the oasis was generally via Bahariya.

Farafra–Bahariya

The ancient Farafra–Bahariya route was always foremost in importance among the desert routes from Farafra. Although the route was approximately 175 kilometers long and took four days to complete, it was blessed with two water sources along its course—thus rendering the journey much less treacherous than any of the other routes that led from the oasis. The first of the water sources is Ain el-Wadi located in Wadi Hannis (see above). The second source is that of Ain el-Hayz, which lies approximately 40 kilometers from the terminus of the route in Bahariya.

Farafra–Siwa

At least two major routes linked Farafra with Siwa and its environs. Each of these, however, first passed through Ain Dallah. From this palm-treed resting place, the heaviest traveled route led northwest across 170 kilometers of barren desert until it intersected the Bahariya–Siwa road at the small oasis of Bahrein. From there, it followed the road westward, via El-Areg, to Siwa. The second route paralleled the first but veered more to the west, bypassing Bahrein and El-Areg and arriving directly at the town of Zaytun at the eastern edge of the Siwa depression.

Farafra–Assiut

The Farafra–Assiut route was the most direct between Farafra and the Nile Valley, but because it crossed almost 300 kilometers of waterless desert it was also the most hazardous—requiring seven to eight days by camel. No doubt it was used primarily during the winter months and then only for urgent business. Otherwise, travelers preferred the longer but much safer routes via the other oases.

Farafra–Libya

Although little is known about the exact location of the Farafra–Libya route—partly because traces of it have vanished under the Great Sand Sea—it is highly probable that at least one ancient route from the Libyan interior entered Farafra via Ain Dallah.

BAHARIYA

The Bahariya depression measures approximately 100 kilometers long and 40 kilometers wide and is completely surrounded by a high escarpment. The depression floor is punctuated by numerous conical hills and small mountains. Prior to the recent discovery of a large Greco-Roman necropolis in Bawiti, scholars (with the exception of Fakhry) had generally ignored the few important sites from that period within the oasis, focusing their attention and resources on the archaeologically richer oases further south. Indeed, until 1999, what little was known about Bahariya during the Roman period came in large part from papyri discovered at the ancient site of Oxyrhynchus in the Nile Valley. These provided glimpses of Bahariya's connections to the outside world: for example, that Bahariya or at least the town of El-Qasr was garrisoned by troops taken from the larger Roman station in Oxyrhynchus; and, on a more mundane level, that in A.D. 75, a man named Sarapion brought two donkeys loaded with barley and onions to Bahariya.[7]

Today, Bahariya is surrounded by impressive stands of date palms, and the modern town of Bawiti has expanded to cover large portions of the ancient settlement whose Egyptian name was Psobthis, now referred to as El-Qasr (The Fortress). Numerous tombs and fragments of ancient buildings, an abundance of pottery, and the presence of an elaborate aqueduct system attest to the possibility that the oasis was heavily populated during the Roman period. Of these sites, the most significant are discussed below.

The Necropolis of Bawiti

In March 1996, an Egyptian antiquities guard assigned to the Temple of Alexander the Great in Bawiti discovered a hole in the desert sand just over a kilometer from the temple. Upon peering into the hole, he glimpsed what appeared to be a man-made chamber. Egyptian archaeologists immediately began excavating the site and soon realized it was a small portion of an enormous necropolis containing perhaps thousands of graves dating from the Greco-Roman period. Remarkably, none of the burial chambers bore evidence of having been pilfered by grave robbers, thus presenting archaeologists with an extraordinary opportunity to examine hundreds of mummies and a great variety of funerary objects in undisturbed condition.

Although it will take years to complete the arduous task of excavating the Bawiti site, archaeologists have already uncovered a treasure trove of artifacts. In 1999, researchers excavated the most prominent among these, more than one hundred gilded mummies. The largest collection was discovered in tomb 54, which contained the remains of thirty-eight such mummies (fig. 9.2). Of these, six bodies

9.2 The upper portion of a gilded mummy from tomb 54 in the Bawiti necropolis.

were those of children, suggesting that the tomb bears the remains of several generations of a single wealthy family. Here, the elaborately decorated mummies were laid to rest in a series of eight niches cut into the sandstone walls of the burial chamber. Each niche contained as many as six bodies laid neatly alongside each other, with additional mummies left on the floor.[8]

Not all the mummies discovered in Bawiti were as splendidly arrayed for the afterlife. Researchers identified roughly four types of mummies. While the first and most impressive were those encased in plaster cartonnage and gold (often inlaid with faience and other semiprecious stones) this type of burial preparation was a privilege of the wealthy few—perhaps merchants—who inhabited the oasis during the Roman period.[9] The second category includes mummies wrapped carefully in linen but with only portions of their upper bodies encased in cartonnage. Upon these coverings are painted depictions of funerary deities. The third category consists of bodies meticulously wrapped in linen but without cartonnage or gilding. Although less impressive than the first two types, these mummies nevertheless were carefully wrapped in different colored linen in such a way as to form intricate geometric patterns over the entire corpse. The final category belongs, predictably, to the poorest residents of the oasis, who, upon their death, were rather carelessly wrapped in linen and buried with little apparent concern for preservation.[10]

Although most of the Bawiti mummies appear to date from the first century A.D., their exact age is uncertain. Further examination of the pottery, coins, and jewelry with which they were interred will give archaeologists valuable information about their age. In the meantime, scientific analysis of several of the mummies has already enabled researchers to gain insights into life in the oasis during antiquity. For example, infectious diseases claimed the majority of lives in the Nile Valley, but there is little evidence that the same illnesses afflicted the people of Bawiti—perhaps owing to the sterility of the dry desert environment. Life, however, was not easy for the people of the oasis. Preliminary data point to a life expectancy slightly higher than that of Egyptians living in the Nile Valley, yet residents of Bawiti still lived, on average, for only twenty-five to thirty-five years, and they suffered a high rate of osteoarthritis before the age of thirty. Scholars hope that additional use of X-rays, CAT scans, and DNA sampling from the Bawiti mummies will yield further information pertaining to the ethnicity, life expectancy, birthrates, diet, labor, and medical practices of the inhabitants of the oasis during the Roman period.[11]

Roman Triumphal Arch

Located in El-Qasr, the famous Roman triumphal arch was probably only part of a larger Roman fortress. It remained standing until at least the mid–nineteenth century, when several European explorers visited it, but virtually nothing of the arch exists today, its stones having been carried off and used in the building of local houses. Fortunately Cailliaud published several drawings of the structure, and Hoskins wrote the following detailed description:

> The most imposing ruin in the Oasis Parva [Small Oasis] is a triumphal arch, evidently Roman. It stands on a platform, 33 ft. in height above the level of the plain and 128 ft. in length, being formed of rough stones thrown without any order into the cement; surrounding which is a wall 7 ft. thick, very much inclined, and curiously constructed of hewn stones, placed alternately crossways and lengthways. The longer side of the stones being three times the measurement of the shorter, one stone of the row placed lengthwise apparently covers three of those beneath. The cornice, which appears to have extended all around the platform, is rather of a good style, being surmounted with triglyphs and dentils. Above is a kind of attic, with its cornice three feet high, forming a parapet to the platform. This latter is uncovered on three sides; but on the fourth side, the ground of the village of Kasr is now and appears to have been always on a level with it. The principal facade is towards the north.
>
> The triumphal arch, situated in the middle of the north facade of the platform, is 25 ft. in length. Only the centre arch now remains, from which a

staircase leads to the ground beneath. The facades are ornamented with pilasters. On each side of the arch is a niche ornamented with small columns. A winding staircase leads to the terrace, the outlet to which is under the arch. There are some traces of Greek letters on the walls.[12]

Aqueducts

Among the ancient structures still visible in Bawiti and El-Qasr is the impressive system of wells and aqueducts that supplied the large quantities of water necessary to cultivate vast tracts of date palms, olive trees, and other crops.[13] The shafts leading down into the aqueducts, which served the local inhabitants until the twentieth century, are still visible along the streets of the town. But the question of who built this impressive system remains unanswered. Although it is often assumed that the aqueducts are the work of the Romans—and there is no doubt they maintained and probably expanded the system during their occupation—Fakhry suggests that they existed at least as far back as the Twenty-sixth dynasty (664–525 B.C.).[14]

The most dramatic ancient spring in El-Qasr is that of Ain Bishmu, whose hot water once flowed from a fissure in the cliff on the northern edge of the town into a large cistern below. One can still see the remains of the ancient catchment walls for channeling the water, but these are now collapsed and filled with garbage. Today, the water emerges via a pipe from a bore-hole at the bottom of the cliff, and from there it flows out into the fields of date palms and olive trees beyond.

Qasr Muharib

Located approximately 12 kilometers east of the modern town of Bawiti, Qasr Muharib (Fortress of the Fighter) contains some of the largest Roman-era buildings still standing in the oasis. Built on the north slope of a hill and surrounded by land that was cultivated in antiquity, the site commanded a clear view of the plains below and thus probably served as an excellent lookout post from which to observe and perhaps regulate traffic entering and leaving the ancient town of El-Qasr via the eastern caravan route. The buildings include the remains of numerous houses, a stone temple, and a mud-brick fortress, all of which presumably date from the late Roman period.

Al-Mi-ysrah

Located just east of Bawiti, Al-Mi-ysrah consists of the remains of a Roman-era village and, until 1939, the three lower courses of a stone chapel containing Greek graffiti. According to Fakhry, who photographed the site in 1938, the large temple stones were removed by government builders in 1939 and used to construct an enclosure for a nearby spring. While excavating the surrounding village, however, Fakhry unearthed a pottery vase hidden in the wall of a house that had been destroyed by fire centuries ago. Upon lifting the lid of the vase, he discovered numerous gold and silver earrings, necklaces, bracelets, and rings and a gold coin depicting Emperor Valens (A.D. 364–78).[15]

Qasr al-Migyhbah

Situated a few kilometers northwest of El-Qasr, at the beginning of the long caravan route to Siwa, Qasr al-Migyhbah contains the remains of a temple complex dedicated to Alexander the Great—the only structure in the entire Western Desert known to have borne the name of the famous conqueror.[16] Excavated by Fakhry in 1938 and 1939, the walled enclosure includes a two-room sandstone temple, the walls of which once contained the effigy and cartouche of Alexander, and a total of forty-five other chambers that served as dwellings for priests, administrative offices, and storerooms. Unfortunately, the temple is now in extreme ruins, and the inscriptions pertaining to Alexander have been severely effaced by blowing sand. Although the building obviously predates the Roman period, Fakhry also discovered pottery, lamps, and Greek and Coptic ostraca within the structure, indicating that the site was occupied at many intervals between its construction and the twelfth century.[17]

El-Hayz

Located approximately 40 kilometers southwest of Bawiti on the principal caravan route to Farafra, the large district of El-Hayz contains the most significant late-Roman sites in Bahariya.[18] The presence of a large fortress, the size and number of the community's other buildings, and the amount of land its ancient inhabitants placed under cultivation, attest that during the Roman period El-Hayz must have been a bustling agricultural and trading community with a population of perhaps several thousand people. Today, the site has at least four springs and the remains of wells, numerous tombs, and buildings. The most important structures are in the vicinity of the spring of Ain el-Ris and include a multistoried fortress, a spacious mansion, a large bathhouse,[19] a thirteen-room building with a well in its courtyard, and a church dedicated to Saint George.

Although much more deteriorated today than it was when Fakhry wrote the following description, the Church of Saint George nevertheless constitutes the most important late Roman structure in the southern district:

> It is the only well-preserved ancient church in the Western Desert and one of the most important Christian monuments in the oases. Of the basilica type, it is built of mud brick in two stories. Its walls are coated with a layer of fine

mud; the interior was white-washed, and its shrine painted with religious scenes. Some few of these paintings still remain, but in 1818 and 1819 there were more. Belzoni and Cailliaud refer to them, mentioning the figure of a man riding a horse. This shows that in all probability the church was dedicated to St. George, in whose name several churches were built in this oasis. The church has two entrances, one at the south which leads to the church proper and one at the north-west corner, which leads to the baptistery. In the southeast corner of the church, just to the right of the chapel, a staircase leads to the upper balconies which were reserved for women as in many oriental churches in ancient and modern times. The roof and the upper part of the walls are now destroyed. We can compare its plan with the remains of the famous church at Dendarah which dates from the 4th-5th century of our era, and we can compare the style of its arches and the ornaments of its pillars with the chapels at Bagawat at Kharga Oasis. As for its date, there is enough evidence to suggest that it is not later than the 5th-6th century.[20]

Scattered throughout the district lie numerous tombs in which early Christian inhabitants were buried. Unfortunately, thieves have either stolen or destroyed whatever artifacts of archaeological value the graves once contained.

DESERT ROUTES FROM BAHARIYA

In addition to the caravan route connecting Bahariya with Farafra, three other important routes entered the oasis from the Nile Valley, the Fayoum, and Siwa Oasis. Although scholars have not surveyed these routes carefully, there is little doubt that all were closely guarded and patrolled, especially during the late Roman period.

Darb el-Bahnasa

The modern town of El-Bahnasa stands near the important ancient city of Oxyrhynchus in the Nile Valley, approximately 190 kilometers due east of Bahariya. From antiquity through the 1930s, when a tarmac road between Cairo and the oasis was completed, this route constituted the main link between Bahariya and the Nile Valley.

Darb el-Fayoum

The area around Lake Fayoum was a major agricultural zone throughout the Roman period and encompassed such important towns as Dionysias, Socnopaiou Nesos, and Karanis—the ruins of which have provided archaeologists with a wealth of information about life in this area.[21] Depending on which of these

9.3 The author's camel en route to Bahariya Oasis on the Darb el-Fayoum.

towns one started in, the distance to Bahariya varied from approximately 210 kilometers to 250 kilometers (fig. 9.3). Initially the roads all headed south so that travelers and their camels could water at the beautiful lakes of Wadi Raiyan; then the tracks turned west and passed through a series of small dune fields separated by wide gravel plains. Although no Roman-era structures exist along this route, one occasionally encounters heavy concentrations of Roman pottery, indicating the presence of an ancient rest stop.[22] After one travels roughly six days on foot from Fayoum, numerous conical hills topped with black iron ore come into view, and the ancient trail descends the eastern escarpment of the Bahariya depression.

Darb el-Siwa

The much-ruined temple to Alexander the Great that stands near the eastern terminus of this route raises the remote possibility that Alexander passed through Bahariya when he returned to the Nile Valley after consulting the oracle at Siwa in 331 B.C.[23] Although this may never be proven, it is certain that this 400-kilometer-long road was used during the Roman period. From El-Qasr, the road heads mainly west-northwest, skirting the southern edges of the massive Qattara depression and winding through a variety of magnificent desert landscapes. Continuing west, it passes the four uninhabited oases of Sitra, Bahrein, Nuwemisah, and El-Areg (see chapter 10), before arriving finally in the town of Zaytun, the easternmost settlement in the Siwa depression.

X

SIWA OASIS

O f the five major oases in the Western Desert, Siwa is the most renowned—and yet also the most mysterious. Located only 45 kilometers
from the modern Libyan border, Siwa is a place of enchanting beauty in
a sea of fire: a cool, green island whose lush palm groves produce some of the
finest dates in North Africa. But despite the quality of its agricultural produce and
its greater fame as the seat of one of the ancient world's most important oracles,
Siwa's early history and its relation with Egypt remain difficult to trace with precision. Like all the oases in the Western Desert, Siwa has been inhabited since Palaeolithic times, but unlike the residents of the other oases, the Siwans boast of an
ethnicity and language that is Berber rather than Egyptian or Arab, and their clothes
and customs set them apart as a unique people. Although Siwa was strongly influenced by Egyptian culture by the Twenty-sixth dynasty (664–525 B.C.), the oasis

10.1 The ruins of the medieval town of Shali, the Siwan name for Siwa.
The original settlement at Aghurmi can be seen atop the hill in
the upper left corner of the photograph.

was considered part of Libya rather than Egypt and managed to retain a high degree of political independence until sometime in the first century A.D.[1]

The Siwa depression is approximately 80 kilometers long from east to west and
averages 18 meters below sea level. The modern town of Siwa lies approximately
in the middle of this depression, surrounding the base of a hill covered by the
mud-brick ruins of the medieval town of Shali, the Siwan name for Siwa (fig. 10.1).
In addition to the modern town, several smaller villages lie scattered across the
depression floor amidst groves of palm and olive trees. These villages, particularly
in the east, stand near the shores of a series of salt lakes, the largest being Birket
Zaytun, which measures 25 kilometers long and averages five kilometers wide.
Indeed, the presence of such sizable bodies of water set in the harsh desert landscape is among the most striking characteristics of Siwa Oasis. The lakes, however, are not the blessing they might seem: they are merely the unfortunate
consequence of the inadequate drainage typical in areas so far below sea level.
Thus, as the water table rises under the depression floor, it brings with it a high
concentration of salt, which in turn severely reduces agricultural productivity and
precludes the possibility of using lake water for irrigation. Undoubtedly, poor

drainage and high salinity were serious issues for ancient farmers as well, but modern irrigation techniques have compounded the problem by permitting farmers to exploit ever-larger volumes of underground water, with the consequence that, today, the land that was agriculturally productive in ancient times is salt-encrusted and sterile.

The difficulties presented by the high salinity of Siwa's soil are not limited to agriculture. Buildings and protective walls constructed from salt-impregnated mud, for example, are vulnerable to the rare, but heavy rains that can fall on the oasis during the winter months. On such occasions, the mud bricks begin to dissolve, causing an immediate and predictable weakening of the structure. Indeed, it was partly because the original ancient settlement of the oasis—located at Aghurmi—had been heavily damaged by rains (and assaults by marauding tribes) that the majority of its inhabitants abandoned the site in A.D. 1203 and moved four kilometers north to a hill upon which they constructed the settlement of Shali. This new town remained inhabited until the early part of the twentieth century, when, again, damage from heavy rains prompted those who still lived in its mud-brick homes to move into the modern, cement buildings that Siwans had begun constructing around the base of the hill.

THE ORACLE OF SIWA

The most famous attribute of Siwa Oasis in ancient times was the presence of the oracle, whose seat was in the great temple dedicated to Ammon, and whose powers were well known throughout the Mediterranean world as far back as the Twenty-first dynasty (circa 1085–945 B.C.), when Siwa was considered part of Libya.[2] In 550 B.C., however, Croesus, the king of Lydia, decided to test the wisdom of all the famous oracles of his time by sending messengers to them and asking each to state in detail what he, Croesus, was doing that very day in far-away Lydia. Alas, not one of the oracles except that of Delphi, in Greece, was able to answer correctly that, on the day in question, Croesus had chopped up a tortoise and some lamb's meat, boiled them together in a bronze cauldron, and placed a bronze lid on the pot.[3]

It does not appear, however, that this setback tarnished the oracle of Siwa's reputation for infallibility. Only twenty-five years later, in 525 B.C., the Persian king, Cambyses, who had conquered Egypt and was on his way south to defeat the Ethiopians, decided to lead his army all the way across the Western Desert to attack the Siwans, then known as Ammonians, and destroy their famous oracle: "He divided off about fifty thousand of his army and ordered them to enslave the Ammonians and burn the oracle of Zeus in Ammon; but he himself, with the rest of his army, marched against the Ethiopians."[4] According to Herodotus, Cambyses' army arrived in Kharga but mysteriously disappeared before reaching Siwa: "What the Ammonians say about them is this: when they were on their road from Oasis [Kharga] to the Ammonia country through the desert and were indeed about midway between the Ammonian country and the Oasis, while they were taking breakfast there blew upon them suddenly a violent southern wind, bringing with it piles of sand, which buried them; thus it was that they utterly disappeared."[5] Although Herodotus probably exaggerated the number of soldiers in Cambyses' army, the story of their disappearance is not entirely implausible. Siwa lies at the northern end of the Great Sand Sea, an awesome, virtually impenetrable expanse of drifting dune fields that extend for 700 kilometers south before ending at the Gilf Kebir Plateau. The dunes within this vast sea are pushed and sculpted by constant northern winds and can attain heights of 100 meters. Indeed, the history of the Western Desert registers numerous accounts of large caravans and military troops disappearing during sudden, violent windstorms that scour the surface of the desert. One account from 1805 relates how blowing sands buried two thousand people and their camels as they traveled from Darfur to Assiut along the Darb el-Arbain.[6]

Although it was the presence of the oracle that made the oasis famous in antiquity, the visit of Alexander the Great in 331 B.C. bestowed upon Siwa a celebrated place in history. Several descriptions of his journey exist, among them that of Callisthenes, Alexander's court historian.[7] His account, and those of others who based their writings on his report, were successful at convincing readers of the divine favor in which the gods held Alexander. Thus, Plutarch, writing in the second half of the first century A.D., gives the following version of the king's march to Siwa:

This was a long and painful, and, in two respects, a dangerous journey; first, if they should lose their provision of water, as for several days none could be obtained; and, secondly, if a violent south wind should rise upon them, while they were travelling through the wide extent of deep sands, as it is said to have done when Cambyses led his army that way, blowing the sand together in heaps, and raising, as it were, the whole desert like a sea upon them, till fifty thousand were swallowed up and destroyed by it. All these difficulties were weighed and represented to him; but Alexander was not easily to be diverted from anything he was bent upon. For fortune having hitherto seconded him in his designs, made him resolute and firm in his opinions, and the boldness of his temper raised a sort of passion in him for surmounting difficulties; as if it were not enough to be always victorious in the field, unless places and seasons and nature herself submitted to him. In this journey, the relief and assistance the gods afforded him in his distresses were more remarkable, and obtained greater belief than the oracles he received afterwards, which, however, were valued and credited the more on account of those occurrences. For first, plentiful rains that fell preserved them from any fear of perishing by drought, and, allaying the extreme dryness of the sand, which now became moist and firm to travel on, cleared and purified the air. Besides this, when they were out of their way, and were wandering up and down, because the marks which were wont to direct the guides were disordered and lost, they were set right again by some ravens, which flew before them when on their march, and waited for them when they lingered and fell behind; and the greatest miracle, as Callisthenes tells us, was that if any of the company went astray at night, they never ceased croaking and making noise till by that means they had brought them into the right way again.[8]

Upon his safe and presumably joyful arrival in Siwa after eight days in the desert, Alexander immediately made his way to the Temple of the Oracle. We shall never know exactly why he made this historic visit—possibly he realized that if he, as a Greek, hoped to rule over the racially diverse population of Egypt, it would be prudent to acknowledge the legitimacy of traditional Egyptian beliefs and to show respect for native Egyptian deities. Thus one might view his journey to pay homage to Ammon as a shrewd political decision.[9] On the other hand, Alexander was a man of supreme confidence and counted among his ancestors Perseus and Hercules, both of whom, according to legend, had consulted the Oracle of Siwa and both of whom were descendants of Zeus. Thus, perhaps he truly believed the oracle might tell him whether or not he, too, was divine. Whatever the case, the surviving ancient texts offer several descriptions of Alexander's meeting with the oracle. One version states that, in the Egyptian tradition of addressing living pharaohs, the priest of Ammon greeted Alexander with the words, "Son of Zeus-Ammon, the master of all countries, unconquered until he is united with the gods." After which, Alexander entered the sanctuary alone and communed with the oracle in secret.[10] Plutarch also relates that the high priest of the temple greeted his visitor with a welcome from Alexander's father, the god Ammon. But the king's first question to the priest was whether any of his father's assassins had escaped punishment. After being reminded by the priest that one who was born of an immortal father should speak with more respect, Alexander rephrased his question by asking specifically about Philip's murderers, then further inquired "whether the empire of the world was reserved for him." To these queries, the priest affirmed that Philip's murders were all slain and that, indeed, he would obtain a world empire. But Plutarch also mentions two other, allegedly later, versions of what transpired in the temple. One is that the priest's responses to

Alexander's questions were indeed made in secret and that Alexander wrote to his mother, Olympias, that he would reveal the substance of the oracle's message to her upon their next meeting. (Alexander, however, died in Babylon eight years after his visit to Siwa and never saw his mother again.) Another version is that, upon greeting Alexander, the priest intended to say, "O Paidion" (My Son), but, mispronouncing the Greek, said, "O Pai Dios" (O Son of Jupiter)—a mistake for which Alexander was supposedly much pleased, for it strengthened his authority as he marched off to conquer all the lands between Egypt and India.

Despite the apparent historical fact of Alexander's visit to Siwa, modern archaeologists have yet to discover any monument or temple that bears his name in the oasis.[11] In February 1995, a Greek archaeologist announced the discovery of Alexander's tomb in the al-Marqi district of the oasis, about 25 kilometers from the town of Siwa, but her claim is generally denounced by leading scholars.[12] No doubt the tomb she uncovered dates to either the Macedonian or Ptolemaic period, and there is some evidence that Alexander had wished to be buried in Siwa, but it is most likely that, upon the insistence of his general, Ptolemy I Soter (304–284 B.C.), Alexander was laid to rest some 450 kilometers further east, in the magnificent city of Alexandria. Although some scholars believe his body lies beneath the Nebi Daniel mosque, the exact location of his tomb will remain one of the great archaeological mysteries of modern times.

It appears that Siwa Oasis had become somewhat of a backwater by the time of the Roman occupation. Upon assuming control of the area, the Romans concerned themselves with expanding and protecting its agricultural output, securing desert roads, and collecting taxes, but they seem to have neglected or even ignored the tradition of consulting the oracle. Instead, they focused their energies on exploiting and taxing the production of olives and olive oil. Indeed, there is strong evidence that the high quality olive oil from Siwa was especially sought after in the second and third centuries and that people were willing to pay 10 percent more for it than for oil from the other oases.[13]

ROMAN SITES OF SIWA

Although archaeologists have yet to identify any major Roman fortresses or temples in Siwa, several ancient structures were certainly used or modified during the Roman occupation of the oasis.

Temples of Ammon

There are at least two temples dedicated to Ammon in Siwa. The first, the famous Temple of the Oracle, stands atop a high, rocky hill at Aghurmi, four kilometers south of the modern town of Siwa. It was within this building's stone chambers that the temple priests received Alexander the Great in 331 B.C. The Greek historian Clitarchus, who wrote in 300 B.C. and whose works were popular among the Romans, recorded the following description of the temple:

> The inhabitants of the Oasis of Amun live in villages; in the middle of the oasis stands the Akropolis which is fortified with three enclosures. The first enclosure contains the palace of the ancient rulers, in the second one are the harem houses of the women, children and the other relatives as well as the guards, and lastly the chapel of the god and the sacred spring in which the offerings of the god are purified. The third one is the soldiers' barracks and the houses of the private guards of the ruler. A short distance from the Akropolis, a second temple of Amun stands in the shade of many large trees. Nearby, is a spring called "Spring of the Sun" because of its nature.[14]

Although the Temple of the Oracle still functioned, with priests officiating at its ceremonies, the influence and prestige of Siwa's oracle had waned by the time of the Roman occupation. One writer who visited Egypt in 23 B.C. claimed that "the Oracle had almost altogether disappeared which had previously enjoyed such high reputation."[15] And yet, according to some sources, the priests of Ammon demonstrated their loyalty to the emperor Hadrian when he visited Egypt in A.D. 130 by placing an inscribed stele in the temple to Ammon.[16] Thirty years later, Pausanius, the Greek writer who traveled to the oasis in A.D. 160, claimed that the oracle and priests were still active and that numerous stele adorned the courtyard of the temple.[17] Indeed, one of two inscribed fragments that Ahmed Fakhry discovered at the temple during excavations there in 1970 date from the second or third century A.D., and, more recently, researchers discovered a fragment dating from the reign of Trajan (A.D. 98–117).[18] Thus it remains unclear when the temple was actually closed. As he did with the temples of the Upper Nile Valley, the emperor Justinian ordered the closing of all pagan temples in Egypt in A.D. 527, and it is likely that the temples of Siwa were subject to that decree, if in fact they were still being used at that time.

Today, the temple is surrounded by—and until recently partly buried by—the crumbling ruins of the village of Aghurmi, which, although now abandoned, was inhabited as late as the first half of the twentieth century. The building dates from Ahmose (Amosis) II, who reigned from 570 to 526 B.C. during the Twenty-Sixth dynasty, but it is possible that it was built on top of an even older foundation. The main structure lies on a north–south axis and consists of one large courtyard with two Doric columns, followed by two smaller courts leading to the entrance of the sanctuary. Another large chamber is located outside the western wall of the sanctuary. The sanctuary itself measures approximately 6 meters long by 3 meters wide, and its side walls contain the only inscriptions found in the temple. These appear to date from the Twenty-Sixth dynasty; none of the walls bear evidence of Roman-era inscriptions. According to Fakhry, however, at least one of the stones used to build more recent additions to the temple dates from the second century A.D.[19]

The second important temple is that of Umm ʿUbaydah, which stands amidst a splendid palm grove only a short distance from Aghurmi village (fig. 10.2). In antiquity, this temple was connected to that of Aghurmi by a processional boulevard and possibly a secret underground tunnel. Most of the large blocks of stone that formed the temple walls have toppled to the ground, but many of the valuable inscriptions on them are well preserved.[20] Like the Temple of the Oracle, however, this structure predates the Roman period, having been built by Nectanebo II, who ruled from 360 to 343 B.C. during the Thirtieth dynasty.

Gebel el-Mawta

Just north of Siwa stands a hill called Gebel el-Mawta (Mountain of the Dead). It constitutes the most important known cemetery in Siwa and holds hundreds of rock-cut tombs, most of which were dug during the late Egyptian period and reused during the Greco-Roman period. Most of these tombs are simple and undecorated, but several (including the Twenty-Sixth-dynasty tomb of Niperpathot, the Ptolemaic-era tomb of Mesu-Isis, and the late Ptolemaic/early Roman tomb of the Crocodile) contain paintings and valuable hieroglyphic inscriptions. A fourth, unfinished tomb, that of Siamun (Man of Ammon), dates approximately from the early Roman period and is adorned by some of the most impressive decorations in the Western Desert.[21] Among the many scenes depicted on the wall of the tomb is a particularly intriguing picture of the bearded Siamun seated before his young son, who rests his hand on his father's knee. One cannot help but wonder if the painting illustrates the father's final good-bye.

Ain el-Gubah

Herodotus was the first to describe Ain el-Gubah (Spring of the Sun) in a discussion of the oases that lie along the ancient route connecting Thebes to Morocco:

> The first of them on the way up from Thebes, and that at ten days' journey, are the Ammonians, who have a temple there derived from the Zeus of Thebes; for in Thebes, too, as I said before, there is an image of Zeus depicted with a ram's face. There is also another spring of water there. Toward dawn it is

10.2 The tumbled remains of the temple of Umm 'Ubaydah in the foreground with the deserted hilltop village of Aghurmi in the background. The temple of the Oracle is located on Aghurmi.

warm; about the time of the crowding of the marketplace it becomes cool; and at noon it is downright cold, and that is when they use it to water their gardens. As the day wanes, the chill relaxes from the water until the sun sinks, and then the water grows warm. It increases in warmth as it draws nearer to midnight, and then it bubbles and boils. Once midnight is past, the chill sets in again until dawn. They call this spring the spring of the sun.[22]

Although this description can, at least in part, be explained by the fact that the warm springwater will feel cooler as the day becomes hotter, one gets the impression that Herodotus enjoyed embellishing his descriptions of places (which he might or might not have seen himself) in order to render them more mysterious and curious to the reader.

SITES WEST OF SIWA

During the Roman period, a considerable number of people lived in the western portion of Siwa Oasis. The remains of these settlements, however, consist mainly of tombs, concentrations of pottery, and a few simple structures.

10.3 Some of the tombs used during the Roman period at
Ghayt Abu Mansur, west of Siwa.

Ghayt Abu Mansur

The site of Ghayt Abu Mansur contains at least twenty-eight rock-cut, undecorated, and thoroughly pillaged tombs. The tombs are simple, containing one or two chambers, and some feature additional niches dug into their walls. Nearby, two kilometers from the spring of Khamisah, are more tombs and pottery dating from the early Roman period. Although also undecorated, one of these tombs holds two square pillars and a niche (fig. 10.3).[23]

Khamisah

Near the famous Khamisah spring, which is surrounded by fertile olive groves, stands a small stone temple, undecorated and much ruined. Just to the west are approximately 150 rock-cut tombs.

Al-Masarah

Located about five kilometers south of Khamisah, Al-Masarah features the remains of a stone gateway and part of a surrounding wall. In 1869, the German explorer Gerhardt Rohlfs discovered a Roman-era statue of a ram's head at this site, which he later donated to the Berlin Museum.

Balad al-Rum

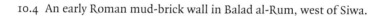

Five kilometers west of Khamisah, Balad al-Rum (Town of Romans) contains numerous rock tombs and the remains of a brick building at the foot of a hill. Nearby are the ruins of a stone temple and the extensive quarries of high quality stone from which the building was made. Eighteenth- and nineteenth-century travelers referred to this structure as a Doric temple, and Fakhry states that it contained "three halls preceded by a colonnade, thirty four meters long; the temple itself was twenty five metres long. The entrances to the halls were decorated but there were no wall inscriptions."[24] The structure, which Cailliaud thought the most beautiful monument in the oasis but which is now almost completely ruined, probably dates from the first century A.D.[25] (fig. 10.4).

An interesting aspect of the ruins of Balad al-Rum is the possibility that they contain evidence of the arrival of Christianity in Siwa. Unlike the other oases, which were generally Christianized by the end of the third century, Siwa has scarce evidence of Christianization. But Fakhry believed that Christianity did

10.4 An early Roman mud-brick wall in Balad al-Rum, west of Siwa.

plant itself in Siwa sometime in the fourth century, and his theory rests in part on the possibility that the structure standing at Balad al-Rum is a church rather than the remains of a Roman fortress. He also cites the following evidence from the Siwan Manuscript:[26] "Bilad al-Rum is a church at the foot of the hill from which some remains still exist and which was built with burnt brick; it is the abode of prostitutes. Khamisah, Mishandid and Dahibah as far as the white mountain belong to their dwelling."[27] Fakhry goes on to argue that people who were regarded as descendants of Romans lived in the village of Aghurmi. In this case Fakhry equates Romans with Christians because after the Arab conquest in the seventh century the term "Romans" was often used to refer to anyone who did not speak Arabic or who was not Muslim. But the date for the establishment of Islam in Siwa is also debatable. Although Muslim armies invaded and captured Alexandria in A.D. 641, at least one prominent work indicates that the Siwans repulsed an attack by the Arab general Musa Ibn Nusayr as late as A.D. 708.[28] Thus Fakhry argues that when Emperor Justinian (A.D. 527–65) ordered the closing of all pagan temples in Egypt (except that of Isis at Philae), the famous temples to Ammon in Siwa would have been forced to comply with his decree. It is therefore quite feasible that Christianity, which had already spread throughout Egypt, including the other oases, had finally taken root in Siwa in the fourth century. If it did take root, the current lack of evidence relating to that period strongly suggests that it did so only weakly and that it gave way quickly to Islam.[29]

SITES EAST OF SIWA

The four principal settlements east of Siwa were larger and more populated during the Roman period than those of the western district.

Ain al-Qurayshat

The Ain al-Qurayshat settlement, located ten kilometers east of Siwa on the north shore of Lake Zaytun, features two major structures, a temple and an administrative building. The limestone temple measures approximately 7 meters by 27 meters, has a spiral staircase in its northwestern corner, and was decorated in a Greco-Egyptian style. Nearby are the remains of an administrative building consisting of a large central room measuring approximately 15 by 16 meters that contains a well and features low benches along its walls. Roman-era artifacts unearthed from the area include a glass bust of a Roman emperor, coins, and numerous oil presses; the presses support the theory that Qurayshat played an

10.5 The late Roman-era temple at Abu Sharuf located approximately
30 kilometers east of Aghurmi.

important role in Siwa's oil production.[30] The settlement was undoubtedly a
large and bustling agricultural community in ancient times, but today its once-
impressive buildings lie in utter ruin owing to the ravages of time and looters.

Abu Sharuf

Located one day's journey from Aghurmi (approximately 30 kilometers) and five
kilometers east of Ain al-Qurayshat, the large stone temple of Abu Sharuf stands
amidst the ruins of a sizable town. Of late Roman construction, the temple remains in fairly good condition, with intact rooms, some featuring barrel vaulting;
but the plastered walls contain neither decorations nor inscriptions (fig. 10.5).
One hundred meters south of the temple is the cemetery.

Al-Zaytun

Al-Zaytun is the easternmost site in the Siwa depression and appears to have
been one of the most prosperous. Located about five kilometers east of

10.6 The abandoned village of Al-Zaytun, the easternmost ancient settlement in the Siwa depression.

Abu Sharuf and two kilometers southeast of the main spring, the unexcavated site dates from the Roman period, but it remained inhabited until the early years of World War II. Contained within its labyrinthine streets are the remains of a modest limestone temple, much of which remains buried under the mud-brick buildings of the recently abandoned village. Only two rooms are now accessible, and these are sparsely decorated in an Egyptian style. The temple and surrounding village stood in the middle of a fertile agricultural area, and its inhabitants produced outstanding olives from antiquity to modern times (fig. 10.6).

Abu Awwaf

Excavations are currently under way at the small but impressive necropolis of Abu Awwaf, located two and a half kilometers north-northeast of Al-Zaytun. In the early nineteenth century, several large buildings were still standing here, but these are now mostly destroyed. The four known buildings display high-quality construction and appear to be mausoleums, each intended for a single family. One contemporary scholar concludes that the site was "a burial ground for some well-to-do officials or landowners in Roman Siwa and the employees of their estates."[31]

DESERT ROUTES FROM SIWA

Siwa to the Mediterranean

Numerous tracks headed northward from Siwa to the Egyptian and Libyan coasts, but the principal route led directly to Paraetonium (modern Marsa Matruh) on the Mediterranean Sea and was called Masrab el-Istabi, or the Sultan's Road. This road, which follows the approximate course of the modern tarmac road, is approximately 300 kilometers long, required seven to nine days to travel, and featured at least seven wells along its course. One of these, Bir el Kanayis, which lies about 65 kilometers from Marsa Matruh, features the remains of a large walled enclosure built of stones, evidence of cultivation of nearby land, and an abundance of Roman-era pottery sherds. This was likely the route taken by Alexander the Great when he traveled to Siwa, although it is not certain whether he returned to the Nile Valley via the same road. After reaching the desert plateau from the north, the route is flat and unattractive until it descends the escarpment into the verdant beauty of Siwa Oasis.

Another, more circuitous route connected Siwa with the coast via Qara, a magnificent and remote settlement on the western edge of the Qattarra depression, 130 kilometers east-northeast of Siwa. Its ancient Greek name was Siropon, then later Qaret Umm al-Soghayyar (the Little Mother). Although the area has not been excavated, such surface evidence as pottery and coins indicates that the original settlement was occupied during the Roman period (fig. 10.7).[32] It is believed that Alexander the Great might have stopped here en route to Memphis, but no ancient stone structures from the Greco-Roman period have been found. After leaving Qara, the route headed northward until it arrived at Ma'atin al-Garawiah, 25 kilometers east of Marsa Matruh.

Siwa to the Nile

This is the longest desert track from Siwa, and travelers of this eastward route (Masrab el-Muhashas) stopped at the fortified town of Qara, passed through the Qattarra depression, then stopped at Ain al-Mughrah and Wadi Natrun before arriving at Kirdasah near the Pyramids of Giza—the entire journey requiring twelve to fourteen days. This important route thus connected Siwa with Memphis, the ancient capital of Egypt, and, according to Fakhry, was used by Alexander to return to the Nile Valley.[33]

10.7 Perched on the edge of the Qattara depression and 130 kilometers east-northeast of Siwa, the ancient village of Qara was an important resting place on the long desert route to the Nile Valley.

Siwa to Libya

Again, numerous routes led from Siwa into Libya, but the principal destinations were the important coastal city of Sallum, 310 kilometers due north, and Jaghbub, approximately 125 kilometers to the northwest.

Siwa to Bahariya

Although this desolate route (Darb el-Siwa) is discussed briefly in chapter 9, it is important to describe the four uninhabited oases through which it passes and which bear evidence of habitation from the Roman era. From west to east, the oases are El-Areg, Bahrein, Nuwamisah, and Sitra.34

El-Areg

Lying approximately 55 kilometers west of Al-Zaytun, El-Areg was the largest and most populated of the four oases that line the ancient route to Bahariya. The oasis consists of two springs that lie at the base of a narrow valley bounded by steep cliffs. Within these cliffs are numerous rock-cut tombs, some of which contain decorations (fig. 10.8). Among the decorations are a portion of text written in an ancient Libyan script and simple paintings depicting the Egyptian gods Nut, Osiris, and Anubis. The most detailed painting yet to be found in the tombs shows a man apparently chopping at the trunk of a date palm, while a cow looks on from the right (fig. 10.9). Although it is possible that some of these paintings were executed by Christian hermits who may have lived in the oasis during the late Roman period, their exact age cannot be determined without further study.

Perhaps the most interesting discovery at El-Areg was made in the late nineteenth century by Rohlfs, who claims to have identified a circular temple containing columns and a marble floor. If such a structure actually exists, however, it must now lie buried beneath the sand because no trace of it is discernible today.[35]

Bahrein

Located 120 kilometers southeast of Siwa and approximately 12 kilometers south of the main caravan route that connected Siwa with Bahariya (Darb el-Siwa), the beautiful, isolated oasis of Bahrein consists mainly of two salt lakes whose southern shores are dotted with scraggly date palms. Just north of the lakes, a fossil-

10.8 Rock-cut tombs at El-Areg, a deserted oasis on the ancient route from Siwa to Bahariya Oasis.

10.9 The painting of a man, a palm tree, and a cow located
on the wall of a tomb at El-Areg.

10.10 One of the many spectacular rock formations near Nuwamisah
on the ancient route from Siwa to Bahariya.

rich escarpment rises to a height of 146 meters at Gebel Bahrein, and it was into this escarpment that the ancient inhabitants of this forlorn place carved numerous caves and tombs. Although archaeologists have not studied these features in detail, the caves appear to date from the Neolithic period, while the tombs are possibly Ptolemaic or Roman.

Nuwamisah

Located on the ancient caravan route some 21 kilometers east of Bahrein, Nuwamisah oasis was also inhabited, albeit minimally, for many thousands of years. Like its neighbor, it features two salt lakes, a sandstone escarpment into which ancient people dug numerous caves, and spectacular rock formations (fig.10.10).

Sitra

Lying 16 kilometers further east of Nuwamisah along the Darb el-Siwa, Sitra contains the largest salt lake in the region. Although it also possesses an escarpment on its northern side, researchers have yet to discover evidence of caves or tombs in the area.

ABBREVIATIONS

AJA	*American Journal of Archaeology*
AJP	*American Journal of Philology*
ANRW	*Aufstieg und Niedergang der Römischen Welt* (Berlin)
ASAE	*Annales du Service d'Antiquités d'Égypte*
AUC	American University in Cairo
BACE	*Bulletin of the Australian Centre for Egyptology*
BAR	*British Archaeological Reports* (Oxford)
BASP	*Bulletin of the American Society of Papyrologists* (Urbana: Department of Classics)
BFA	*Bulletin of the Faculty of Arts* (Cairo: Fouad University)
BGU	*Berliner Griechische Urkunden* (Berlin, 1895)
BIE	*Bulletin de l'Institut d'Égypte*
BIFAO	*Bulletin de l'Institut Francais d'Archéologie Orientale*

BSOAS	*Bulletin of the School of Oriental and African Studies* (University of London)
CE	*Chronique d'Égypte*
CIL	*Corpus Inscriptionum Latinarum.* Edited by T. Mommsen et al. (Berlin: G. Reimerum, 1862)
CHE	*Cahiers d'histoire égyptienne*
CNWS	Centre of Non-Western Studies (Leiden)
CR	*The Classical Review*
CSSH	*Comparative Studies in Society and History* (Cambridge: Cambridge University Press)
DAIK	Deutches Archäologisches Institute Kairo
DFIFAO	*Documents de Fouilles, Institut Français d'Archéologie Orientale*
Eph. Epig.	*Ephemeris Epigraphica, Corpus Inscriptionum Latinarum Supplementum* (Berlin: Institutus archaeologici romani, 1872)
GRBS	*Greek, Roman and Byzantine Studies*
GRBM	*Greek, Roman and Byzantine Monograph* (Durham: Duke University)
IFAO	Institut Français d'Archéologie Orientale (Cairo)
IG	*Inscriptiones Graecae Siciliae et Italiae additis Graecis Galliae, Hispaniae, Britanniae, Germaniae Inscriptionibus.* Edited by G. Kaibel (Berlin: G. Reimerum, 1890)
IGRR	*Inscriptiones Graecae ad Res Romanae Pertinentes.* Edited by R. Cagnat et al. (Paris: E. Leroux, 1901–21)
ILS	*Inscriptiones Latinae Selectae.* Edited by H. Dessau (Berlin: Weidmann, 1892–1916)
I. Portes	*Les portes du désert: recueil des inscriptions grecques d'Antinooupolis, Tentyris, Koptos, Apollonopolis Parva et Apollonopolis Magna.* By A. Bernand. (Paris: Editions du Centres National de la Recherche Scientifique, 1984)
JAC	*Jahrbuch für Antike und Christentum*
JARCE	*Journal of the American Research Center on Egypt*
JEA	*Journal of Egyptian Archaeology*
JNES	*Journal of Near Eastern Studies* (University of Chicago)
JRA	*Journal of Roman Archaeology*
JRS	*Journal of Roman Studies* (London: Society for the Promotion of Roman Studies)
JSSEA	*Journal of the Society for the Study of Egyptian Antiquities*
KUSH	*Journal of the Sudan Antiquities Service* (Khartoum: Commissioner for Archaeology; Oxford: J. Thornton and Sons)
MC Inv.	Mons Claudianus Inventory number. Quoted for material not yet published.

MDAIK	*Mitteilungen des Deutschen Archäologischen Instituts Kairo* (Mainz/Rhein: Verlag Phillipp von Zabern)
MIFAO	*Mémoires de l'Institut Français d'Archéologie Orientale*
NARCE	*Newsletter of the American Research Center in Egypt* (New York: American Research Center in Egypt)
O. Claud.	*Mons Claudianus: Ostraca Graeca et Latina I.* Edited by J. Bingen, A. Bülow-Jacobsen, W. Cockle, H. Cuvigny, L. Rubinstein, and W. Van Rengen. (Cairo: DFIFAO, 1992, 1997)
OGIS	*Orientis Graeci Inscriptiones Selectae.* Edited by W. Dittenberger (Leipzig: S. Hirzel, 1903–05)
PBA	*Proceedings of the British Academy* (London: Oxford University Press)
P. Giss.	*Griechische Papyri im Museum des Oberhessischen Geschichtsverein zu Giessen.* Edited by O. Eger, E. Kornemann, and P. Meyer (Leipzig-Berlin: B. G. Teubner, 1910–12)
P. Oxy.	*Oxyrhynchus Papyri.* Edited by B. P. Grenfell and A. S. Hunt et al. (London: Egypt Exploration Fund, 1898)
RFS	*Roman Frontier Studies*
SB	*Sammelbuch Griechischer Urkunden aus Ägypten.* Edited by F. Preisigke, F. Bilabel, and E. Kiessling (Strassburg-Berlin-Leipzig: K. J. Trübner, 1913–15)
SNR	*Sudan Notes and Records*
TAPA	*Transactions (and Proceedings) of the American Philological Association* (Chico, California: Association of Scholars Press)
TAPAS	*Transactions of the American Philosophical Society* (Philadelpia)
YCS	*Yale Classical Studies*
ZAS	*Zeitschrift für Agyptische Sprache und Altertumskunde*
ZPE	*Zeitschrift für Papyrologie und Epigraphik*

NOTES

PREFACE

1. Notably Vivian, *The Western Desert of Egypt: An Explorer's Handbook*.

INTRODUCTION

1. Herodotus, *History*, trans. George Rawlinson (Chicago: William Benton, 1952), 2:35.
2. Herodas, *Mimes* I, lines 26–35.
3. Shakespeare, "Antony and Cleopatra" (*The Riverside Shakespeare*, 2d ed. Boston: Houghton Mifflin Company, 1997), V,ii.
4. Skeat, "The Last Days of Cleopatra," 98–100.
5. For a thorough discussion of the Roman army in Egypt, see Alston, *Soldier and Society in Roman Egypt*.

6. For general works on Roman Egypt, see Bagnall, *Egypt in Late Antiquity*; Bowman, *Egypt after the Pharaohs: 332 B.C.–A.D. 642*; and Rowlandson, ed., *Women and Society in Greek and Roman Egypt: A Sourcebook*.

CHAPTER I. THE HILLS OF SMOKE

1. Weigall, *Travels in the Upper Egyptian Deserts*, 109.
2. Esther, 1:6. *The New Oxford Annotated Bible*, Revised Standard Version, 1977.
3. This is a small quarry for black porphyry that lies north of the main settlement at the base of Gebel Dokhan. It was discovered in 1991 by the American geologist James Harrell, but it was not named and its location was not made known until 1994, when a British researcher, Nicholas Bradford, published its location.
4. According to Wilfried Van Rengen, Caius Cominius Leugas was a Roman citizen, but the fact that the inscription does not mention a rank or unit indicates that he was not a soldier. Van Rengen, "New Paneion at Mons Porphyrites," 242.
5. Ibid.
6. Peacock and Maxfield, "On the Trail of Imperial Porphyry," 24.
7. Explanations vary as to why the mountain is referred to as the Mountain of Smoke. In 1949, Leo Tregenza's Egyptian guide stated that it was because "on hot days the air shimmering all around it looks like smoke from a distance." Tregenza had also heard, however, that it was due to the fact that when the Romans were working the quarries, one could see the smoke of their fires from the desert beyond the mountains. Tregenza, *Red Sea Mountains of Egypt*, 126.
8. The inscription of A.D. 29, which was discovered in a hut in the village of the Northwest Quarry, states, "The adoration of Apollodonius, son of Longinus, of the god Pan." Ibid., 136.
9. Aelius Aristeides, *Aigyptios* 48:349. Quoted in Meredith and Tregenza, "Mons Porphyrites: The North-West Village and Quarries," 142.
10. The *Ala Vocontiorum* was a branch of cavalry of the *Vocontii*, a people inhabiting Narnonese Gaul, and the date shows that it was stationed in Mons Porphyrites in A.D. 113. Tregenza, *Red Sea Mountains of Egypt*, 120.
11. Cockle, "Inscribed Architectural Fragment from Middle Egypt Concerning the Roman Imperial Quarries," 26.
12. Tregenza, *Red Sea Mountains of Egypt*, 120.
13. Meredith and Tregenza, "Mons Porphyrites: The North-West Village and Quarries," 132–33.
14. Sidebotham, Zitterkopf, and Riley, "Survey of the 'Abu Sha'ar-Nile Road," 596.
15. James Harrell, personal correspondence, October 20, 1995.
16. Sidebotham, Zitterkopf, and Riley, "Survey of the 'Abu Sha'ar-Nile Road," 596.
17. James Harrell discovered this tool in 1994.
18. Scaife, "Note on a Visit to the Imperial Porphyry Quarries at Gebel Dokhan," 145.

19. Scaife, "Note on Certain Inscriptions at Gebel Dokhan, and on a Small Station Hitherto Unrecorded, on the Road from Kainopolis to Myos Hormos," 106.

20. Ibid., 108.

21. As Leo Tregenza pointed out, local bedouin sometimes use this charcoal for cooking. While camping in these mountains in January 1996, I, too, was able to employ the ancient fuel to prepare afternoon tea.

22. Van Rengen, "The Ostraca," 18.

23. For example, a papyrus states, "Subatianus Aquila [Prefect of Egypt] to Theon, strategos of the Arsinoite nome, greeting. Niger, slave of Papirius, condemned to the alabaster quarry for five years by his Honour Claudius Julianus, now that he has completed the term of his sentence, I release. Good-bye." (December A.D. 209). SB 4639, quoted in Lewis, *Life in Egypt Under Roman Rule*, 138.

24. Van Rengen, "The Ostraca," 18.

25. Scaife, "Note on Certain Inscriptions at Gebel Dokhan, and on a Small Station Hitherto Unrecorded, on the Road from Kainopolis to Myos Hormos," 109. Steven Sidebothem points out that it is unclear which Hermopolis this inscription refers to, since there were two: Hermopolis Parva (Damanhur, in the Delta), and Hermopolis Magna (Asmunein, in Upper Egypt). Both of these were heavily Christian. Sidebotham, Zitterkopf, and Riley, "Survey of the 'Abu Sha'ar-Nile Road," 576.

26. Sidebotham, Zitterkopf, and Riley, "Survey of the 'Abu Sha'ar-Nile Road," 576. Approximately 20 km south of Gebel Dokhan, atop the headwall of Wadi Qattar, a small stone church dating from the fourth century marks the site of a Christian hermitage.

27. These pockets of water date from the Halocene, which began approximately 11,000 years ago.

28. A first-century ostracon discovered in the rubbish heap of the Badia fortress requests palm leaves "to crown the *hydreuma*." Maxfield and Peacock, "Archaeology of an Industrial Landscape: An Interim Report on the Work of the Imperial Quarries (Mons Porphyrites) Project," 188.

29. Unfortunately, the future of these graffiti and, indeed, of all the Roman remains in the area is in jeopardy from the ravages of tourism. With the rapid proliferation of Red Sea beach resorts, many hotel owners who are eager to expand their profits now offer "desert safaris" to their customers. Tour guides who know little or nothing of the history of the region now bring jeep-loads of tourists to the Gebel Dokhan range. Lacking regulation or oversight, this activity has predictable effects: tourists pick up potentially valuable artifacts as souvenirs, climb atop the unstable walls of the fortress, and etch or paint their names on the sides of the buildings. "SABRI, 27–11–91 MISR TRAVEL" is now the most conspicuous graffito in the fragile plaster of the ancient pillars mentioned above.

30. Sidebotham, "Ship Graffiti from Mons Porphyrites," 339–44.

31. Quoted in Hobbs, *Bedouin Life in the Egyptian Wilderness*, 98.

32. According to Joseph Hobbs, the Romans are only partly to blame for the present situation. Bedouins in the nineteenth and early twentieth centuries also cut large numbers

of trees to be sold as charcoal, and hunters in the twentieth century have devastated the remaining populations of animals. These hunters are generally not bedouin, since bedouin are forbidden to own guns. Egyptian soldiers stationed along the Red Sea, however, still drive far into the desert to cut trees, which they burn in their camps, and regularly shoot gazelle and ibex for sport. Ibid., 99–101.

33. Scholars continue to debate the type of animal the Romans used for hauling stone from the quarries. The possibility that they used camels is supported by limited textual evidence such as a papyrus dating from A.D. 163, in which a man named Satabous, from Dimê in the Fayoum, complains that one of his four camels was requisitioned for service on the "porphyry road" (Murray, *Dare Me to the Desert*, 117). This does not prove, however, that camels were primarily draft animals, for they might also have been requisitioned to carry supplies, food, water, messengers, or soldiers along the porphyry road.

34. Maxfield, "The Eastern Desert Forts and the Army in Egypt During the Principate," 18.

35. Sidebotham, Zitterkopf, and Riley, "Survey of the 'Abu Sha'ar-Nile Road," 577.

36. Ibid., 578. *Limes* is a Latin term that historians have traditionally used to refer to a Roman defensive system consisting of permanent fortifications linked by roads in a frontier zone. Recently, however, scholars have debated this definition. Citing first- and second-century sources, Benjamin Isaac states that *limes* did not necessarily mean "fortified line," nor was it always defensive. Moreover, the meaning of the term seems to have changed over time. From the first through the third centuries, it was used to indicate a demarcated land border of the Roman Empire. But from the fourth century onward, it was used to designate a frontier district under the command of a governor. The soldiers who served under the governor were called *limitanei*, and their task was to take care of road security in the frontier districts. Isaac, "The Meaning of the Terms *Limes* and *Limitanei*," 125–47.

37. Tregenza, *Red Sea Mountains of Egypt*, 145.

38. Murray, *Dare Me to the Desert*, 118.

39. Ibid., 116–18.

40. F. Corsi, *Delle pietre antiche* (Rome, 1845), 203, 295, 385. Quoted in Peña, "P.Giss. 69: Evidence for the Supplying of Stone Transport Operations in Roman Egypt and the Production of Fifty-Foot Monolithic Column Shafts," 127–28, n. 7.

41. Ibid., 128.

42. Cockle, "Inscribed Architectural Fragment from Middle Egypt Concerning the Imperial Quarries," 25; also Murray, *Dare Me to the Desert*, 118.

43. Cockle, "Inscribed Architectural Fragment from Middle Egypt Concerning the Imperial Quarries," 25.

44. Galerius, one of several joint rulers of the eastern empire, had the rank of Caesar from A.D. 293 to 305, during the First Tetrarchy, and held the rank of Augustus from A.D. 305 to 311 during the Second Tetrarchy.

45. Scarre, *Chronicle of the Roman Emperors*, 219.

46. Ibid.

47. Constantine died on May 22, A.D. 337, in Ankyrona, Turkey. His body was returned to Constantinople and was buried in the mausoleum he had built called the Church of the Holy Apostles. His own sarcophagus—which was not of porphyry—was placed in the middle of a row of twelve empty sarcophagi, one for each of the apostles.

CHAPTER II. MONS CLAUDIANUS

1. The most recent studies indicate that the settlement went through cycles of occupation. After Trajan there were twenty years of possible abandonment, then a busy period from the twenty-first year of the reign of Hadrian to that of Antoninus (A.D. 138–61). Documents also attest to the site's occupation during the reigns of Commodus (A.D. 180–92), Septimius Severus (A.D. 193–211), and Severus Alexander (A.D. 222–35). See Peacock and Maxfield, Mons Claudianus Survey and Excavation 1987–1993: Topography and Quarries; J. Bingen et al., Mons Claudianus: Ostraca graeca et latina I. (O. Claud. 1 à 190); and J. Bingen et al., Mons Claudianus. Ostraca graeca et latina II. (O. Claud. 191 à 416).

2. Quoted in Murray, Dare Me to the Desert, 33.

3. Cockle, "Inscribed Architectural Fragment from Middle Egypt Concerning the Imperial Quarries," 26.

4. Weigall, Travels in the Upper Egyptian Deserts, 126. The full titles of Roman emperors became longer as the empire aged. At the time of his death in A.D. 14, Augustus had six official titles: Imperator Caesar Divi Filius Augustus, Pontifex Maximus, Consul XIII, Imperator XXI, Tribuniciae potestatis XXXVII, and Pater Patriae. By the beginning of the fourth century, Diocletian could boast of having fifteen titles.

5. Ibid.

6. Bernand, Pan du désert, 90. Quoted in Aufrère, Galvin, and Goyan, L'Égypte Restituée, 2:221. Translated from the French by the author.

7. Researchers did uncover an ostracon near the hydreuma dating from the time of Nero (A.D. 54–68), but all other evidence points to the settlement beginning during the reign of Domitian. Peacock, "The Hydreuma," in Peacock and Maxfield, Mons Claudianus Survey and Excavation: Topography and Quarries, 140–48.

8. According to Leo Tregenza, Diqal refers not to Roman columns, but to narrow, meter-long stones that predynastic people used as anchors for their gazelle traps. These can still be found in the area. The Arabic word for the Roman column is amud. Tregenza, Red Sea Mountains of Egypt, 55.

9. Peacock and Maxfield, Mons Claudianus Survey and Excavation 1987–1993: Topography and Quarries, 151–73.

10. Ibid., 197.

11. Weigall, Travels in the Upper Egyptian Deserts, 127.

12. This column is not, however, the largest monolithic column ever hewn. Obelisks of much larger dimensions were produced during the Pharaonic period. Hatshepsut, for example, had two obelisks erected in the Karnak Temple in Luxor. The northern obelisk, the only one still standing, is 27.5 meters high and weighs approximately 320

tons. Larger still is the unfinished obelisk abandoned in the northern quarry near Aswan, which is 42 meters long and weighs 1,000 tons.

13. The following six examples are from Peña, "*P. Giss.* 69: Evidence for the Supplying of Stone Transport Operations in Roman Egypt and the Production of Fifty-Foot Monolithic Column Shafts," 130–31.

14. The later time frame is probably more accurate. In the early twentieth century, a papyrus (*P. Giss.* 69) dated December 29, A.D. 118, was published in Germany. The writer of the document requested that a large quantity of grain be sent to Mons Claudianus, "for we have a great number of animals for the purpose of bringing down a fifty-foot column, and already we are nearly out of barley." It is conceivable that the column mentioned in the document was among those destined for Trajan's Forum.

15. Scaife, "The Origin of Some Pantheon Columns," 37.

16. The splendidly carved base of this column is now in the Vatican Museum. It depicts Antoninus Pius and his beloved wife, Faustina, ascending to heaven on the back of a winged angel.

17. The stone used in the columns of these buildings is a quartz diorite known as *granito bianco e nero*. It was quarried by the Romans in Wadi Barud, approximately ten kilometers south of Mons Claudianus. Peacock, "The Quarries and Settlement of Tiberiane (Wadi Barud)," 275.

18. Peacock et al., "Characterization Studies and the Use of Mons Claudianus Granodiorite," 333–34.

19. Tregenza, *Red Sea Mountains of Egypt*, 52.

20. These figures are taken from unpublished ostraca (*MC Inv.* 1538 and 2921) that record the distribution of water to 920 people. Maxfield, "Eastern Desert Forts and the Army During the Principate," 19.

21. Weigall, *Travel in the Upper Egyptian Deserts*, 134.

22. Murray, *Dare Me to the Desert*, 33.

23. Cockle, "An Inscribed Architectural Fragment from Middle Egypt Concerning the Imperial Quarries," 26.

24. Cuvigny, "The Amount of Wages Paid to the Quarry-Workers at Mons Claudianus," 139–40.

25. *O. Claud.* 4751.

26. Other ostraca suggest that there was a slight increase in this payscale after A.D. 150.

27. Cuvigny, "The Amount of Wages Paid to the Quarry-Workers at Mons Claudianus," 141. Surprisingly, the wages were based not on the occupation, but on the age of the worker.

28. Ibid.

29. All documents are from Bingen et al., *Mons Claudianus, ostraca graeca et latina I* (*O. Claud.* 1 à 190).

30. Isidorus and his two sons lived in the desert. The sons, however, probably lived at the main settlement at Mons Claudianus and had easier access to mail and provisions than their father, who appears to have lived at one of the outlying quarries.

31. I.e., the Nile Valley.

32. The meat referred to in this ostracon is probably beef. Although cattle were not kept at Mons Claudianus, this and other ostraca indicate that beef and beef products were imported from the Nile Valley.

33. Twelve letters addressed to Successus were discovered. Although his exact rank and title are unknown, he was apparently the keeper of materials for the quarries.

34. The writer could be referring to the type of leather water bags that archaeologists have recovered at Mons Claudianus. They held 28 liters of water and were designed to be carried by camels. Four such bags were the standard load for one camel. When the bags were no longer suitable for carrying water, they were cut up and used as leg-protectors by the stone masons in the quarries.

35. "Feathers" were small iron plates inserted into wedge holes to create a tighter fit for the wedge.

36. The person authorizing the travel is probably the centurion of Mons Claudianus, but the destinations of the travelers are uncertain.

37. Cuvigny, "Nouveaux ostraca grecs du Mons Claudianus," 276.

38. Red Sea fish included parrotfish, seabass, and groupers, but it is unclear whether these were dried or brought fresh to Mons Claudianus.

39. For more information on vegetable cultivation at Mons Claudianus, see van der Veen, "Gardens in the Desert."

40. Cuvigny, "The Amount of Wages Paid to the Quarry-Workers at Mons Claudianus," 141.

41. By today's standards, five liters per day is generally accepted as the minimum necessary to keep a man adequately hydrated in such an environment.

42. Bingen, "Dumping and the Ostraca at Mons Claudianus," 31.

CHAPTER III. QUARRY ROADS TO THE RIVER NILE

1. Sidebotham, Zitterkopf, and Riley, "Survey of the 'Abu Sha'ar-Nile Road," 571–600.

2. Sidebotham, "A Limes in the Eastern Desert of Egypt: Myth or Reality?" 494–96.

3. From northeast to southwest, these wadis are Wadi Belih, Wadi Qattar, Wadi el-Atrash, and Wadi Qena.

4. Sidebotham, Zitterkopf, and Riley, "Survey of the 'Abu Sha'ar-Nile Road," 595–600.

5. Ibid., 580–82.

6. Ibid., 582–83.

7. Dates are based on information from Wadi Abu Qwei, in Redford and Redford, "Graffiti and Petroglyphs Old and New from the Eastern Desert."

8. A third, similar warrior is located several meters to the north on the same wall.

9. Tregenza, "Notes on Inscriptions and Graffiti at Mons Claudianus and Mons Porphyrites and on the 'Flavius' Stone in Wadi Qattar, Collected during a Visit to the S.E. Desert in the Summer of 1949," 146–50. George Murray removed the block containing this inscription and brought it to Luxor in 1949.

10. From Palladius's *Historia Lausiaca*, quoted in Tregenza, *Red Sea Mountains of Egypt*, 179.

11. Sidebotham, Zitterkopf, and Riley, "Survey of the 'Abu Sha'ar-Nile Road," 584–87.

12. Ibid., 587.

13. Given that this well dates from the third or fourth century, it was apparently not used to support the transportation of stone from Mons Claudianus. Sidebotham, "Newly Discovered Sites in the Eastern Desert," 183.

14. Tregenza, *Red Sea Mountains of Egypt*, 212–13.

15. Sidebotham, Zitterkopf, and Riley, "Survey of the 'Abu Sha'ar-Nile Road," 591.

16. Weigall, *Travels in the Upper Egyptian Deserts*, 96.

17. Tregenza, *Red Sea Mountains of Egypt*, 229.

18. Fuchs, "Notes on the Archive of Nicanor," 207–16; and Meredith, "The Myos Hormos Road: Inscriptions and Ostraca," 356–57.

19. Tregenza, *Red Sea Mountains of Egypt*, 97–98.

20. Sidebotham, "Newly Discovered Sites in the Eastern Desert," 191.

21. Tregenza, *Red Sea Mountains of Egypt*, 41–48

22. MC Inv. O.7334

23. Written descriptions of the wagons typically used in Roman Egypt to haul agricultural produce do exist. One papyrus contains the following description: "The transport wagon belonging to you, covered with iron and equipped, that is, the two wheels with the iron outer coverings and the hubs and rims and basket seat with rings and pole and yoke with chains and axle and wooden wagon box." Bagnall, "The Camel, the Wagon, and the Donkey in Later Roman Egypt," 2.

24. The Military Museum in Lisbon features an eighteenth-century stone-carrying wagon that bore its load underneath its platform. The wagon was rolled lengthwise over the column, which was then raised into place by winches. Peacock, "Routes and Transportation," 261–62, 271 (for drawing of the cart).

25. Steven Sidebotham identified the track of a "three- (or multiple of three) wheeled cart with a gauge of 4.0 m." Perhaps this suggests that the Romans added a third wheel in the middle of the axle to provide additional support. Sidebotham, "Newly Discovered Sites in the Eastern Desert," 183.

26. Peacock, "Routes and Transportation," 262–63.

27. If one estimates that the largest columns could be rolled at a rate of 500 meters per hour, then transporters could cover five kilometers in a ten-hour day. At this rate, they would complete the 120-km distance to the Nile in twenty-four days.

28. There is some documentary evidence supporting the theory that the transportation of columns occurred only during the winter months. The dates from a group of third-century inscriptions concerning a stone transport guild at the sandstone quarries of Kertassi are concentrated between February and April. See Peña, "*P. Giss.* 69: Evidence for the Supplying of Stone Transport Operations in Roman Egypt and the Production of Fifty-Foot Monolithic Column Shafts," 130, n. 19.

29. Camels were introduced into Egypt on a large scale during the reign of Ptolemy II (284–246 B.C.), who is famous for importing many new varieties of plants and animals into Egypt. Bagnall, "The Camel, the Wagon, and the Donkey in Later Roman Egypt," 1–6.

30. *P. Oxy.* 3.498.

31. Peña, "*P. Giss.* 69: Evidence for the Supplying of Stone Transport Operations in Roman Egypt and the Production of Fifty-Foot Monolithic Column Shafts," 127.

32. Socnopaios Nesos was the Greco-Roman settlement on the north coast of Lake Fayoum. The site is now called Dimê.

33. BGU III (163 p.c) in Lesquier, *L'armée romaine d'Égypte d'Auguste à Dioclétien*, 370–71.

34. Bulliet, *The Camel and the Wheel*, 23.

35. Today, camels are used extensively as draft animals only in northern India, northeastern Turkey, southern Yemen, and on the west coast of Morocco. Ibid., 176–77.

36. Peacock, "Routes and Transportation," 263.

37. Ibid., 264.

38. Grain was the most vital international commodity in the ancient world. Egypt supplied Rome with a third of its grain requirements—an estimated 135,000 tons per year. A grain shortage was a major fear of Roman leaders because it could easily lead to riots and possibly threaten the stability of the government.

39. Modern historians, however, do not have to rely solely on these drawings and ancient descriptions to study the nautical genius of the Romans. In the early 1920s, two of Emperor Caligula's magnificent houseboats were discovered at the bottom of Lake Nemi, 35 kilometers southeast of Rome. From 1928 to 1936, an ambitious rescue project—which required the temporary draining of the lake—succeeded in recovering and displaying both ships in a special museum built on the shore of the lake. One ship measured 71.4 m × 19.8 m, and the second measured 65 m × 23.5 m. The splendid accommodations included patterned marble floors and walls, numerous statues, and bronze railings. Unfortunately, members of a German artillery unit intentionally burned the museum to the ground when they were forced to withdraw from their position near the museum on June 2, 1944. The ships were consumed in the inferno.

40. Fitzgerald, "The Ship of Saint Paul, Part II: Comparative Archaeology," 31–39.

41. Casson, *Ships and Seafaring in Ancient Times*, 123.

42. Hirschfeld, "The Ship of Saint Paul, Part I: Historical Background," 27.

CHAPTER IV. PORTS ON THE RED SEA COAST

1. The order of the location of the ports north to south varies among several ancient authors.

2. An ostracon from Thebes, dated circa A.D. 112, refers to the "Potamos Babylonos," suggesting that the canal commenced at or near the large Roman military fort of Babylon. Sidebotham, *Roman Economic Policy in the Erythra Thalassa 30 B.C.–A.D. 217*, 68.

3. See Mayerson, "The Port of Clysma (Suez) in Transition from Roman to Arab Rule."

4. Sidebotham, *Roman Economic Policy in the Erythra Thalassa 30 B.C.–A.D. 217*, 68.

5. Mayerson, "Egeria and Peter the Deacon on the Site of Clysma (Suez)," 64.

6. Wilkinson, trans. and annot., *Egeria's Travels to the Holy Land*, 205, quoted in Mayerson, "Egeria and Peter the Deacon on the Site of Clysma (Suez)," 62.

7. Ibid., 101, quoted in Mayerson, "Egeria and Peter the Deacon on the Site of Clysma (Suez)," 62.

8. Sidebotham, "Ports of the Red Sea and the Arabia-India Trade," 487.

9. Strabo, *Geography* 17.1.45. "Ethiopia" here refers to any African lands south of the Egyptian border. Strabo's comment regarding Ethiopia indicates that its exports not destined for Arabia were brought into Egypt via caravan routes through the desert.

10. Strabo traveled through Egypt in 25–24 B.C.. He wrote, "Not far from Berenice is Myos Hormos, a city with a naval station for vessels which navigate this sea." Strabo, *Geography*, 17.1.45. The name Mussel Harbor probably derives from the abundance of large clams and mussels that thrive along this part of the coast.

11. Although the fort has been exposed to the elements, not all the damage was caused by nature. In 1982, the Egyptian army intentionally dismantled portions of the ancient walls and towers and used the stones to construct a building (now destroyed) 200 meters north of the fort. Sidebotham, "Preliminary Report on the 1990–1991 Seasons of Fieldwork at 'Abu Sha'ar (Red Sea Coast)," 146.

12. As quoted in Thompson, *Sir Gardner Wilkinson and His Circle*, 59.

13. Sidebotham, "Preliminary Report on the 1990–1991 Season of Fieldwork at 'Abu Sha'ar (Red Sea Coast)," 133.

14. Seeger, "The Hydraulic Systems at Abu Sha'ar." Also see Sidebotham, "Abu Sha'ar."

15. Baths were often located outside of forts to reduce the danger of fire.

16. Sidebotham, "Preliminary Report on the 1990–1991 Seasons of Fieldwork at Abu Sha'ar (Red Sea Coast)," 157.

17. By this time, Rome was ruled by a tetrarchy—four joint rulers. These tetrarchs constantly conspired against each other, until, finally they were reduced to only two, Constantine and Licinius. Constantine defeated Licinius in the battle of Chrysopolis in Asia Minor in September A.D. 324. Licinius was hanged in A.D. 325, and Constantine became the sole ruler of the Roman world. Bagnall and Sheridan, "Greek and Latin Documents from 'Abu Sha'ar, 1990–1991," 159–63.

18. See chapter 1, n. 36 for a definition of *limes*.

19. Sidebotham, "Preliminary Report on the 1990–1991 Seasons of Fieldwork at Abu Sha'ar (Red Sea Coast)," 157–58.

20. Bagnall and Sheridan, "Greek and Latin Documents from 'Abu Sha'ar: 1990–1991," 167.

21. The monastery of the great hermit Saint Anthony was constructed during the reign of Emperor Julian the Apostate, between A.D. 361 and 363. The building of Saint Paul's monastery is more difficult to ascertain, but it probably took place slightly later, in the early fifth century. Meinardus, *Monks and Monasteries of the Egyptian Deserts*, 5, 35. St. Catherine's monastery in the Sinai was completed in A.D. 565 by Emperor Justinian. Hobbs, *Mount Sinai*, 74.

22. Based on evidence from Judea, Syria, and Palestine, the conversion of abandoned Roman forts into monasteries was common in late antiquity. Sidebotham, "University of Delaware Archaeological Project at 'Abu Sha'ar: The 1992 Season," 7. Also see Hirschfeld, *The Judean Monasteries in the Byzantine Period*, 47–54.

23. Sidebotham, "University of Delaware Archaeological Project at 'Abu Sha'ar: The 1992 Season," 6.

24. Bagnall and Sheridan, "Greek and Latin Documents from Abu Sha'ar: 1990–1991," 164.

25. Ibid.

26. At least one historian, however, Richard Alston, believes that Abu Sha'ar could still be the site of Myos Hormos. He suggests that either an older building or buildings lie beneath the present structure, or, because ancient trade was seasonal, that the port did not possess permanent buildings and therefore left no archaeological remains. Alston, *Soldier and Society in Roman Egypt*, 194.

27. Whitcomb and Johnson, *Quseir al-Qadim 1980: Preliminary Report.*

28. *Terra sigillata* was among the finest pottery produced in ancient Rome. With its smooth, glossy finish and bright red color, it was intended to be used at the dining table. Included in the pieces from Quseir al-Qadim were Arrentine wares from the Italian town of Arezzo. These highly prized pieces were often copied, and, indeed, the Quseir collection included many imitations from Cyprus, Asia Minor, and North Africa. Whitcomb and Johnson, "Egypt and the Spice Trade," *Archaeology*, 17–20.

29. Whitcomb and Johnson, *Quseir al-Qadim 1980: Preliminary Report*, 7.

30. Excavations conducted at the site of Arikamedu in the 1940s by the British archaeologist Sir Mortimer Wheeler uncovered Roman pottery that included Arrentine wares and amphorae. Wheeler, "Arikamedu: An Indo-Roman Trading Station on the East Coast of India," 17–124. Also see Begley et al., *The Ancient Port of Arikamedu: New Excavations and Researches 1989–1992*, vol. 1.

31. Whitcomb and Johnson, "Egypt and the Spice Trade," 18.

32. Peppercorns were also discovered at Quseir al-Qadim, but only in the strata corresponding to the Islamic period of occupation.

33. Bagnall, "Epigraphy—Greek and Latin," 243–44.

34. The presence of Himyarite reflects the fact that prior to the arrival of the Romans, the Sabaeans had controlled the lucrative spice and incense trade. Once the Romans took over, Sabaeans probably continued working in the business as middlemen. Whitcomb and Johnson, "Egypt and the Spice Trade," 21.

35. Bagnall, "Papyri and Ostraka from Quseir Al-Qadim," 5.

36. Ibid., 8–9.

37. After the Romans departed, Quseir al-Qadim remained generally deserted until it became a port for Qus, the capital of Upper Egypt from the Fatamid period onward. Discoveries of Chinese porcelain from the Sung and Ming dynasties attest to Quseir al-Qadim's functioning as a trading port with the East in the thirteenth and fourteenth centuries. Whitcomb and Johnson, *Quseir al-Qadim 1980: Preliminary Report*, 2.

38. Dumreicher, *Trackers and Smugglers in the Deserts of Egypt*, 124.

39. Bülow-Jacobsen, Cuvigny, and Fournet, "The Identification of Myos Hormos: New Papyrological Evidence," 27–42.

40. *O. Max.* 175, in ibid., 29–30.

41. The fish sauce mentioned here was called *garum*. It was made from rotten fish and was used throughout the Roman Empire. One historian recently suggested that it was the Roman equivalent to ketchup.

42. *O. Max.* 279 and 467, in Bülow-Jacobsen, Cuvigny, and Fournet, "The Identification of Myos Hormos: New Papyrological Evidence," 32–33.

43. *O. Max.* 267, in ibid., 33–34.

44. *O. Max.* 254, in ibid., 34–35.

45. On the Leukos Limen–Myos Hormos debate, see Whitcomb, "Quseir al-Qadim and the Location of Myos Hormos," 747–72.

46. Sidebotham, "Survey of the Hinterland," 364–68.

47. It is unclear when or if Myos Hormos eclipsed Berenike as the principal Red Sea port. As mentioned earlier, Strabo states that in the early first century Myos Hormos was the more important of the two ports. But one scholar suggests that for any given year the winds determined whether ships could sail all the way to Myos Hormos or whether they had to put in at Berenike. Bülow-Jacobsen, "Traffic on the Roads Between Coptos and the Red Sea," 65.

48. Forest elephants, used by the Ptolemies in battle, are much smaller than bush elephants: they rarely exceed a height of 2.5 m at the shoulder. Casson, *Periplus Maris Erythraei: Text with Introduction, Translation, and Commentary,* 108.

49. Diodorus Siculus, 3.39.3, quoted in Sidebotham and Wendrich, eds., *Berenike 1994,* 6. No archaeological evidence of such activity has been discovered on Ras Banas, mainly because the area is under the strict control of the Egyptian military and is off-limits to archaeological research. Perhaps when the military permits a thorough examination of the peninsula, evidence of a slipway will appear.

50. Wendrich, "Fringes are Anchored in Warp and Weft: The Relations Between Berenike, Shenshef and the Nile Valley," 243–49.

51. The highest elevations of the site were also damaged during the construction of a military installation by the Egyptian army in 1973. A wide area around the temple was leveled by bulldozers, and several buildings on the western side of the site appear to have been buried. Sidebotham and Wendrich, *Berenike 1994,* 13.

52. Serapis was a Hellenized version of the god Osirapis, who in turn was a combination of Osiris and the Apis bull. As the primary god of the great port city of Alexandria, Serapis was regarded as the protector of sailors and travelers.

53. Sidebotham and Wendrich, *Berenike 1994,* 13–17.

54. St. John's Island, known as Gezira Zeberged in Arabic, lies approximately 50 kilometers southeast of Ras Banas and is a renowned source of peridots, a yellowish green mineral used as a gem. Casson, *Periplus Maris Erythraei: Text with Introduction, Translation and Commentary,* 94.

55. Ibid., 16.

56. Casson, *Rome and India,* 9–11. There are many unanswered questions concerning the ships of Roman Egypt. First, archaeologists have not discovered the remains of any Roman or Roman-era ship in the Red Sea. Second, while it is true that Roman ships

were impressively strong in the Mediterranean, one cannot assume that the same ships were used for the eastern trade routes. Owing to the lack of wood in the desert, it is doubtful that such ships could have been built on the Egyptian Red Sea coast, thus raising the question of how such large ships got to the Red Sea. While it is possible that they were brought to the Red Sea via Trajan's Canal (Babylon–Clysma), so little is known about the canal that ones hesitates to make such a speculation. Another possibility is that the Romans simply used Arab vessels for their trade, but these were small, and it is unlikely that they could have carried the volume of goods the Romans imported from the East. In short, almost no objective evidence exists concerning the dimensions and structure of the ships of the Roman–Indian trade. Bedouin in the vicinity of Berenike claim that an ancient ship rests at the bottom of the harbor, but no evidence of a wreckage has yet been found. See Casson, The Periplus Maris Eryhraei: Text with Introduction, Translation, and Commentary, 284–85.

57. Tacitus, Annals 3. 53.
58. Pliny, Natural History, 6. 102.
59. Quoted in Casson, The Periplus Maris Erythraei: Text with Introduction, Translation, and Commentary, 296. (Note: the Periyar River is on the southwest coast of India).
60. During the Roman period, this site was known as Rhapta (meaning "sewn" and referring to the sewn boats of the area). Chami, "Roman Beads from the Rufiji Delta, Tanzania: First Incontrovertible Archaeological Link with the Periplus (1)," 237.
61. Casson, The Periplus Maris Erythraei: Text with Introduction, Translation, and Commentary, 61.
62. Ibid., 30–31, 85.
63. Wendrich, "Fringes are Anchored in Warp and Weft: The Relations Between Berenike, Shenshef and the Nile Valley," 246.
64. Rose, "Report on the Handmade Sherds," 41–43.
65. Propus, Historia Augusta, 19,7, quoted in Wiedemann, Emperors and Gladiators, 13.
66. Procopius, History of the Wars 1.19.3–33. Given that these groups apparently continued their raids, it seems that these payments were unsuccessful.
67. Van Hecke et al., Martyrium Sancti Arethae (27,28,29), 1970, 743, 747, cited in Sidebotham and Wendrich, eds., Berenike 1996, 452.
68. Sidebotham, "The Excavations," Berenike 1996, 120.
69. Wendrich, "Fringes are Anchored in Warp and Weft: The Relations Between Berenike, Shenshef and the Nile Valley," 248.
70. Verhoogt, "Greek and Latin Textual Material," in Sidebotham and Wendrich, Berenike 1996, 194–95. (Preliminary transcription by J. Dieleman.)
71. Dijkstra and Verhoogt, "The Greek-Palmyrene Inscription," 207–18.
72. Cappers, "A Botanical Contribution to the Analysis of Subsistence and Trade at Berenike (Red Sea Coast, Egypt)," 77.
73. Ball, The Geography and Geology of South-Eastern Egypt, 31. Quoted in Sidebotham and Wendrich, Berenike 1994, 93.
74. Murray, "Note on the Ruins of Hitan Shenshaf, Near Berenice," 166–67. Quoted by Sidebotham, Berenice 1994, 96.

75. Aldsworth and Barnard, "Survey of Shenshef," 427–43.
76. Aldsworth and Barnard, "Berenike Survey," 120.
77. Sidebotham and Wendrich, "Interpretative Summary and Conclusions," 453–54.

CHAPTER V. DESERT TRADE ROUTES

1. The fourth road has only recently been discovered; it links Marsa Nakari (Port of Nechesia?) with Edfu on the Nile. See Sidebotham, "Survey of the Hinterland," 364–68.
2. Lewis, *Life in Egypt Under Roman Rule*, 141.
3. Sidebotham and Zitterkopf, "Survey of the Via Hadriana," 354.
4. Clement of Alexandria, *Protrepticus* IV 49.1. Quoted in Montserrat, *Sex and Society in Graeco-Roman Egypt*, 143–44.
5. Murray, "The Roman Roads and Stations in the Eastern Desert of Egypt," 149–50.
6. Sidebotham and Zitterkopf, "Survey of the Via Hadriana by the University of Delaware: The 1996 Season," 221–37; and Sidebotham and Zitterkopf, "Survey of the Via Hadriana by the University of Delaware: The 1997 Season," 353–65.
7. Whether the port of Myos Hormos is located at Quseir al-Qadim or is as yet undiscovered under the modern town of Quseir, their close proximity to each other suggests that it is still appropriate to refer to this desert route as the Myos Hormos road.
8. During the Islamic period, this route was known as the Pilgrimage Road.
9. Whitcomb and Johnson, *Quseir al-Qadim 1978: Preliminary Report*, 6. As early as 2400 B.C., the Egyptians sent expeditions to Punt—on the Red Sea coast near the present border between Sudan and Ethiopia—to obtain myrrh and frankincense.
10. Evidence of one such attack was recently discovered at El-Zerkah. On March 13, A.D. 118, nomads attacked the El-Muweih station, killing one man and kidnapping several women and children. Cuvigny, "Women in the Ostraca of Mons Claudianus and of the Myos Hormos Road."
11. A detailed description of each of the stations can be found in Zitterkopf and Sidebotham, "Stations and Towers on the Quseir–Nile Road," 159. Another station, Bir Nakheil, was located approximately halfway between Quseir and El-Iteima and about ten kilometers north of the main road. In addition, other stations might have existed closer to Myos Hormos.
12. Ibid., 163–64.
13. I. *Koptos* 1 = SB I 1006; I. *Koptos* 2 = CIL III 6628. Quoted in Alston, *Soldier and Society in Roman Egypt*, 194. The second Roman legion stationed in Egypt in the first century was the XXII Deiotariana. For a discussion of these inscriptions, see Bernand, *De Koptos à Kosseir*, 37–39.
14. Strabo, *Geography*, 17, 1, 45.
15. Archaeologists from the French Archaeological Institute in Cairo are currently studying the *hydreuma* at El-Zerqah. The site's excellent state of preservation has provided scholars with a better understanding of Roman architecture. In addition, excavations

have revealed more than one thousand ostraca, mostly letters, which, once translated, will help researchers learn a great deal more about life along this important Roman highway.

16. Zitterkopf and Sidebotham, "Stations and Towers on the Quseir-Nile Road," 166–69.

17. Bülow-Jacobsen et al., "Les Inscriptons d'Al-Muwayh," 104–05.

18. ILS I.2483 = CIL III.6627 = Eph. Epig. V (1884), 5, no. 15. Cited in Steven E. Sidebotham, Roman Economic Policy in the Erythra Thalassa 30 B.C.–A.D. 217, 65.

19. Alston, Soldier and Society in Roman Egypt, 200.

20. Sidebotham, Roman Economic Policy in the Erythra Thalassa 30 B.C.–A.D. 217, 64. Also see Zitterkopf and Sidebotham, "Stations and Towers on the Quseir-Nile Road," 180–89.

21. Bagnall, "Upper and Lower Guard Posts," 125–28.

22. OGIS 674 = IGRR I 1183 = IG Portes 67, in Johnson, Roman Egypt to the Reign of Diocletian, 593–94.

23. The drachma, minted in silver and bronze, was the standard unit of currency and weight in Egypt during the Ptolemaic and Roman periods. One drachma weighed 3.5 grams. An obol was equivalent to one-sixth of a drachma.

24. Campbell, "The Marriage of Soldiers Under the Empire," 153–66. An example of the legal implications of this law is the case of two married citizens of Alexandria. The husband joined the army, and, while he was in service, his wife gave birth to a son. The case was presented to Rutilius Lupus, governor of Alexandria, who ruled that the son was illegitimate on the grounds that a soldier cannot have a legitimate child, even by his wife of a preexisting marriage.

25. Herodian, 3.8.4–5, quoted in ibid., 160.

26. Montserrat, Sex and Society in Graeco-Roman Egypt, 120–35.

27. The theory of a group rate rests on the probability that if the tariff for a prostitute were disproportionately high, she would be inclined to lie about her profession, thus making that tariff category meaningless. Ibid., 130–31.

28. One recent estimate is for two thousand camel loads per month to Berenike. (K. Ruffing, "Das Nikanor—Archiv und der römische Sud- und Osthandel," Münsterische Beiträge zur antiken Handelsgeschichte 12.2, 4–7, stated in Bülow-Jacobsen, "Traffic on the Roads Between Coptos and the Red Sea," 66.) However, this figure is based on the existence of approximately two thousand houses in Berenike, while the most recent estimates indicate that the main settlement contained about one hundred houses and that the population was therefore approximately five hundred people (Wendrich, "Fringes are Anchored in Warp and Weft," 244). Even if one considers the sizable populations that inhabited the outlying settlements around Berenike, perhaps a monthly figure of between two hundred to five hundred camels is more accurate.

29. Strabo, Geography 17, 1, 5.

30. Sidebotham and Zitterkopf, "Routes Through the Eastern Desert of Egypt."

31. Meredith, Tabula Imperii Romani (Map of the Roman Empire) Sheet N.G. 36 Coptos, note: Meredith's list is now incomplete. Surveys done between 1990 and 2000 have revealed

several dozen additional sites along the Berenike–Edfu–Coptos roads. The updated maps of this region, however, have not yet been published. For a brief interim report, see Sidebotham and Zitterkopf, "Routes Through the Eastern Desert of Egypt," 39–52.

32. Bernand, *Le Paneion d'El-Kanaïs: les inscriptions grecques*, 70 (translation from the French by the author).

33. Casson, *The Periplus Maris Erythraei: Text with Introduction, Translation and Commentary*, 14.

34. For ancient inscriptions along this route and its environs, see Colin, "Les Paneia d'El-Buwayb et du Ouadi Minayh sur la piste de Bérénice à Coptos: inscriptions égyptiennes," 89–125; and Cuvigny and Bülow-Jacobsen, "Inscriptions rupestres vues et revues dans le désert de Bérénice," 133–75.

CHAPTER VI. THE GATEWAY TO AFRICA

1. The Aswan High Dam was built by the late President of Egypt Gamal Nasser with financial assistance from the Soviet Union. Lake Nasser (or Lake Nubia, as it is called in the Sudan), which built up behind the dam, averages ten kilometers wide and stretches southward for 500 kilometers into northern Sudan. The formation of this lake resulted in the forced relocation of 100,000 Nubians from their traditional lands and the destruction of their villages along with numerous ancient monuments.

2. Unlike Mons Porphyrites and Mons Claudianus, which lay deep in the mountains of the Eastern Desert, the Aswan quarries were close to the Nile, thus greatly reducing the labor and transportation costs incurred in conveying the quarried stone to its destination. It was from the Aswan quarries, for example, that Fourth dynasty engineers extracted the nine fifty-ton slabs that form the ceiling of the King's Chamber in the Pyramid of Cheops at Giza. Here, too, Roman stonemasons, in A.D. 300, quarried the enormous pillar now located in Alexandria that honored the emperor Diocletian, but that has been mistakenly referred to as Pompey's Pillar ever since the publication of Napoleon's *Description de l'Égypte* in the early nineteenth century.

3. Jaritz and Rodziewicz, "Syene—Review of the Urban Remains and its Pottery," 119.

4. Culliford, ed., *David Roberts, From an Antique Land: Travels in Egypt and the Holy Land*, 56.

5. Herodotus, *History*, II, 28.

6. Ibid., II, 29.

7. Shinnie, "Trade Routes of the Ancient Sudan: 3,000 B.C.–A.D. 350," 49.

8. Juvenal, Satire XI, 124. As a result of Juvenal's occasional literary stabs at the emperor, Trajan allegedly banished the eighty-year-old writer to the ends of the known world, Syene.

9. Researchers have discovered numerous similar drawings of feet on the paving stones of the temples throughout the Roman world. See Dunbabin, "*Ipsa deae vestigia* . . . Footprints divine and human on Graeco-Roman monuments," 85–107.

10. Shortly after Julius Caesar arrived in Alexandria on the heels of Pompey, an insurrection by the Egyptian army forced him to seek refuge in the royal palace of Cleopatra VII. During the ensuing violence, several buildings were set ablaze. The fire spread and

eventually consumed a portion of the library of Alexandria, the greatest center of learning in the ancient world.

11. Strabo, *Geography*, 17, 1, 48.

12. Pliny the Elder, *Natural History* 5.58. Pompey was Caesar's rival for control of the Roman Empire. After losing the battle of Pharsalus in August 48 B.C., Pompey and his wife fled to Alexandria, where he hoped to use the great wealth of Egypt to raise another army against Caesar. But servants of Pothinus, an officer of Ptolemy XII, stabbed, then decapitated Pompey as he stepped ashore in Alexandria.

13. Today, only portions of the middle section of the wall can be seen, but these are destined to crumble in the near future. Some 3.5 kilometers of the wall's northern portion have been destroyed because of the construction of modern roads and buildings. About 1.7 kilometers of the southern end disintegrated when they were submerged by the waters of the reservoir created by the first Aswan dam in the early twentieth century. Jaritz, "The Investigation of the Ancient Wall Extending from Aswan to Philae: Second Preliminary Report," 113.

14. Jaritz, "The Investigation of the Ancient Wall Extending from Aswan to Philae: First Preliminary Report," 69.

15. Adams, *Nubia: Corridor to Africa*, 344.

16. Ibid., 74.

17. Rodziewicz, "The Pottery from the Watch-Tower at Tell Asmar," 119–21. An unusually high tower can still be seen on the west bank, at the beginning of the ancient Farshout road that heads across the desert to Kharga Oasis.

18. Curzon, *Visits to the Monasteries of the Levant, 1834.* Quoted in Save-Söderbergh, ed., *Temples and Tombs of Ancient Nubia: The International Rescue Campaign at Abu Simbel, Philae and Other Sites,* 151.

19. Edwards, *A Thousand Miles up the Nile*, 139.

20. Like several other monuments of Nubia, the magnificent buildings of Philae were moved in the early 1970s to save them from the rising waters behind the Aswan Dam. In a remarkable feat of engineering and planning that took ten years to complete, the entire complex was dismantled, moved to the island of Agilqiyyah, and reerected.

21. Save-Söderbergh, *Temples and Tombs of Ancient Nubia: The International Rescue Campaign at Abu Simbel, Philae and Other Sites,* 151.

22. Ibid., 162.

23. Ibid.

24. Haeny, "A Short Architectural History of Philae," 197–233.

25. Adams, *Nubia: Corridor to Africa*, 336–37.

26. Haeny, "A Short Architectural History of Philae," 232.

27. Zabkar, "Six Hymns to Isis in the Sanctuary of her Temple at Philae and their Theological Significance," 130.

28. Save-Söderbergh, *Temples and Tombs of Ancient Nubia: The International Rescue Campaign at Abu Simbel, Philae and Other Sites,* 240.

29. Ibid., 241.

30. Adams, Nubia: Corridor to Africa, 337.
31. Ibid., 338.
32. Welsby, The Kingdom of Kush: The Napatan and Meroitic Empires, 66–67.
33. Speidel, "Nubia's Roman Garrison," 779. Speidel suggests that Iunius Sabinus commanded the Syene troops during the Nubian campaigns of Petronius in 24–22 B.C.
34. Strabo, Geography, 17, 1, 12. CIL III 14147.2 = Dessau 8907 indicates that the three cohorts were still in Aswan in A.D. 99.
35. In contrast to Aswan's contingent of fifteen hundred men, for more than fifty years a full Roman legion (five thousand men) was stationed in Thebes. Although their job was to control unrest in Thebes, no doubt their proximity to Aswan gave the troops stationed there an added measure of authority. Speidel, "Augustus' Deployment of the Legions in Egypt," 122.
36. Strabo, Geography, 17, 1, 53.
37. Török, "Economic Offices and Officials in Meroitic Nubia (A Study in Territorial Administration of the Late Meroitic Kingdom)." Quoted in Welsby, The Kingdom of Kush: The Napatan and Meroitic Empires, 68.
38. From one such statue, the Kushites removed a superb bronze head of Augustus. It was unearthed during the British excavation of the temple at Meroe in 1910 and is now on display in the British Museum in London.

CHAPTER VII. ROMAN NUBIA

1. The origin of the term "Nubia" is unclear. The ancient Egyptians often referred to the land as Ta-sety, "Land of the Bow," but the meaning of "Kush," which appears to be the name used by the inhabitants of Nubia to designate their territory, is uncertain. Given that most of the land and villages that once constituted Nubia now lie under the waters of Lake Nasser, Nubia as a political reality does not exist. Today, geographical Nubia straddles the Egyptian-Sudanese border. The term "Nubian," which has been used since the Middle Ages, refers to the "settled farming peoples of the Nile valley south of Aswan, whose cultures, although not originally derived from Egypt, were strongly influenced by their Egyptian neighbors" (Adams, Nubia: The Corridor to Africa, 44).
2. Egyptian influence is clearly evident in the use of the Egyptian hieroglyphic language for royal inscriptions, and in the royal burial customs of the later Napatan rulers. After the death of King Piankhy, the first Napatan king of Egypt, for example, all Napatan and subsequently all Meroitic royal burials were under steeply angled pyramids, and the traditional bed burials were replaced by the use of wooden or stone sarcophagi (Shinnie, Ancient Nubia, 100–01).
3. Details of Piankhy's invasion of Egypt were discovered on a stele at Gebel Barkal in 1862. The stele is now in the Egyptian National Museum. After King Taharqa (690–664 B.C.), Kushite kings never actually ruled Egypt but maintained the pretense of such authority by using Pharaonic titles. Ibid., 101.

4. The exact time this transition to Meroë occurred is unclear, but archaeological evidence suggests that Meroë became the seat of government and the royal residence even before the Kushites began to bury their kings there in approximately 300 B.C. Ibid., 102.

5. Little is known about the personality of Ptolemy I. One ancient sources states, "A member of Alexander's bodyguard and a first-rate soldier, Ptolemy was even more talented at, and better known for, the civilian rather than military skills. His manner was modest and unassuming, and he was superlatively generous and approachable, having assumed none of the pride of royalty" (Yardley, trans., *Quintus Curtius Rufus: The History of Alexander*, 59). The only extant biography of Ptolemy I is Ellis, *Ptolemy of Egypt*.

6. Some scholars believe that by the time of the Ptolemies, the ancient name for the region lying between Aswan and Wadi Allaqi was forgotten. Therefore, the Ptolemies, who wished to reassert Egypt's claim to this portion of Nubia in order to control the gold mines located in Wadi Allaqi and to gain access to the lands further south from whence they could obtain war elephants, simply renamed the territory according to its size: one *schenoi* = 10 kilometers, twelve *schoenus*, or *Dodekaschoenus* = 120 kilometers. Adams, *Nubia: Corridor to Africa*, 334.

7. It is possible, however, that the *Triakontaschoenus*, or "thirty *schoenoi*," refers to the entire distance from the first to the second cataract because it corresponds fairly well to the actual distance (i.e., 325 km). This means that the *Dodekaschoenus* might have been enclosed within the *Triakontaschoenus* rather than being separate from it. Griffith, *Meroitic Inscriptions*, part 2, note 12. Quoted in Adams, *Nubia: Corridor to Africa*, chap. 12, n. 15.

8. Updegraff, "The Blemmyes I: The Rise of the Blemmyes and the Roman Withdrawal from Nubia under Diocletian," 50–52.

9. Although the Romans called them Ethiopians, the Nubians had little in common with the people who live in the modern country of Ethiopia.

10. Strabo, *Geography*, 17, 1, 1–2. It seems likely that, at least in the early period (i.e., first century A.D. or possibly earlier), the Blemmyes had a close but as yet not fully understood relationp with Meroë. The oldest inscriptions commissioned by the Blemmyes, for example, were written in Meroitic, a language that has not yet been fully translated. Updegraff, "The Blemmyes I: The Rise of the Blemmyes and the Roman Withdrawal from Nubia under Diocletian," 79.

11. Macadam, *The Temple of Kawa I*, plate 16, lines 18–20. Quoted in Updegraff, "The Blemmyes I: The Rise of the Blemmyes and the Roman Withdrawal from Nubia under Diocletian," 56.

12. Ibid., 60–61.

13. Pliny the Elder, *Natural History*, book 5, 44 and 46.

14. Rufius Festus Avienus, *Orbis Terrae*. Quoted in Updegraff, "The Blemmyes I: The Rise of the Blemmyes and the Roman Withdrawal from Nubia under Diocletian," 66.

15. Shinnie, *Ancient Nubia*, 73.

16. Lichtheim, *Ancient Egyptian Literature* 1:119–20. Quoted in ibid., 73–76. The stele containing this message is dated 1862 B.C.—the sixteenth year of Sesostris's reign.

17. Scholars have identified ancient Iken as Mirgissa, which was the largest of the Middle Kingdom fortresses and was located approximately 55 km to the north of Semna, overlooking the second cataract.

18. Emery, *Egypt in Nubia*, 157. Quoted in Shinnie, *Ancient Nubia*, 76. This inscription dates from 1870 B.C.—the eighth year of Sesostris's reign.

19. Welsby, *The Kingdom of Kush: The Napatan and Meroitic Empires*, 69.

20. Speidel, "Nubia's Roman Garrison," 770.

21. Ibid., 790.

22. Ibid. The use of horsemen in the Nubian garrison is attested by several documents. One (*P. Oxy.* IV, 735), dated September 4, A.D. 205, records that wheat was given to fifty horsemen of the Syene garrison. Another document (BGU XI, 2024) from the Fayoum records a similar allotment of barley to horsemen from the same garrison. Ibid., 794.

23. Shinnie, "Trade Routes of the Ancient Sudan: 3,000 B.C.–A.D. 350," 49.

24. Another major desert route began on the west bank about 15 km north of Qasr Ibrim, continued west through the remote Dunqul Oasis, and ended at Dush, in Kharga.

25. Adams, *Nubia: Corridor to Africa*, 344.

26. This list does not include Philae, discussed in chapter 6, although it is technically in Nubia. In addition, the list does not include Ramses II's great temple of Abu Simbel, which does not appear to have played a significant role during the Roman occupation.

27. Baikie, *Egyptian Antiquities in the Nile Valley: A Descriptive Handbook*, 764.

28. Save-Söderbergh, ed., *Temples and Tombs of Ancient Nubia: The International Rescue Campaign at Abu Simbel, Philae and Other Sites*, 127.

29. Weigall, *Guide to the Antiquities of Upper Egypt from Abydos to the Sudan Frontier*, 530.

30. Edwards, *A Thousand Miles Up the Nile*. Quoted in ibid.

31. Although its elevated position prevented Qasr Ibrim from suffering the ignoble fate of being moved, the creation of Lake Nasser nevertheless turned the hilltop fortress into an island. Since the mid 1980s, the waters of the lake have been rising steadily and are now lapping at the base of the fortress itself. The unfortunate consequence of this is that water seepage is causing the deterioration of thousands of yet-uncovered artifacts—particularly textiles and papyrus—and erosion from waves has destroyed large segments of the outer wall. In addition, two unforeseen dangers, tourism and vandalism, are also threatening the site. In 1991, the Egyptian government gave permission for the first cruise ships to begin plying the length of Lake Nasser, enabling tourists to visit the Nubian monuments. Qasr Ibrim was on the itinerary for three years, and the weekly visits of several hundred tourists not only impeded the work of archaeologists, but also caused considerable damage to many of the structures within the complex. Fortunately, the Egyptian government listened to the protests of the Egyptian Exploration Society (EES), which sponsors the excavations, and as of 1995 tourists are no longer permitted to visit Qasr Ibrim. But the end of tourism does not mean that the fortress is safe from damage. Local fishermen who visit this remote region occasionally land at the site and dig up its ancient timbers to burn as firewood. In addition, the presence of archaeologists has convinced other local inhabitants that treasures are buried

at Qasr Ibrim, and they often search for artifacts when the researchers have left for the season. In the process, they have smashed an altar, torn up stone pavement in the main temple, and dug numerous pits throughout the site. As of this writing, the EES has been unsuccessful in its attempts to have a year-round guard assigned to the fortress.

32. Horton, "Africa in Egypt: New Evidence from Qasr Ibrim," 264.

33. Adams, "Primis and the 'Aethiopian' Frontier," 95.

34. Two faunal discoveries at Qasr Ibrim are of particular interest. The first was of the remains of a ritually killed domestic chicken dating from A.D. 450–550—among the earliest known incidence of such a fowl in Africa south of the Tropic of Cancer and evidence that domestic chickens might have arrived in Africa via the "Nubian corridor." MacDonald and Edwards, "Chickens in Africa: The Importance of Qasr Ibrim," 584–90. (Domestic chicken bones were also discovered during the excavations at Berenike.) The second discovery was of the remains of a camel and camel dung dating from the very earliest occupation of the fortress (1250–810 B.C.) Given that previous studies have suggested that camels did not enter Egypt until the Ptolemaic period, this discovery advances their introduction by more than five hundred years and suggests that camels entered Egypt from the south, after they had been imported there from Arabia. This earlier date greatly increases the probability that desert tribes like the Blemmyes used camels long before the Romans arrived in Nubia. Rowley-Conwy, "Camel in the Nile Valley: New Radiocarbon Accelerator (AMS) Dates from Qasr Ibrim," 245–48.

35. Adams, "Primis and the 'Aethiopian' Frontier," 96.

36. [P. Qasr Ibrim inv. 78-3-11/I (LI/2)] The page is difficult to date with precision, but, given the context in which it was discovered, it was probably produced sometime between 50 B.C. and 20 B.C., and, most likely, within the lifetime of Gallus himself (i.e., before 26 B.C.). As such, it constitutes the oldest surviving manuscript of Latin poetry. Anderson, Parsons, and Nisbet, "Elegiacs by Gallus from Qasr Ibrim," 127–28.

37. Ovid, Amor. I.15. 29. Quoted in ibid., 155.

38. Ibid., 125–55.

39. Ibid., 127.

40. Adams, "Primis and the 'Aethiopian' Frontier," 97.

41. The discovery of thousands of stone ballistae (catapult balls) at a level corresponding to the later phases of Roman occupation suggests that a greater military threat was perceived at that time than there was in the beginning. Ibid., 97.

42. Adams, "Ptolemaic and Roman Occupation at Qasr Ibrim," 16–17.

43. Kirwan, The Oxford University Excavations at Firka. Quoted in Adams, "Primis and the 'Aethiopian' Frontier," 100.

44. Adding credence to this theory is that the ancient Egyptian name for the fortress at Qasr Ibrim meant "Repelling the Medjay," the Medjay being the possible ancestors of the Blemmyes. Adams, "Ptolemaic and Roman Occupation at Qasr Ibrim," 17.

45. Adams, "Primis and the 'Aethiopian' Frontier," 95.

46. Skeat, "A Letter from the King of the Blemmyes to the King of the Noubades," 159–70.

47. Cassius Dio (53, 23, 5). Scholars are not in agreement on the date of his suicide: some suggest it might have occurred in 27 B.C.
48. Jameson, "Chronology of the Campaigns of Aelius Gallus and C. Petronius," 79.
49. Ibid., 72.
50. Strabo, Geography, 17, 1, 54.
51. There is some confusion over the tenure of each of these men as prefects, since they seem to overlap in that office.
52. Strabo, Geography, 17, 1, 54.
53. The term "Candace" (or Kandake) was not a personal name, but a title given to the queens of Nubia, including its principal cities of Meroë and Napata. It is likely that the Candace who engaged Petronius was Queen Amanishakhete, who ruled in 41–12 B.C. Archaeologists have discovered the pyramid graves of several Candaces near Meroë that date from 300 B.C. to A.D. 300. Interestingly, it was the eunuch of one such Candace whom Philip met on the road between Jerusalem and Gaza: "Now an Ethiopian had been on a pilgrimage to Jerusalem; he was a eunuch and an officer at the court of the kandake, or queen, of Ethiopia." Acts 8:27.
54. Strabo, Geography, 17, 1, 54.
55. Ibid.
56. Adams, Nubia: Corridor to Africa, 341.
57. Strabo, Geography, 17, 1, 54.
58. Jameson, "Chronology of the Campaigns of Aelius Gallus and C. Petronius," 81.
59. Scholars are not in accord on this theory. Discoveries at Qasr Ibrim, including numerous papyrus fragments of Greek and Latin documents dating from the first century B.C. through the first century A.D., raise the possibility that Qasr Ibrim continued to serve as the southern border at least for the duration of the reign of Augustus (30 B.C.–A.D. 14).
60. Adams, Nubia: Corridor to Africa, 344.
61. Seneca, VI, 8.3. Quoted in ibid., 342.
62. Moorehead, The White Nile, 83–84.
63. Braund, Rome and the Friendly King: The Character of Client Kingship.
64. Bersina, "Milanese Papyrus No. 40," 217–23.
65. A Demotic inscription indicates that the road to the south had been closed for three years. Given that the inscription was written at about the time of the first Blemmye invasion of Egypt, it is likely that they were responsible for the closure of the road. Updegraff, "The Blemmyes I: The Rise of the Blemmyes and the Roman Withdrawal from Nubia under Diocletian," 82, n. 235.
66. Chronicon Paschale, CSHB I, 1832, 504f. Quoted in ibid., 69.
67. Scriptiores Histotiae Augustae Tyranni triginta 22, 6. Quoted in ibid., 69.
68. Scriptiores Histotiae Augustae Vita Firmi 3, 3. Quoted in ibid., 70.
69. Scriptiores Histotiae Augustae Vita Aur. 33, 4. Quoted in ibid., 70.
70. Scriptiores Histotiae Augustae Vita Probi 19, 2 and 8. Quoted in ibid., 71.
71. Scarre, Chronicle of the Roman Emperors, 200. On his coinage, Aurelius Achilleus used the name L. Domitius Domitianus.

72. Updegraff, "The Blemmyes I: The Rise of the Blemmyes and the Roman Withdrawal from Nubia under Diocletian," 73.

73. Procopius, *History of the Wars*, book I, 19.

74. Updegraff, "The Blemmyes I: The Rise of the Blemmyes and the Roman Withdrawal from Nubia under Diocletian," 74–76.

75. Welsby, *Kingdom of Kush: Napatan and Meroitic Empires*, 196–97.

76. Constantine engaged the former emperor Maxentius in battle at the Milvian bridge just west of Rome on October 28, A.D. 312. The traditional story of his conversion claims that prior to the battle, he saw a cross of light in the sky with the inscription, "Conquer by this sign." Inspired by this apparition, he led his troops to victory, and from that point on his armies carried shields bearing painted crosses. Some scholars, however, question the veracity of this story. The crosses the soldiers painted on their shields, for example, closely resembled the symbol for the sun god Sol Invictus, a popular military deity. Yet Constantine was a deeply spiritual man, and although he continued to issue coins bearing the sign of Sol Invictus until A.D. 324, it remains probable that he truly did experience a religious conversion to Christianity after A.D. 313—despite the fact that it was only on his deathbed in A.D. 337 that he was officially baptized.

77. In A.D. 553, Emperor Justinian I convened a meeting in Constantinople to reformulate the earlier interpretation of Christ's dual nature (i.e., fully God and Man), which had been established by the Council of Chalcedon in A.D. 451. The new convocation resulted in a Christology that retained the balanced dual nature of Christ but more clearly emphasized the centrality of his divine nature. Monophysitism, however, is the doctrine that in the person of Christ there was but a single divine nature.

78. Bury, *History of the Later Roman Empire from the Death of Theodosius I to the Death of Justinian (A.D. 395–A.D. 565)*, 328.

79. Ibid., 329.

80. Ibid. The conversion of the Nobatai occurred about A.D. 540.

81. Ibid., 330.

82. Save-Söderbergh, ed., *Temples and Tombs of Ancient Nubia: International Rescue Campaign at Abu Simbel, Philae and Other Sites*, 241.

OVERVIEW OF THE WESTERN DESERT

1. A sixth, the great Qattara depression, is located near the Mediterranean coast between the Nile and Siwa Oasis. It is the largest and deepest depression in Egypt. Covering an area of thousands of square kilometers, and lying 130 meters below sea-level, the depression is uninhabitable because of the salty water beneath its surface.

2. Beadnell, *An Egyptian Oasis: An Account of the Oasis of Kharga in the Libyan Desert*, 2–6.

3. Hoskins, *Visit to the Great Oasis of the Libyan Desert*, 25.

4. Many of the older implements in Egypt date from the late Lower Palaeolithic (Acheulean) period and are between 250,000 and 90,000 years old, while the more

finely worked "Neolithic" tools date from 7,000 to 4,000 B.C. Hoffman, *Egypt Before the Pharaohs*, 53, 232–33.

5. These early dates are derived from pottery discovered in the Dakhleh Oasis. Mills, "The Dakhleh Oasis Project: Report on the Second Season of Survey, September–December, 1979," 254.

6. Wagner, *Les Oasis d'Égypte*, 120.

7. Coptic was derived from the spoken form of Late Egyptian, the administrative tongue of the New Kingdom, and became the final version of the ancient Egyptian language. Used mainly by the native peasant population, it received its written form in approximately the second century A.D., supplementing the twenty-four letters of the Greek alphabet with seven forms borrowed from Demotic. It was written from left to right, and, although its vocabulary was highly influenced by Greek, its grammar and syntax were rooted in Egyptian. Of the six dialects of Coptic that existed, Sahidic and Bohairic were the most important. By the fourth century, Sahidic was the standard literary language of the Nile Valley and the western oases.

8. Wagner, *Les Oasis d'Égypte*, 247.

9. Ibid., 397.

10. Ibid., 395.

CHAPTER VIII. THE GREAT OASIS

1. From the poem "The Oasis of Sidi Khaled," by Wilfred S. Blunt

2. Even today, banishing criminals to the desert is practiced. Northeast of the modern town of Kharga, for example, stands a high-security prison to which the Egyptian government has sentenced hundreds of criminals and Islamic extremists.

3. Domitius Ulpianus (Ulpian) was an assistant to Emperor Severus Alexander (A.D. 222–35) and an ardent persecutor of Christians. He was appointed commander of the praetorian guard but was eventually assassinated by a group of his own men in A.D. 224. Edmonstone, *A Journey to the Two Oases of Upper Egypt*, 137–38.

4. Ibid., 138.

5. Athanasius was removed from his post in Alexandria because of his adherence to the orthodox Christian doctrine—formulated at the Council of Nicaea in A.D. 325—which maintained that Jesus was "of the same substance" with God. Emperor Constantius II (A.D. 337–61), along with many others in the eastern empire, supported the conflicting doctrine, advanced by Arius of Alexandria (d. A.D. 335), which argued that Jesus Christ could not be "of the same substance" as his Father, because the substance of the Father must be indivisible. In an ultimately unsuccessful attempt to end this bitter theological debate, Constantius deposed and exiled Athanasius, along with several western bishops who supported the original Nicene doctrine. Nestorius, who served as the patriarch of Constantinople from A.D. 428 to 431, taught that the humanity of Jesus should be emphasized rather than his divinity. This contradicted the beliefs of the patriarch Cyril of Alexandria, who believed that Christ was essentially divine. In the ensuing con-

frontation at Ephesus in A.D. 431, both patriarchs excommunicated the other, but Cyril was able to restore his position through bribery. Meanwhile, Nestorius was exiled, first to a monastery in Antioch and then to Kharga in A.D. 434. He died in Panopolis, Egypt, about A.D. 447. Downey, *The Late Roman Empire*, 37–43, 89–90.

6. Evagrius, *Hist Ecl. Lib.* 1 Cap 5. Quoted in Edmonstone, *Journey to Two Oases of Upper Egypt*, 140.

7. Wagner, *Les oasis d'Égypte*, 117–18.

8. Ibid., 117, n. 7 (translated by the author).

9. Emperor Julian became known as the Apostate because of his attempt to replace Christianity with the traditional Roman religion. He died during his invasion of Persia of wounds sustained in a fight near the city of Ctesiphon, but it is rumored that he was killed by an angry Christian rather than a Persian.

10. Wagner, *Les oasis d'Égypte*, 117, n. 7 (translated by the author).

11. Ibid.

12. Ibid., 118 (translated by the author).

13. Ibid. (translated by the author).

14. Beadnell, *An Egyptian Oasis: An Account of the Oasis of Kharga in the Libyan Desert*, 7–9.

15. There is, however, a long history of foreign invasion into the Western Desert. During the reign of Ramses II, for example, the viceroy Setain captured a band of Libyans in either the Dungul or Kurkur Oases (south of Kharga) and forced them to work on the construction of the temple in Wadi el-Sebua. Libyans also later attacked Bahariya and Kharga Oases. Morkot, "The Darb el-Arbain, the Kharga Oasis and its Forts, and Other Desert Routes," 92.

16. Reddé, "A l'ouest du Nil: Une frontière sans soldats, des soldats sans frontière," 485–92.

17. Winlock, *El Dakhleh Oasis: Journal of a Camel Trip Made in 1908*, 61.

18. In addition to the major sites discussed below, the remains of numerous other Roman-era buildings exist in Kharga. Many of these, such as Qasr el Geb and Qasr el Sumeria, were small outposts that have never been excavated and about which little is known.

19. Morkot, "The Darb el-Arbain, the Kharga Oasis and its Forts, and Other Desert Routes," 84.

20. In 1996, French archaeologists discovered a small bronze statue, possibly of Persian origin, which might suggest that the Dush was occupied before the Romans constructed the present edifice.

21. Beadnell, *An Egyptian Oasis: An Account of the Oasis of Kharga in the Libyan Desert*, 13.

22. Reddé, *Le trésor de Douch (Oasis de Kharga)*.

23. Annia Galeria Faustina was fifteen when she married the twenty-four-year-old Marcus Aurelius in May A.D. 145. Of their fourteen children, only six survived beyond childhood. In her later life, Faustina was known for her infidelities with gladiators and members of the imperial court. Yet Marcus grieved upon her death and chose never to remarry. Scarre, *Chronicle of the Roman Emperors*, 115.

24. *Ostraca Douch*, no. 284, in Cuvigny and Wagner, *Les ostraca grecs de Douch: Fascicule I, II and III*, 48.

25. Gascou and Wagner, "Deux voyages archéologiques dans l'oasis de Khargeh," 7.

26. It is difficult to determine the age of a camel carcass in the desert. Although camel bones can last for hundreds of years when buried, if they remain on the surface of the desert, sun and wind-blown sand can cause them to disintegrate completely in a few years.

27. Gascou et al., "Douch: rapport préliminaire des campagnes de fouilles de l'hiver 1978/1979 et de l'automne 1979," 337.

28. A fortified well named Ain Borek was located approximately eight kilometers northeast of Dush, at the base of the trail leading up the escarpment.

29. Troops in the Roman army were trained diligently in marching. During the summer, the standard "military pace" was four Roman miles per hour, while the "full pace" equaled just under five Roman miles per hour. (A Roman mile equals 1.08 statute miles.) Watson, *The Roman Soldier*, 54–55.

30. See Arkell, *A History of the Sudan from the Earliest Times to 1821*, 43–44. Until approximately twenty years ago, the Darb el-Arbain was used to import camels from their breeding grounds in Darfour to the Egyptian markets at Assiut and Daraw. Although portions of the route are still used for this purpose, new tarmac roads in the Sudan and Egypt have altered the ancient route, and today large trucks haul the camels to their destination, replacing this once-adventurous journey with diesel fumes and the confines of a truck bed. For a recent account of this route, see Asher, *In Search of the Forty Days Road*.

31. Burckhardt, *Travels in Nubia*, 4.

32. Cailliaud, *Travels in the Oases of Thebes, and in the Deserts situated East and West of the Thebaid, in the Years 1815, 1816, 1817, and 1818*. Quoted in Beadnell, *An Egyptian Oasis: An Account of the Oasis of Kharga in the Libyan Desert*, 34.

33. Beadnell, *An Egyptian Oasis: An Account of the Oasis of Kharga in the Libyan Desert*, 99; and Edmonstone, *Journey to Two Oases of Upper Egypt*, 67–68.

34. Sauneron, "Quelques sanctuaires égyptiens des oasis de Dakhleh et de Khargeh," 291.

35. Aufrère, Galvin and Goyon, *L'Égypte restituée*, vol. 2, *Sites et temples des déserts*, 100.

36. Of the three Persian kings who ruled Egypt, only Darius I visited the country.

37. Owing to the structural damage being caused by the high water table at its current location, the Egyptian government is currently planning to move the entire temple to higher ground nearby.

38. These inscriptions are of enormous importance to an understanding of the history of the Roman occupation of Kharga Oasis. For the original Greek, see White and Oliver, *The Temple of Hibis in El Khargeh Oasis*, part 2, *Greek Inscriptions*, 1938.

39. Beadnell, *An Egyptian Oasis: An Account of the Oasis of Kharga in the Libyan Desert*, 95–96.

40. This codex was not recovered from Hibis during archaeological excavations. Instead, it was looted from the site, probably by a local farmer, and ended up in the antiquities market in Luxor, where, in 1906, the Reverend Archibald H. Sayce, a professor of Assyriology at Oxford University, purchased the wooden tablets. They are now in the col-

lection of the Ashmolean Museum, Oxford, and catalogued under "Bodleian Greek Inscriptions 3018."

41. Parsons, "The Wells of Hibis," 65–180.

42. Winlock, El Dakhleh Oasis: Journey of a Camel Trip Made in 1908, 48–49.

43. Ibid., 49.

44. The Coptic church adopted a calendar that began with the reign of Emperor Diocletian, whom Egyptians regarded as the most terrible of all Roman persecutors.

45. Edmonstone, Journey to Two Oases of Upper Egypt, 63.

46. Hoskins, A Visit to the Great Oasis of the Libyan Desert. Quoted in Beadnell, An Egyptian Oasis: An Account of the Oasis of Kharga in the Libyan Desert, 104–05.

47. Wagner, Les oasis d'Égypte à l'époque grecque, romaine et byzantine d'après les documents grecs, 63–65.

48. Romans 8:32.

49. Devauchelle and Wagner, Les graffites du Gebel Teir: textes demotiques et grec, 50.

50. Ibid., 41, 36.

51. Ibid., 19.

52. During the summertime, caravans often traveled during the cool of night, so a fire atop a tower such as this would have been a valuable navigational aid. Up until the early part of this century, lamps were often hung from high minarets in Egyptian towns and cities for the same purpose. See Reddé, "Sites militaires romains de l'oasis de Kharga," 381.

53. Local inhabitants often refer to Roman-era buildings in Kharga as El Deir. During the Christian period, many but by no means all of these buildings did, indeed, house Christian communities.

54. This latter route, via the Ramia pass, constituted the final portion of the Darb el Arbain, which began in Darfour, Sudan, and arrived in Kharga via Selima Oasis. From the top of the pass, the ancient traveler still had to cover another 210 kilometers of waterless desert before arriving at Assiut in the Nile Valley.

55. Wagner, Les oasis d'Égypte à l'époque grecque, romaine et Byzantine d'après les documents grecs, 170. Also see Naumann, "Bauwerke der Oase Khargeh," 2.

56. The fortress measures approximately 75 m ×x 75 m, and its walls are 10 m high and 3.5 m thick.

57. The Sanussi, an austere and influential sect of Islam in the late nineteenth and early twentieth centuries, were based in the Libyan oases of El Jaghbub and El Kufrah. As a result of several hostile encounters with English officials and travelers, the Sanussi were denounced by the European press as Islamic fanatics. The so-called Sanussi danger, however, never resulted in a widespread outbreak of hostilities within Egypt. See Dumreicher, Trackers and Smugglers in the Deserts of Egypt, 25.

58. Darnell and Darnell, "The Luxor–Farshut Desert Road Survey," 49.

59. This temple bears at least twelve devotional inscriptions, several of which date from the reign of Antonius Pius. See Wagner, "Les inscriptions grecques d'Ain Labakha (stèles - graffites - depinti)," 97–114.

60. Labekha's beautiful setting and its accessibility to the modern town of Kharga have made it a popular stop for adventure tour companies based in Cairo. As they do at Roman sites in the Eastern Desert, the tourists who visit Labekha inflict serious damage on the site when they climb through its fragile, mud-brick buildings.

61. Jenkins, McBride, and Rossi, "Brief Report on the 1998 'Ain Umm el Dabadib Project."

62. Gascou and Wagner, "Deux voyages archéologiques dans l'oasis de Khargeh," 15–16.

63. An estimated 20,000 cubic meters of solid rock were removed in the process of digging the four aqueducts. Beadnell, *An Egyptian Oasis: An Account of the Oasis of Kharga in the Libyan Desert*, 179.

64. According to Beadnell, who visited the area in January 1905, almost a dozen acres were reclaimed by this effort, and the aqueduct was discharging 30 to 35 gallons of water per minute. Several years later, however, the farm was abandoned, and the aqueduct was left to fill with sand and silt. Ibid., 171–72.

65. I have made two attempts to discover what might lie at the end of the aqueduct. On both occasions, I was forced to turn back within an estimated 500 meters of the end because major blockages of sand and silt in the confined space made further progress too hazardous.

66. Beadnell, *An Egyptian Oasis: An Account of the Oasis of Kharga in the Libyan Desert*, 182–83.

67. Some maps indicate that this route passed along the west side of Gebel Tarif. Although the western route might have been used, the eastern road is the most direct, and the numerous shards of ribbed amphora and other Roman-era pottery I observed while hiking this route in 1995 suggest that this was the principal track between Dabadib and Hibis during the Roman period.

68. Because of the steepness of the ascent up the escarpment, this route was probably not used by caravans. In addition, the degree to which this route might have been used—or whether it was used at all—during the Roman period is unknown.

69. An early twentieth-century traveler reported that the old Arabic name for the well at Ain Amur was Mu-allakeh, or "the Hanging." Winlock, *El Dakhlah Oasis: Journey of a Camel Trip Made in 1908*, 48.

70. The Roman-era pottery shards that lie in and around the enclosure are ribbed amphora, red coarse-ware bowls, and fragments of blue faience.

71. Winlock, *El Dakhlah Oasis: Journey of a Camel Trip Made in 1908*, 49. Inscribed in the stones that once featured these paintings is the name of A. Edmonstone, who in February 1819 became the first European to visit Ain Amur. Just above Edmonstone's name, is that of I. Hyde, who visited the site in December of the same year.

72. Ibid., 49.

73. These blocks were in place when I visited Ain Amur in early January 1995 but were missing when I returned to the site in December of that same year. Judging from tracks I observed on the plateau above Ain Amur, it appears that someone managed to drive a tractor or tractor-like vehicle from Dakhleh all the way to the top of the pass that leads down to Ain Amur. From there, they walked to the site and eventually carried whatever items they thought worth stealing back up to their vehicle.

74. Winlock, *El Dakhlah Oasis: Journey of a Camel Trip Made in 1908*, 7–16.

75. "Furthermore, it is obvious that no one, from now on, will waste his time making the trip on foot and camel back, and it seems to me that there is some interest in recording one of the last trips that will ever be so made" (Winlock, *El Dakhlah Oasis: Journal of a Camel Trip Made in 1908*, 3).

76. One does occasionally encounter low, crescent-shaped windbocks made from loose piles of stones, but these are most likely of fairly recent construction.

77. Given that the ancient Egyptians appear to have inhabited only the eastern portion of Dakhleh Oasis, it is probable, although not proven, that this area of desert existed in antiquity and served to divide the oasis into its current eastern and western regions. The possibility remains, however, that further ruins—of the Pharaonic or even Roman period—might yet be discovered under the sand.

78. Mills, "Dakhleh Oasis Project: Report on the First Season of Survey (October–December 1978)," 180–81.

79. Mills, "Lively Paintings: Roman Frescoes in the Dakhleh Oasis," 21.

80. Winlock, *El Dakhlah Oasis: Journey of a Camel Trip Made in 1908*, 42, and plate 32. Vivian, *The Western Desert of Egypt*, 131–32.

81. Despite the seemingly impenetrable vastness of the Western Desert, it was not as formidable an obstacle to invasion as it might seem. Libyans launched numerous attacks on the oases and the Nile Valley during the Pharaonic period, and even the modern history of the oasis is punctuated by hostile invasions from the west, mainly from the Sanussi, a radical Islamic sect, of Libya. In 1816, for example, an army of four hundred desert invaders descended on the oasis, causing great loss of life and carrying away a large quantity of plunder. Edmonstone, *Journey to Two Oases of Egypt*, 55. Even in the twentieth century, the oasis suffered attacks and occasional occupations by Libyans. The Sanussi briefly occupied Dakhleh Oasis in 1916. Fearing that the Sanussi might be planning an attack on Kharga, British forces based in Kharga flew over Mut, Dakhleh's capital, and dropped a few bombs just outside the city as a show of strength. Shortly afterward, the Sanussi troops, under the command of Ahmed el Sharif, abandoned the oasis.

82. As indicated earlier, Dakhleh contains important Roman sites beyond the four discussed here. Mut el-Kharab, for example, which lies southwest of the modern town of Mut, contains a fortified enclosure with mud-brick walls. The pottery from the site dates from the Roman period, but thus far archaeological excavations have not been conducted there. Mills, "Dakhleh Oasis Project: Report on the First Season of Survey (October–December 1978)," 175.

83. One scholar has suggested that the etymology of the word "Teneida" comes from the Coptic term for "monastery." Guy Wagner, *Les oasis d'Égypte à l'époque grecque, romaine et byzantine d'après les documents grecques*, 196.

84. Alternatively, the last line could be translated as "he has overthrown the gang in [this] town." Kaper, "How the God Amun-Nakht Came to Dakhleh Oasis," 151.

85. Ibid., 151–54.

86. Winlock, *El Dakhlah Oasis: Journey of a Camel Trip Made in 1908*, 17.

87. In 1987, archaeologists working at Kellis unearthed several Greek texts written on papyrus. One of these dates from the early fourth century and states that Kellis was in the Mothite *nome*, which derived its name from the town of Mothis, the modern Mut. This discovery was the first clear indication that Dakhleh Oasis was a separate administrative zone from those of the Nile Valley. Hope, "Three Seasons of Excavation at Ismant el-Gharab in Dakhleh Oasis," 169.

88. During the third century, at the height of its population, Kellis contained approximately two thousand inhabitants.

89. Hope, "Excavations at Ismant el-Kharab in the Dakhleh Oasis," 17.

90. The cult of Tutu was popular during the reigns of Trajan, Hadrian, and Antoninus Pius (A.D. 98–161, collectively). Neith wore the red crown of Lower Egypt and carried a shield and crossed arrows. One of the great Egyptian deities, she was the goddess of the ancient Delta town of Sais, capital of the fifth nome of Lower Egypt.

91. Translated by the author from Wagner, "Les inscriptions grecques des oasis de Dakhleh et Bahriyeh découvertes par le Dr. Ahmed Fakhry," 178.

92. Mills, "Dakhleh Oasis Project: Report on the 1990–1991 Field Season," 14.

93. Although wooden tablets containing multiple leaves were often used by the fifth century B.C., the codex form of the book was rarely used for Greek literature before A.D. 200, and it was not until approximately A.D. 300 that codices matched that of the scroll as a form of book production. The codices from Dakhleh span this transition from wooden tablet to parchment codex. Sharpe, "Dakhleh Oasis Project: The Kellis Codices," 192–93.

94. Hope, "Kellis in the Mothite Nome: Regional Contacts."

95. Hope, "The Dakhleh Oasis Project: Ismant el-Kharab 1988–1990," 166.

96. Ibid.

97. Manichaeism was founded in the second century A.D. by a Parthian named Mani (circa A.D. 216–77), who believed himself to be the Paraclete, or intercessor, promised by Jesus. ("I shall ask the Father, and he will give you another Paraclete to be with you forever." John 14:16.). The faith combines elements of Christianity, Judaism, Zoroastrianism, Buddhism, and Hinduism in an elaborate mythology largely determined by Gnostic and Zoroastrian dualism. Mani taught that the two opposing forces of God (light) and matter (darkness) in the universe were originally separated but are commingled in the present world, including humanity. Knowledge of this dualism is the only way by which humans can deliver themselves from evil. Humans must protect the spark of light within them so that it might pass into the realm of light upon the death of the body, rather than passing into another body. The modern age of mixed light and darkness will end with the final judgment and the burning of the world, after which light and darkness will be eternally separated.

   The Manichaean "elect" lived a strict monastic life of celibacy, vegetarianism, and abstinence from alcohol and agricultural work, while Manichaean "hearers," who could only hope to enter the next life as members of the elect, lived spiritually and morally strict, but more normal, lives. Eerdmans, *The Eerdmans Bible Dictionary*, 686.

98. Gardner, *Kellis Literary Texts* 1:xi.

99. Ibid., x–xi.

100. Ibid., vii.

101. Worp, Whitehorne, and Daniel, eds., *Greek Papyri From Kellis* 1:167–69.

102. Ibid., 220–22.

103. Ibid., 201–02.

104. Ibid., 29–31.

105. The reference to Kellis being in the Mothite nome is illuminating. During the first three centuries of Roman rule in Egypt, Dakhleh Oasis was administered by a provincial official stationed at Hibis in Kharga Oasis. This official had an assistant in Dakhleh, who probably maintained his office in Mothis. By the time of this letter, however, Dakhleh was a separate province. Ibid., 122–23.

106. Ibid., 64–67.

107. Ibid., 136–38.

108. Ibid., 183–84.

109. Ibid., 178–79.

110. Ibid., 184–88.

111. Thanheiser "Fruits, Nuts, Spices and Other Luxurious Commodities at Kellis."

112. El Molto and Sheldrick, "Death and Dying in the Roman Period of Egypt's Dakhleh Oasis." Several mummies from the west cemetery featured elaborately decorated gilded cartonnage similar to those discovered in Bawiti in 1996. See Birrell, "Excavations in the Cemeteries of Ismant el-Kharab," 33–38.

113. Mills, "The Dakhleh Oasis Project: Report on the Second Season of Survey (September–December, 1979)," 272.

114. In this story, one of the favorites of ancient Greece, Perseus was the son of Danae, the beautiful daughter of King Acrisius, who had been condemned to live underground in a bronze chamber with only a hole open to the sky. Upon stopping in Ethiopia during his return journey from having killed the great snake-haired Medusa of the Gorgons, Perseus discovered that a beautiful maiden had been sacrificed to a sea monster. The beauty, of course, was Andromeda, the daughter of Cassiopeia, queen of Ethiopia, who had made the error of boasting that she was more beautiful than the daughters of Nereus, the sea god. Andromeda was chained to a rock in the middle of the sea, about to be sacrificed to the sea serpent sent by the gods as punishment for Cassiopeia's arrogance. Perseus slayed the monster, rescued Andromeda, and eventually married her.

115. Mills, "Lively Paintings: Roman Frescoes in the Dakhleh Oasis," 19–25; and Leahy, "Dakhleh Oasis Project: The Roman Wall-paintings from Amheida," 331–78.

116. While the painting of Odysseus is unique in Egypt, the story of the Odyssey was widely known and revered during both the Ptolemaic and Roman periods, and fragments of Homeric poetry are abundant among the Greek literary papyri found in Egypt.

117. Homer, *The Odyssey*, book 19, lines 443–46, 528–38, 563, 566–67. Trans. by Robert Fagles (New York: Viking Press, 1996).

118. Leahy, "Dakhleh Oasis Project: The Roman Wall-Paintings from Amheida," 341–46.

119. Ibid., 354.

120. Homer, *The Odyssey*, book 8, lines 347–53.

121. Leahy, "Dakhleh Oasis Project: The Roman Wall-Paintings from Amheida," 364–78.

122. Mills, "Dakhleh Oasis Project: Report on the Second Season of Survey (September–December 1979)," 269–270.

123. After years of meticulous study, members of the Dakhleh Oasis Project and the Supreme Council of Antiquities reconstructed this important temple and have now opened it to visitors.

124. Kaper and Worp, "Dipinti on the temenos wall at Deir el-Haggar (Dakhleh Oasis)," 233–57.

125. Kaper, "The Astronomical Ceiling of Deir El-Haggar in the Dakhleh Oasis," 175–95.

126. Ibid., 193–95.

127. Kaper, "How the God Amun-Nakht Came to Dakhleh Oasis," 154.

128. King, *Mysteries of the Libyan Desert: Record of Three Years of Exploration in the Heart of that Vast and Waterless Region*, 58–59.

129. Whitehouse, "Roman in Life, Egyptian in Death: The Painted Tomb of Petrosiris in the Dakhleh Oasis," 253–65.

130. Osing et al., "Denkmaler der Oase Dachla aus dem Nachlass von Ahmed Fakhry," 92. Quoted in ibid, 258.

131. Wagner, *Les oasis d'Égypte à l'époque grecque, romaine et byzantine d'après les documents grecques*, 81.

132. King, *Mysteries of the Libyan Desert: A Record of Three Years of Exploration in the Heart of that Vast and Waterless Region*, 204.

133. Ibid., 205.

134. Ibid., 206.

135. Edmonstone, *Journey to Two Oases of Upper Egypt*, 20–21.

136. Ibid., 26.

137. King, *Mysteries of the Libyan Desert: A Record of Three Years of Exploration in the Heart of that Vast and Waterless Region*, 305.

138. The tarmac road that now connects Dakhleh to Farafra first heads west-northwest from Dakhleh via Bir Abu Minqar, then turns north toward Farafra.

139. I made these observations during a six-day walk from Dakhleh to Farafra in the early 1980s. Since that time, the Darb el Farafra has been used at least twice as part of the annual Pharaoh's Rally in which hundreds of jeeps, trucks, and motorcycles race across Egypt's deserts. Predictably, the rallies have severely scarred this ancient caravan road.

CHAPTER IX. THE SMALL OASIS

1. Fakhry, *Oases of Egypt*, vol. 2, *Bahriyah and Farafra Oases*, 157.

2. Ibid., 158

3. The ruins of a large stone and mud-brick fortress stand atop the palm-covered hill located in the center of the modern town of Qasr el-Farafra. Ahmed Fakhry, however, states that this structure dates from the medieval rather than the Roman period. It stood largely intact until 1958, when it collapsed as a result of several years of unusually heavy rains.

4. Fakhry, *Oases of Egypt*, vol. 2, *Bahriyah and Farafra Oases*, 163.

5. Numerous pictographs and simple inscriptions are located on the sandstone outcroppings in Wadi Hannis. Many of them resemble the "Libyan inscriptions" discovered by Ahmed Fakhry in Qasr al-Zabw, but they have never been systematically cataloged or studied, so their age and origin remain uncertain.

6. Fakhry, *Oases of Egypt*, vol. 2, *Bahriyah and Farafra Oases*, 164–65.

7. P. Oxy. 1439. Quoted in Wagner, *Les oasis d'Égypte à l'époque grecque, romaine et byzantine d'après les documents grecques*, 147. Wagner cites numerous texts that refer to Baharia Oasis, 146–51.

8. Hawass, *Valley of the Golden Mummies*, 33–41.

9. Several of Bawiti's gilded mummies bear a strong resemblance to some of the mummies from the Nile Valley—for example, that of a woman from Panopolis (modern Akhmim), which dates from the second century. See Doxiadis, *The Mysterious Fayum Portraits: Faces from Ancient Egypt*, 90–91.

10. Hawass, *Valley of the Golden Mummies*, 53–69.

11. Ibid., 88.

12. Hoskins, *Visit to the Great Oasis of the Libyan Desert*, 225–27.

13. Aqueducts of this type are not unique to Qasr. Similar structures are located near the spring of Ain al-Izzah near El-Hayz, and in the other western oases. But the supreme example of this kind of water delivery system is that found at Ain Umm Dabadib in Kharga.

14. Fakhry, *Oases of Egypt*, vol. 2, *Bahriyah and Farafra Oases*, 34.

15. Ibid., 102–05.

16. Although no detailed records describing Alexander's travels in Egypt exist, it is possible that after consulting the famous oracle of Siwa in 331 B.C., Alexander returned to the Nile Valley via the southern route, which required that he pass through Bahariya.

17. Fakhry, *Oases of Egypt*, vol. 2, *Bahriyah and Farafra Oases*, 99–101.

18. Some scholars argue, however, that El-Hayz constitutes a separate oasis from Bahariya. A Ptolemaic-era text discovered in the Temple of Edfu lists seven major oases in the Western Desert: Kharga, Dakhleh, Farafra, "The oasis which is established in the place of the 'Noun' 13,000 trees," the Northern Oasis (Bahariya), Siwa, and Wadi al-Natrun, which lies just west of the Nile Delta. For years scholars have speculated about the exact location of the mysterious "fourth oasis." Some believed it was Ain el-Wadi north of Farafra, but based on the number of its ruins, the abundance of water, and the obvious size of its population in late antiquity, Fakhry argues that it is probably El-Hayz. Ibid., 110.

19. The ruins of this well-constructed building lie just west of the fortress. Given the apparent quality of the wine produced in this area during antiquity, at least one scholar believes that this structure served as a wine factory rather than a bathhouse. See Hawass, *Valley of the Golden Mummies*, 164–66.

20. Fakhry, *Oases of Egypt*, vol. 2, *Bahriyah and Farafra Oases*, 114. In recent years, archaeologists have discovered and cleared an ancient well a few meters from the southeast corner of the church.

21. For information about these Roman towns, see Boak, ed., *Soknopaiou Nesos: The University of Michigan Excavations at Dime in 1931–32*; and Husselman, *Karanis: Excavations of the University of Michigan in Egypt, 1928–1935*.

22. I traveled this route by camel before the modern road was built between Wadi Raiyan and Bahariya. It is probable that the ancient campsites were obliterated during the construction of this road.

23. Built of mud brick and sandstone and containing forty-five chambers, this temple is among the largest in the oasis. The walls of the temple contain numerous faded but visible reliefs, at least two of which purportedly represent Alexander the Great. See Hawass, *Valley of the Golden Mummies*, 195–201.

CHAPTER X. SIWA OASIS

1. Although Cyrenaica, a former province of Eastern Libya that included Siwa, became part of the Roman Empire in 74 B.C., neither Siwa nor Paraetonium appear to have come under Roman control at that time. Kuhlmann, "Roman and Byzantine Siwa: Developing a Latent Picture," 164.

2. The Athenians reportedly kept a special ship ready at all times to convey important questions across the sea to the oracle of Siwa.

3. Herodotus, *History*, I.46–48.

4. Ibid., III.26.

5. Ibid.

6. Fakhry, *The Oases of Egypt*, vol. 1, *Siwa Oasis*, 82.

7. For classical descriptions of the journey to Siwa, see Leclant, "Témoignages des sources classiques sur les pistes menant à l'oasis d'Ammon," 193–253.

8. Plutarch, *The Lives of the Noble Grecians and Romans*, Dryden Translation (New York: Modern Library Edition, 1992), 2:160–61. Arrian relates a similar story but says that it was a pair of hissing snakes that saved the travelers. Arrian, *The Campaigns of Alexander*, 152.

9. It was characteristic of Alexander to treat his newly conquered peoples and their religions with respect. Unlike Cambyses, for example, who had actually stabbed the sacred Apis bull at the temple of Memphis (Herodotus, *History*, III.27–28), Alexander made a special sacrifice to Apis when he visited Memphis. Arrian, *The Campaigns of Alexander*, 148.

10. Fakhry, *Oases of Egypt*, vol. 1, *Siwa Oasis*, 146–47.

11. Upon deciding that Alexander would be buried in Alexandria, Ptolemy sent gifts to the priests of Ammon in Siwa and ordered that a stele be erected in the Temple of the Oracle. Pausanius (9:16,1) claims to have seen this stele when he visited Siwa in the second century A.D. Ibid., 150.

12. Souvaltzi, "Discovering a Macedonian Tomb in Siwa Oasis," 511–13.

13. Kuhlmann, "Roman and Byzantine Siwa: Developing a Latent Picture," 173. For evidence concerning Siwan olive oil, see P. Oxy. 2423, vs. III, 22, and P. Oxy. 2783, 6–9.

14. Clitarchus (Kleitarchos), quoted by Fakhry, *Oases of Egypt*, vol. 1, Siwa Oasis, 152.

15. Strabo, *Geography*, 17, 1, 43

16. The stele is now in the Greco-Roman museum of Alexandria.

17. Pausanius, 9:16.1

18. Fakhry, *Oases of Egypt*, vol. 1, Siwa Oasis, 89.

19. Ibid., 163.

20. The temple remained remarkably intact until it was partly destroyed by an earthquake in 1811. Later, in 1887, it suffered even more damage when a local governor dynamited the structure to extract stone blocks that he used to build a staircase for his home.

21. For a detailed description of this tomb, see Fakhry, *Oases of Egypt*, vol. 1, Siwa Oasis, 190–206. Scholars disagree on the age of this tomb. Fakhry believed it dated from the second to fourth centuries B.C., while Kuhlmann argues for an early Roman date. Kuhlmann, "Roman and Byzantine Siwa: Developing a Latent Picture," 171.

22. Herodotus, *History*, IV.181.

23. Fakhry, *Oases of Egypt*, vol. 1, Siwa Oasis, 125.

24. Ibid., 126.

25. Caillaud, *Voyage à Meroé, au Fleuve Blanc, au-délà de Fazoql dans le Midi du Royaume de Sennar, à Syouah et dans cinq autres oasis, fait dans les années 1819, 1820, 1821 et 1822*, 72–74.

26. The Siwan Manuscript is an Arabic history of Siwa Oasis written in the fifteenth century and maintained by one family until this century. According to one European who saw it and enjoyed listening to readings of its contents by the local sheik, the manuscript was "a muddled collection of loose sheets of manuscript kept in a leather bag." Belgrave, *Siwa: The Oasis of Jupiter Ammon*, 75.

27. *Siwan Manuscript*, quoted by Fakhry, *Oases of Egypt*, vol. 1, Siwa Oasis, 90.

28. Ibn al-Wardi, *Kharidat al-'Aja'ib*, fourteenth century, as quoted by Fakhry, *Oases of Egypt*, vol. 1, Siwa Oasis, 93.

29. Fakhry, *Oases of Egypt*, vol. 1, Siwa Oasis, 90–91.

30. Kuhlmann, "Roman and Byzantine Siwa: Developing a Latent Picture," 166–67.

31. Ibid., 168–69.

32. Wagner, *Les oasis d'Égypte à l'époque grecque, romaine et byzantine d'après les documents grecs*, 151, 212.

33. Fakhry, *Oases of Egypt*, vol. 1, Siwa Oasis, 15.

34. Cosson, "Notes on the Bahren, Nuwemisah, and El-A'Reg Oases in the Libyan Desert," 226–29.

35. Rohlfs, *Drei Monate in der Libyschen Wüste*, 194–95.

BIBLIOGRAPHY

Adams, William Y. "Ecology and Economy in the Empire of Kush." ZAS 108 (1981).
———. "Kush and the Peoples of Northeast Africa." In Fritze Hintze, ed., Meroit-
ica 5: Africa in Antiquity: The Arts of Ancient Nubia and the Sudan. Proceedings of the
Symposium held in conjunction with the Exhibition, Brooklyn, September
1978. Berlin: Akademie-Verlag, 1979.
———. "Primis and the 'Aethiopian' Frontier." JARCE 20 (1983).
———. "Ptolemaic and Roman Occupation at Qasr Ibrim." In Mélanges offerts à
Jean Vercoutter. Edited by F. Geus and F. Thill. Paris: Editions Recherche sur les
Civilisations, 1985.
———. Nubia: Corridor to Africa. London: Allen Lane, Penguin Books, Ltd.; Prince-
ton: Princeton University Press, 1977.
Adams, William Y., J. A. Alexander, and R. Allen. "Qasr Ibrîm 1980 and 1982." JEA
69 (1983).

Addison, Frank. "Second Thoughts on Jebel Moya." *KUSH* 4 (1956).

Alcock, A., I. Gardner, and P. Mirecki. "Magical Spell: Manichaean Letter." In *Emerging from Darkness to Light*. Edited by P. Mirecki and J. BeDuhn. Leiden: E. J. Brill, 1997.

Alcock, A., I. Gardner, and W.-P. Funk, eds. *Coptic Documentary Texts*. Dakhleh Oasis Project: Monograph 9. Oxford: Oxbow Books, 1999.

Aldsworth, F., and H. Barnard. "Berenike Survey." In *Berenike 1996: Report of the Excavations at Berenike (Egyptian Red Sea Coast) and the Survey of the Eastern Desert*. Edited by Steven E. Sidebotham and Willemina Z. Wendrich. Leiden: Research School CNWS, 1996.

————. "Survey of Shenshef." In *Berenike 1996: Report of the Excavations at Berenike (Egyptian Red Sea Coast) and the Survey of the Eastern Desert*. Edited by Steven E. Sidebotham and Willemina Z. Wendrich. Leiden: Research School CNWS, 1996.

Alexander, J. A. "The Saharan Divide in the Nile Valley: The Evidence from Qasr Ibrim." *African Archaeological Review* 6 (1988).

Alexander, J. A., and B. Driskell. "Qasr Ibrim: 1984." *JEA* 71 (1985).

d'Almasy, V. E. *Récentes explorations dans le désert libyque (1932–1936)*. Cairo, 1936.

Alston, Richard. "Roman Military Pay from Caesar to Diocletian." *JRS* 84 (1994).

————. *Soldier and Society in Roman Egypt: A Social History*. London: Routledge, 1995.

Anderson, Robert D. "Qasr Ibrim: Watchdog of the Nile." *Archaeology* 35 (September/October 1982).

Anderson, Robert D., and William Y. Adams. "Qasr Ibrîm: 1978." *JEA* 65 (1979).

Anderson, Robert D., P. J. Parsons, and R. G. M. Nisbet, "Elegiacs by Gallus from Qasr Ibrîm." *JRS* 69 (1979).

Andrew, Gerald. "On the Imperial Porphyry." *BIE* 20 (1937–38).

Arkell, A. J. *A History of the Sudan from the Earliest Times to 1821*. 2d ed. London, 1961.

Arnold, Dorothea, and Janice Bourriau, eds. *An Introduction to Ancient Egyptian Pottery*. Mainz am Rhein: Verlag Philipp Von Zabern, 1993.

Arrian, Flavius. *The Campaigns of Alexander*. Translated by Aubrey de Sélincourt. Revised, with a new introduction and notes by J. R. Hamilton. Middlesex: Penguin Books, 1971.

Asher, Michael. *In Search of the Forty Days Road*. London: Longman Group Limited, 1984.

Attia, Mahmoud Ibrahim. "A Diorite Quarry of the Roman Period in Wadi Barud (Eastern Desert)." *BIE* 28 (1947).

Aufrère, S. "La nécropole sude de Qila al-Dabba (Oasis de Dakhla, secteur de Balat): un palimpseste archéologique." *BIFAO* 90 (1990).

Cockle, Walter E. Helen. "The Breaking of an Altar at Mons Claudianus (IG Pan. 37)." CE 67 (1992).

———. "An Inscribed Architectural Fragment from Middle Egypt Concerning the Imperial Quarries." In *Archaeological Research in Roman Egypt: The Proceedings of the Seventeenth Classical Colloquium of the Department of Greek and Roman Antiquities, British Museum, held on 1–4 December 1993.* Edited by Donald M. Bailey. JRA Supplementary Series, no. 19 (September 1996).

———. "State Archives in Graeco-Roman Egypt from 30 b.c. to the Reign of Septimius Severus." JEA 70 (1984).

———. "Pottery Manufacture in Roman Egypt: A New Papyrus." JRS 71 (1981).

Colin, Frédéric. "Les Paneia d'el Buwayb et du Ouadi Minyah sur la piste de Bérénice à Coptos: inscriptions égyptiennes." BIFAO 98 (1998).

Connolly, Peter. "The Roman Fighting Technique Deduced from Armour and Weaponry." RFS 1989.

Cook, M. "The Mummies of Dakhleh." In *Strength in Diversity: A Reader in Physical Anthropology.* Edited by A. Herring and L. Chan. Toronto: Canadian Scholars' Press, 1994.

Cosson, Anthony de. "Notes on the Bahren, Nuwemisah, and El-'Areg Oases in the Libyan Desert." JEA 23 (1937).

Coulston, J. C. "Roman Archery Equipment." In *The Production and Distribution of Roman Military Equipment,* BAR International Series, no. 275 (1985).

Couyat, J. "La route de Myos-Hormos et les carrières de porphyre rouge." BIFAO 7 (1910).

———. "Ports gréco-romains de la mer rouge, et grandes routes du desert arabique." *Comptes Rendus* (Paris), 1910.

Cullivord, Barbara, ed. *David Roberts, From an Antique Land: Travels in Egypt and the Holy Land.* New York: Weidenfeld and Nicolson, 1989.

Curzon, Robert. *Visits to the Monasteries of the Levant, 1834.* Quoted in Torgny Save-Söderbergh, ed., *Temples and Tombs of Ancient Nubia: The International Rescue Campaign at Abu Simbel, Philae and Other Sites.* London: Thames and Hudson, 1987.

Cuvigny, Hélène. "The Amount of Wages Paid to the Quarry-Workers at Mons Claudianus." JRS 86 (1996).

———. "Inscription inédite d'un ergodotis dans une carrière du Mons Claudianus." In *Itinéraires d'Égypte: Mélanges offerts au père Maurice Martin s.j.* Edited by C. Décobert. Cairo: IFAO, 1992.

———. "Nouveaux ostraca grecs du Mons Claudianus." CE 61 (1986).

———. "Women in the Ostraca of Mons Claudianus and of the Myos Hormos Road." Lecture delivered on December 12, 1996 at the Italian Cultural Institute, Cairo, Egypt.

Cuvigny, Hélène, and Adam Bülow-Jacobsen. "Inscriptions rupestres vues et re-vues dans le désert de Bérénice." *BIFAO* 99 (1999).

Cuvigny, Hélène, Abdel Hussein, and Guy Wagner. *Les ostraca grecs d'Ain Waqfa (Oasis de Kharga)*. DFIFAO, no. 30, 1993.

Cuvigny, Hélène, and Guy Wagner, *Les ostraca grecs de Douch: Fascicule I, II, and III*. Cairo: IFAO, 1986, 1988, 1992.

Dabrowa, Edward. "Dromedarii in the Roman Army: A Note." *RFS* (1989).

Daniels, Charles. *Africa*. Vol. 2 of *The Roman World*. Edited by John Wacher. London: Routledge and Kegan Paul, 1987.

Darnell, John Coleman, and Deborah Darnell. "The Luxor–Farshut Desert Road Survey." *1992–3 Annual Report*. Chicago: Oriental Institute.

———. "The Luxor–Farshut Desert Road Survey." *1993–4 Annual Report*. Chicago: Oriental Institute.

———. "The Luxor–Farshut Desert Road Survey." *1994–5 Annual Report*. Chicago: Oriental Institute.

David, Ch. *Frontier and Society in Roman North Africa*. Oxford: Oxford University Press, 1998.

Davies, P., D. Hemsoll, and M. Wilson-Jones. "The Pantheon: Triumph of Rome or Triumph of Compromise?" *Art History* 10 (1987).

Davies, R. W. *Service in the Roman Army*. Edinburgh: University Press, 1989.

Davies, W. V. "Egypt and Africa in the British Museum." In *Egypt and Africa: Nubia from Prehistory to Islam*. London: British Museum Press, 1991.

de Jong, T., and K. A. Worp. "A Greek Horoscope from a.d. 373." *ZPE* 106 (1995).

De Kuyffer, Herman Frances Valerie. "Het Romainse Leger in Egypte (30 b.c.–284 N.C.)." Ph.D. diss., Katholieke Universiteit Leuven (Belgium), 1989.

Delia, Diane. "Review of *Les ostraca grecs de Douch*." *JARCE* 28 (1991).

Delia, Robert D. "First Cataract Rock Inscriptions: Some Comments, Maps, and a New Group." *JARCE* 30 (1993).

Demicheli, Anna Maria. *Rapporti di pace e di guerra dell' Egitto romano con le popolazioni dei deserti africani*. Milan: A. Giuffrè, 1976.

Denon, D. V. *Voyage dans la basse et la haute Égypte pendant les campagnes du général Bonaparte*. Paris, 1802.

Derchain, P. "Présence romaine dans l'oasis de Thebes." *Bulletin de l'Association des classiques de l'université de Liege* 3 (1955).

Devauchelle, Didier, and Guy Wagner. *Les Graffites du Gebel Teir: Textes demotiques et grecs*. Cairo: IFAO, 1984.

Devijver, H. "The Roman Army in Egypt (with Special Reference to the 'Militiae Equestres')." *ANRW* 2.1 (1974).

Dijkstra, M., and A. M. F. W. Verhoogt. "The Greek-Palmyrene Inscription." In *Berenike 1997: Report of the 1997 Excavations at Berenike and the Survey of the Egyptian Eastern Desert, including Excavations at Shenshef.* Edited by Steven E. Sidebotham and Willemina Z. Wendrich. Leiden: Research School CNWS, 1999.

Dixon, D. M. "A Meroic Cemetery at Sennar (Makwar)." *KUSH* 11 (1963).

Dodgeon, M. H., and S. N. C. Lieu. *The Roman Eastern Frontier and the Persian Wars a.d. 226–363: A Documentary History.* London: Routledge, 1991.

Downey, Glanville. *The Late Roman Empire.* New York: Robert E. Krieger, 1976.

Doxiadis, Euphrosyne. *The Mysterious Fayum Portraits: Faces from Ancient Egypt.* Harry N. Abrams, 1995.

Driel-Murray, C. van. "A Roman Tent: Vindolanda Tent I." *RFS* (1989).

Driskell, Boyce Norman. "Quantitative Approaches to Nile Valley Basketry: Basketry Analysis at Qasr Ibrim." *Meroitica* 10 (1988).

Driskell, Boyce Norman, N. K. Adams, and P. G. French. "A Newly Discovered Temple at Qasr Ibrim: Preliminary Report." *Archéologie du nil moyen* 3 (1989).

Drovetti, Bernardino, M. Jomard, and Frèdèric Cailliaud. *Voyage à l'oasis de Syouah.* Revised and published by M. Jomard. Paris, 1823.

Dudas, Gregory Steven. "Pharaoh, Basileus and Imperator: The Roman Imperial Cult in Egypt." Ph.D. diss., University of California at Los Angeles, 1993.

Dumreicher, André von. *Trackers and Smugglers in the Deserts of Egypt.* London: Methuen, 1931.

Dunand, Françoise, and Roger Lichtenberg. "Une tunique brodée de la nécropole de Douch." *BIFAO* 85 (1985).

Dunand, Françoise, J-L. Heia, et al. *La nécropole de Douch (oasis de Kharga).* DFIFAO 26 (1992).

Dunbabin, Katherine M. D. "*Ipsa deae vestigia . . .* Footprints Divine and Human on Graeco-Roman Monuments." *JRA*, 1998.

Dunbar, J. H. *The Rock-Pictures of Lower Nubia.* Cairo: Government Press, 1941.

Dunham, D., and J. M. A. Janssen. *Semna Kumma: Second Cataract Forts.* Boston, 1960.

Dworakowska, Angelina. *Quarries in Roman Provinces.* Translated by Jerzy Bachrach. Warsaw: Polish Academy of Sciences, 1983.

Eadie, J. W. "Strategies of Economic Development in the Roman East: The Red Sea Trade Revisited." In *The Eastern Frontier of the Roman Empire: Proceedings of a Colloquium held at Ankara in September 1988.* Edited by D. H. French and C. S. Lightfoot. British Institute of Archaeology at Ankara, Monograph no. 11. BAR International Series, no. 553(ii) (1989).

Edmonstone, Sir Archibald. *A Journey to Two Oases of Upper Egypt.* London: John Murray, 1822.

Edwards, Amelia. *A Thousand Miles Up the Nile*. London: George Routledge and Sons, 1888.

Edwards, D. N. *Archaeology and Settlement in Upper Nubia in the 1st Millennium A.D.* BAR International Series, no. 537 (1989).

Eerdmans, William B. *The Eerdmans Bible Dictionary*. Michigan: William B. Eerdmans, 1987.

Ellis, Walter M. *Ptolemy of Egypt*. London: Routledge, 1994.

El-Saghir, M., J.-C. Golvin, Hegazy El-Sayed, and Guy Wagner. "Le camp romain de Louqsor (avec une étude des graffites gréco-romains du temple d'Amon)." *MIFAO* 83 (1986).

Emery, Walter B. *Egypt in Nubia*. London: Hutchinson, 1965. Quoted in P. L. Shinnie, *Ancient Nubia*. London: Kegan Paul International, 1996.

Evans-Pritchard, E. E. *The Sanusi of Cyrenaica*. London: Oxford University Press, 1949.

Fakhry, Ahmed. *The Egyptian Deserts: Bahria Oasis*. Cairo: Government Press, 1942 (Vol. 1) and 1950 (Vol. 2).

———. *The Necropolis of El-Bagawat in Kharga Oasis*. Cairo: Government Press, 1951.

———. *The Oases of Egypt*. Vol. 2, *Bahriyah and Farafra Oases*. Cairo: AUC Press, 1973.

———. *The Oases of Egypt*. Vol. 1, *Siwa Oasis*. Cairo: AUC Press, 1973.

———. *Recent Explorations in the Oases of the Western Desert*. Cairo: IFAO, 1942.

———. "The Tombs of El 'Areg Oasis in the Libyan Desert." *Annals du service* 39 (1939).

Falls, J. C. Ewald. *Three Years in the Libyan Desert*. Translated by Elizabeth Lee. London: T. Fisher Unwin, 1913.

Fitzgerald, Michael. "The Ship of Saint Paul, Part II: Comparative Archaeology." *Biblical Archaeologist* 53 (March 1990).

Fitzler, K. *Steinbruche und Bergwerke in Pyolemaischen und romischen Aegypten*. Leipzig, 1910.

Floyer, Ernest Ayscoghe. *Étude sur le nord-etbai entre le nil et la mer rouge*. Cairo: Imprimerie Nationale, 1893.

———. *Further Routes in the Eastern Desert of Egypt*. London: Clowes, 1893.

Fournet, Jean-Luc. "Les inscriptions grecques d'Abu Ku' et de la route Quft-Qusayr." *BIFAO* 95 (1995).

Fraser, P. M. *Ptolemaic Alexandria*. Oxford: Clarendon Press, 1972.

French, D. H., and C. S. Lightfoot, eds. *The Eastern Frontier of the Roman Emp.* BAR International Series, no. 553 (1989).

Frend, W. H. C. "Augustus' Egyptian Frontier: Q'asr Ibrim?" *RFS* (1979).

———. "The Podium Site at Qasr Ibrim." *JEA* 60 (1974).

Fuchs, A. "Notes on the Archive of Nicanor." *Journal of Juristic Papyrology* 5 (1951).

Gardner, E. W. "Notes on a Temple at 'Ain Amur in the Libyan Desert." *Ancient Egypt and the East* (London and New York: MacMillan), Part 1 (1934) and Part 2 (1935).

Gardner, Iain. "An Abbreviated Version of Medinet Madi Psalm 68 found at Kellis." In *The Manichaean*. Edited by A. van Tongerloo. Louvain: International Association of Manichaean Studies, 1995.

———. "Glory be to Mani!" *Divitae Aegyptae* (1995).

———. *Kellis Literary Texts*. Vol. 1. Dakhleh Oasis Project: Monograph 4. Oxford: Oxbow Monograph 69, 1996.

———. "The Manichaean Community at Kellis." In *Emerging from Darkness to Light*. Edited by P. Mirecki and J. BeDuhn. Leiden: E. J. Brill, 1997.

———. "The Manichaean Community at Kellis: Progress Report." *Manichaean Studies Newsletter*, no. 11 (1993).

———. "A Manichaean Liturgical Codex found at Kellis." *Orientalia* 62 (1993).

Gardner, Iain, and S. N. C. Lieu. "From Narmouthis (Medinet Madi) to Kellis (Ismant el-Kharab): Manichaean Documents from Roman Egypt." *JRS* 86 (1996).

Gardner, Iain, and K. A. Worp. "Leaves from a Manichaean Codex." *ZPE* 117 (1997).

Garnsey, Peter, and Richard Staller. *The Roman Empire: Economy, Society and Culture*. Berkeley: University of California Press, 1987.

Garstang, John, A. H. Sayce, and F. LL. Griffith. *Meroë: The City of the Ethiopians*. Oxford: Clarendon Press, 1911.

Gascou, Jean, and Guy Wagner. "Deux voyages archéologique dans l'oasis de Khargeh." *BIFAO* 79 (1979).

———. "Rapport sur un voyage à l'oasis de Khargeh, 15–19 mai 1977: Site de l'ain Labakha." *BIFAO* 77 (1977).

Gascou, Jean, et al. "Douch: rapport préliminaire des campagnes de fouilles de l'hiver 1978/1979 et de l'automne 1979." Condensed by Jean Vercoutter. *BIFAO* 80 (1980).

Gazda, Elaine K., ed. *Karanis: An Egyptian Town in Roman Times*. Ann Arbor: University of Michigan, Kelsey Museum of Archaeology, 1983.

Ghonaim, Omar Abd El-Hady. *Die Wirtschaftsgeographische Situation der Oase Siwa (Agypten)*. Stuttgart: Geographisches Institut der Universitat Stuttgart, 1980.

Giddy, Lisa L. *Egyptian Oases: Bahariya, Dakhla, Farafra and Kharga During Pharaonic Times*. Warminster: Aris and Phillips Ltd., 1987.

Gilliam, James F. "The Ostracon from Mons Claudianus." *CE* 28 (1953).

———. *Roman Army Papers*. Vol. 2. Edited by M. P. Speidel. Amsterdam: J. C. Gieben, 1984.

Golenischeff, W. "Une excursion à Bérénice." *Recueil de travaux relatifs à la philologie et à l'archéologie égyptienne et assyriennes* 13 (1890).

Golvin, J.-C. "The Luxor Cache." *Egyptian Archaeology* 2 (1992).

Golvin, J.-C., and M. Reddé. "Quelques recherches récentes sur l'archéologie militaire romaine en Égypte." *Comptes-rendus des séances de l'Acadamie des inscriptions et belles lettres*, 1986.

Green, B. A. "Ancient Egyptian Stone Vessels." Ph.D. diss., University of California at Berkeley, 1989.

Griffith, F. L. *Meroitic Inscriptions.* Part 2, *Archaeological Survey of Egypt*, Memoir 20, 1912. Quoted in William Y. Adams, *Nubia: Corridor to Africa*. London: Allen Lane, Penguin Books, Ltd. and Princeton: Princeton University Press, 1977.

Gueraud, O. "Ostraca grecs et latins de l'Wâdi Fawâkhir." *BIFAO* 41 (1942).

Haeny, Gerhard. "A Short Architectural History of Philae." *BIFAO* 85 (1985).

Hardy, E. R. "The Egyptian Policy of Justinian." *Dumbarton Oaks Papers* 22, 1968.

Harrell, James A. "An Inventory of Ancient Egyptian Quarries." *NARCE*, no. 146 (1989).

Harrell, James A., and V. Max Brown. "The Oldest Surviving Topographical Map from Ancient Egypt: (Turin Papyri 1879, 1899, and 1969)." *JARCE* 29 (1992).

Harrell, James A., V. Max Brown, and Lorenzo Lazzarini. "Two Newly Discovered Roman Quarries in the Eastern Desert of Egypt." In *Archéomatériaux: Marbres et autres roches. ASMOSIA (Association for the Study of Marble and Other Stones in Antiquity) IV: Actes de la IVième conférence internationale, France Bordeaux-Talence, 9–13 octobre 1995, organisée par le Centre de Recherche en Physique Appliquée à l'Archéologie.* Bordeaux: Presses Universitaires de Bordeaux (1995).

Hassanein, Ahmed. *The Lost Oases*. London: Thorton Butterworth, 1925.

Hawas, Zahi. *Valley of the Golden Mummies*. Cairo: AUC Press, 2000.

Haycock, B. G. "Landmarks in Cushite History." *JEA* 58 (1972).

Hinkel, F. W. "Les Pyramides de Meroe." *Les dossiers d'archéologie* 196 (1994).

Hirschfeld, Nicolle. "The Ship of Saint Paul, Part I: Historical Background." *Biblical Archaeologist* 53 (March 1990).

Hirschfeld, Yiznar. *The Judean Monasteries in the Byzantine Period*. New Haven: Yale University Press, 1992.

Hobbs, Joseph J. *Bedouin Life in the Egyptian Wilderness*. Cairo: AUC Press, 1990.

———. *Mount Sinai*. Austin: University of Texas Press, 1995.

Hobson, Deborah W. "House and Household in Roman Egypt." *YCS* 28 (1985).

———. "Women as Property Owners in Roman Egypt." *TAPA* 113 (1983).

Hodge, A. Trevor. *Roman Aqueducts and Water Supply*. London: Gerald Duckworth, 1992.

―――. "Témoignages des sources classiques sur les pistes menant à l'oasis d'Ammon." *BIFAO* 49 (1950).

Le Quesne, Charles. "Old Cairo: Fortress into City." *Egyptian Archaeology*, no. 7 (1995).

Lesquier, J. "L'armée romaine d'Égypte d'Auguste à Dioclétien." *MIFAO* 41 (1918).

Letsios, Demetres G. *Vyzantio kai Erythra Thalassa: scheseis me te Nouvia, Aithiopia kai Notia Aravia hos ten aravike kataktese (Byzantium and the Red Sea: Relations with Nubia, Ethiopia and South Arabia until the Arab Conquest).* Athens: Historikes ekdoseis St. D. Vasilopoulos, 1988.

Lewis, Naphtali. "The Compulsory Public Services of Roman Egypt." *Papyrologica Florentina* 11 (1982).

―――. "Leitourgia Papyri: Documents on Compulsory Public Service in Egypt Under Roman Rule." *TAPAS* 53 (1963).

―――. *Life in Egypt Under Roman Rule.* Oxford: Clarendon Press, 1983.

―――. "A Reversal of a Tax Policy in Roman Egypt." *GRBS* 34 (Spring 1993).

―――. "The Romanity of Roman Egypt: A Growing Consensus." In *Atti del XVII Congresso, Internazionale di Papirologia.* Naples: Centro internazionale per lo studio papri Ercolansei, 1984.

―――. "Soldiers Permitted to Own Provincial Land." *BASP* 19 (1982).

Lewis, M. J. T. "Roman Methods of Transporting and Erecting Obelisks." *Trans. Newcomen Soc.* 56 (1985).

Lichtheim, M. *Ancient Egyptian Literature.* Vol. 1. Quoted in P. L. Shinnie, *Ancient Nubia.* London: Kegan Paul International, 1996.

Littman, E., and David Meredith. "An Old Ethiopic Inscription from the Berenice Road." *Journal of the Royal Asiatic Society*, 3d ser. (1954).

Luttwak, E. N. *The Grand Strategy of the Roman Empire from the First Century a.d. to the Third.* Baltimore: Johns Hopkins University Press, 1976.

Lythgoe, A. M. "The Oasis of Kharga." *Bulletin of the Metropolitan Museum of Art* 3 (1908).

Macadam, M. F. L. *The Temple of Kawa I: The Inscriptions.* London: Oxford University Press, 1949. Quoted in Robert T. Updegraff, "The Blemmyes I: The Rise of the Blemmyes and the Roman Withdrawal from Nubia under Diocletian." *ANRW* 2, 10.1 (1988).

MacAlister, D. A. "The Emerald Mines of Northern Etbai." *Geographical Journal* 16 (1900).

MacDonald, Kevin C., and David N. Edwards. "Chickens in Africa: The Importance of Qasr Ibrim." *Antiquity* 67 (September 1993).

MacDowall, D. W. "The Evidence of the Gazetteer of Roman Artifacts in India." In *Tradition and Archaeology: Early Maritime Contacts in the Indian Ocean. Proceedings of* the International Seminar—Techno-Archaeological Perspectives of Seafaring in the Indian Ocean (4th century b.c.—15th century a.d. New Delhi, February 28–March 4, 1994. New Delhi-Lyon: Manohar, 1996.

MacMullen, Ramsay. Soldiers and Civilians in the Later Roman Empire. Cambridge: Harvard University Press, 1963.

MacQuitty, W. Island of Isis: Philae, Temple of the Nile. New York: Scribner, 1976.

Mann, John Cecil. "The Frontiers of the Principate." ANRW 2.1 (1974).

———. Legionary Recruitment and Veteran Settlement During the Principate. London: Institute of Archaeology, 1983.

———. "Power, Force and the Frontiers of the Empire." JRS 69 (1979).

Maspero, G. Egypt: Ancient Sites and Modern Scenes. London: T. Fisher Unwin, 1910.

———. "Les stations anciennes entre Coptos et Bérénice d'après des rélèves faits dans 1873 par l'état-major egyptien." ASAE 3 (1902).

Maspero, Jean. L'organisation militaire de l'Égypte Byzantine. Paris: Libraire ancienne Honoré Champion, 1912.

Matthews, J. F. "The Tax Law of Palmyra: Evidence for Economic History in a City of the Roman East." JRS 74 (1984).

Mayerson, Philip. "Egeria and Peter the Deacon on the Site of Clysma (Suez)." JARCE 33 (1996).

———. "The Port of Clysma (Suez) in the Transition from Roman to Arab Rule." JNES 55 (1996).

Maxfield, Valerie. "The Eastern Desert Forts and the Army in Egypt During the Principate." In Archaeological Research in Roman Egypt: The Proceedings of the Seventeenth Classical Colloquium of the Department of Greek and Roman Antiquities, British Museum, held on 1–4 December 1993. Edited by Donald M. Bailey. JRA Supplementary Series, no. 19 (September 1996).

———. "The Imperial Porphyry Quarries Project." JEA 81 (1994–95).

———. Soldier and Civilian: Life Beyond the Ramparts. Cardiff: National Musem of Wales, 1995.

Maxfield, Valerie, and David P. S. Peacock. "The Archaeology of an Industrial Landscape: An Interim Report on the Work of the Imperial Quarries (Mons Porphyrites) Project." In Life on the Fringe: Living in the Southern Egyptian Deserts During the Roman and Early-Byzantine Periods. Leiden: Research School CNWS, 1998.

———. "Mons Porphyrites." JEA 83 (1997).

———. "The Roman Imperial Porphyry Quarries Project, Gebel Dokhan." JEA 82 (1996).

Meinardus, Otto F. A. Monks and Monasteries of the Egyptian Deserts. Cairo: AUC Press, 1989.

Meredith, David. "Annius Plocamus: Two Inscriptions from the Berenice Road."
   JRS 43 (1953).

———. "Berenice Troglodytica." JEA 43 (1957).

———. "Contributions to the Roman Archaeology of the Eastern Desert of
   Egypt." Ph.D. diss., University of London, Institute of Archaeology, 1954.

———. "Eastern Desert of Egypt: Notes on Inscriptions." CE 28 (1953).

———. "Eastern Desert of Egypt: Notes on Inscriptions." CE 29 (1954).

———. "How the Romans Worked the World's Sole Source of Imperial Porphyry." Illustrated London News, Issue 217, December 16, 1950.

———. "Inscriptions from the Berenice Road." CE 29 (1954).

———. "The Myos Hormos Road: Inscriptions and Ostraca." CE 31 (1956).

———. "The Roman Remains in the Eastern Desert of Egypt." JEA 38 (1952) and
   39 (1953).

———. Tabula Imperii Romani (Map of the Roman Empire) Sheet N.G. 36 Coptos. Oxford:
   Society of Antiquaries of London, 1958.

Meredith, David, and Leo A. Tregenza. "Notes on Roman Roads and Stations in
   the Eastern Desert." BFA 11, part 1 (1949).

———. "Mons Porphyrites: The North-West Village and Quarries." BFA 12, part 1
   (1950).

Meyer, Carol. "The Bir Umm Fawakhir Project, 1992: A Gold Mining Camp in the
   Eastern Desert." Chicago House Bulletin 3, no. 2 (1992).

———. "The Bir Umm Fawakhir Survey: 1991–1992 Annual Report."
   http://www-oi.uchicago.edu/OI/AR/91–92/91–92_Fawakhir.html (May 20,
   1997, 10:36:29).

———. "The Bir Umm Fawakhir Survey: 1992–1993 Annual Report."
   http://www-oi.uchicago.edu/OI/AR/92–93/92–93_Fawakhir.html (May 20,
   1997, 10:33:47).

———. "A Byzantine Gold-Mining Town in the Eastern Desert of Egypt: Bir Umm
   Fawakhir, 1992–1993." JRA 8 (1995).

———. Glass from Quseir al-Qadim and the Indian Ocean Trade. Chicago: Oriental Institute, 1992.

Meyer, Carol, and Lisa Heidorn. "Three Seasons at Bir Umm Fawakhir in the Central Eastern Desert." In Life on the Fringe: Living in the Southern Egyptian Deserts During the Roman and Early-Byzantine Periods. Edited by Olaf Kaper. Leiden: Research
   School CNWS, 1998.

Milburn, Mark. Secrets of South Sahara. New York: Vantage, 1979.

Millar, Fergus. The Roman East: 31 b.c.–a.d. 337. Cambridge: Harvard University
   Press, 1993.

Millar, Fergus, and E. Segal, eds. *Caesar Augustus: Seven Aspects*. Oxford: Clarendon Press, 1984.

Mills, A. J. *The Cemeteries of Qasr Ibrim*. Cairo: Egyptian Exploration Society, Excavation Memoir 51, 1982.

———. "The Dakhleh Oasis Columbarium Farmhouse." *Bulletin de la société archéologique d'Alexandrie*, no. 45 (1993).

———. "Dakhleh Oasis: Dynastic and Roman Sites." In *The Archaeology of Ancient Egypt: An Encyclopedia*. Edited by K. Bard. London and New York: Routledge, 1999.

———. "The Dakhleh Oasis Project: Report on the First Two Seasons." ASAE 68 (1979).

———. "Dakhleh Oasis Project: Report on the First Season of Survey (October–December 1978)." JSSEA 9 (1979).

———. "The Dakhleh Oasis Project: Report on the Second Season of Survey (September–December 1979)." JSSEA 10 (1980).

———. "Dakhleh Oasis Project: Report on the Third Season of Survey (September–December 1980)." JSSEA 11 (1981).

———. "Dakhleh Oasis Project: Report on the Fourth Season of Survey (October 1981–January 1982)." JSSEA 12 (1982).

———. "Dakhleh Oasis Project: Report on the Fifth Season of Survey (October 1982–January 1983)." JSSEA 13 (1983).

———. "Dakhleh Oasis Project: Report on the Sixth Season of Survey (1983–1984)." JSSEA 14 (1984).

———. "Dakhleh Oasis Project: An Interim Report on the 1984–1985 Field Season." JSSEA 15 (1985).

———. "Dakhleh Oasis Project: A Preliminary Report on the Field Work of the 1985/1986 Season." JSSEA 15 (1985).

———. "The Dakleh Oasis Project: Report on the 1986/1987 Field Season." JSSEA 16 (1986).

———. "The Dakhleh Oasis Project: Report on the 1987/1988 Field Season." JSSEA 17 (1987).

———. "The Dakhleh Oasis Project: Report on the 1988–1989 Field Season." JSSEA 20 (1990).

———. "The Dakhleh Oasis Project: Report on the 1989–1990 Field Season." JSSEA 20 (1990).

———. "The Dakhleh Oasis Project: Report on the 1990–1991 Field Season." JSSEA 20 (1990).

———. "The Dakhleh Oasis Project: Report on the 1991–1992 Field Season." JSSEA 20 (1990).

———. "Rome in the Desert: A Symbol of Power." Inaugural Lecture at University of Southampton, 1992.

———. "Routes and Transportation." In *Survey and Excavations at Mons Claudianus: 1987–1993*. Vol. 1, *Topography and Quarries*. Edited by David P. S. Peacock and Valerie Maxfield. Cairo, IFAO (1997).

———. "The Site of Myos Hormos: A View from Space." JRA 6 (1993).

———. "On the Trail of Imperial Porphyry." *Egyptian Archaeology*, no. 5 (1994).

Peacock, David P. S., and Valerie Maxfield. *Mons Claudianus—Survey and Excavations: 1987–1993*. Vol. 1, *Topography and Quarries*. Cairo: IFAO (1997).

———. "The Roman Imperial Porphyry Quarries: Gebel Dokhan, Egypt. Interim Report, 1996." Southampton: Privately printed.

Peacock, David P. S., Olwen Williams-Thorpe, R. S. Thorpe, and A. G. Tindle. "Characterization Studies and the Use of Mons Claudianus Granodiorite." In *Mons Claudianus—Survey and Excavations: 1987–1993*. Vol. 1, *Topography and Quarries*. Edited by David P. S. Peacock and Valerie Maxfield. Cairo: IFAO (1997).

———. "Mons Claudianus and the Problem of the '*granito del foro:*' A Geological and Geochemical Approach." *Antiquity* 68 (1994).

———. "The Roman Quarries of Mons Claudianus, Egypt: An Interim Report." In *Classical Marble: Geochemistry, Trade. Proceedings of the NATO Advanced Workshop on Marble in Ancient Greece and Rome*. Edited by N. Hertz and M. Waelkens. Boston: Kluwer Academic Publishers, 1988.

Peña, J. Theodore. "*P.Giss.* 69: Evidence for the Supplying of Stone Transport Operations in Roman Egypt and the Production of Fifty-Foot Monolithic Column Shafts." JRA 2 (1989).

Plumley, J. Martin. "Qasr Ibrîm: 1963–64." JEA 50 (1964).

———. "Qasr Ibrîm: 1966." JEA 52 (1966).

———. "Qasr Ibrîm: 1969." JEA 56 (1970).

Plumley, J. Martin, and W. Y. Adams. "Qasr Ibrîm: 1972." JEA 60 (1974).

Plumley, J. Martin, W. Y. Adams, and Elizabeth Crowfoot. "Qasr Ibrim: 1976." JEA 63 (1977).

Pococke, Richard. *A Description of the East and Some Other Countries*. London: W. Bowyer, 1743 and 1745.

Pomeroy, Sarah B. "Women in Roman Egypt: A Preliminary Study based on Papyri." ANRW 10.1 (1988).

Posener-Krieger, P. "(Works on Mons Claudianus)." BIFAO 93 (1987).

Price, R. M. "The Limes of Lower Egypt." In *Aspects of the Notitia Dignitatum: Papers Presented to a Conference in Oxford, December 13 to 15, 1974*. Edited by R. Goodburn and P. Bartholomew. Oxford: BAR Supplement, no. 15 (1976).

Purdy, Col. "Une reconnaissance entre Bérénice et Berber: Expedition Purdy-Colston." *Bulletin de la Société Khediviale de Géographie de l'Égypte*. 2d ser., no. 8 (1886).

Raschke, M. G. "New Studies in Roman Commerce with the East." ANRW 2.9 (1978).

Rathbone, Dominic W. *Economic Rationalism and Rural Society in Third-Century a.d. Egypt*. Cambridge: Cambridge University Press, 1991.

Raven, Susan. *Rome in Africa*. 3d ed. London: Routledge, 1993.

Rea, John R. "A Cavalryman's Career: a.d. 384 (?)–401." ZPE 56 (1984).

Reddé, Michel. "A l'ouest du Nil: Une frontière sans soldats, des soldats sans frontière." *RFS 1989: Proceedings of the 15th International Congress of Roman Frontier Studies*. Exeter: Exeter University Press, 1991.

———. "Quinze années de recherches françaises à Douch: vers un premier bilan." BIFAO 90 (1990).

———. "Sites militaires romains de l'oasis de Kharga." BIFAO 99 (1999).

———. *Le trésor de Douch (Oasis de Kharga)*. DFIFAO, no. 28 (1992).

———. "Une ville romaine dans le désert occidental d'Égypte: Douch." *Revue Archéologique* 1 (1988).

Reddé, Michel, and J.-C. Golvin. "Du Nil à la mer rouge: documents anciens et nouveaux sur les routes du désert oriental d'Égypte." *Karthago* 21 (1987).

Redford, Susan, and Donald B. Redford. "Graffiti and Petroglyphs Old and New from the Eastern Desert." JARCE 26 (1989).

Rees, B. R. "Popular Religion in Graeco-Roman Egypt: The Transition to Christianity." JEA 36 (1950).

Reid, James S. *The Municipalities of the Roman Empire*. Cambridge: University Press, 1913.

Reisner, G. A. *The Archaeological Survey of Nubia: Report for 1907–1908*. Cairo: National Printing Department, 1910.

Rengen, Wilfried Van. "A New Paneion at Mons Porphyrites." CE 70 (1995).

———. "The Ostraca." In *The Roman Imperial Porphyry Quarries: Gebel Dokhan, Egypt: An Interim Report*. Edited by David P. S. Peacock and Valerie Maxfield. Southampton: Privately printed, 1996.

Roberts, C. H. "The Antinoë Fragment of Juvenal." JEA 21 (1935).

Robins, F. W. "Graeco-Roman Lamps from Egypt." JEA 25 (1939).

Rodziewicz, Mieczyslaw. "Introduction à la céramique à Egnobe Rouge de Kharga (Kharga Red Slip Ware)." In *Cahiers de la Céramique Égyptienne*. Vol. 1. Cairo: IFAO, 1987.

———. "The Pottery from the Watch-Tower at Tell Asmar." MDAIK 49 (1993).

Rohlfs, Gerhardt. *Drei Monate in der Libyschen Wüste*. Cassel, 1875.

————. *Quer Durch Afrika-Reise Vom Mittelmeer nach dem Tchadsee.* Leipzig, 1879.

Rose, Pamela J. "The Aftermath of the Roman Frontier in Lower Nubia." Ph.D. diss., Cambridge University, 1992.

————. "Qasr Ibrim: 1995." JEA 81 (1994–5).

————. "Qasr Ibrim: 1996." JEA 82 (1996).

————. "Qasr Ibrim: 1997." JEA 83 (1997).

————. "Report on the Handmade Sherds." In *Berenike 1994: Preliminary Report on the 1994 Excavations at Berenike (Egyptian Red Sea Coast) and the Survey of the Eastern Desert.* Edited by Steven E. Sidebotham and Willemina Z. Wendrich. Leiden: Research School CNWS, 1994.

Rose, Pamela J., and P. Rowley-Conwy. "Qasr Ibrim Regional Survey: Preliminary Results." *Archéologie du Nil Moyen* 3 (1989).

Rostovtzeff, M. *A Large Estate in Egypt in the Third Century B.C.* Revised edition. New York: Arno Press, 1979.

————. *Social and Economic History of the Roman Empire.* Oxford: Clarendon Press, 1926.

Rostovtzeff, M., and Elias Bickerman, eds. *Rome.* Translated from Russian by J. D. Duff. London: Oxford University Press, 1960.

Rothe, Russell D., and William K. Miller. "More Inscriptions from the Southern Eastern Desert." JARCE 36 (1999).

Rowlandson, Jane, ed. *Women and Society in Greek and Roman Egypt: A Sourcebook.* Cambridge: Cambridge University Press, 1998.

Rowley-Conwy, Peter. "The Camel in the Nile Valley: New Radiocarbon Accelerator (AMS) Dates from Qasr Ibrim." JEA 74 (1988).

Roxan, Margaret M. "Women on the Frontiers." RFS (1989).

Russel, Thomas. *Egyptian Service 1902–46.* London: John Murray, 1949.

Sadr, K. "Preliminary Report on an Archaeological Reconnaissance in the Eastern Desert, Southeast Egypt." In *Études nubiennes: actes du VIIe congrès international d'études nubiennes, 3–8 septembre 1990.* Vol. 2. Edited by Ch. Bonnet. Geneva.

Sauneron, Serge. "Les temples gréco-romains de l'oasis de Khargéh." BIFAO 55 (1955).

————. "Quelques sanctuaires égyptiens des oasis de Dakhleh et de Khargeh." CHE 7 (1955).

Sauneron, Serge, et al. "Douch: Rapport préliminaire de la campagne de fouilles 1976." BIFAO 78 (1978).

Save-Söderbergh, Torgny, ed. *Temples and Tombs of Ancient Nubia: The International Rescue Campaign at Abu Simbel, Philae and Other Sites.* London: Thames and Hudson, 1987.

Scaife, C. H. O. "A Note on Certain Inscriptions at Gebel Dokhan, and on a Small Station, Hitherto Unrecorded, on the Road from Kainopolis to Myos Hormos." BFA 2 (1934).

———. "Note on a Visit to the Imperial Porphyry Quarries at Gebel Dokhan." BFA 1 (1933).

———. "The Origin of Some Pantheon Columns." JRS 43 (1953).

———. "Two Inscriptions at Mons Porphyrites (Gebel Dokhan), also a Description, with Plans, of the Stations between Kainopolis and Myos Hormos together with some Other Ruins in the Neighborhood of Gebel Dokhan." BFA 3 (1935).

Scarre, Chris. Chronicle of the Roman Emperors. London: Thames and Hudson, 1995.

Schwartz, Jacques, et al. Qasr Qarun/Dionysias 1950: Fouilles franco-suisses, Rapports 2. Cairo: IFAO, 1969.

Schweinfurth, G. "Die Steinbrüche am Mons Claudianus in der östlichen Wüste □gyptens." Zeit. Gesell. Erdkunde Berlin 32 (1897).

———. Auf unbetretenen Wegen in Agypten. Hamburg and Berlin, 1909.

Scullard, Howard Hayes. The Elephant in the Greek and Roman World. Ithaca: Cornell University Press, 1974.

Seeger, John. "The Hydraulic Systems at Abu Sha'ar." Lecture given at the American Research Center in Egypt, Cairo, December 13, 1995.

Seton-Williams, Veronica, and Peter Stocks. Blue Guide: Egypt. London and New York: Black-Norton, 1988.

Sharpe, John L. "Dakhleh Oasis Project: The Kellis Codices." JSSEA 17 (1987).

———. "Exciting Discoveries in the Egyptian Desert." Duke University Libraries 5 (1991).

Shaw, I., and R. Jameson. "Amethyst Mining in the Eastern Desert: A Preliminary Survey at Wadi el-Hudi." JEA 79 (1993).

Sheldrick, P. G. "Human Remains from the Dakhleh Oasis." JSSEA 10 (1980).

———. "Pathologically Slender Human Long Bones from the Dakhleh Oasis." In Reports from the Survey of Dakhleh Oasis, Western Desert of Egypt: 1977–1987. Edited by C. S. Churcher and A. J. Mills. Dakhleh Oasis Project: Monograph 2. Oxford: Oxbow Monograph 99, 1999.

———. "'Skinny Bones' from the Dakhleh Oasis." Paleopathology Newsletter, no. 30 (1980).

Shinnie, P. L. Ancient Nubia. London: Kegan Paul International, 1996.

———. Meroe: A Civilization of the Sudan. London: Thames and Hudson, 1967.

———. "Trade Routes of the Ancient Sudan: 3,000 b.c.–a.d. 350." In Egypt and Africa: Nubia from Prehistory to Islam. London: British Museum Press, 1991.

Shinnie, P. L., and R. J. Bradley. "The Murals from the Augustus Temple, Meroe." In *Studies in Ancient Egypt: The Aegean and the Sudan.* Edited by W. K. Simpson and W. M. Davies. Boston, 1981.

Sidebotham, Steven E. "Abu Sha'ar." *Dumbarton Oaks Papers* 48 (1994).

———. "The Excavations." In *Berenike 1996: Report of the Excavations at Berenike (Egyptian Red Sea Coast) and the Survey of the Eastern Desert.* Edited by Steven E. Sidebotham and Willemina Z. Wendrich. Leiden: Research School CNWS, 1998.

———. "Fieldwork on the Red Sea Coast: The 1987 Season." *JARCE* 26 (1989).

———. "A Limes in the Eastern Desert of Egypt: Myth or Reality?" In *Roman Frontier Studies 1989: Proceedings of the 15th International Congress of Roman Frontier Studies.* Edited by Valerie A. Maxfield and M. J. Dobson. Exeter: University of Exeter Press, 1991.

———. "Lure of the Desert Road." *Archaeology* (July/August 1989).

———. "Newly Discovered Sites in the Eastern Desert." *JEA* 82 (1996).

———. "Ports of the Red Sea and the Arabian-Indian Trade." In *The Eastern Frontier of the Roman Empire: Proceedings of a Colloquium held at Ankara in September 1988.* Edited by D. H. French and C. S. Lightfoot. British Institute of Archaeology at Ankara, Monograph no. 11. BAR International Series, no. 553(ii) (1989).

———. "Preliminary Report on the 1990–1991 Seasons of Fieldwork at 'Abu Sha'ar (Red Sea Coast)." *JARCE* 31 (1994).

———. *Roman Economic Policy in the Erythra Thalassa 30 b.c.–a.d. 217.* Leiden: E. J. Brill, 1986.

———. "Ship Graffiti from Mons Porphyrites." *BIFAO* 90 (1990).

———. "Survey of the Hinterland." In *Berenike 1997: Report of the 1997 Excavations at Berenike and the Survey of the Egyptian Eastern Desert, Including Excavations at Shenshef.* Edited by Steven E. Sidebotham and Willemina Z. Wendrich. Leiden: Research School CNWS.

———. "University of Delaware Archaeological Project at 'Abu Sha'ar: The 1992 Season." *NARCE*, no. 161/162 (Spring/Summer 1993).

Sidebotham, Steven E., John A. Riley, Hany A. Hamroush, and Hala Barakat. "Fieldwork on the Red Sea Coast: The 1987 Season." *JARCE* 26 (1989).

Sidebotham, Steven E. and Willemina Z. Wendrich, eds. *Berenike 1994: Preliminary Report of the 1994 Excavations at Berenike (Egyptian Red Sea Coast) and the Survey of the Eastern Desert.* Leiden: Research School CNWS, 1995.

———. *Berenike 1995: Preliminary Report of the 1995 Excavations at Berenike (Egyptian Red Sea Coast) and the Survey of the Eastern Desert.* Leiden: Research School CNWS, 1996.

———. *Berenike 1996: Report of the Excavations at Berenike (Egyptian Red Sea Coast) and the Survey of the Eastern Desert.* Leiden: Research School CNWS, 1998.

———. *Berenike 1997: Report of the 1997 Excavations at Berenike and the Survey of the Egyptian Eastern Desert, including Excavations at Shenshef.* Leiden: Research School CNWS, 1999.

———. "Interpretative Summary and Conclusions." In *Berenike 1996: Report of the Excavations at Berenike (Egyptian Red Sea Coast) and the Survey of the Eastern Desert.* Edited by Steven E. Sidebotham and Willemina Wendrich. Leiden: Research School CNWS, 1998.

Sidebotham, Steven E. and Ronald E. Zitterkopf. "Routes through the Eastern Desert of Egypt." *Expedition* 37 (1995).

———. "Survey of the Via Hadriana by the University of Delaware: The 1996 Season." *BIFAO* 97 (1997).

———. "Survey of the Via Hadriana by the University of Delaware: The 1997 Season." *BIFAO* 98 (1998).

———. "Survey of the Via Hadriana by the University of Delaware: The 1998 Season." *JARCE* 37 (2000).

Sidebotham, Steven E., Ronald E. Zitterkopf, and John A. Riley. "Survey of the 'Abu Sha'ar-Nile Road." *AJA* 95 (1991).

Simpson, G. E. *The Heart of Libya: The Siwa Oasis, Its People, Customs and Sport.* London: H. F. & G. Witherby, 1929.

Skeat, T. C. "The Last Days of Cleopatra: A Chronological Problem." *JRS* 43 (1953).

———. "A Letter from the King of the Blemmyes to the King of the Noubades." *JEA* 63 (1977).

Smith, Harry S., and Lisa L. Giddy. "Nubia and Dakhla Oasis in the Late Third Millennium b.c.: The Present Balance of Textual and Archaeological Evidence." In *Mélanges offerts à Jean Vercoutter.* Edited by F. Geus and F. Thill. Paris: Editions Recherche sur les civilisations, 1985.

Snowden, Frank M., Jr. *Blacks in Antiquity.* Cambridge: Harvard University Press, 1970.

Souvlatzi, Liana. "Discovering a Macedonian Tomb in Siwa Oasis." *Sesto Congresso Internazionale di Egittologia, Atti.* Vol. 2. Turin, 1993.

Speidel, Michael P. "Augustus' Deployment of the Legions in Egypt." *CE* 47 (1982).

———. "Nubia as a Roman Frontier." *ANRW* 2 (1983).

———. "Nubia's Roman Garrison." *ANRW* 10 (1988).

———. *Roman Army Studies.* Vol. 1. Amsterdam: J. C. Gieben, 1984.

———. *Roman Army Studies.* Vol. 2. Stuttgart: Steiner, 1992.

Spencer, A. Jeffrey. *Brick Architecture in Ancient Egypt.* Warminster, 1979.

Stanley, C. V. B. "A Report on the Oasis of Siwa." *Journal of African Society.* London and Cairo (1911).

Steindorff, Georg. *Durch die Libysche Wüste zur Ammonsoase*. Bielefeld/Leipzig, 1904.

Straus, Jean A. "L'esclavage dans l'Égypte romaine." ANRW 10 (1988).

Tait, J. G., et al. *Greek Ostraca in the Bodleian Library at Oxford and Various Other Collections*. Vol. 1. London, 1930–64.

Thanheiser, Ursula. "Fruits, Nuts, Spices and Other Luxurious Commodities at Kellis." Lecture delivered at the "Life on the Fringe" conference at the Netherlands Institute for Archaeology and Arabic Studies in Cairo, Egypt, December 1996.

Thomas, J. D., and R. W. Davies. "A New Military Strength Report on Papyrus." JRS 67 (1977).

Thompson, F. H. "Mons Claudianus, Egypt, 1988." *Archaeological Journal* 145 (1988).

Thompson, Homer Armstrong. "The Transportation of Government Grain in Graeco-Roman Egypt." Ph.D. diss., University of Michigan, 1929.

Thompson, Jason. *Sir Gardner Wilkinson and His Circle*. Austin: University of Texas Press, 1992.

Titherington, G. W. "A Roman Fort in the Sudan." SNR (1923).

Tod, Marcus N. "The Scorpion in Graeco-Roman Egypt." JEA 25 (1930).

Tomber, R. "Early Roman Pottery from Mons Claudianus." In *Cahiers de la céramique égyptienne*. Vol. 3. Cairo: IFAO, 1992.

———. "The Pottery Survey." In *The Roman Imperial Porphyry Quarries: Gebel Dokhân, Egypt. Interim Report: 1994*. Edited by David P. S. Peacock and Valerie A. Maxfield. Southampton: Privately printed, 1994.

———. "Provisioning the Desert: Pottery Supply to Mons Claudianus." In *Archaeological Research in Roman Egypt: The Proceedings of the Seventeenth Classical Colloquium of the Department of Greek and Roman Antiquities, British Museum held on 1–4 December 1993*. Edited by Donald M. Bailey. JRA Supplementary Series, no. 19 (September 1996).

Tomlin, R. S. O. "The Roman 'Carrot' Amphora and its Egyptian Provenance." JEA 78 (1992).

Török, László. "Augustus and Meroe." *Orientalia Suecana* 38–39 (1989–90).

———. "Economic Offices and Officials in Meroitic Nubia (A Study in Territorial Administration of the Late Meroitic Kingdom)." *Studia Aegyptiaca* (Budapest) 5 (1979). Quoted in Derek A. Welsby. *The Kingdom of Kush: The Napatan and Meroitic Empires* London: British Museum Press, 1996.

———. "Economy in the Empire of Kush: A Review of the Written Evidence." ZAS 111 (1984).

———. "To the History of the Dodekaschoenos between ca. 250 b.c. and a.d. 298." ZAS 107 (1980).

———. "Kush and the External World." *Meroitica* 10 (1988).

Tregenza, Leo A. "The Curator Inscription and Other Recently Found Fragments from Wadi Semna." BFA 13 (1951).

———. *Egyptian Years*. London: Oxford University Press, 1958.

———. "A Latin Inscription from Wadi Semna." BFA 12 (1950).

———. "Notes on Inscriptions and Graffiti at Mons Claudianus and Mons Porphyrites, and on the 'Flavius' Stone in Wadi Qattar, Collected during a Visit to the S.E. Desert in the Summer of 1949." BFA 11 (1949).

———. *The Red Sea Mountains of Egypt*. London: Oxford University Press, 1955.

Trench, R. *The Forbidden Sands*. London: Murray, 1978.

Turner, E. G. "Papyrus 40 'della raccolta Milanese.'" JRS 40 (1950).

———. "Roman Oxyrhynchus." JEA 38 (1952).

Updegraff, Robert T. "The Blemmyes I: The Rise of the Blemmyes and the Roman Withdrawal from Nubia under Diocletian." ANRW 2, 10.1 (1988).

Van Neer, W., and A. Ervynck. "The Faunal Remains." In *Berenike 1996: Report of the Excavations at Berenike (Egyptian Red Sea Coast) and the Survey of the Eastern Desert*. Edited by Steven E. Sidebotham and Willemina Z. Wendrich. Leiden: Research School CNWS, 1996.

Van Rengen, Wilfried. "A New Paneion at Mons Porphyrites." CE 70 (1995).

———. "The Ostraca." In *The Roman Imperial Porphyry Quarries: Gebel Dokhan, Egypt. An Interim Report*. Edited by David P. S. Peacock and Valerie Maxfield. Southampton: Privately printed, 1996.

Veen, Marijke van der. "Gardens in the Desert." In *Life on the Fringe: Living in the Southern Egyptian Deserts during the Roman and Early-Byzantine Periods*. Edited by Olaf Kaper. Leiden: Research School CNWS, 1998.

———. "The Plant Remains from Mons Claudianus, a Roman Quarry Settlement in the Eastern Desert of Egypt. An Interim Report." *Vegetation History and Archaeobotany* 5 (1996).

Verhoogt, A. M. F. W. "Greek and Latin Textual Material." In *Berenike 1996: Report of the Excavations at Berenike (Egyptian Red Sea Coast) and the Survey of the Eastern Desert*. Edited by Steven E. Sidebotham and Willemina Z. Wendrich. Leiden: Research School CNWS, 1996.

Vivian, Cassandra. *Father of Rivers: A Traveler's Companion to the Nile Valley*. Cairo: Trade Routes Enterprises, 1989.

———. *Islands of the Blest: A Guide to the Oases and Western Desert of Egypt*. Cairo: International Publications, 1990.

———. *The Western Desert of Egypt: An Explorer's Handbook*. Cairo: AUC Press, 2000.

Wagner, Guy. *Elephantine 13: Les papyrus et les ostraca grecs d'Elephantine (P. et O. Eleph DAIK)*. Mainz am Rhein: Verlag Philipp von Zabern, 1998.

———. "Les inscriptions et graffiti grecs inédits de la grande oasis." *BIFAO* 76 (1976).

———. "Les inscriptions grecques d'Ain Labakha (stèles—graffites—depinti)." *ZPE* 111 (1996).

———. "Les inscriptions grecques des oasis de Dakhleh et Bahriyeh découvertes par le Dr. Ahmed Fakhry." *BIFAO* 73 (1973).

———. *Les oasis d'Égypte à l'époque grecque, romaine et byzantine d'après les documents grecs.* Cairo: IFAO, 1987.

———. "Les ostraca grecs de Douch." *Proceedings of the 16th International Congress of Papyrology, New York, 21–28 July 1980.*

Wainwright, G. A. "The Date of the Rise of Meroë." *JEA* 22 (1936).

———. "Zeberged: The Shipwrecked Sailor's Island." *JEA* 36 (1937).

Wallace, Sherman L. *Taxation in Egypt from Augustus to Diocletian.* Princeton: Princeton University Press, 1938.

Wareth, Usama Abdel, and Pierre Zignani. "Nag al-Hagar: A Fortress with a Palace of the Late Roman Empire." *BIFAO* 92 (1992).

Warmington, E. H. *The Commerce Between the Roman Empire and India.* Cambridge: Cambridge University Press, 1928.

Watson, G. R. *The Roman Soldier.* 4th ed. New York: Cornell University Press, 1996.

Webster, Graham. *The Roman Imperial Army of the First and Second Centuries a.d.* 3d ed. New Jersey: Barnes and Noble Books, 1981.

Weigall, Arthur. *A Guide to the Antiquities of Upper Egypt from Abydos to the Sudan Frontier.* 2d ed. London: Methuen, 1913.

———. *A Report on the Antiquities of Lower Nubia.* Oxford, 1907.

———. *Travels in the Upper Egyptian Deserts.* London: William Blackwood and Sons, 1909.

Weinstein, M. E., and E. G. Turner. "Greek and Latin Papyri from Qasr Ibrîm." *JEA* 62 (1976).

Wells, C. M. "The Problems of Desert Frontiers: Chairman's Comments on the Session." *RFS* (1989).

Wellsted, J. R. "Notice on the Ruins of Berenice." *Journal of the Royal Geographical Society* 36 (1836).

Welsby, Derek A. *The Kingdom of Kush: The Napatan and Meroitic Empires.* London: British Museum Press, 1996.

———. "The Northern Dongola Reach Survey." *Egyptian Archaeology,* no. 5 (1994).

Wendrich, Willemina. "Fringes are Anchored in Warp and Weft: The Relations Between Berenike, Shenshef and the Nile Valley." In *Life on the Fringe: Living in the Southern Egyptian Deserts during the Roman and Early-Byzantine Periods.* Edited Olaf Kaper. Leiden: Research School CNWS, 1998.

West, Louis C. "Phases of Commercial Life in Roman Egypt." *JRS* 7 (1917).

West, Louis C., and A. C. Johnson. *Currency in Roman and Byzantine Egypt.* Princeton: Princeton University Press, 1944.

Wheeler, Sir Robert Eric Mortimer. *Rome Beyond the Imperial Frontiers.* London: G. Bell, 1954.

Wheeler, R. E. Mortimer, A. Ghosh, and Krishna Deva. "Arikamedu: An Indo-Roman Trading Station on the Coast of India." *Ancient India* 2 (1946).

Whitcomb, David. "Quseir al-Qadim and the Location of Myos Hormos." *Topoi* 6 (1996).

Whitcomb, Donald S., and Janet H. Johnson. "Egypt and the Spice Trade." *Archaeology* 34 (November/December 1981).

———. "The Port of Quseir al-Qadim 1980." *Field Museum of Natural History Bulletin* 51 (June 1980).

———. *Quseir al-Qadim 1978: Preliminary Report.* Princeton: Cairo–American Research Center in Egypt, 1979.

———. *Quseir al-Qadim 1980: Preliminary Report.* Malibu: Undena Publications, 1982.

White, A. S. *From Sphinx to Oracle: Through the Libyan Desert to the Oasis of Jupiter Ammon.* London, 1899.

White, H. G. Evelyn. "Graeco-Roman Ostraka from Dakka, Nubia." *CR* 34 (May-June 1919).

White, Hugh G. Evelyn, and James H. Oliver. *The Temple of Hibis in El Khargeh Oasis.* Part 2, *Greek Inscriptions.* New York: Metropolitan Museum of Art Egyptian Expedition, 1938.

White, K. D. *Greek and Roman Technology.* Ithaca: Cornell University Press, 1984.

Whitehouse, Helen. "Roman in Life, Egyptian in Death: The Painted Tomb of Petrosiris in the Dakhleh Oasis." In *Life on the Fringe: Living in the Southern Egyptian Deserts during the Roman and Early-Byzantine Periods.* Edited by Olaf Kaper. Leiden: Research School CNWS, 1998.

Wiedemann, Thomas. *Emperors and Gladiators.* Trade Paperback, 1995.

Wilkinson, J., trans. and annot. *Egeria's Travels to the Holy Land.* Jerusalem, 1981. Quoted in Philip Mayerson, "Egeria and Peter the Deacon on the Site of Clysma (Suez)." *JARCE* 33 (1996).

Wilkinson, Sir John Gardner. *Modern Egypt and Thebes: Being a Description of Egypt, Including the Information Required for Travelers in that Country.* London: J. Murray, 1843.

———. "Notes on a Part of the Eastern Desert of Egypt." *Journal of the Royal Geographic Society* 2 (1832).

INDEX